BLACK HISTORY EVERYDAY
PART ONE
BLACK HISTORY EVERYDAY

PART ONE
FREDERICK MONDERSON

SUMON PUBLISHERS

FREDERICK MONDERSON

Black History Everyday - Part One
Photo. At the "Tribute to Prof. George Simmonds" at the Victoria 5 Theater in Harlem, "Young" Fred Monderson sat at the feet of his heroes Dr. Ben-Jochannan and with Prof. George Simmonds in full-chiefly regalia and Elombe Brathe, Brother X, Leonard Jeffries, Michael Carter and Sister Camile Yarbrough, among others.

ISBN 978-1-61023-059-9
LCCN – 201-7907788

Black History Everyday - Part One
Photo. Marcus Garvey's Red, Black and Green, symbol of the African-American experience.

BLACK HISTORY EVERYDAY PART ONE

ABOUT THE AUTHOR

Frederick Monderson is a retired college professor and school teacher who taught African History in the City University of New York and American History and Government in the New York public schools. He has written more than 1000 articles in the New York Black Press, *Daily Challenge*, *Afro Times* and *New American* newspapers. In this venture, Monderson lends his expertise as a historian, Egyptologist, journalist and author of several books including *When is a "Gangster Government" a "Gangster Government?" Ladies in the House*; *Michael Jackson: The Last Dance*; *50 on Point*; *Barack Obama: Ready, Fit to Lead*; *Barack Obama: Master of Washington D.C.*; *Obama: Master and Commander*; *Sonny Carson: The Final Triumph*; *Black Nationalism: Alive and Well*; *Black Nationalism: Still Alive and Well*; *African Nationalist: Poetry and Prose*; and on ancient Egypt *Seven Letters to Mike Tyson on Egyptian Temples*; *10 Poems Praising Great Blacks for Mike Tyson*; *Research Essays on Ancient Egypt*; *Temple of Karnak: The Majestic Architecture of Ancient Kemet*; *Where are the Kamite Kings?*; *Abydos and Osiris*; *Temple of Luxor*; *Medinet Habu: Mortuary Temple of Rameses III*; *The Quintessential Book on Ancient Egypt*: *"Holy Land"* (A Novel on Egypt); *Hatshepsut's Temple at Deir el Bahari*; *The Majesty of Egyptian Gods and* Temples (a book of *Egyptian* Poems); *Egypt Essays on Ancient Kemet*; *The*

FREDERICK MONDERSON

Ramesseum: Mortuary Temple of Rameses II; The Colonnade: Then and Now; Reflections on Ancient Kemet; Grassroots View of Ancient Egypt; Into the Egyptian Mind; Glory of the Ancestors: 19 Letters to O.J. Simpson on Ancient African History; and (a Trilogy on Dr. Ben) as Celebrating Dr. Ben-Jochannan; Black History Extravaganza; and Let's Liberate the Temple. A student of the esteemed Dr. Yosef ben-Jochannan, Dr. Monderson conducts tours to Egypt. **SuMon Publishers**, PO Box 160685, Brooklyn, New York 11216

For Tour information: Please contact Orleane Brooks-Williams at Nostrand Travel, 730 Nostrand Avenue, Brooklyn, New York 11216. Phone Number 718-756-5300. **Next Tour of Egypt** - July 24-August 7, 2020.

Black History Everyday - Part One
Photo. "Mother Africa" in colorful splendor.

BLACK HISTORY EVERYDAY
PART ONE

Black History Everyday - Part One
Photo. A heart of love in "Mother Africa."

FREDERICK MONDERSON

Black History Everyday - Part One
Photo. "Justice or Else" is the **MESSAGE**!

Black History Everyday - Part One
Photo. Respect Human Rights!

BLACK HISTORY EVERYDAY
PART ONE
TABLE OF CONTENTS

1. "PRAISING THE BLACK WOMAN" — 10
2. ASA PHILIP RANDOLPH'S MARCH ON WASHINGTON, D.C. - 1941 — 44
3. REV. AL. SHARPTON: THE NEXT LEVEL AND EARNED ASCENT — 69
4. ARC OF THE MORAL UNIVERSE — 85
5. BARACK OBAMA: MASTER OF WASHINGTON, DC — 97
6. BARACK OBAMA – PRESIDENT — 100
7. BETTY DOPSON, WARRIOR QUEEN! — 114
8. BLACK HISTORY EVERYDAY — 125
9. BLACK INFLUENCE ON THE SUPREME COURT — 133
10. BOB LAW'S TRIBUTE TO NELSON MANDELA — 152
11. CALLING OUT OBAMA — 170
12. CELEBRATING DR. BEN - PART I — 179
13. CELEBRATING DR. BEN PART II — 194
14. "CHICKENS COMING HOME" — 214

15. CULTURE FOR LIBERATION   226
16. DR. YOSEF A.A. BEN-   239
    JOCHANNAN - A TRIBUTE
17. ELOMBE BRATHE "ULTIMATE   265
    NATIONALIST SOLDIER"
18. GOD SEND - SONNY CARSON   272
    AT NEW YORK CITY COUNCIL
19. JITU WEUSI   283
    "MOUNTAIN OF A MAN"
20. "LIKE IT IS" AND   291
    IMPERIALISM
21. SHARPTON AND CRUMP'S   336
    MARCH ON WASHINGTON
22. MICHAEL! "A SONG OF   341
    PRAISE!"
23. MILLION MAN MARCH: 350
    SUBSTANCE AND SIGNIFICANCE
24. MILLIONS MORE MOVEMENT: 368
    "I WAS THERE!"
25. NO TO REPUBLICAN   385
    BULLYING!
26. "OBAMA: 'A BAD YEAR' NO!"   391
27. OBAMA AND EXECUTIVE   403
    ORDER
28. OBAMA AND LEADERSHIP   420
29. PIPELINE WISE,   434
    INFRASTRUCTURE FOOLISH

BLACK HISTORY EVERYDAY
PART ONE

30.	REFLECTIONS ON RACE IN AMERICA IN 2006 AND TODAY	440
31.	SALVATION THROUGH PAN-AFRICANISM	463
32.	SONNY CARSON: AT THE GATES	481
33.	SPIRITUAL VALUES VERSUS SECULAR MATERIALISM	495
34.	THE BLACK WOMAN	505
35.	THE ILLUSTRIOUS QUEEN MOTHER	532
36.	THE OBAMA LEGACY II	546
37.	THE "SOUTHERN FIREWALL"	554
38.	THE TRIANGULAR TRADE	567
39.	TRUMP AND OBAMA I	594
40.	WHEN MCCONNELL MEETS OBAMA!	607
41.	DEFENDING A MYTH!	614
42.	MR. MANDELA'S LONG WALK	630
43.	"LYNCHING AS RACIAL TERROR"	663

FREDERICK MONDERSON

Black History Everyday – Part One
Photo. I LOVE BLACK PEOPLE!

"The Black woman has deep wells of spiritual strength. She doesn't know how she's going to feed her family in the morning, but she prays and, in the morning out of thin air, she makes breakfast." [William Thomas] Billy Strayhorn from Brian Lanker, *I Dream a World* [1989]"

1. "PRAISING THE BLACK WOMAN" BY DR. FRED MONDERSON

As we celebrate **Women's History Month** in March this year, commentary and praises are due to Black Women who for long have given so much,

BLACK HISTORY EVERYDAY
PART ONE

from the earliest times up to now; giving birth, been companion, leader, visionary, perfectly planned, a dish of the gods, who improves with love, appreciation and so much more.

Science, utilizing DNA reconstruction, has demonstrated that the earliest surviving progenitor of the human race has been a woman who roamed the plains of East Africa nearly two hundred and fifty thousand years ago. Earlier, a paleo-anthropologist named Johansson discovered the most complete human fossil. It was of a woman in the Hadar region of Ethiopia, who was subsequently, nicknamed "Lucy," and dated to more than two million years old. Dr. Ben-Jochannan correctly pointed out her name was *Denk Nesh*. Science has also confirmed, again through DNA reconstruction, that the individual thought to be "Eve" and most probably the mother of all humanity, was an African woman who roamed the plains of East Africa more than 200,000 years ago. From this woman all races, as we know it, trace a lineal descent. Thus, together with Black Goddesses and equally the "Black Madonna," this puts the Black woman in the most sacred and divine company. Perhaps this is why the respected elder, historian, Egyptologist, tour guide, etc., Dr. Ben-Jochannan in praising the 'Sacred Womb of the Black Woman,' began the Keynote Address at the Second Annual Ancient Egyptian Conference (**ASCAC**) from February 28 through March 3, 1985 by saying: "Brothers of the Craft and Sisters of the House: 'Heaven is between a Black Woman's Legs.'" In this she has given life, been supportive and played a role of great distinction as woman, mother, warrior, entrepreneur, supportive and even being told "woman behold thy son." Sometimes witty, tactful, sometimes a pleasure, always a treasure, lovely in her bones, faithful; Mighty Sparrow says "using guile with a pretty smile," assertive often with a tiger's heart, the woman's work is never done.

Black History Everyday Part One - Photo. BLACK LIVES MATTER!

That essential element of Professor Len Jeffries' "Male-female complimentarity principle" is equally what Marcus Garvey said in his *Philosophy and Opinions*, that woman is: "What the night is to day, is woman to man. The period of change that brings us light out of darkness, darkness out of light, and semi-light out of darkness are like the changes we find in woman day by day. She makes one happy,

BLACK HISTORY EVERYDAY
PART ONE

then miserable. You are to her kind, then unkind. Constant yet inconstant. Thus, we have **WOMAN**. No real man can do without her." Even Shakespeare said, "She is a woman, therefore may be woo'd; She is a woman, therefore may be won." And this is what we strive for! Let us not go with Hyponex 570-520 B.C.: "There are two days when a woman is a pleasure: the day one marries her and the day one buries her." Never forget as Longfellow said: "As onto the bow the cord is, so unto the man is woman, though she bends him, she obeys him, though she draws him, yet she follows, Useless each without the other."

Black History Everyday Part One - Photo. Betty Dopson, Co-Chair of **CEMOTAP** (**Committee to Eliminate Media Offensive to African People**).

FREDERICK MONDERSON

Black History Everyday - Part One Photo. Faces in the crowd for the 50th Anniversary March on Washington.

Black History Everyday - Part One Photo. We Shall Not be Moved March. Faces in the Crowd.

As such then, in the chronological development of female assertion, the next great flowering of African womanhood occurred in the Nile Valley, where, as

BLACK HISTORY EVERYDAY
PART ONE

Nornelia Otis Skinner said in 1901, "a woman's virtue is man's greatest invention."

Black History Everyday - Part One Photo. Faces in the Crowd for the 50th Anniversary March on Washington. "Keep Calm and Protect Civil Rights!"

FREDERICK MONDERSON

As a result, the role of women in ancient Egypt/Kemet has been essential, appreciated, respected and necessary. From the earliest times the indispensable position of Egyptian women has been depicted in the graves of the prehistoric period and in the tombs of deceased nobles. Their roles as goddesses, queens, princesses, mothers, and plain old folks, were demonstrated and the impact on numerous pharaohs as well as Egyptian society has been recounted.

Many women have ruled as queens of Egypt but Hatshepsut of the Eighteenth Dynasty has been the most significant woman bold enough to rule, as King or Pharaoh, of this ancient land.

The female principle in Egypt, as in Africa, is divine in nature. In Egyptian cosmogony and religious beliefs, female divinities have played important roles. They have featured prominently in triads, and in a number of instances, shapely as a swan, females were a part of pharaonic triads.

With her brother Geb, the earth god, Nuit, the sky goddess, Shu and Tefnut (air and moisture), together with Osiris and Isis, and Seth and Nephthys, they completed the Heliopolis Ennead of nine headed by Ra. Thus, Goddess Nuit or Nut, was from the earliest times a water goddess who formed part of a divine company of nine. The Hermopolis Ennead, headed by Thoth comprised divinities of whom the males were Nu and Heru, Keku and Kerh. The females were

BLACK HISTORY EVERYDAY
PART ONE

Kerhet, Keruit, Hehut and Nut. Not much is known about the other goddesses but, in the New Empire, Nut was represented as a woman and as a cow.

Black History Everyday – Part One Photo. We Shall Not be Moved March. Faces in the Crowd.

According to the *Book of the Dead* or the *Hieratic Transcript of the Papyrus of Ani*, translated by E.A. Wallis Budge, there were a number of female deities in the Egyptian religious drama. The male Shu and the female Tefnut were children of Ra, the Sun God. Tefnut formed the third member of the company of gods of Anu. Tefnut is sometimes shown as moisture and at other times as sunlight. This goddess originated in the Nubian Desert. She had a lion head and wore a disk or uraeus or both. She drank her enemies' blood and had fire in her eyes.

The next female divinity of importance was Isis or Auset. She was the seventh member of the company of Anu, wife of Osiris and mother of Horus, the younger. She is usually depicted as a woman with a headdress in the shape of a seat or throne. Her principal temple is located at Philae, now moved to the nearby Agilka Island. Some early names ascribed to her are "the great goddess, the divine mother, the mistress of words of power and enchantment." In later times she is called "mother of the gods" and the "living one." Isis is sometimes shown as the cow goddess Hathor who wears a solar disk between her horns with a throne or seat, and she also has plumes or feathers. Her most famous depiction is as the mother suckling her child Horus. The original "Madonna and Child" concept is based on this depiction. Naturally, she was Black like the sky, hence, the **Black Madonna**.

Nephthys was Isis' sister and wife of the evil god Seth. "When the sun rose at the creation of the primeval waters Nephthys occupied a place in his boat with Isis and other deities; as a nature goddess she either represents day before sunrise or after sunset, but not associated with night. Her hieroglyphic name means "lady of the house." Plutarch tells of a legend that said she was the mother of Anubis by Osiris, who later became judge of the dead. She is shown as the companion of Isis and was grieved during Osiris' murder.

BLACK HISTORY EVERYDAY
PART ONE

The next female divinity was Ma'at, the female counterpart of Thoth. The Heliopolitan tradition makes her a daughter of Ra. She was the wife or daughter of Thoth, the god of writing. A feather symbolizes her name and she also hold a scepter in one hand and an ankh in another. The name Ma'at means straight; her name stands for righteousness, right, genuine, righteous, just, real, truth, balance, order, steadfast, unalterable, etc.

Hathor, the "House of Horus," was the goddess of the sun where the sun god rose and set. Hathor is depicted as a woman with a disk and horns on her head. She is also shown as a cow with a disk between her horns. Budge says that as a "Cow-goddess she is probably of Sudani origin." That is Africa proper, to the south of Egypt.

Neith has been called "the divine mother, the lady of heaven, the mistress of the gods." She is mentioned in the *Pyramid Texts* as the mother of Sobek, the crocodile god. Neith was believed to be self-produced and an ancient Saite tradition made her to be the mother of Ra, the Sun God. She is depicted in the form of a woman, having upon her head the shuttle or arrows, or she wears the Red Crown and holds arrows, a bow and a scepter in her left hand.

FREDERICK MONDERSON

Black History Everyday - Part One Photo. We Shall Not be Moved March.
Faces in the Crowd.

Sekhmet was the wife of Ptah, and the mother of Nefer-Temu and of I-Em-Hetep. She personified the terrible heat of the desert. "When Ra determined to punish mankind with death, because they scoffed at him, he sent Sekhmet, his 'Eye' to perform the work of vengeance; illustrative of this aspect of her is a figure wherein she is depicted with the sun's eye for a head." Bast was a sort of opposite to Sekhmet. She personified the gently and fructifying heat of the sun. She is usually pictured as cat-headed.

Nekheb-ka is the name of a goddess represented by a serpent. Utchait and Nekhabit were very special goddesses. They personified Upper and Lower Egypt and comprised the Pharaoh's "Two Ladies" name. Utchait, a form of Hathor, is depicted as a woman with the crown of the north and a scepter. Nekhabit was the vulture goddess, tutelary deity of Upper Egypt from the city of Hekheb. Mut the earth goddess was wife of Amon Ra, the "Sun-God," and

BLACK HISTORY EVERYDAY
PART ONE

mother of Khonsu the "Moon-God." She was an essential part of the Theban triad, of Amon-Ra, Mut and Khonsu and sometimes shown as a vulture.

As a result, female roles in the divine cosmogony and religious drama of the Egyptians gave them a special place in the social fabric of the society. Whether as wife, mother or sister, females were respected, cared for, and had equal status at home and before the law. They cold inherit property, become literate and were able to conduct business.

Black History Everyday – Part One Photo. Erik Monderson can later boast "I was there! My father took me to the **50th Anniversary March on Washington**, August 2013."

FREDERICK MONDERSON

Black History Everyday – Part One Photo. Sharpton and Crump's March on Washington. Faces in the crowd.

Black History Everyday - Part One Photo. Faces in the crowd for the 50th Anniversary March on Washington.

The graves of the Badarian and Naqada I burials show much evidence of some association between the

BLACK HISTORY EVERYDAY
PART ONE

dead and women. What we call female paraphernalia can be found in many graves of the time. These include combs, rings, bracelets, and studs for the nose, jewelry of shells, carnelian and coral around the neck. There, earrings and dresses are also included. These early people utilized dyes with green malachite and castor oil for cleansing and softening the skin.

By the time of the Gerzean culture or Naqada II, figurines of the fertility goddess are found in graves. Carved bone and ivory figurines of women are also found in graves designed to accompany men into eternity.

Female jewelry was made from a wide variety of materials including amethyst, button-pearl, amber, agate, onyx, and glass. Jewelry included necklaces, girdles, bracelets, and a circlet or diadem for the head. Therefore, in the pre-dynastic time, before 3000 B.C., the role of women was considered important enough to receive the attention indicated in graves. Even more so, in the Mythology they traveled with and were counterparts of the gods.

From the time of the First Dynasty, c. 3000 B.C. onwards, the position of women is seen as advanced, appreciated, and respected. On the **Narmer Macehead** the king is shown beneath a pavilion. His wife, Queen Neithhotep is also shown seated beside and facing him. Some feel this is probably a marriage ceremony. However, it clearly shows an

FREDERICK MONDERSON

elevated position for his wife or more important, a female. They had a son named Aha, who succeeded his father to the throne.

While Narmer was buried in a regular sized Mastaba tomb at Abydos; Aha built an elaborate tomb for his mother, Queen Neithhotep. The indications of this are that the husband and son, in ancient Egypt, loved and respected the wife and or mother. The same care and concern could be found for the daughter and for the sister. Many men married their sisters.

Black History Everyday - Part One Photo. We Shall Not be Moved March. Faces in the Crowd.

In this reality, the basis for the love, respect and proper consideration of women or females in Egypt is clear. Thus, this treatment is evident by the roles of and respect for the goddesses, queens, mothers and princesses. It stands to reason that the ordinary

BLACK HISTORY EVERYDAY PART ONE

woman also enjoyed some of this special attention. However, it must also be pointed out, there were women who held positions as household help and slaves, as in many societies in the ancient world.

The significance of women in Egypt is further indicated by their status before the law. The Supreme Court, according to an inscription on the walls of a tomb at Sakkara, upheld a certain woman's right to inheritance. Schafik Allam's *Everyday Life in Ancient Egypt*, argues that women could "inherit moveable things, house and landed property."

Even more, however, women were held accountable for their actions in the society. In this, they could also engage in business or represent their husbands in business transactions. They could receive loans, mediate between two parties and were allowed to bear witness in many judicial proceedings. Much more significant, women had the legal right to conduct legal affairs without the prior authorization of their husbands.

The inscription at Sakkara tells of a woman named Ornero, who was "designated by the courts as representative for a group of heirs and who consequently had to administer on trust all the property in question." Women could sue in court. Many wives of officials were "responsible for regulating their husbands' affairs and looking after their husbands' interests." Many were authorized to act in his absence. Therefore, it's clear that a number

FREDERICK MONDERSON

of dynamic African women have impacted on three thousand years of socio-political-religious cultural expression in dynastic Egypt. Dr. Diop contrasted the dynamic of this equality before the law and in social relations with the virtual absence of queens and general women relations in Greece and Rome and in many other ancient societies, outside of Africa.

The Third Dynasty began the first golden age in Egypt. It also began the Old Empire or Old Kingdom.

The accomplishments of the preceding Pre-dynastic and Archaic periods set the stage for the new era. The Step-Pyramids and the great Mastaba tombs became prototype in size, techniques and building strategy for the true pyramids of the Fourth Dynasty.

Black History Everyday - Part One Photo. **Pam Africa** and **Dr. Adelaide Sanford**, former Regent of the State of New York, Department of Education, at **CEMOTAP**' 31st Anniversary celebration.

BLACK HISTORY EVERYDAY
PART ONE

The pharaohs who dominated the Fourth Dynasty were Sneferu, Khufu, Khafre and Menkaure. The first built two pyramids at Dashur and Meydum. The other three built the famous Giza group. What is significant, however, is the role Queen Hetep-Heres played in influencing these four great African kings. Queen Hetep-Heres was the wife of Pharaoh Sneferu, mother of Khufu, grandmother of Khafre and great-grandmother of Menkaure, as the evidence seems to indicate. What a progeny! She must have been a powerful African woman.

In 1925, excavators in an expedition from Harvard University worked at Giza. Behind the pyramid of Khufu, they discovered the "only intact tomb chamber from the Old Kingdom" found up to that time. According to J.E. Manchip White's *Ancient Egypt: Its Culture and History*, a "wonderful collection was unearthed."

Black History Everyday - Part One Photo. Brother Walter Brown and a friend at the 50th Anniversary Reunion in Augusta, Georgia.

FREDERICK MONDERSON

Black History Everyday - Part One Photo. We Shall Not be Moved March. Faces in the Crowd.

Archaeologists found, "there was a canopy, a bed, two chairs and a carrying chair, all sheeted in gold. There were alabaster vessels, a copper and gold manicure instrument. There was a toilet box with cosmetics contained in eight little alabaster pots, and a jewel case with twenty silver anklets inlaid with lapis lazuli, carnelian and malachite. Inlaid gold hieroglyphs on the ebony panels of the carrying chair carried the fourfold inscription: 'Mother of the King of Upper and Lower Egypt, follower of Horus, guide of the Ruler, favorite whose every command is carried out for her, daughter of the god (born) of his body Hetep-Pheres.'"

BLACK HISTORY EVERYDAY
PART ONE

Black History Everyday - Part One
Photo. Faces in the crowd for the 50th Anniversary March on Washington.

Black History Everyday - Part One
Photo. Faces in the crowd for the 50th Anniversary March on Washington.

FREDERICK MONDERSON

In the tradition of powerful African women, Hetepheres was one of the greatest. The bust of Pharaoh Khufu is so African with his broad nose and thick lips; one can only wonder what his mother and father looked like. Naturally, we must accept, in the African mold, they were wonderful to behold.

However, who's better than the greatest? The answer is Teti-Sheri!

The Eighteenth Dynasty was the most remarkable of all others. This was so because of the females who provided the progeny and inspiration for this greatest golden period. Teti-Sheri was the wife of Sekenenra II. In *Temples, Tombs and Hieroglyphs*, Barbara Mertz wrote: "Teti-Sheri survived him; she lived to see her daughter marry her own brother, Sekenenra the Brave. [His son Kamose married Aahotep and their children were Aahmose and Nefertari.] Her grand-daughter Aahmose-Nefertari also married her brother, Ahmose .... Ahmose's queen was a lovely woman, and a great lady, who was deified in later times." Sekenenra was killed with an axe-blow to the head in the war of liberation against the Hyksos, or Asiatic invaders.

The family relationship of Teti-Sheri's progeny is important for it clearly establishes the Blackness of the Eighteenth Dynasty. In *The Splendor That Was Egypt* Margaret Murray describes Ahmose, the founder of the dynasty as, a "strongly built man, broad-shouldered, and with curly brown hair; he was

BLACK HISTORY EVERYDAY
PART ONE

not good-looking for he had projecting front teeth, and his portraiture suggests an admixture of Negro blood."

Black History Everyday - Part One Photo. We Shall Not be Moved March. Faces in the Crowd.

From her portrait in the British Museum the beautiful Ahmes-Nefertari leaves no doubt about her Black Ethiopian origin. Her grand-daughter Queen Hatshepsut had to contend with the fact of her "Ethiopian blood" as the heiress to the throne after her father Thutmose I's death, she seemed proud being part of the "Aahmes-Nefertari lineage." This equally remarkable woman challenged male dominance and ruled for two decades. Senmut, her favorite and architect who built the magnificent Deir el-Bahari temple at Thebes, headed her personal circle.

Senmut also quarried and erected two obelisks for the queen. Another architect, Amenhotep, erected two others. Two have disappeared and one still stands at Karnak while another remains where it has fallen. The standing obelisk measures 105 feet and is the tallest in Egypt. This queen who described her-self as "beautiful to look at above all things; her voice was that of a god; her frame that of a god; her spirit was like a god," maintained the prosperity of her nation but succumbed to male rage and dominance. Nevertheless, her name still ranks as one of the most beautiful and powerful of African heroines.

Queen Tiye was the wife of Amenhotep III and the mother of Amenhotep IV. Her husband ruled Egypt at the height of the New Kingdom's "Golden Age." She played a prominent role in events of her time. Amenhotep III built a palace called Malcata for his beautiful Black Queen Tiye. She had a significant impact on her son Amenhotep IV. He changed his name to Akhenaten and ushered in a new religious movement. Also, the art of the time was probably influenced by his ideas. Critics have credited her with influencing the rebellion in religion and art her son introduced.

Dushrata's daughter Thadukhippa, renamed Nefertiti, was a Mitanni princess who came to Egypt and married Queen Tiye's son Akhenaton or Ikhnaton. She came into a powerful family and played a significant role in her husband's rule. She

BLACK HISTORY EVERYDAY
PART ONE

bore him five daughters and visibly displayed her love for him in a number of representations.

In the Nineteenth Dynasty Rameses II, the great builder and warrior Pharaoh built the Abu Simbel temple in Nubia. He married Nefertari, a Nubian princess and built her a temple next to his at Abu Simbel. This was the supreme test of love, which clearly indicates the power of this African woman. Tausert, buried in the Valley of the Kings was the last ruler of the Nineteenth Dynasty.

This selection seeks to highlight the majesty, power, beauty and everlasting testimony of the greatness of African and African-American womanhood. Clearly, no nation on earth can boast such a splendid line of outstanding women as Egypt and the influence these exerted on their state in the young age of the world. They remain to be admired and serve as role models of integrity and accomplishment for an entire race of people. These were indeed great African women and they set powerful examples for progeny of the African race.

Queen Amendaris, sister of Piankhy of the Twenty Fifth Dynasty was a beautiful woman who became God's wife to Amon-Ra at Thebes following the Ethiopian conquest of Egypt. A temple was erected for her in the outer enclosure Migdol at Medinet Habu, mortuary temple of Rameses III, 20th Dynasty. Isis, the Ethiopian mother of Taharka was well-liked by her son and so she influenced him tremendously.

FREDERICK MONDERSON

Queen Cleopatra was beautiful and had to contend with the changing geo-political realities thrust upon her nation and she rose to the occasion. Ethiopia produced a strong line of queens called Candace who were warrior Queens and represented their nation and people with distinction. These followed in the tradition of Queen of Sheba, who while not a warrior, was Black and beautiful and a lover as well.

Black History Everyday – Part One Photo. We Shall Not be Moved March. Faces in the Crowd.

In West Africa, the role of Queen and Queen Mother was very significant contributing much to that culture cluster comprising the Ghana, Mali and Songhay empires. The descendants of these women were dragged off to be slaves in the New World. One of the first of those was **Angela** who disembarked

BLACK HISTORY EVERYDAY
PART ONE

from the Dutch Man O' War in 1691 and **Isabela** who in 1624 gave birth to the first Black-African child born in the New World. Tonya Bolden in *The Book of African-American Women* mentions 150 crusaders, creators and up-lifters of Black men in America. These women were in every walk of life, from slave to plantation owner. Some were entrepreneurs, preachers, abolitionists, activist-lecturers, thinkers, conductors of the Underground Railroad, writers, singers, mothers, nurses, spies, real estate investors, playwrights, cooks, poets, journalists, educators, civil rights activists, doctors, pharmacists, aviators, army officers, judges, lawyers, anthropologists, historians, dancers, psychologists, politicians, athletes, mathematicians and even more. Some were lynched and there were the "**Four Little Girls**," victims in a Birmingham Church bombing.

In looking at James Allen's exhibit on "Lynching across America" a grandmother in the line said: "I must get my grandchild to come over to look at this" as she viewed the Black woman **Laura Nelson who was lynched in Oklahoma in 1911**. That day both mother and son were lynched! Interestingly enough, there is no question that in the more than one hundred slave rebellions Herbert Aptheker chronicled in this hemisphere, women played a significant role, and we can add to this **Angela Davis** and **Assata Shakur**.

FREDERICK MONDERSON

Recognition is due the dignity and accomplishments of the ancient "Sheroes" mirrored in the struggles and untiring efforts of many modern women.

Black History Everyday – Part One
Photo. Faces in the crowd for the 50th Anniversary March on Washington.

Black History Everyday – Part One
Photo. Sign greeting visitors to the James Brown Statue in Augusta, Georgia. "Say it loud, I'm Black and I'm Proud!"

BLACK HISTORY EVERYDAY
PART ONE

Black History Everyday – Part One Photo. Faces in the crowd for the 50th Anniversary March on Washington.

They are all so beautiful and it's so hard to snub a beautiful woman. As Winston Churchill said: "It is hard, if not impossible, to snub a beautiful woman - they remain beautiful and the rebuke recoils." Let us remember the **Bible** says: "A virtuous woman is a crown to her husband." **George Meredith** (1829-1909) believed: "A witty woman is a treasure; a witty beauty is a power" and **Wordsworth** opined as so many here recounted: "A perfect woman, nobly planned, To warm, to comfort and command." So, to coin a phrase from **Charles Farrar Browne** (1834-1867), "The female woman is one of the greatest institutions of which this land can boast." The black man can echo similar sentiments as he cherishes, appreciates and is thankful for his woman, lover, heart throb, charming companion and fine specimen of nature. Of course, don't ever cross them, for as **William Congreve** (1670-1729) affirmed: "Heaven has no rage like love to hatred turned, Nor hell a fury like a woman scorned."

Black History Everyday - Part One Photo. **Pam Africa** and **Nickey Pinckney** at **CEMOTAP's** 31st Gala.

The African-American male is therefore fortunate to have such powerful women to stand with, beside and behind him to help guide his endeavors. Perhaps **William Dean Howells** (1837-1920) was right when he said: "They were Americans, and they knew how to worship a woman." Therefore, this tribute to these women is well deserved. There are conduits in the tradition of strong Black women bequeathing the strong yet tender and ferocious African womanism in

BLACK HISTORY EVERYDAY
PART ONE

the American experience. It's been said in this year of the tenth anniversary of the **Million Man March** (2005) we must have women this time for they were so essential in the March on October 16, 1995. Black men, make your women proud, they understand!

Black History Everyday – Part One Photo. We Shall Not be Moved March. Faces in the Crowd.

FREDERICK MONDERSON

Black History Everyday – Part One Photo. **Brother Walter Brown** of Atlanta, Georgia, stands before Peace and Justice Memorial Center in Montgomery, Alabama.

Black History Everyday – Part One Photo. Faces in the crowd for the 50th Anniversary March on Washington.

BLACK HISTORY EVERYDAY
PART ONE

Black History Everyday – Part One Photo. Brother Walter Brown stands before the Legacy Museum, in Montgomery, Alabama.

Black History Everyday Part One Photo. Faces in the crowd for the 50th Anniversary March on Washington.

FREDERICK MONDERSON

Black History Everyday - Part One Photo. Lest we forget how we were brought here!

"Salvation for a race, nation or class must come from within." **Asa Philip Randolph**. *The World Crisis and the Negro People Today.* [1940]

"Freedom is never Granted, it is won. Justice is never given, it is exacted." Asa Philip Randolph. *The World Crisis and the Negro People Today.*

Black History Everyday - Part One Photo. Rev. Herbert Daughtry stands for **JUSTICE**!

BLACK HISTORY EVERYDAY
PART ONE

Black History Everyday - Part One. Brother Walter Brown doing the "James Brown" alongside his buddy Brother Fred Monderson in Augusta, Georgia, all before images of "The Godfather of Soul."

Black History Everyday - Part One Photo. Plaza, so named for James Brown who brought great fame to his hometown, Augusta, Georgia. "The Sex Machine!"

2. A. PHILIP RANDOLPH'S MARCH ON WASHINGTON, DC IN 1941
BY
DR. FRED MONDERSON

Who was A. Philip Randolph? If we read his writings, we would realize he was one of the most brilliant minds of his age, Black or white. Randolph was confronted with the problems facing Black people in the first half of the 20th Century and he ably articulated and effectuated a leadership role that raised the issues and advanced the cause of Black freedoms and quest for equality in the Depression and Post-Depression age. A die-hard advocate of labor, Randolph saw Black salvation in America from a position of labor, activism that sought and brought integration in the workplace but more importantly, allowed the worker to demand and receive a decent wage to help raise the family. Beyond this milestone, he advocated mass movements and demonstrations to secure equality and social justice, and civil and human rights.

BLACK HISTORY EVERYDAY
PART ONE

Black History Everyday - Part One Photo. Labor Leader A. Philip Randolph in Union Station, Washington, D.C.

To understand the struggles of A. Philip Randolph, one has to understand the condition of Black people by the time of the **Great Depression** in 1929 and the significance of the election that followed in 1932.

From the time of Abraham Lincoln's *Emancipation Proclamation* (1863), and election of the **Radical Republicans** in Congress who were instrumental in securing the 13th, 14th, and 15th Amendments to the Constitution (1865-1868) as well as numerous Civil Rights legislations in the 19th Century particularly

FREDERICK MONDERSON

those of **Reconstruction** (1865-1877), Blacks have voted Republican, the "Party of Lincoln." Yet, substantive issues were not fully addressed in the age of terror, especially in the South. Gains made consistent with new Black voting strength were later lost in a systematic and concerted campaign of disfranchisement as whites eventually regained power.

Black History Everyday - Part One Photo. We Shall Not be Moved March. Faces in the Crowd.

John P. Davis in *The American Negro Reference Book* (1967: 63) recounts how after disappointments with the Teddy Roosevelt and Howard Taft Administrations, things got no better and Blacks looked for relief. "In 1912 they were willing to turn to any group that promised some hope. To some Negroes, Woodrow Wilson seemed to provide some hope when he said, during his campaign, that he wished to see 'justice done to the colored people in every matter; and not mere grudging justice, but

BLACK HISTORY EVERYDAY
PART ONE

justice executed with liberality and cordial good feeling." Shortly after Wilson's inauguration, it became clear to most Negroes that they could not rely on Wilson or his party for support in their efforts. Soon, segregation was reintroduced in the nation's capital and in the offices of the Federal government."

Still, Black commitment to the Republican Party continued through World War I (1914-1918), the great economic advances of the 1920s and passed the great **Stock Market Crash** in 1929, which ushered in the **Great Depression**. Yet, despite their loyalty to the Republican Party that generally won most elections, Blacks were for the most part, ignored and their condition never improved in the age of terror through which they lived.

In this, the first few years of the Depression hit home hard and Blacks were doubly affected, being the last hired and first fired. Therefore, Blacks decided to switch parties in 1932 and voted overwhelmingly for the Democrat Franklin Delano Roosevelt, who proclaimed and promised the "**New Deal**." They repeated this support again in 1936 and again in 1940. As such then, while the "New Deal" sought to seriously confront the wrenching conditions of the Depression with its "**Alphabet Programs**," the issue of the day was jobs. Interestingly enough, as the "drums of war" in Europe began to beat louder and louder in the minds and hearts of the American people, the war industry of the "home front" geared

FREDERICK MONDERSON

for the inevitable. This one place where jobs were in great supply as the nation fed the "**Lend-Lease Program**," the ugly face of racism and discrimination sought to exclude the Black man, confining him to a few jobs in the most degrading and dead-end positions of janitor, sweepers and elevator operators. The record seems to show, for example, of the thirty thousand jobs in New York City, only 142 were held by Blacks in the above-mentioned positions and this example was indicative of the broader social condition of Blacks in the nation's workforce.

Accordingly, **Executive Order 8802** issued June 25, 1941 highlighted the evident situation: "Whereas there is evidence that available and needed workers have been barred from employment in industries engaged in defense production solely because of considerations of race, creed, color, or national origin, to the detriment of workers' morale and of national unity."

Bradford Chambers in *Chronicles of Black Protest* (1968: 174) recounts: "In the armed forces, segregation was still the official government policy, a carry-over from the Civil War. Black newspapers reported 'race riots at Fort Oswego; discrimination at Fort Devens; Jim Crow Conditions at Camps Blanding and Lee; and the edict – 'Not to shake a Nigger's hand at Camp Upton.' The *Baltimore Afro-American* called for thousands of Black men to desert rather than serve in army camps in the South."

BLACK HISTORY EVERYDAY
PART ONE

Black History Everyday - Part One
Photo. Faces in the crowd for the 50th Anniversary March on Washington.

Black History Everyday - Part One
Photo. Faces in the crowd for the 50th Anniversary March on Washington.

FREDERICK MONDERSON

Into this mix, A. Philip Randolph had been active for more than two decades, primarily as a labor-unionist but more interested in the well-being of Black people, then generally referred to as Negroes. As early as 1935 he became **President of the Brotherhood of Sleeping Car Porters** on the railroad, but also active in the **National Negro Congres**s, Co-Chairman of **The American Committee on Africa**, as well as Co-Chairman of **The American Negro Leadership Conference on Africa**.

BLACK HISTORY EVERYDAY PART ONE

Black History Everyday - Part One Photo. Real engaging image of **James Brown,** the "**God Father of Soul!**"

Philip Foner in *The Voice of Black America* (1972: 808) tells about A. Philip Randolph. "Born April 15, 1889, in Crescent City, Florida, Randolph finished high school in Florida, worked his way North and subsisted on odd jobs while attending City College of New York. (He never earned a college degree, and was mostly self-taught). Together with Chandler Owen, a young black law student at Columbia University, Randolph became active in the Socialist Party, and both edited The Messenger, a radical black journal of opinion which endorsed Socialism and was a leading voice of the "New Negro" in the post-World War I period. Randolph was asked by the Pullman porters to help them organize, and in 1935, after twelve years of hard struggle, the Brotherhood of Sleeping Car Porters, with Randolph as President, forced the Pullman Company to recognize it."

In his Address to the **National Negro Congress** held in Chicago February 14, 15, 16 in 1936 of which a pamphlet is in the **Schomberg Library** in Harlem, New York, and in Foner (1972: 810-811) where after speaking of the problems facing Europe on the eve of World War II, Randolph turned to the condition of the Black man in America in that "Depression" and "New Deal" era. To this he stated,

FREDERICK MONDERSON

"Our contemporary history is a witness to the stark fact that Black-America is a victim of both class and race prejudice and oppression. Because Negroes are black, they are hated, maligned and spat upon, lynched, mobbed and murdered. Because Negroes are workers, they are browbeaten, bullied, intimidated, robbed, exploited, jailed and shot down. Because they are black, they are caught between the nether millstones of discrimination when seeking a job to join a union."

"Thus, voiceless in thirteen states; politically disregarded and discounted in the others; victims of lynch terror in Dixie, with a Scottsboro frame-up of notorious memory; faced with the label of the white man's job and the white man's union; unequal before the law; Jim-Crowed in schools and colleges throughout the nation; segregated in the slums and ghettos of the urban centers; landless peons of a merciless landlordism; hunted down, harassed and hounded as vagrants in the Southern cities, the Negro people face a hard, deceptive and brutal capitalist order, despite its preachments of Christian love and brotherhood."

Further he indicated, Black progress must come through admission into the industrial and craft unions, to which he opined, "the craft union invariably has a color bar against the Negro worker, but the industrial union in structure renders race discrimination less possible, since it embraces all the workers included in the industry, regardless of race, creed, color, or craft, skilled or unskilled. Thus, this

BLACK HISTORY EVERYDAY PART ONE

Congress should seek to broaden and intensify the movement to draw Negro workers into labor organizations and break down the color bar in the trade-unions that now have it. The next instrumentality which the workers must build and employ for their protection against economic exploitation, war and fascism, is an independent working-class political party. It should take the form of a farmer-labor political organization. This is indispensable in view of the bankruptcy in principles, courage and vision of the old-line parties, Republican and Democratic."

Black History Everyday – Part One Photo. Outstanding stalwarts being honored at **CEMOTAP's** 31st Anniversary Luncheon.

Randolph says further, in Foner (1972: 813-814), pointing out: "The fight for civil and political rights of the Negro peoples can effectively be carried on if only those organizations that are pushing the struggles are broadened and built with a wider mass

FREDERICK MONDERSON

base. Those organizations that are serving on the civil-rights front effectively for the Negro are the **National Association for the Advancement of Colored People** and the **International Labor Defense**. It needs to be definitely understood, however, that the fight in the courts for civil and political rights cannot be effective except when backed by a broad nationwide, if not international, mass protest through demonstrations in the form of parades, mass meetings and publicity."

Black History Everyday – Part One Photo. Former NY State Assemblyman Karim Camara at Rev. Al Sharpton's "Power and Policy forum" on MLK's Birthday, January 20, 2020.

BLACK HISTORY EVERYDAY PART ONE

Black History Everyday - Part One Photo. Luis makes a point that **Black Lives Matter** at Sharpton and Crump's March to Freedom Square in Washington, DC.

FREDERICK MONDERSON

Black History Everyday - Part One Photo. Memorial in praise of the **Tuskegee Airmen** who performed admirably in World War II.

Randolph cautioned, Philip Foner (1972: 814) continued: "The task of overcoming the enemies of democratic institutions and constitutional liberties is too big for any single organization. It requires the united and formal integrating and coordinating of the various Negro organizations – church, fraternal, civil, trade-union, farmer, professional, college and what not – into the framework of a united front, together with the white groups of workers, lovers of liberty and those whose liberties are similarly menaced for a common attack upon the forces of reaction, backed by the embattled masses of black and white workers. The united front strategy and tactics should be executed through methods of mass demonstration, such as parades, picketing, boycotting, mass protests, the mass distribution of propaganda literature, as well as legal action."

BLACK HISTORY EVERYDAY
PART ONE

Black History Everyday - Part One Photo. One of James Brown's famous hats, now famously remembered in an Augusta, Ga. Museum.

Black History Everyday - Part One Photo. Faces in the crowd for the 50th Anniversary March on Washington.

FREDERICK MONDERSON

"The salvation of the Negro like the workers, must come from within," he believed. Then he chronicled challenges facing Blacks, particularly during the 1930s. He indicated: "These issues should be obvious, clear and simple, such as prevention of stoppage of relief, cuts in relief allotments, layoffs of relief workers or workers in any industry, discrimination in the giving of relief, exorbitant rents, evictions, rent increases, police brutality, denial of free assembly, freedom of the press, freedom of speech to unpopular groups, denial of civil rights to Negroes, access to public utilities and forms of transportation, such as the Pullman car."

He called on Blacks to be involved and advocated: "Wage struggles around war upon Ethiopia by the fascist dictator Mussolini, strikes and lockouts of black and white workers, the amendment to the federal constitution or the adoption of social legislation such as the Retirement Pension Act for railroad workers, fight for the freedom of **Angelo Herndon**, the **Scottsboro Boys**, the **Wagner-Costigan anti-lynching bill**, the violations of the **Wagner Labor Disputes Bill**, the forcing of teachers to take the oath, the goose-stepping of the students in the school system thru the R.O.T.C., the abolition of the color bar in trade-unions, the **murder of Shoemaker in Tampa**, Florida, exposing the **menace of the American Liberty League**, **William Randolph Hearst** and the **Ku Klux Klan**, and

BLACK HISTORY EVERYDAY
PART ONE

supporting the movement of **John L. Lewis** for industrial unionism."

Such is the task of the Negro people as Randolph outlined them. Nevertheless, continued Randolph: "To meet the task, the Negro peoples, pressed with their backs against the wall, must face the future with heads erect, hearts undaunted and undismayed, ready and willing and determined to pay the price in struggle, sacrifices and suffering that freedom, justice and peace shall share and enjoy a more abundant life."

Black History Everyday - Part One Photo. We Shall Not be Moved March. Faces in the Crowd.

In a further speech, upon its 150th anniversary entitled *The Crisis of the Negro and the Constitution* in Foner (1972: 816-817), Randolph stated: "Freedom is never

FREDERICK MONDERSON

given; it is won. And the Negro people must win their freedom. They must achieve justice. This involves struggle, continuous struggle. True liberation can be acquired and maintained only when the Negro masses possess power; and power is the product and flower of organization - organization of the masses, the masses in the mills and mines, on the farms, in the factories, in churches, in fraternal organizations, in homes, colleges, women's clubs, student groups, trade-unions, tenants' leagues, in co-operative guilds, political organizations and civil-rights associations."

Black History Everyday - Part One Photo. The sign is crystal clear at **Sharpton and Crump's March at Freedom Square in Washington, DC**.

BLACK HISTORY EVERYDAY
PART ONE

Still, despite the organizing and speech-making, Blacks continued to face major obstacles and difficulties in the society. All this, and despite the sympathetic attitude of the President's wife, Eleanor Roosevelt and even the efforts of the "Black Cabinet" who consulted with President Roosevelt himself. As the war unfolded in Europe, Blacks sought meaningful jobs in the war industries from which they were generally excluded. It was time for action!

In January, 1941, A. Philip Randolph, as head of *The Brotherhood of Sleeping Car Porters Union* issued a call for a "March on Washington, D.C.," insisting "Ten, twenty, fifty thousand Negroes" would gather on the White House Lawn on July 1, 1941, to demand the federal government end discrimination in civilian and military job contracts. Importantly, however, if we look to Randolph's activism, we get a broader view of the overall condition of Black in the depression years leading to the war, despite their voting record as Democrats.

Randolph was joined by other Black leaders Walter White, Adam Clayton Powell, Jr., and Frank Crosswaith to demand, according to Chambers (1968: 175) that the "federal government take action to stop discrimination in the defense industries and the armed forces." Imagine, 9 years later and three significant Democratic victories and Blacks were still waiting for significant changes in the American social and civic order. Chambers (1968: 175) continued: "The idea of a black revolt in a time of

FREDERICK MONDERSON

crisis threw Washington into a panic. President Roosevelt called the March leaders to Washington and tried to persuade them to call it off." They refused! Interesting, for people don't generally refuse the President.

The **Program of the March on Washington** on July 1, 1941 was as follows:

"We demand, in the interest of national unity, the abrogation of every law which makes a distinction in treatment between citizens based on religion, color, or national origin. This means an end to Jim Crow in education, in housing, in transportation and in every other social, economic, and political privilege; and especially, we demand, in the capital of the nation, an end to all segregation in public places and in public institutions."

"We demand legislation to enforce the Fifth and Fourteenth Amendments guaranteeing that no person shall be deprived of life, liberty or property without due process of law, so that the full weight of the national government may be used for the protection of life and thereby may end the disgrace of lynching."

"We demand the enforcement of the Fourteenth and Fifteenth Amendments and the enactment of the Pepper Poll Tax Bill so that all barriers in the exercise of the suffrage are eliminated."

BLACK HISTORY EVERYDAY
PART ONE

"We demand the abolition of segregation and discrimination in the Army, Navy, Marine Corps, Air Corps, and all other branches of national defense."

"We demand an end to discrimination in jobs and job training. Further, we demand that the FEPC be made a permanent administrative agency of the U.S. Government and that it be given power to enforce its decisions based on its findings."

"We demand that federal funds be withheld from any agency which practices discrimination in the use of such funds."

"We demand colored and minority group representation on all administrative agencies so that these groups may have recognition of their democratic rights to participate in formulating policies."

Black History Everyday - Part One Photo. Faces in the crowd for the 50th Anniversary March on Washington.

FREDERICK MONDERSON

Black History Everyday - Part One
Photo. Brother Walter Brown with "Hands Up" at the Lynching Memorial in Montgomery, Alabama.

Black History Everyday - Part One
Photo. Faces in the crowd for the 50th Anniversary March on Washington.

BLACK HISTORY EVERYDAY
PART ONE

We demand representation for the colored and minority racial groups on all missions, political and technical, which will be sent to the peace conference so that the interests of all people everywhere may be truly recognized and justly provided for in the postwar settlement.

The **March** never happened, because of **necessity President Roosevelt** signed **Executive Order 8802** in June 25, 1941, days before the March date. This **Executive Order** banned discrimination in the war industries and government training programs, and established a **President's Commission on Fair Employment Practices**.

Black History Everyday - Part One Photo. Faces in the crowd for the 50th Anniversary March on Washington.

FREDERICK MONDERSON

Nevertheless, while **FEPA** (Fair Employment Practices Act) banned selective job discrimination, desegregation of the Armed Forces had to wait until the death of FDR, end of World War II and the new Harry Truman Administration, when the **Armed Forces Act** officially ended discrimination in the military.

Notwithstanding, most of the other issues mentioned in the program had to be hard won in the late 1940s, the 1950s and well into the Civil Rights struggles of the 1960s and beyond. We can never forget Frederick Douglass' statement: "Power concedes nothing without a struggle. It never did and it never will."

Black History Everyday - Part One Photo. Brother Walter Brown poses with a visiting couple before chained captive at the Equal Justice Initiative Memorial.

BLACK HISTORY EVERYDAY PART ONE

It was Randolph who actually originated the 1963 March on Washington. Davis (1967: 476) wrote: "The march on Washington originated with A. Philip Randolph, militant head of the **Brotherhood of Sleeping Car Porters**. It was organized and programmed by Bayard Rustin, former field Secretary of **CORE**, who also organized the New York City school boycott. Every Negro protest organization working for integration was represented, as were a number of white or mixed supporting organizations representing labor, churches and civic and various liberal groups. Martin Luther King, Jr., James Farmer, Roy Wilkins, A. Philip Randolph and John Lewis were the principal speakers."

Randolph was unquestionably a brilliant mind, consummate activist, jailed for 2 years while editor of the *Messenger* during World War I and whose ideas laid the foundation strategies for the later Civil Rights Movement. He initially called for a **United Front Movement** that Malcolm X later championed and Jitu Weusi and Conrad Worrill and Rev. Herbert Daughtry subscribed to. Unfortunately, Randolph has not gotten the credit he deserves for the pivotal and *Avant Garde* role he played as a Civil Rights activist who made a difference.

FREDERICK MONDERSON

Black History Everyday - Part One Photo. Members stand and applause for words spoken at the Dais during **CEMOTAP's** 31st Anniversary Luncheon.

Black History Everyday - Part One Photo. Faces in the crowd for the 50th Anniversary March on Washington.

"It is true that Mr. Lincoln singed the **Emancipation Proclamation**, after which there was a commitment to give forty acres and a

BLACK HISTORY EVERYDAY
PART ONE

mule. That's where the argument, to this day, of reparation starts. We never got the forty acres.... We didn't get the mule. So, we decided we'd ride this donkey as far as it would take us. Alfred Sharpton. *Speech to the Democratic National Convention* [2004]

"There's a difference between peace and quiet. Quiet means shut up. Quiet means suffer in silence. Peace means justice. We want peace, but won't get quiet until we get justice." *Speech at the funeral of Sean Bell* [December 1, 2006]

3. REV. AL. SHARPTON: THE NEXT LEVEL AND EARNED ASCENT BY DR. FRED MONDERSON

In recent months a number of friends have approached me with a single question: "What do you think of this Sharpton thing?" As a free and critical thinker, I could only respond: "I think it was the best thing that has happened to Sharpton and certainly his constituency." Then they would assume a puzzling countenance with a follow up: "Well, explain." In as much as I have not done so, I now venture to offer my considered opinion.

FREDERICK MONDERSON

I thought then and now the government made a mistake with putting Sharpton in Jail! They should have thought it out first and then said, pardon the pun: "Rev. Sharpton, we know you are concerned about this matter and are moving to resolve this issue, so you should go home." They did not and this set-in motion a consciousness raising and mobilization of people and sentiment, unimagined. The Pope called for the First Crusade; **Jitu Weusi** called for the First **African Arts "Street" Festival**; and when Sharpton does and calls for people to get arrested, they come running. Talk about Love Offering!

Importantly, after his lengthy imprisonment, Sharpton emerged, thinner, fitter, more conscious and with a vision of salvation for the nation's downtrodden, silent victims and the dispossessed, disenfranchised and discriminated against. All this, with a view to polishing and brightening America's image at home and abroad. Yet still, as such, it leaves one to wonder who are making those decisions in Washington.

BLACK HISTORY EVERYDAY
PART ONE

Black History Everyday - Part One Photo. We Shall Not be Moved March. Faces in the Crowd.

As a young activist, some friends were expecting me to run for Congress. That notwithstanding, so much has happened since those days with family, college, community, job, etc., that such a dream was not realized. Still, along the way, and trained as a historian, I see a litany of parallels in governments making similar mistakes that left them in the dust. Even more important, the individuals who "spoke truth to power" ended up having significant impacts on the issues of their time and the challenged governments ended up with cake on their face, to say the least.

FREDERICK MONDERSON

Black History Everyday - Part One Photo. Rev. Al Sharpton addressing **NAN's** "Keepers of the Dream Conference" in 2018.

If we look back far enough, we can see; first, Moses who was imprisoned challenged Pharaoh and the end result was catastrophic for that nation and antiquity as some evidence seem to indicate. The Bible tells of **Daniel in the Lion's Den** and the brothers **Shadrack**, **Meshack** and **Abednego**, whom Nebuchadnezzar imprisoned in the fire were protected and this did not do much for the King's image. The establishment and its interests had Delilah cut Samson's hair and both columns and the walls came tumbling down. Herod had Salome dance, then cut off John the Baptist's head. However, he served his function in validating the coming messiah. Then, the Romans and their corroborators killed Jesus and two millennia later his movement,

BLACK HISTORY EVERYDAY
PART ONE

Christianity, boasts a following of more than a billion believers.

Black History Everyday - Part One Photo. Faces in the crowd for the 50th Anniversary March on Washington.

Black History Everyday - Part One Photo. Faces in the crowd for the 50th Anniversary March on Washington.

FREDERICK MONDERSON

The Church censured Copernicus and look where we are today, in the heavens. Then Napoleon imprisoned Toussaint L'Ouverture and this emboldened Dessalines and Christophe to create in Haiti, a Black beacon of hope in a raging sea of enslavement and racial turbulence. This in the aftermath of the British iron fist against the American colonists that forced the "founding fathers" to challenge that juggernaut and the result was an American nation, the tenacity of whose founders created a system that has survived for centuries and is a great beacon and hope for mankind. In this, Nathan Hale, challenged the British, and was sorry he only had one life to give for his country. Denmark Vesey, in 1822, after his failed revolt faced his captors and proudly spoke: "I know you intend to shed my blood. What then is the purpose of a trial? I have only one life to give for the liberation, freedom of my people as would George Washington, had he been captured by the British. So, take me quickly to be executed." As testimony to such martyrdom, and in the tradition of its purpose, this country is being challenged today to enact reforms to live out its creed. Lest we forget, Thomas Jefferson is quoted as saying: "When I think there is a just God, I tremble for this nation."

In Harlem, Marcus Garvey was betrayed and imprisoned after he had galvanized Black people worldwide, resuscitated their cultural history, created their "men of big affairs" and began economic organization that was to have national and global repercussions. All the while he emphasized "Africa for the Africans, those at home and abroad." That

BLACK HISTORY EVERYDAY
PART ONE

Africans should have a voice in their own destiny, he argued, while upholding their right to own the land they lived on that they and their ancestors had lived on and equally tilled. In this effort, he was able to found the **UNIVERSAL NEGRO IMPROVEMENT ASSOCIATION (ANIA)** and **AFRICAN COMMUNITIES LEAGUE (ACL)**, that created the **Black Cross Nurses**, the historic and mystical **Red, Black and Green** flag, and ushered in the notion of and Philosophy of Garveyism with its Garveyite followers. He was betrayed, this "Moses of his people," accused, tried and imprisoned. On way to the Atlanta Federal Prison, handcuffed, he prophesized: "Look for me in the whirlwind. You have caged the tiger but the cubs are running free out there." Today Marcus Garvey is regarded as an authentic Black hero, an ancestor of merit and substance. Many of his ideas have stood the test of time. His organization, the UNIA still thrives and the Red, Black and Green once flew over the nation's Capital Building during the Million Man March on October 16, 1995.

We will not be turned back! "I feel no way tired," Rev. Cleveland often exclaimed: "Get out there and protest." In calling for such action, he admonished, "Let your blood flow in the street." "We've come too far to turn back now. I don't think he brought me this

FREDERICK MONDERSON

far to leave me now." Sharpton is a significant leader in this forward thrust.

Black History Everyday - Part One Photo. We Shall Not be Moved March. Faces in the Crowd.

The British government imprisoned Mahatma Gandhi and his non-violent creative protest won, ending in establishment of a nation state of India. So overwhelming had been his noon-violent, creative protest movement, the British simply walked away, out of frustration.

In Africa, Kwame Nkrumah, Jomo Kenyatta, Albert Luthuli, Sekou Toure, Namdi Azikwe, Ahmed Ben Bella, and many others were imprisoned in struggle to decolonize their respective African nations ending cultural, educational, political and economic dehumanization and exploitation of African people and their natural resources. Patrice Lumumba was imprisoned then killed in the Congo but his

BLACK HISTORY EVERYDAY PART ONE

martyrdom was a victory for the people, defeat for colonialism and a realignment of "North-South" relationships.

In the ensuing political and historical thunderstorm of the times, Harold Macmillan labeled the "winds of change," the odious system of apartheid imprisoned Nelson Mandela and the gentleman, possessing Chieftainship wherewithal, weathered decades of that racist storm. Truly, one man can become a majority if his truth is sound and he persists in the ideals of his conviction. The world finally caught up with Mandela, and then globally people saw the light, the true nature of the man, and the prize he struggled for. The end result was not simply the end of apartheid, the creation of a non-racial South Africa, but empowered a Truth Commission that exposed the horrors of the oppressive government apparatus the system of apartheid had perpetuated. Revealed, were the methods of oppression where the government killed Steven Biko among others in **The Graves at Dimbaza**, as these martyrs sought to right the wrongs of a society warped by the notion of racial superiority and untold wealth and political power enjoyed exceedingly by a racist minority at the expense of the African majority.

At home, Rosa Parks was arrested for sitting on a segregated bus. Significantly, however, the defiance set in motion a firestorm that did wonders for the image of America as it was forced to examine itself and expose the insidious lacerations of its actions against itself, against its citizens. In that turbulence forcing creative social protest, Martin Luther King, Jr., emerged and in forcing the American system to confront itself, he was imprisoned, where he penned his famous "Letter from a Birmingham Jail." This action of imprisonment did more for the cause of social justice in America than most would ever understand. These creative yet correct thoughts undergirded the struggle and laid the foundation for the significance of Dr. King's "Dream." Now, decades later, the "King Holiday Marches" of protest that keep alive his ideas, enable observers to see the wisdom of Dr. King's creative protests, recognizing his was a battle cry as a "Drum Major" to improve the rights of the poor and downtrodden. Certainly Jesse Jackson, Andrew Young, John Lewis, Julian Bond, Fannie Lou Hamer, Rev. Shuttlesworth, Medgar Evers, and others got their heads busted and were imprisoned but the collective successes of their efforts has helped in transforming America, where so many people, ethnicities, persuasions and physicalities benefited.

BLACK HISTORY EVERYDAY
PART ONE

Black History Everyday - Part One Photo. Luis and Erik were there at **Sharpton and Crump's March** on Washington, DC, at Freedom Square.

Black History Everyday - Part One Photo. Faces in the crowd for the 50th Anniversary March on Washington.

FREDERICK MONDERSON

Sonny Carson was arrested and ended up fighting the system by keeping tabs on the Prison Industrial Complex and its attitudes towards Blacks, Hispanics and other peoples of color. In addition, Carson extended his activism to honoring Black Heroes through the Committee to Honor Black Heroes. He was effective in naming streets, schools, etc., in their honor, viz., Martin Luther King Boulevard, Malcolm X Boulevard, Malcolm X School, Akbar Place, Harriet Tubman Boulevard, etc., in Brooklyn. With far reaching implications, Sonny was instrumental in returning a runaway slave; his ancestor, Samuel Carson, to Ghana, West Africa. In 1845, he served in the United States Navy and in the 1990s the Navy discovered his bones, buried in the then segregated Brooklyn, Navy Yard where one marine was identified as early as 1801. The bones were turned over to his grand-nephew Sonny Carson. Thus, the **Repatriation of Samuel Carson** opened the "**Door of Return**." This historic action was a highlight of the 1998 **First Emancipation Day Festival** held in that West African nation on August 1, 1998. That significant gesture remained Sonny's guiding light until the end as he continued to struggle to reclaim the bones of so many other enslaved Africans.

Many of our progressive ministers were jailed. Institutional builder Rev. Herbert Daughtry and iconic Malcolm X, made their contributions to raising the consciousness of African people.

BLACK HISTORY EVERYDAY
PART ONE

Black History Everyday - Part One Photo. We Shall Not be Moved March. Faces in the Crowd.

Rev. Al Sharpton came of age in the backdrop of all these happenings. He carved his own path of activism in his climb from humble beginnings. His is the true story of living the American Dream. Yet, some say the legal system was unfair to Sharpton in giving him 90 days of imprisonment over Vieques. Perhaps not so, for the instrument of that action, the presiding judge was simply following the law for repeat offenders, which Sharpton was. Consider that he had been arrested before as he forced New York City to confront its racial attitudes when four New York City policemen shot the West African merchant Amadou Diallo 41 times. One cop, Witherspoon argued for 42, perhaps 43 shots were fired at Amadou. Look at the litany of high and low who followed this African American genius, Al Sharpton,

FREDERICK MONDERSON

to be arrested in systematic protest in front of One Police Plaza. Can I just mention David Dinkins, Ed Koch, Charles Rangel, Major Owens, even Floyd Flake, and the rest you know? It was work of a visionary who, in the tradition of the American system that shed light beyond the Blue Wall. All this coming after Howard Beach, Bensonhurst, Tawana Brawley, Abner Louima, Anthony Baez, James Byrd, racial profiling, etc., statesmanship following the wrongful verdict in the "Rodney King" trial and so many other "trials."

In 1994, when this writer endorsed Al Sharpton for Senator against Daniel Moynihan, I believed then and still do, Sharpton is the quintessential American nationalist steeped in the tradition of the founding patriots as Crispus Attucks, America's first authentic hero. Then as now, I measured his idealism, as it became refined, tempered in struggle to give voice to those victimized by society's institutions and its mindless minions who perpetuate racial, religious, political, and sexual violence and discrimination. This is the record the judge saw when he "threw the book at Sharpton." He saw Sharpton as championing causes that were not popular. His well-documented acts of civil disobedience gave voice of concern to the powerless and many not so powerless. After all, Sharpton helped to raise national attention to urban, youth, education, police brutality, prison reform, senseless violence, homelessness and other social problems that affect Blacks, women, Native Americans, immigrants, disabled, and particularly people from the Caribbean. Strange, many

BLACK HISTORY EVERYDAY
PART ONE

victimized by racial violence were from the Caribbean and Africa. And, as a true Pan-Africanist, Garveyite in outlook, Sharpton was there, not questioning their national origin. He has been outspoken on Somalia, Haiti, Uganda, shown interest in Jamaica, West Indies, slavery in Sudan and is known around the world, from Algeria to Zimbabwe. This is why institutions as the *New York Post* among others character assassinate Al Sharpton because he makes these people nervous when eh shines light on the many problems minorities and the poor face. Rather than focus on such ills, they attack Sharpton but in doing so, they raise his profile and his value to the oppressed.

The Vieques incident, therefore, was a culmination of a strategy and tactic of civil disobedience in form of demonstrations, sit-ins, boycotts, sanctioned by the American constitution and used so effectively in the civil rights struggle. It is what Dr. King called **creative protest**! Now, as he moves to the next level, progressives around the nation can help mold Sharpton's vision as he charts a course for betterment of the American system. But, why not Sharpton? When we consider, what Blacks got out of the 2000 presidential election? They turned out en-masse and voted primarily Democratic. In Florida there was significant disfranchisement and perhaps in other locations too. Following the questionable results, nothing has been said regarding this constituency. It's like Prof. John Clarke used to say: "When I look

FREDERICK MONDERSON

for our picture in **All of US**, we are not there." Paul Robeson's picture is not in that famous one at Rutgers, though he was their star running back. Consider how he was treated and equally Al Sharpton.

Black History Everyday - Part One Photo. Faces in the crowd for 50th Anniversary March on Washington.

"How Long? Not long, because the Arc of the Moral Universe is long, but it bends toward Justice." **Martin Luther King, Jr**. *Sermon on the Vietnam war, Riverside Church*. New York [April 4, 1967]

"The Ultimate measure of a man is not where he stands in moments of comfort and convenience, but where he stands at times of challenge and controversy." **Dr. Martin Luther King**. *Strength to Love*.

BLACK HISTORY EVERYDAY
PART ONE
4. ARC OF THE MORAL UNIVERSE
BY
DR. FRED MONDERSON

Dr. Martin Luther King exhorted, "The arc of the moral universe is long, but it bends towards justice!" Sadly, it may have taken Donald Trump a long time to realize this!

At his **2005 Inaugural**, the **Republican President George W. Bush decried the prevalence of racism in the country** up to that date, one hundred and fifty years after the **Dred Scott Decision of 1857**, **Emancipation Proclamation** and subsequently the **Civil War Amendments**. Through **Jim Crow** (1865-1890), *Plessey v. Ferguson* (1896), *Brown v. Board of Education* (1954), the **Civil Rights Acts** (1964) and the **Voting Rights Act** (1965) in response to activism of the **Civil Rights Movemen**t these milestones demonstrated earned advances in the American social order. The 1965 Voting Rights Act empowered African-Americans to gain political representation across the different states, culmination in the 2008 election of Barack Obama as the first African-American President. In response, the then

FREDERICK MONDERSON

Mayor of Newark, New Jersey, Cory Booker characterized Mr. Obama's election victory as ushering in a new post-racial America. Naturally, there was a difference of opinion on both sides of the issue, Black and White.

Black History Everyday - Part One Photo. We Shall Not be Moved March. Faces in the Crowd.

Then along came Mr. Mitch McConnell (R. Kentucky), Minority Leader in the Democratic controlled Senate of the United States Congress. First, Mr. McConnell made a publicly advertised statement, "I intend to make Barack Obama a one-term president."

This statement, Mr. Morgan Freeman, the actor, on Piers Morgan's CNN program, characterized as "blatantly racist!" Mr. McConnell's next ground-

BLACK HISTORY EVERYDAY
PART ONE

breaking and outrageous act was, after an important round of negotiations with the President, where bright-eyed and bushy tailed, a smiling Mr. McConnell emerged and gave that now infamous "thumbs up" signal to likeminded cohorts on television who were probably in the treasonous gathering. Observers with penetrating vision saw this for what it was, "a coded signal to his handlers" that "I got that Nigger in the White House!" Some five years later in October 6, 2013, *The New York Times* newspaper published a "big write-up" indicating in the run-up to the 2012 election, a group of influential Republicans and their backers met and strategized on how to deny Mr. Obama a second term; that is, after they universally opposed him in every way, politically, legislatively, even morally, and certainly with the help of "right wing media." and in conjunction with Donald Trump and his venomous "birther" falsity. The article named Ed Meese as principal along with CEOs of some 20 Republican affiliated non-governmental organizations. Many were involved in training programs designed to propagandize falsity to generate opposition to Mr. Obama's **Affordable Care Act**. Astute observers characterized the gathering as a treasonous conspiracy to subvert the legally elected representative of the United States Government. Today the names and faces of all so involved has become public knowledge. With the 2012 act now manifest, the "long plot" by McConnell "the plotter," now seems evident thought Mr. Obama proved clever and victorious on "both go-rounds."

FREDERICK MONDERSON

Because Mr. Obama is African-American who had the audacity to declare for the presidency, beat back his democratic challengers and be chosen to represent his party, a number of racial cross-currents began to emerge directed at Barack Obama. While Blacks accused him of "not being Black enough," Whites accused him of "being too Black." As a result, a whole flurry of activity mobilized to denounce Mr. Obama's quest. Republican propaganda helped spread false notions Mr. Obama would change the Constitution, that he was a Muslim, and this fueled right-wing militias to purchase and stock up on enormous armaments, exhibited camped training sessions for the coming "race war" which, up to this date, have yet to materialize.

An unregistered plumber named "Joe the Plumber" accused Mr. Obama of promoting socialism and this garnered him enormous but short-lived fame. "I can see Russia from my front porch" "Lipstick on a pig" Sarah Palin then accused Mr. Obama of "Palling around with terrorists." Questions of his patriotism, ability to effectively lead and lack of foreign policy experience proved enormous capital for the Anti-Obamaites. Still Mr. Obama forged ahead with an effective organizational strategy driven by a tremendous work ethic and an unfailing desire to be successful while not paying much attention to nay-Sayers. Simmering but now more visibly active, the "Birther" movement escalated with its queen and king Trump on their fools' errand and while this falsity emboldened anti-Obama forces which gave

BLACK HISTORY EVERYDAY
PART ONE

birth to the "Tea Party" formation. Through all this, Mitch McConnell's parallel quest remained in full stride. All the while, the "Party of No's" obstructionist agenda blocked every legislative effort of Mr. Obama designed to improve the condition and advance the cause of the American people through Executive Action he achieved much. Meanwhile, Senator Mitch McConnell, having been issued his charge set about leading the plowed path of opposition as part of the grand scheme we could come to learn of later.

Black History Everyday - Part One Photo. Prof. James Smalls in full effect at **CEMOTAP** expounding on Pan-African philosophy and esoteric and spiritual significance.

Undaunted, President Obama continued to repair the faltering auto industry; lending money to banks and

FREDERICK MONDERSON

bailed out Wall Street. It strengthening the nation's economy; assessed the nation's crumbling infrastructure; and providing for "shovel ready" jobs. Next Mr. Obama sought to overhaul the nation's economic and financial systems by instilling effective regulation including Dodd-Frank; and expressed concern about the environment, thereby initiating efforts to generate clean energy supplies while underwriting research and development of future resources. Nevertheless, Republicans turned up the heat on the President. As a result, a climate of hatred and disrespect targeted Mr. Obama and his administration. Surprisingly, as Republicans and their allies peppered Mr. Obama, perhaps unmindful that Edmund Burke once wrote, "The only thing necessary for evil to triumph is for good men to do or say nothing;" yet, among the higher echelon of Republican leadership nothing was said or done against such mis-characterization. Nothing!

Black History Everyday - Part One Photo. We Shall Not be Moved March.
Faces in the Crowd.

BLACK HISTORY EVERYDAY PART ONE

Despite their failure to achieve anything but block the President's every move and falsely characterize the man and his work, they hood-winked the American people, and so Republicans made gains in the 2010 and 2014 mid-tern elections. Despite the vituperative Republican mischief, President Obama continued his efforts to scale down the wars in Iraq and Afghanistan, contend with Somali pirates and pursuit of Osama Bin Laden and Al Qaeda affiliates. As this unfolded, Obama continued his responsibilities as Chief Executive and Commander-in-Chief. Meanwhile the Republicans convened, in a "tunnel vision focus" on how the new Congressional House majority would seek to hamstrung Mr. Obama in the incoming Congress. Throughout it all, as Mr. Obama played it cool, in response to unfolding events, the Grand Jury decisions happened more than once in response to the killing of Black men and women and this galvanized protests.

The "Arc of the Moral Universe" swung back when people of goodwill, young and old, across all ethnic spectrums, took to the streets in city after city. The "Chickens had come home!" Republicans were caught off-guard. They said nothing and had nothing to say as the people staged numerous "Die-In" protests across the various cities and states.

FREDERICK MONDERSON

Black History Everyday - Part One Photo. That **Eric Garner Rest in Peace** is indicative **Black Lives Matter** as the signs say.

Black History Everyday - Part One Photo. Two of the "**Godfather of Soul's**" outfits.

BLACK HISTORY EVERYDAY
PART ONE

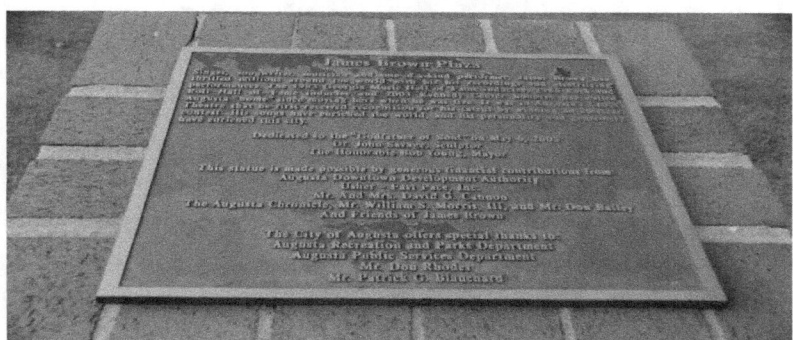

Black History Everyday - Part One Photo. Plaque explaining the commemoration of the James Brown Statue in Augusta, Georgia.

Black History Everyday - Part One Photo. Faces in the crowd for the 50th Anniversary March on Washington. Right On, young man!

FREDERICK MONDERSON

Black History Everyday - Part One
Photo. Faces in the crowd for the 50th Anniversary March on Washington.

After **Officer Wilson shot Michael Brown in Ferguson, Missouri**, a spontaneous protest movement coalesced in a boiling cauldron of social outrage that challenged political, economic and social injustice; unchecked and unrepentant police killing of Black men; as well as discriminatory practices emanating from institutional racism and practices that contradict the American ideals of the Declaration of Independence and Constitution. The nation remained divided, essentially, because a Black man presided at the helm of the state.

The people, Black, Brown, White, Gay and straight, etc., in numerous instances protested, demonstrated and chanted "Justice for Michael Brown," "I am Michael Brown" and "Hands-Up, Don't Shoot!"

BLACK HISTORY EVERYDAY
PART ONE

Following the incident of his death, in New York and as far away as California protesters chanted Eric Garner's last words, "I Can't breathe!" and "Justice for Eric Garner!" as well as "Black Lives Matter!" As this unfolded, prominent Athletes in the NFL and NBA joined the fray with "Hands Raised" in a "Hands Up, Don't Shoot" gesture in sympathy realizing they were not immune.

Again, Republican, caught in a vulnerable position, were in a quandary. The hatred and disrespect they sowed was now being called into question by young people who want an America with justice for all. If, as some predicted, this consciousness would into future elections, then the country may be transformed in more ways than one. This is what happened in the 2018 Mid-Term election.

Black History Everyday - Part One Photo. Michael Hardy at the Podium for the "Power and Policy Forum" at Sharpton's **NAN**.

FREDERICK MONDERSON

"In the white community, the path to a more perfect union means acknowledging that what ails the African-American community does not just exist in the minds of Black people; that the legacy of discrimination – and current incidents of discrimination, while less overt that in the past – are real and must be addressed. Not just with words, but with deeds." Barack Obama. *Speech, Philadelphia Pennsylvania.*

"We lose ourselves when we compromise the very ideals that we fight to defend. And we honor those ideals by upholding then not when it is easy, but when it is hard." **Barack Obama**. Noble lecture, Oslo [December 10, 2009]

5. BARACK OBAMA: MASTER OF WASHINGTON, DC BY DR. FRED MONDERSON

With nearly fifty books that negatively portray the President (2005), *Barack Obama: Master of Washington, DC* (2010) seeks to reverse that trend focusing on some positive traits that characterize the man, the office and the human and material challenges he faced in his short time in office as reflected by this writer in newspaper articles for New York's Black Press written as Mr. Obama's tenure unfolded.

BLACK HISTORY EVERYDAY
PART ONE

From "Proud to Be President," "Leadership," "Obama in Africa," "Eternal Optimist," "President's Many Hats," "Excitement," "Obama Doctrine," "Quintessential Obama," "Powers of the Presidency," "War Powers," "Great Visionary," "Cabinet and Order of Succession," "Health Care Reform," "The Supreme Court" and character assassination to "The Obama Years," "Rally Around Barack," "Vote or Die!, Well," in which 73 essays paint a vivid picture of unwavering support for Mr. Obama, while highlighting the work of Republican obstructionists, their allies and nefarious efforts designed to **STOP OBAMA**; to his perseverance to enact Health Care Reform, prolifically legislate for financial, economic, social and environmental reforms to changing America's image abroad, rescuing the nation's economic structure, combating unemployment and the housing crisis while emphasizing and encouraging the need for innovative means of energy production, offering educational incentives to restore competitiveness in the fields of teaching and learning all with an intensity to assure a brighter future for his nation; all this while simultaneously waging wars in Iraq and Afghanistan, combating terrorism at home and abroad and still be blessed to come home to a wonderful and loving family. Even his wife Michelle has come in for some harsh treatment, though her detractors got the message when the President laid down the law, "Lay off my wife!"

FREDERICK MONDERSON

Clearly Mr. Obama is a great, hardworking and visionary leader with a view to the future and these essays point to his intent to chart a path for his nation to remain competitive and innovative as he prepares a way for the youth of tomorrow. His vision emphasizes education, science and environmental sustainability in an America that respects the rights of Americans irrespective of race, gender, religion, physical stature or sexual orientation. Some 300 photographs help paint a picturesque image of the domain over which Mr. Obama not only presides but is a true Master of the 'City on a Hill,' Washington, DC.

"It's been a long time coming, but tonight, because of what we did on this day, in this election, at this defining moment, change has come to America."
Barack Obama. *Presidential Victory Speech, Grant Park, Chicago* [*November 4, 2008*]

Black History Everyday - Part One Photo. **We Shall Not be Moved March**.
Faces in the Crowd.

BLACK HISTORY EVERYDAY
PART ONE

Black History Everyday - Part One Photo. The message is: "Seek Knowledge and Make a Difference."

"We remain a young nation, but in the words of scripture, the time has come to set aside childing things. The time has come to reaffirm our enduring spirit; to choose our better history; to carry forward that precious gift, that noble idea, passed on from generation to generation; the God-given promise that all are equal, all are free, and all deserve a chance to pursue their full measure of happiness." **Barack Obama**. *Inaugural Address*, January 20, 2019.

6. BARACK OBAMA - PRESIDENT!
BY
DR. FRED MONDERSON

Barack Obama's tenure as President can be considered historic because he is the first African-American to be elected President of these United States of America, but even more important for the things he accomplished and the invective avalanche launched against him and his Presidency. However, because of the nature of causality, as Dr. Leonard James often iterated, "The higher monkey climbs, the more he exposes himself." Meaning, as the many have flung the filth of disgusting epithets at President Obama, in fact, they revealed the deep-seated inner workings of their true selves and the view is nauseating. Yet still, in deflecting, Obama affirmed, "Politics is a contact sport. "Even those Black commentators who attacked President Obama for not doing enough for Black people, have been forced to realize the dynamics at play, if they have; they must seek to understand the nature of the opposition's obstructionism, their lies and falsification of facts and their unabashed racist rancor that truly characterize the "ugly American" for who he really is, certainly not Obama!

BLACK HISTORY EVERYDAY
PART ONE

Black History Everyday - Part One
Photo. Faces in the crowd for the 50th Anniversary March on Washington.

President Obama must be numbered among the great presidents of this nation for he has had to heal the ills of the nation's domestic and foreign economic policies and practices; repair its relationships with the wider world whose image of America was severely tarnished and to operationalize the workings to successfully conclude American military deployment in Iraq and Afghanistan while challenging Somali Pirates and contending with a ubiquitous global war on terrorism. Equally, while the business of nation states never takes a holiday, President Obama has had to deal with nuclear non-proliferation involving Iran and North Korea, seeking progress on the perennially illusive Middle East peace process and all the other responsibilities of the President as steward of the nation including America's role in global economics, trade, cultural affairs, etc., all relying on his unfailing good government.

FREDERICK MONDERSON

Mr. Obama inherited a dire economic situation and has demonstrated exemplary leadership in formulating purposely orchestrated policies and practices that halted the crises despite Republican opposition and obstructionism.

1. A TREASONOUS PLOT TO OVERTHROW A LEGITIMATE AMERICAN GOVERNMENT!

On the day Mr. Obama was inaugurated as President of the United States, a form of overthrowing the government can be considered treason and all perpetrators should have been arrested and put on trial. Treasonous intent has been manifesting in Republican Party opposition to the legally constituted American government. First, we knew of Ed Meese and 20 NGOs Presidents but today we know of some two-dozen top Republican Operatives and Congressional Leaders who signed on "day One" to shamefully sabotage or oppose Barack Obama in every way possible. Yet he succeeded!

BLACK HISTORY EVERYDAY
PART ONE

Black History Everyday - Part One Photo. We Shall Not be Moved March. Faces in the Crowd.

I.   The McConnell Mandate - "My job is to make Barack Obama a one term president."

II.   Mr. Obama set out to execute the responsibilities of the Office of the President of the United States as Chief Executive Officer of the nation. Recognizing the grave situation, he inherited as President, Mr. Obama took a number of prudent but rapid steps to address the nation's problems. The first of these was legislative passage of:

a.   Lilly Ledbetter Fair Pay for Equal Work Act designed to enable women to be compensated for the same work as men.

b. Auto Industry Rescue had become necessary for, since America invented the automobile to have allowed this important engine of the American economy to go bankrupt as Mr. Romney suggested, would have been both an economic and psychological as well as moral let down for the nation.

c. Bank Bailout was essential for as the banks began to crumble, the reverberations would have been far-reaching with potential for global panic.

d. Health Care Reform or the Affordable Care Act is an idea whose time had come and Mr. Obama very early saw the need, formulated a strategy to deal with it, campaigned for this measure during the Primary and Presidential campaigns and upon being elected moved to legislate it into law.

e. With the nation hemorrhaging jobs at an enormously unhealthy rate, Mr. Obama created a Jobs Bill to address problems of domestic infrastructure and put significant segments of the work force back to work. As we have seen, one clear plan of obstruction was to kill the jobs bill! "Don't give the Black guy a win!"

III. As Commander-In-Chief, President Obama next turned to address the military engagement in

BLACK HISTORY EVERYDAY
PART ONE

Iraq to stem the loss of American lives, decrease the economic costs and seek a way out of the quagmire, to "bring the boys and girls home" to their families and friends. Ultimately, he was able to create an agreement enabling the end of American forces deployment after training Iraqi forces to assume responsibilities for military action in their nation. In Afghanistan, Mr. Obama deployed a surge and after ongoing engagements he was able to begin to negotiate an agreement that American forces will leave that nation in 2014.

Black History Everyday - Part One Photo. Mr. Larry Hamm, founder of People Organized for Progress (**POP**) at **CEMOTAP**.

Osama bin-Laden, leader of Al Qaeda and many others were responsible for the 9/11 catastrophic attack on the World Trade Towers, forced Mr.

FREDERICK MONDERSON

Obama to intensify efforts to find and eliminate such terror masterminds. After some time and extensive preparation, the Commander gave the go ahead to launch the assault on bin-Laden's compound in Pakistan, certainly mindful of the consequences of a failed operation. Not unmindful of the last time American forces had launched an operation of a similarly significant nature to rescue Americans held captive in Iran during the Carter Presidency and the fallout that resulted, Mr. Obama took the chance with full faith in the capabilities of the Seal Team Six force. The rest is known! The same leadership daring that brought success with bin-Laden was applied to Somali Pirates who rampaged off the coast of East Africa. When the necessity demanded, Mr. Obama, not simply as Commander-in-Chief but with exemplary leadership, gave the order sending a stern message to these Somali terrorists.

Black History Everyday - Part One Photo. We Shall Not be Moved March.
Faces in the Crowd.

BLACK HISTORY EVERYDAY
PART ONE

2. EVIDENCE OF TREASONOUS REPUBLICAN BEHAVIOR

In an escapade of "non-cooperation," Republican lawmakers with allies outside of government began a series of obstructionist behaviors and practices designed to curtail and destroy Mr. Obama's tenure as President in their intent to "Deny Obama a win!"

a. **BUSH TAX CUT** - The first of these came when the President took bold steps not to extend the "Bush Tax Cuts" that primarily benefitted the wealthy "One percent;" it's generally but falsely thought, if the tax cuts are enacted then these people will re-invest in American businesses and other venues to provide jobs for the American people. As this had not worked during the Bush years, Mr. Obama could not envision it working during his term. Republicans launched a non-cooperation "scorched earth" strategy designed to obstruct administration efforts even threatening to shut down the government. Rather than allow that dire consequence to manifest, Mr. Obama relented but extended the Tax Cuts for a limited time, not indefinitely as Republicans wanted. This is when Senator Mitch McConnell was shown with that broad duplicitous smile and he gave the now-infamous "Thumbs Up" signal many read as "I got that **NIGGER** in the White House!"

FREDERICK MONDERSON

Black History Everyday - Part One

Photo. Faces in the crowd for the 50th Anniversary March on Washington.

Black History Everyday - Part One

Photo. Faces in the crowd for the 50th Anniversary March on Washington.

BLACK HISTORY EVERYDAY
PART ONE

b. **DEBT CEILING DEBATE** - By the mid-term election, as the insidious treasonous plot thickened, Republicans gained control of the House of Representatives and John Boehner replaced Nancy Pelosi as Speaker of the House. The next significant agenda item was the Debt Ceiling issue, which in debate, Mr. Obama again relented for the better good of the nation to move it forward out of gridlock. At the conclusion of events, Speaker Boehner sarcastically boasted "We got 98 percent of what we wanted!" which is predictable as a pattern of obstruction and insidious greed. Even more important, when the President reached out to him, Speaker Boehner refused to return the phone calls of the nation's Chief Executive Officer. This behavior was not only treasonous but contemptuous of the Office of the President as part of the insidious plot. It is difficult to divorce former Speaker Boehner, the now marijuana merchant, from the "McConnell Cabal," that failed in its intent as "plotters!"

Mr. Obama was aware of the treasonous actions but his sense of personal dignity and the dignity of the Office would not allow him to respond in kind to the inelegance of the Speaker of the House. This pernicious continuum of disrespect for both the Office of the Presidency and person of the President is identifiable from the day of the President's Inauguration to the present and it is a manifestation of the intent of the political leaders gathered on the day of Inauguration to plot his political demise.

FREDERICK MONDERSON

To his profound credit, his political sophistication and personal determination that despite the obstructionism, through exemplary leadership, he has been able to accomplish much; as former President Bill Clinton said, "what no other President" including him-self was unable to accomplish," given the enormous obstacles Mr. Obama faced and dire economic conditions of the time.

So, let me identify some examples of Barack Obama's "elegance of mind and nobility of spirit."

1. BANK BAILOUT - The nation was on a trajectory of financial ruin that would most likely engulf the world in a depression far worse than 1929. Not only was he assailed by people within the Congress but ordinary Americans were quite concerned that the President cared more about Wall Street than "Main Street," let alone "Back Street." But he had the self-confidence and the confidence in the nation that once the precipitous fall was avoided, the natural resilience of the nation's economic capabilities would rectify itself to the benefit of all.

2. AUTO INDUSTRY RESCUE - Chrysler and General Motors are two of the most important economic elements of American society. The ancillary impact in employment entities which support these companies is incalculable in their support of the Middle Class and Lower Income class of the nation.

BLACK HISTORY EVERYDAY
PART ONE

The President was quite aware that these 2 economic sources were absolutely vital to any recovery from the terrifying economic realities of the day. Concerted opposition to his effort to save these companies was starkly expressed by the Presidents opponent Mr. Mitt Romney who said, "Let Detroit Go Bankrupt!"

Black History Everyday - Part One Photo. We Shall Not be Moved March. Faces in the Crowd.

With President Obama's vision and support, Detroit has remade itself, regained its "Market Share" and continues to produce cars of a high quality. These efforts and more, despite determined and relentless opposition, some say, racist machinations and disrespect, Mr. Obama achieved much and has left office with one of the highest ratings ever, nearly 60 percent just behind Bill Clinton at 68 percent and Ronal Reagan at 64 percent. But let us not forget -

FREDERICK MONDERSON

Lilly Ledbetter; Student Loan and Credit Card Adjustment; Affordable Care Act; Same Sex Marriage recognition; Climate Change Agreement; Iran Nuclear Deal; "Good-bye" Bin Laden; the Cuban-American Initiative; The Dreamers; many sentences were commuted in Prison Reform efforts; 72-months of positive job growth helped strengthen the American Economy; and most certainly the Dodd-Frank Economic and Financial Reform measures. He was a great Conservationist; initiating "My Brothers' Keeper;" Encouraging Mothers to Return to College; Recognition and Support of Community Colleges; Clean Energy Research and Development; and "Race to the Top;" as well as speaking out on Racial Matters; and most important, singing "Amazing Grace" in Mother Emanuel Church Commemorating the 9-Martyrs, killed by a racist white supremacist. Thank You, President Barack Hussein Obama.

Black History Everyday - Part One Photo. The Lincoln Memorial on the day of Sharpton and Crump's March on Washington, DC.

BLACK HISTORY EVERYDAY
PART ONE

Black History Everyday - Part One Photo. Faces in the crowd for the 50th Anniversary March on Washington.

"The work of **CEMOTAP** has been to address misrepresentation, discrimination and distortion in the media. Like a rolling stone, it will continue until it uproots and banishes all gathered moss." Betty Dopson. Co-Chair of **CEMOTAP**.

Black History Everyday - Part One Photo. New York State Assemblyman Nick Perry extolls **Justice for Eric Garner**.

FREDERICK MONDERSON

"The Board of Education for People of African Ancestry salutes the work of our esteemed elder, Dr. John Henrik Clarke and we will continue to pursue the enlightening path he set for us and set us on." Betty Dopson in **Clarke House**, Harlem.

7. BETTY DOPSON, WARRIOR QUEEN!
BY
DR. FRED MONDERSON

In a splendid and colorful turnout members and friends of **CEMOTAP** came to the **Robert Johnson Life Center** in Queens, New York, on May 31, 2015, to recognize, complement, praise, honor and offer a heartfelt "Thank You and Farewell to Betty Dopson at her Going Away Party." More importantly, however, these people came out not simply to celebrate Betty Dopson, Co-Chair of **CEMOTAP** along with Dr. James McIntosh for their unrelenting, uncompromising and steadfast nurturing of an organization brought to adult manhood/womanhood while standing unflinching in the face of misdirected, pernicious and deplorable depiction of African people in the various modes of media, whether TV, print or radio. They came to praise a movement nurtured in an oasis of intellectuality and activist daring that challenged false representation of African people.

BLACK HISTORY EVERYDAY
PART ONE

Black History Everyday - Part One Photo. Sister Betty Dopson with Erik Monderson making an announcement about **CEMOTAP**.

Black History Everyday - Part One Photo. Faces in the crowd for the 50th Anniversary March on Washington.

FREDERICK MONDERSON

This courageous leader of men and women, Betty Dopson, standing next to her Co-Chair, Dr. James McIntosh, for some three decades demonstrated and spoke truth to power! Their message was clear! Stop mischaracterizing our people in your presentation or we will use every strategy in our arsenal, whether to boycott you and your sponsors, picket your place of establishment unending to shine the light of truth and correction or, write and publish exposure of your malicious depiction of African people and more. This message remained consistent and has not let up!

CEMOTAP simultaneously educated its members by inviting and presenting enriching discussions, where untold numbers of trained and effective professionals and activists all baptized in the "arena of fire," made enemies of African people stand up and take notice. Appearing on TV, whether "**Like It Is**" or other programs, on the radio or presenting carefully crafted position papers in print, conducting college tours to expose young people to this higher form of liberation protest, holding forums, sponsoring activist outings, etc., **CEMOTAP** enshrined its image and stature in the annals of African American activism. Simultaneously the organization promoted education with a resolve designed to achieve success in every endeavor to encourage African upliftment and mental liberation.

BLACK HISTORY EVERYDAY
PART ONE

Black History Everyday - Part One Photo. We Shall Not be Moved March. Faces in the Crowd.

In the Opening Prayer, Rev. Simmons characterized **Betty Dopson** as possessing tenacity, courage, a stick-to-it-iveness dynamic resilience while emphasizing "Faith without works is dead." Recognizing that she is "a gem" he asked the Creator to sustain and bless her insisting we give thanks for Betty Dopson. He thanked the Lord for filling our time with joy, peace, hope and his unending love for us and the world. That "Your blessing is food for us and the mingling of our spirits is a testament of how great a Creator you are," was a well-deserved going away prayer gift.

Dignitaries on the Dais included: (1) Professor James Blake, Chairman of Queens **Million Man March**

FREDERICK MONDERSON

Committee; (2) Sister Betty; (3) Mr. and Mr. John White who stood up for blackness! (4) Reverend Charles Norris, "Spiritual father" of the **CEMOTAP** movement; (5) The People's Chancellor, Warrior "Queen Mother" Adelaide Sanford; (6) Reverend Herbert Oliver; and (7) Sister Frederika Bey. Those in attendance, easily recognized, included Dr. Arthur Lewis and Wife; Dr. Jack Felder and son Nova; Michael Greys of "**100 Blacks in Law Enforcement Who Care**;" Attorney Dr. Joseph Mack; Prof. James Smalls; Pam Africa; Sister Viola Plummer; Omowale Clay and others too many to mention. Such persons as Brother Fuller, Razakhan Shaheen, Father Lawrence Lucas, Brother Harold, Brother Bryan, Sister Penny, Olmeda and Shazanne Williams and Ed Ward, original **CEMOTAP** members were also there.

There was the "New Jersey crew" with Sister Frederika Bey including Poet Brother Ladine Kalibah as well as Radio personality Bernard White, **NAKO** representative Bokim, Shadini, Brokaby, Richadena Theodore and Molefi, among the "Sons of **CEMOTAP**." Artist Brother Lucian Pinckney was in the house!

Throughout, Stephanie Juneau and Shawn Broughata sang "Love Train," "Just My Imagination Running Away with Me;" "My Girl" and many other old sentimental favorites.

BLACK HISTORY EVERYDAY
PART ONE

Dr. Adelaide Sanford began with her customary "Beloved," and acknowledged the opportunity to be with Sister Betty all over the world. She pointed out; Betty Dopson brought a lightning rod spirit to activism. Equally, as Co-Chair of **BEPAA** (Board of Education of People of African Ancestry) at **Dr. Clarke Elders' House** Sister Betty strove to promote liberation through education for her people. She established policies for education for liberation. On a lighter note, "She makes fantastic biscuits. You must taste those famous Betty Dobson biscuits."

Black History Everyday - Part One Photo. Brother John, Dr. MacIntosh, Brother Larry Hamm and another Brother at **CEMOTAP**.

FREDERICK MONDERSON

Reverend Oliver was happy to celebrate this wonderful occasion. He classed Betty Dopson as "mediating on young, gifted and black! She is educated and black! A community activist and black! A woman of character, a woman of integrity, compassion and beautifully black! Personable and black! Black, proud and happily Black!"

The St. Alban Church congregation offered a heartfelt "Thank you for blessing us in a wonderful way. Yours is a foundation of faith!"

Rev. Norris praised the Beacon School, IS 8, affiliated with **CEMOTAP**, and offered his continued praise, support and elicited a wonderful blessing. Jokingly he mused that his "Teeth are like the stars that come out at night!"

Mr. John White offered a praise that Betty Dopson and **CEMOTAP** were "There when we needed them. They supported so many groups there and then." His wife classed Betty as gorgeous, a warrior woman. She is a giant alongside people who appreciate freedom. More especially, 'You look beautiful. Happy Birthday!'"

Prof. James Blake thought, "Jitu even made this event. Give me my flowers while I'm alive." Speaking of Betty, he insisted "She is a flower. She pollinates. She challenged Mayor Koch. She closed "strip joints" and racist merchants. Closed "drug dens." She "organized college tours" after the Million

BLACK HISTORY EVERYDAY
PART ONE

Man March. She has tenacity, continuity and consistency. 'God brought you into this world to help our people,'" he reminded the beautiful lady.

Inez Baron thought Betty Dopson the complete, thoughtful package, being bold, innovative and on the battlefield in all our struggles. She was fortunate to work with Charles Baron, Chukwe Lumumba, Sonny Carson, Jitu Weusi, Dr. Ben Jochannan and Dr. Clarke. Viola Plummer of the **New York 8** and the **December 12 Movement** insisted she "Keep it going!"

Mr. Bernard White characterized Betty Dopson with Dr. McIntosh as a "Tag Team." He confessed, "They recognized I was worthy of support." Father Lucas, in paying tribute to "Our warrior sister" explained, "The wives are known by their wisdom but the great are known by their actions and work. And in this Betty Dopson was supreme!"

Sister Shahid offered Asante Sana and thought it was an honor and privilege to know and work with Betty. Molefi McIntosh recounted "She took care of me" and that "Betty the Belly Dancer" is a beautiful lady.

Yusuf Salaam-Hanlon reflected, "They were moving people who were intellectuals while depicting filthy images of our people and **CEMOTAP** stood up." Professor James Smalls reminded, "Betty you are a goddess having a human experience. We make a pact with god. You have done your duty."

Black History Everyday - Part One Photo. **We Shall Not be Moved March**. Faces in the Crowd.

Michael Greys of "**100 Blacks in Law Enforcement Who Care**" confessed, "I am because we are. **CEMOTAP** is like home. Once there is a need, **CEMOTAP** is there. God speed sister!" Attorney Mack insisted, "Great women are known by what they do and leave behind. We must do and continue the work of Betty!" While her brother reminded, "We made Betty fight boys not girls!" and Dr. Arthur Lewis mentioning "Africans Helping Africans" offered, "We Love You, Betty!"

BLACK HISTORY EVERYDAY
PART ONE

The artist classed Betty Dopson as among "People who bright a light to everything." She was connected to her African-ness. She cracks the whip and make people stand at attention. On her own behalf, Betty offered a promise and that the, "Remarks are so remarkable and reassuring, of which I am very appreciative. I thank you from the bottom of my heart where Betty Dopson was a mere 81 years old, you made me feel good."

In total, all wished Sister Betty Dopson the very best in the future and she promised to be back in New York at every opportunity time and circumstance permitted.

Black History Everyday - Part One Photo. Faces in the crowd for the 50th Anniversary March on Washington.

FREDERICK MONDERSON

Black History Everyday - Part One
Photo. Faces in the crowd for the 50th Anniversary March on Washington.

"[*On Black History Month*] Ridiculous. You're going to relegate my history to a month? I don't want a Black History Month. Black History is American History." **Morgan Freeman**. *Television Interview, 60 Minutes* [2005]

"Mitch McConnell's pubic statement: 'I intend to make Barack Obama a one-term President' was indeed racist!" Morgan Freeman *Piers Morgan - CNN*

Black History Everyday - Part One
Photo. ZULU

BLACK HISTORY EVERYDAY
PART ONE
8. BLACK HISTORY EVERYDAY
BY
DR. FRED MONDERSON

Ancient Egypt in North-East Africa, as **Black history**, should be celebrated every day, 365 days per year. Naturally this admonition flies in the face of the falsity taught by those imperialists who colonized the intellectual and artifactual history of ancient Egypt. Dr. John Henrik Clarke taught, "The people who preached racism colonized history" and "When Europe colonized the world, she colonized the world's knowledge." To that end, the true history of Egypt is taught both from black and white perspectives. The European and American (white) dominated perspective teaches the intrinsic beauty of the art, architecture, science and mythology of Egypt which is underscored by the wonderful artifactual displays contained and "Photo Shopped" and "Sanitized," in Museums and private collections in cities across Europe and America. That is, interestingly enough, the displays are highlighted under wonderful lighting that obfuscates their true ethnological origins.

The perpetual fabrication began more than two centuries ago when Africa and Africans were prostrate in chains and justification used to deny the humanity of Black Africans. In this age of "naked imperialism" the clash of empires led to a discovery of ancient Egypt. Napoleon's soldiers and savants found the Rosetta stone and began the study of ancient Egypt leading to Champollion's decipherment of hieroglyphics in 1822. In this early beginning, the African connection to Egypt was evident but Prof. Clarke's observation emerged in a divergent strand of scholarship. Just then the true history became distorted through pronouncements of individuals as Auguste Hegel who taught, "Africa is out of the historical realm of history" and the defender of slavery Samuel Cartwright in *Slavery and Ethnology* (1857) as well as other theories as the "Hamitic Hypothesis." The movement to remove Africans from Egypt and Egypt from Africa began at this time.

Black History Everyday - Part One Photo. We Shall Not be Moved March.
Faces in the Crowd.

BLACK HISTORY EVERYDAY
PART ONE

Yet still, there were credible European scholars who decried and challenged the emerging falsification of the historical record. The first is Baron Vivant Denon who was part of Napoleon's expedition; Count *Volney's Ruins of Empires* (1798); Godfrey Higgins' *Anacalypsis* in 2 volumes (1836); later Lenormant and Emile Amelineau, etc. were some of those who sought very early to set the record straight. By the end of the 19th Century, Gerald Massey's *Book of the Beginnings* (2 volumes), *Natural Genesis* (2 volumes) and *Ancient Egypt: Light of the World* (2 volumes) were ground breaking. Then came his "disciples" Raymond Dart and Albert Churchward whose works were restricted to limited editions. Unfortunately, it was a terrible time for Africans who were victims of the Piranhic mentality of the age when, in contradiction, men of Europe and America spoke of freedom, justice, humanity, even the "fatherhood of god and the brotherhood of man." Then the notion of "polygenesis" as opposed to "monogeneses became an arguable position. But "truth crushed to the earth shall rise" and from mid-nineteenth century Blacks became involved in the intellectual fray regarding Egypt. First Edward Wilmot Blyden, the West Indian cleric who went to West Africa began arguing for a Black Egypt from Biblical references. Then Martin Delaney and other religious Blacks, with very scant sources available to them began to question the incorrect portrayal of ancient Blacks in Egypt.

FREDERICK MONDERSON

From mid-19th Century onward a new impetus on Egypt Emerged. Concomitant with the whitening of Egypt, the search for antiquities for private and museum collections unleashed a "Rape of the Nile." This was all masked under the umbrella of ensuing "enlightened imperialism" of the last haft of the 19th Century. Under this banner, "intellectual imperialism" emerged and unleashed a multitude of ethnological, botanical, mineralogical, and zoological inquiries of areas of the world under colonization. In this, Egypt received a full share of the attention from explorers, archaeologists, writers, publishers and others whose efforts were fired by the dynamic promise of adventure the evolving "penny press" and rapid publication of any discovery of an archaeological nature.

The years from 1870 until around 1930 saw an unrelenting effort to excavate and analyze then publish the findings in the resurrection of Egypt and the Nile Valley culture. Here the "ancient records of the ancient records" were systematically retrieved and conventions established about how Egypt was to be interpreted. Naturally the role of Europe loomed paramount in this effort and the principal beneficiaries became Europe and America while the role of Blacks in Egypt diminished to a lowly status. Fortunately, by the turn of the Twentieth, Blacks were in the ascent intellectually, freed from the constraints of slave trade and slavery and now they began to view Egypt as part of the African creation and legacy.

BLACK HISTORY EVERYDAY
PART ONE

Marcus Garvey the great nationalist met Duse Mohammed in London who impressed him on the role of Blacks in ancient Egypt. Then W.E.B. DuBois wrote *The Negro* (1915), that with very little resources available to him he was able to produce a masterpiece, yet almost a century later, much of his findings go unchallenged. His later work *The World and Africa* (1946) though dealing with the continent on a broader scale had significant information about Egypt. Drusilla Dunjee wrote about the *Wonderful Ethiopians* in 1926 and Carter G. Woodson contributed his share about the role of Africans in the shaping of ancient world history, but more especially *The Mis-Education of the Negro* and *Education of the Negro*. John Jackson and John Huggins wrote their first *Introduction to African Civilizations* in the 1930 and this was followed by J.A. Rogers' *Sex and Race* 3 volumes and *World Great Men of Color* in 2 volumes. From then on, a whole litany of African scholars has dealt with the question on and the lack of credit given to Black people in this civilizational experience. There is no need to recount the names of the great Africans who have wrestled with this topic in the Twentieth Century. From ben-Jochannan and John Clarke to Ivan Van Sertima and Runoko Rashidi, prodigious research was conducted on the topic of African intellectual redemption, not simply in Africa *per se*, but globally.

FREDERICK MONDERSON

Black History Everyday - Part One

Photo. Faces in the crowd for the 50th Anniversary March on Washington.

BLACK HISTORY EVERYDAY
PART ONE

An interesting observation can be made here. Certainly, the black scholar has as much credibility as his white counterpart. In the business of intellectual endeavor thirty years is a long time. Equally it must be granted that one can unearth a great deal of new information and this should sharpen and crystallize one's view of the pursued subject. However, while a black scholar may spend thirty years of research and writing and solidify his position taken earlier in his research this cannot be said about his white counterpart. Seldom, if, any white scholar has corrected his earlier views about Blacks in Egypt even after some thirty years of researching the field. Is the work of Africana scholarship credible or not?

Black History Everyday - Part One Photo. The Master, Dr. James McIntosh, Co-Chair of **CEMOTAP**, presiding at the Dias, doing what he loves.

FREDERICK MONDERSON

"When I think of your appointment to the Supreme court, I see not only the result of your own ambition, but also the culmination of years of heartbreaking work by thousands who preceded you. I know you may not want to be burdened by the memory of their sacrifices. But I also know that you have no right to forget that history. Your life is very different from what it would have been had these men and women never lived." **Aloyisus Leon Higginbotham, Jr**. in *An Open Letter to Justice Clarence Thomas* [November 29, 1001]

Black History Everyday - Part One Photo. We Shall Not be Moved March. Faces in the Crowd.

"The Supreme Court has ruled on many occasions to correct the wrongs of past Court decisions, but unless their pronouncements on law are strictly adhered to, those whose duty is to uphold such rulings fail to do so, dishonors the spirit of the law." **Anonymous**.

BLACK HISTORY EVERYDAY
PART ONE
9. BLACK INFLUENCE ON THE SUPREME COURT
BY
DR. FRED MONDERSON

No ethnic group has had more of an impact on the United States Supreme Court than African-Americans for the Court has ruled against Black interest and has even had to reverse itself, before making its most significant rulings in favor of Blacks. However, huge as this influence has been, it has been excluded from the narrative of history. Thus, we must follow its most important cases and even measure how blacks have wielded their influence whether as attorneys before the bar or as in the extraordinary work of Jurist Thurgood Marshall who rose from the law ranks to be one of the most influential voices on the bench; or still, being the subject of judicial interpretation. Now, in his tenure the African-American President Barack Obama has appointed two women to the Court. In the history of the Republic, Presidents Washington, Jackson, Lincoln, Grant, Harrison, Taft, Harding, Franklin Roosevelt, Truman, Eisenhower and Nixon have appointed four or more members of the Court. In the event of his being re-elected, President Obama will have the opportunity to impact the Court even more with one, possibly two additional appointments and join this exclusive group. This latter reality is especially troubling for many people who are disposed to see him defeated in the up-coming 2012 election. As such, this election will be truly historic to determine whether the nation moves forward or return to its tattered conservative past.

Thus, to understand the Black influence and how it has shaped the Constitution through the Court one has to even antedate the Supreme Court sitting for the **"Three Fifths Clause"** or Compromise or **Compromise of 1787**, of the Constitution. This Compromise had to do with apportioning of enslaved Africans for Southern representation initially in the political and taxation dispensation to create the National instrument of government. Make no mistake; the **Compromise of 1820** more fully defined the condition of Blacks! Even with the **Compromise of 1850** the Court remained silent on the condition of Blacks as chattel, meaning property. However, within less than a decade the Court could no longer hide behind the fait accompli in silence and was forced to show its true colors in the 1857 case of *Dred Scott*. After Dred Scott, while there were others of a lesser import, the 1896 *Plessey v. Ferguson* case affirming "separate but equal," the culmination of "Jim Crow," is another milestone in landmark Supreme Court rulings. Again, while the "Grandfather Clause" reversal in 1915 is also of minor import among others whittling away at the second-class Black condition, cases such as *Smith v. Albright* outlawing the "white primary" in 1944, and the more landmark 1954 *Brown v. Board of Education of Topeka, Kansas* affirming "segregation

BLACK HISTORY EVERYDAY
PART ONE

is illegal" represented the next and most significant Black impact on the Court. Thurgood Marshall, the man who led that fight would ultimately wield untold influence on the Court and at his death praised for his efforts, even by his adversaries on the bench. To his efforts we could add the various Civil Rights and Voting Rights Acts passed to strengthen previous legislation and to protect Black gains that also benefitted all Americans. Now, President Obama is poised to add even more Black influence regarding the direction of the Court.

Black History Everyday - Part One Photo. We Shall Not be Moved March. Faces in the Crowd.

Historically speaking, the **"Three-Fifths Compromise"** of 1787 was instrumental in moving forward with acceptance of the Constitution.

FREDERICK MONDERSON

However, as Chief Justice Roger Taney later pointed out in the **Dred Scott decision of 1857**, Africans then enslaved were not considered citizens! In fact, they were not considered as fully human at the time of the formation of the Constitution, but only "Three-fifths" of persons. Equally, that year of 1787, the Compromise also outlawed the importation of slaves after 1808 but this practice continued unabated surreptitiously in the "Internal Slave Trade" until the Civil War. To get their way, the South played hardball because their economy depended on slavery. This is made clear by Mary Frances Berry (1971: 7) who point out: "The **Fugitive Slave Clause** was scarcely noticed by northern delegates to the ratifying conventions, but in the South, it was used as a definitive selling point. James Madison particularly emphasized its usefulness in Virginia, as did some of the Federalists in the North Carolina convention. These debates lend credence to the view that the southern states would not have ratified the Constitution without the proslavery compromises." The Compromise required two thirds of the Senate to approve treaties and prohibited the national government from taxing exports or interfering with the slave trade until 1808, the year after the British finally outlawed their involvement in the trade.

In the *American Political Dictionary* (1989: 29-30) Plano and Greenberg make reference to the significance of this agreement. They state, Southern delegates, "feared that northern majorities might cut off the slave trade and discriminate against the profitable cotton trade …. It was believed that a

BLACK HISTORY EVERYDAY
PART ONE

sufficient number of slaves would be available by 1808, although illegal slave trade continued until the Civil War of 1860. The treaty and foreign commerce provisions continued to influence the making of American foreign policy." To this we may also add the "**Internal Slave Trade**" with its tremendously depraved practices on Southern "Slave Farms." Yet, the Supreme Court chose not to be "activist" in this respect and in its silence upheld the institution of slavery that denied Africans any rights and in turn supported the falsely construed sub-human status of African. To be sure, in a *Brief Review of United States History and Government* (2001: 94) Briggs and Peters write: "Until the Civil War, the Constitution had recognized and protected slavery in three ways: The *Three-Fifths Compromise*, the provision that Congress could not end the importing of slaves before 1808, and the fugitive slave clause. These compromises had been made in order to encourage southern states to ratify the Constitution. With the expansion of American territory in the West, controversy brewed over whether these new territories should allow slavery or not."

After the Louisiana Purchase by Thomas Jefferson, the status of the states, free and slave, became a **Sectional** issue regarding division of the new territory. The North wanted more Free States; the South wanted more Slave States. To settle this matter, Irving L. Gordon's *American Studies* (1984: 106-

107) point out: "The North and South agreed to the **Missouri Compromise of 1820** admitting Maine as a free state and Missouri as a slave state and prohibiting slavery in most of the Louisiana Territory." Thus, Sectional balance was maintained.

Black History Everyday - Part One Photo. Faces in the crowd for the 50th Anniversary March on Washington.

Black History Everyday - Part One Photo. NYC stands with Charleston Against Hate!

BLACK HISTORY EVERYDAY
PART ONE

Black History Everyday - Part One Photo. Faces in the crowd for the 50th Anniversary March on Washington.

The **Industrial Revolution** in America was spurred by Eli Whitney's **Cotton Gin of 1793** among other inventions that ultimately saw "Cotton become king!" And, in 1815 at the end of the **War of 1812**, Internal Improvements opened the way to infrastructure improvements and westward expansion. As labor demands of the agrarian South expanded with continued plantation culture of tobacco, rice, sugarcane, and cotton, **Encyclopedia Britannica's** *The U.S. Government: How and Why it Works* (1978: 210) explained: "By 1850 there were 3,204,000 slaves in the area, and it has been estimated that 1,815,000 were connected with the cultivation of cotton. Perhaps this is why the Court cast a blind eye to

FREDERICK MONDERSON

abolition and reform until the **Compromise of 1850** tried to settle the significant issue of expanding states. Three key provisions were agreed to in this measure, that include:

California entered the Union as a free state.

The Fugitive Slave Law required that escaped slaves be returned to their owners, providing Slave Catchers with unchecked power.

Through a vote, people living there would determine whether a territory in the **Mexican Cession** chose to be slave or free.

Black History Everyday - Part One Photo. We Shall Not be Moved March. Faces in the Crowd.

BLACK HISTORY EVERYDAY
PART ONE

Mary Frances Berry's *Black Resistance, White Law* (1971:7) pointed out: "The Fugitive Slave Clause and the commitment of the national government to protect slavery, but not interfere with it, were indispensable parts of the Constitution. However, this band aid solution as part of denial of black rights was short lived in the abolitionist and reform era, forcing the 1957 *Dred Scott v. Sandford* landmark decision which clearly defined the status of the African in America.

According to the evidence, Dred Scott was an enslaved African whose master took him into a Free State in 1834 then brought him back into a Slave State. Upon his return in 1846, Mr. Scott sued for his freedom on grounds of having set foot on free soil; he therefore claimed he was entitled to be free. Finally reaching the Supreme Court in 1857, Chief Justice Roger Taney (1836-1864) ruled in this historic case. In *American Historical Documents*, Edited and with an **Introduction** by Harold C. Syrett (New York: 1965, 250), we are told: "The Court considered the following points: whether Scott was a citizen of Missouri (if he was not, he could not sue in a federal court); whether residence in a free area gave Scott his freedom following his return to Missouri; and whether the **Missouri Compromise** (under the terms of which slavery was prohibited in the Wisconsin territory) was constitutional."

FREDERICK MONDERSON

In answer, Bonnie-Anne Briggs and Catherine Fish Petersen in *Brief Review in United States History and Government* (2001: 95-96) have argued: "The ruling held that no African-Americans, slave or free, were citizens, and therefore, they were not entitled to constitutional protection. The ruling also held that the **Missouri Compromise** was unconstitutional because Congress could not deprive people of their right to property - slaves - by banning slavery in any territory." That, no African-Americans, free or slave were citizens makes a mockery of Crispus Attucks martyrdom as the first authentic American hero, even large Black landowners who could not vote. Still, we know Lincoln's "House divided" speech loomed large and its subsequent implications resulted in the Civil War.

Soon, however, despite Taney's decision on Dred Scott, John S. Rock of Massachusetts was the first Black invited to practice at the Supreme Court under the new Chief Justice Salmon P. Chase (1864-1873). Entering the bar and wearing 'Buck Wheat,' to plead his case he stood defiantly, as Page Smith in *The Constitution: A Documentary and Narrative History* (1978: 440) stated, "[I]n the monarchial power of recognized American manhood and American Citizenship, within the bar of the Court which had solemnly pronounced that Black men have no rights which white men were bound to respect.... By Jupiter the sight was grand!" Even further, Smith (1978: 441) noted: "The Court in the case of *Ex parte* Milligan ruled that Lincoln had acted unconstitutionally when he ordered military courts in places where civil courts

BLACK HISTORY EVERYDAY
PART ONE

were functioning." Lincoln saw this action as necessary, notwithstanding Chief Justice Chase's contention: "The Constitution of the United States is a law for rulers and people, equally in war and peace, and covers with the shield of its protection all classes of men, at all times, and under all circumstances."

This was a powerful statement for the War settled two questions as *Encyclopedia Britannica* (1978: 215) states: "First, it killed the idea of state sovereignty and the right of secession. Second, it ended the institution of slavery." It did, however, little to change the agrarian basis of the South's economy, since slavery was an economic system of slave ownership and racial control. Still, *Britannica* (1978: 215) continued: [T]he institution of slavery was replaced by three others. The economic system of sharecropping, the political system of one-party politics, and the social system of segregation supported both by law and by custom." Clearly then, despite the Civil War Amendments, Reconstruction was betrayed and white southern backlash gave birth to "Jim Crow." Aided by **Black Codes**, this new state of affairs began to curb the newly secured rights of African-Americans. As part of the grand strategy to gain political power in the South, while some whites sought legal means, some conservative southerners employed terror groups as the Ku Klux Klan, Red Shirts and Knights of the White Camelia to intimidate and terrorize Blacks from going to the polls. With the 1877 "betrayal" that brought Rutherford B. Hayes to the Presidency and the end of

Reconstruction, whites now emerged successfully in control; and as such, southern legislators-imposed poll taxes and literacy tests on the Freedmen and used the "Grandfather Clause" to empower poor whites who could not pass the literary tests imposed on Blacks! Thus, "Jim Crow" laws created segregation of African Americans and whites in schools, parks, public buildings and on public transportation. In challenges to these practices, in the 1883 Civil Rights Cases, the Court ruled the "Thirteenth Amendment abolished slavery but did not prohibit discrimination and that the Fourteenth Amendment prohibited discrimination by government but not by individuals."

In this period of "The Nadir," the mood of the country fueled by "Jim Crow" practices forced the Supreme Court to consider the case of *Plessey v. Ferguson* in 1896. The Court upheld "**Jim Crow**" by ruling in favor of "equal but separate" or "**separate but equal**" facilities which in fact was actually "**separate and unequal**." Plano and Greenberg (1989: 296) pointed out: "Under this doctrine, a wide pattern of segregation developed in schools, transportation, recreation and housing." As such, the ruling encouraged the highest forms of social depravity visited upon Blacks until the conscience of the Supreme Court really began to stir. First, it outlawed the "**Grandfather Clause**" in 1915 and several minor racist rulings until the 1940s when even the armed forces became desegregated that also saw abolition of the "White primary."

BLACK HISTORY EVERYDAY
PART ONE

In the 1954 *Brown v. Board of Education of Topeka, Kansas* the Supreme Court ruled "separate but equal" inherently unequal and therefore unconstitutional. In *United States History and Government*, Paul Stich, Susan Pingel and John Farrell (1989: 241) recognize the roles of the Truman and Eisenhower administrations in facilitating integration despite southern senators' use of the "filibuster" to stymie legislation. However, the Supreme Court was not hamstrung by these tactics. They write: "After World War II, in a series of civil cases brought by the **National Association for the Advancement of Colored People (NAACP)**, the court began applying 14th Amendment's 'equal protection of the laws' phrases against various state segregation laws. In 1954, the Court issued its decision in *Brown v. the Board of Education of Topeka, Kansas*, which reversed the doctrine of 'separate but equal' put forth in the 1896 Plessey case. At the time of Brown, racially segregated schools were the norm in nearly 20 states. In *Brown*, the Court used a procedure called 'orbiter dictum' to 'speak beyond' the Topeka situation and announced that racial segregation of schools was inherently wrong and must cease throughout the nation." This, they moved expeditiously to correct!

FREDERICK MONDERSON

**Black History Everyday - Part One
Photo**. Dr. James McIntosh, Co-Chair of **CEMOTAP** is about to introduce Brother Larry Ham, President of **POP**, (People Organized for Progress), a New Jersey based organization.

Often times the work of a single person is overlooked but that of Thurgood Marshall, first as a lawyer influencing the Court, and then as jurist influencing the Court's direction is unparalleled among American men of law. This enormous capability is best reflected in the laudatory commentary by the trustees of Howard University after Marshall, ten years out of law school, successfully argued *Smith v. Allwright* overthrowing the "white primary" in 1944. According to Michael Davis and Hunter R. Clark in *Thurgood Marshall*: *Warrior at the Bar*, *Rebel on the Bench* (1994: 11) the University's citation read: "You are winning significant and enduring victories for a disadvantaged people. Your increasing labors are opening the way for the achievement of an even greater measure of justice and equality under the law.

BLACK HISTORY EVERYDAY PART ONE

Your star still rises, and though it is not yet at its zenith the brilliance of your accomplishments and the value of your service to your fellow man already marked you as an advocate, a legal scholar and humanitarian of the highest magnitude."

Black History Everyday - Part One Photo. Walter Brown among the iron pillars that recount horrors of intimidation, terror and lynching, affirmed: "My ancestors lived through this."

Equally, the **Eulogy** at his death summed up the work and influence of this extraordinary man of law. Davis and Clarke (1994: 385) additionally say: "[I]nscribed above the front entrance to the Supreme Court building are the words 'Equal justice under law.' Surely no one individual did more to make these words a reality than Thurgood Marshall." Thus, with the all-inclusive phrase 'no one,' Rehnquist

FREDERICK MONDERSON

ranked Marshall alongside Washington, Jefferson, and Lincoln. This statement was from the same man who, as a law clerk some thirty years earlier, had urged that *Plessey's* separate-but-equal doctrine be upheld." William T. Coleman, former transportation secretary who also worked on *Brown*, observed, "History will ultimately record that Mr. Justice Marshall gave the cloth and linen to the work that Lincoln's death left undone." And Vernon E. Jordan of the **National Urban League** and advisor to President Clinton said Marshall's mission, according to Davis and Clarke (1994: 388) had been "to cleanse our tattered Constitution and our besmirched legal system of the filth of oppressive racism and to restore to all Americans a Constitution and a legal system newly alive to the requirement of justice."

Black History Everyday - Part One
Photo. Faces in the crowd for the 50th Anniversary March on Washington.

BLACK HISTORY EVERYDAY
PART ONE

Black History Everyday - Part One Photo. Faces in the crowd for the 50th Anniversary March on Washington.

Clarence Thomas replaced Thurgood Marshall as the only Black on the bench. However, his policies and writings were utterly opposed to those of Marshall. Davis and Clarke (1994: 376) write, in 1990 President Bush No. 41 appointed Thomas to the U.S. Court of Appeals and in 1992 he was appointed to the Supreme Court. "At first, Thomas's nomination appeared to be a shrewd political move on the part of the president. By making effective, if cynical use of the skin color of a nominee opposed to racial preferences, Bush threatened the Democratic coalition of liberals, women's groups, and blacks. Liberal feminists were aligned against Thomas because of his conservatism and outspoken opposition to abortion. At the same time these groups risked antagonizing blacks whose paramount goal

FREDERICK MONDERSON

was to have an African-American succeed Marshall. The white liberal leadership of the Democratic party knew that by opposing Thomas, they also risked further alienating white middle-class voters - the so-called Reagan Democrats - who regarded racial preferences as reverse discrimination." Even further, Davis and Clarke (1994: 378) continued: "During the 1991-92 term, his first as an associate justice, Thomas demonstrated himself to be exactly what his conservative proponents had hoped and his liberal opponents had dreaded. Most often, he aligned himself with the Court's two most conservative members, Rehnquist and Scalia. He has voted to restrict constitutional protection accorded prison inmates; he has called for softening the wall that has traditionally separated church and state; and, dissenting from the Court's ruling in *Planned Parenthood of Southeastern Pennsylvania v. Casey*, decided on June 29, 1992, he has called for *Roe v. Wade* to be overturned outright." Still, Justice Thomas characterized Thurgood Marshall as "a great lawyer, a great jurist and a great man."

Nevertheless, so much has transpired once the Court assumed an "activist" posture recognizing and safeguarding the rights of African-Americans. Given the vote, educational and other social and economic opportunities, and flexing new won power, economic and political especially, Blacks began making strides in electing representatives and finally became an election force owing to the backing of the Court. Now, an African-American President is poised to move this historic legal institution even further in

BLACK HISTORY EVERYDAY
PART ONE

recognizing and securing a more just future for all America's people. Without question, rights gained by Blacks have benefitted all segments of the American populace whether Black or White, Jew, Gentile, Catholic, Protestant, Asian and Latino, Gays and Lesbians, handicapped and especially women and the work of the Supreme Court has been instrumentally prodded by Black influence.

Black History Everyday - Part One Photo. We Shall Not be Moved March. Faces in the Crowd.

"The time for the healing of the wounds has come. The moment to bridge the chasms that divide us has come. The time to build is upon us. We have, at last, achieved our political emancipation. We pledge ourselves to liberate all our people from the continuing bondage of poverty, deprivation, suffering, gender and other discrimination." *Inaugural Address* [May 10. 1994]

FREDERICK MONDERSON

"The challenge for every prisoner, particularly every political prisoner, is how to survive prison intact, how to emerge from prison undiminished." *Long Walk to Freedom.*

10. BOB LAW'S TRIBUTE TO NELSON MANDELA BY DR. FRED MONDERSON

The incomparable Bob Law of "Night Talk" fame sponsored another of his tremendously informative Forums at historic **Church of God in Christ** on Kingston Avenue in Brooklyn, December 17, 2013, 7:00 - 10:00 pm, this time in tribute to Nelson Mandela. After Bob Law had laid the foundation for comprehensive understanding of this recent phenomenon of Mr. Mandela's passing, Dr. Leonard Jeffries provided a scintillating analysis and then synthesis for some 100 persons who braved the inclement weather to see beyond the outward appearance of global, even South African, tribute to the fallen leader, icon and freedom fighter. Both Mr. Law and Dr. Jeffries were painstakingly meticulous in turning on its head much of the Mandela tribute from world leaders and Western media by focusing not on the man as a mountain, but as a "tree" in a forest of freedom fighters.

Mr. Bob Law first educated his audience about Mr. Mandela's heritage.

BLACK HISTORY EVERYDAY
PART ONE

This point was lucidly elucidated in "Mandela and the Unfinished Freedom Struggle" *Daily Challenge*, 12/17/13, p. 5, where Ron Daniels wrote, "Mandela was the 'tallest tree' in a forest that included many movements and stellar leaders, e.g., the **Pan African Congress**, and the **Black Consciousness Movement**, Mass Democratic Movement, Steve Biko, Bishop Desmond Tutu, Allan Boesak, Cyril Ramaphosa, Albertina and Walter Sisulu and Oliver Tambo to mention a few. This is an important note because there is a tendency to cast successful movements as the result of the acts of a solitary heroic figure." We should also include the Afrikaner cleric Byers Naude, though White, he stood up for Blackness! Many attributes as demonstrated loyalty to Mr. Mandela's tribal heritage, his education and profession as a lawyer, his activism and daring; and his role as student, husband and family man were highlighted and emphasized. These scholars who conceptualize so readily and well, were quick to point out the cliché, he went from "Prisoner to President" and his steadfast "commitment to reconciliation;" does not tell the full story that he was forced into armed struggle; convicted and while in prison those 27 years became a symbol, an icon; yet, the struggle continued to be waged by others on the outside suffering at the hands of the oppressive and repressive regime that banned, tortured and killed many.

FREDERICK MONDERSON

It's universally recognized, the Afrikaners who perpetrated the racist, evil system of apartheid, did not suddenly have an epiphany and decided to free Nelson Mandela. Like Ian Smith of Rhodesia, they hoped to rule for another 1000 years, though in 1000 days power was wrestled from Smith by "the boys in the bush." In the case of South Africa, it was the insistence, commitment and unrelenting struggle of the women, the young people, the African National Congress cadre and the global mobilization of protest for divestment to rid the world of the evil system that apartheid represented, despite President Reagan and Chester Crocker's policy of "constructive engagement" that contributed to and prolonged Mandela's and South Africa's freedom struggle. This is what forced the half-hearted offer by President Pieter Botha's offer to free or release Mandela in 1988. Such release, however, was dictated only if he would renounce violence! Clearly, if Mr. Mandela did accept an early release under those conditions it would have undermined everything he stood for, what he spent those many years incarcerated to achieve, and he would have lost the respect of the South African people whom he represented as well as the people of the world who stood with him and forcefully pressured the Apartheid system through change agents demanding his release.

It has been acknowledged; globally Africans all over see the world differently because of their shared racist imperial and colonial experience. That is why Mr. Law wanted his audience to begin to understand

BLACK HISTORY EVERYDAY
PART ONE

the continuity of that experience. That is why he insisted "We not let others tell the story," for when they do it's with a twist that actually distorts the experience. The "Prison to President" cliché is thus not correct! First of all, he did not commit a crime; yet, as a man of principle, he was willing to forgive all the wickedness of the apartheid regime and this demonstrated his humanity was of a higher standard than theirs. This philosophic and moral guidepost is what separates "us" from "them."

Though he was called a terrorist, he was actually a freedom fighter who became President! Prison was only a step on the way! In the horrendous experience, there was a long history of struggle against the murderous, vicious racist expropriators of the very best African land confining Africans to "black spots," then removing them into balkanized and barren reserves called "Bantustans" that were supposed independent nations, yet dependent on South Africa, of course, with the whites in control, politically and economically. This behavior and much more forced the African National Congress to pick up the gun. These African people of that nation were actually pressed into the armed struggle amidst the hopelessness and dehumanization instituted through fear and intimidation and use of stooges such as the **Inkatha Movement** of Chief Buthelezi. That is why Mr. Mandela insists Xhosa, Sotho, Zulus, all Africans, are one people suffering under the same oppressive system. The racists fermented a blood bath between the Africans before they could fight the

FREDERICK MONDERSON

white man! Yet, Mr. Mandela would say, "Let us forgive these wicked people who have oppressed us for so long!" Importantly, nobody went behind his back-seeking vengeance! No one sought to assassinate or injure those who perpetrated the system. Much more significant, because Mr. Mandela refused to compromise his principles, his was liberation in a real sense! This demonstrated the tremendous patience of the African people while these so-called "superior white folks" were stealing their land and its riches. Showing magnanimity, in his uncompromising stance, he denounced violence from both black and white elements. This is because Mr. Mandela understood the potency of violence and its impact on the people and nation in its policy, infrastructure and view of the world.

Black History Everyday - Part One Photo. Each column lists different numbers of how many Africans were lynched in each county from 1870-1950.

BLACK HISTORY EVERYDAY
PART ONE

Black History Everyday - Part One Photo. We Shall Not be Moved March. Faces in the Crowd.

Naturally, most people never really or fully understood Mr. Mandela or his strategy. It can be assumed Mr. Mandela went to prison an angry man after his trial but he was still a proud man! Observe his walk into prison! He probably never expected to be freed one day. In that "Long Walk," he experienced much and had the time to reflect, think and strategize. He said he matured! He knew he represented the people; he had them on his side. He also studied his enemy. He learned Afrikaans, the language of the oppressor, so he better understood their history and culture and this was important in his negotiations to end apartheid.

FREDERICK MONDERSON

Black History Everyday - Part One Photo. African masks sandwiching **Dr. Fred Monderson's** coverage of the **Queens Million March Organizing Committee** March for the *Daily Challenge* in 1995, hanging on the wall at **CEMOTAP**.

In reflecting, Madiba, as he was known, probably thought "We may be able to kill some whites but Africans would suffer more in any bloodbath." They knew he was coming and expected riotous behavior, so they stockpiled their armaments. They strategized and erected their forts and barriers, their "Alamos" to create their "Amritsars." Madiba outfoxed the devils! He said no recrimination! "Africans, let us forgive the white citizens of our nation." Thus, their arms were useless, ineffective, their barriers yet showed their thinking and bunker mentality! As Sun Tzu advised, "Win the battle before taking the field!" To recall, even more, Nkrumah had said, "Seek ye first the political kingdom." In the South African system,

BLACK HISTORY EVERYDAY
PART ONE

whites-controlled economics and politics. Mandela realized he could not dislodge them from economic control. However, by virtue of the Black majority and to keep democracy alive, he chose the democratic way to political power. Ron Daniels said it best. Mandela theorized through political power the African people will whittle away at the preponderance of white economic dominance. One African lady explained why she loved Mandela in part; Soweto had no electricity, the night belonged to whites! Now they have electricity and she now has a fridge and TV. The muddy roads are now paved. These were government efforts initiated by Mandela. Unrelenting political effort over time will economically empower Africans much further!

Black History Everyday - Part One Photo. Faces and signs in the crowd for the 50th Anniversary March on Washington.

FREDERICK MONDERSON

Much more significantly, Mr. Mandela's humanity pulled the mask off the white racists and he exposed their true selves. He was well-versed in his historical responsibility, coming as he did from a community with a royal duty to the people of his land. That is why we must seek to fully understand in putting him in proper perspective. The Western and American media does not tell or focus on Mr. Mandela's and the ANC's true role in the total liberation of African people and the struggles of pushing back colonialism as well as the significance of true elimination of the immoral system of apartheid. In reality, it's who he forgave rather than what he forgave them for is really the issue and this forces another look at the Afrikaner Boers, South Africa and Mr. Mandela.

Black History Everyday - Part One Photo. We Shall Not be Moved March. Faces in the Crowd.

Dr. Leonard Jeffries emphatically made his point about Mr. Mandela and the South African struggle.

BLACK HISTORY EVERYDAY
PART ONE

In one of the features run in the media recently about an Afrikaner Museum, a young woman visiting boasted of her need to know her history! It is clear the museum would not recount the brutality, the killing, the African humiliation, the wrongs, so that is why the Africans must know and tell their story to get a more balanced view for historical recounting. Mandela's insistence on the **Truth and Reconciliation Commission** was a masterful stroke! In the many confessions it gave the "monsters" a chance to reveal their mechanism of control for the world to realize how right they were that apartheid must go!

Changing pace, in a musical interlude Craig Crawford played a beautiful jazz rendition of a tribute and he followed this up with another really great song. Also, Xavier Bost sang two wonderful pieces, "Shattered but not Broken" and "A Hero Lies in You." Bob Law then praised the musicians and audience for being "Credoso Africans" who were "strong and resilient." He even tied this personality trait to the tenacity of braving the inclement weather to attend the event, insisting more such forums are planned.

Not discounting that Mr. Mandela was a good man; they however, pointed out, but he was not unique as a freedom fighter! Mr. Law expressed, "We came from a long line of freedom fighters who fought courageously in liberation struggles." This is why he insisted, "It is important that we claim our own history." At that point he mentioned African leaders of Mr. Mandela's stature such as Ghana's Kwame Nkrumah, Guinea's Sekou Toure, and Congo's Patrice Lumumba who liberated their country and gave their all in its cause. These leaders were uncompromising liberation fighters. Of course, Mr. Machel of Mozambique must also be numbered in this lot. At this point Mr. Law waxed philosophical by telling the audience, "When you celebrate Mr. Mandela, you celebrate yourself; you celebrate the African liberation struggle." He spoke of "something on the inside that is so strong, Holy Spirit, Holy Ghost," that cannot be touched or conquered that contributed to his and others' successes. Then he reflected on an old African liberation saying, "The higher they build the barriers, the taller you will rise." Even further, "To celebrate Mr. Mandela, let every leader be a Mandela" who refused to hate, was uncompromising, principled, and a man of great integrity. Despite his circumstances, he continued to fight which showed his character. He fought for what was right and would not compromise. This is what his enemies had to recognize. He fought against poverty, against inhumanity of man to man. He recognized gay rights and praised education.

Bob Law insisted, we must guard against "People who will come to confuse us, who will betray us." Because Mr. Mandela would not compromise, would not back down, Mr. Law quoted biblical wisdom to reflect his strong, principled personality, for "No weapon formed against me will prosper." Even more

BLACK HISTORY EVERYDAY
PART ONE

philosophical and spiritual, he offered, "You think you are doing it on your own," but divinely guided forces are at work and play in guiding your every move! To explain where Mr. Mandela got his strength poses a profound proposition; for Mr. Law quotes Isaiah the prophet who wrote, "They that wait on the Lord shall renew their strength, they shall mount up with wings of eagles; they shall run and not be weary; they shall walk and not faint." This strength, this life in commitment to struggle, is a reminder of how great as a people the audience really is! This again is why we must not let them separate Madiba Mandela from the continuity of the history of his people.

Bob Law used analogies to get his point across. He asked the audience to Google two interviews between Malcolm X and Mike Wallace and Farrakhan and Wallace on "**The Hate that Hate Produced**." He veered off to speak on the disrespect Blacks receive, especially when shopping at high-end stores such as Barney's. He spoke of the young lady at Barney's who "Was not arrested for shoplifting but for spending too much" when she bought the $2700.00 ladies' bag! He also talked about new and upcoming ventures of the church in addressing the suffering of families, families of loved ones in prisons. People never really understand the hurt they put their families through when they commit a crime and go to prison. The family, the mothers, brothers and sisters, sons and daughters, also do the time on the outside. This suffering is what the church will now address.

Next it was Leonard Jeffries' turn, arriving late as he always is! Jokingly Mr. Law referred to the keynote speaker as "The Late Dr. Jeffries." Pulling no punches, he focused not just on Nelson Mandela but the movement of African Liberation. While the focus today is on Mr. Mandela, Dr. Jeffries insisted, for 27 years he was only a symbol! At the funeral Winnie and Graca demonstrated the strength of the black woman. These women were the wind that powered their husbands' sails!

There were many similarities in the struggles of the **ANC** (1910) and the **NAACP** (1912) who sought to restore African humanity in a world of white rapaciousness. In South Africa it was the **African National Congress**, the **Pan-African Congress**, the **Student Movement** that gave the world Steve Biko and of course the church, in close association with the **World Council of Churches** under the leadership of Dr. Philip Potter in which Dr. Jeffries and Professor Scobie, in Geneva, were lending assistance to coordinate activities in the South African struggle. From this vantage position he realized and stated emphatically, "The most devastating destruction of the Black man was in South Africa."

In that horrific experience was the 1962 Sharpsville massacre and the June 16, 1976 student uprising in

BLACK HISTORY EVERYDAY
PART ONE

Soweto that demonstrated the viciousness of the white minority regime. However, efforts to brainwash the students in demands that they learn Afrikaans was "more than a bridge too far," it was a tremendous miscalculation! The Africans suffered but the move failed!

First, in laying out his presentation, Dr. Leonard Jeffries reminded the audience, the Boers comprised Dutch, German and French elements from Europe mingled with Britons. With the discovery of the gold and diamond wealth of South Africa in late 19th Century, his "3 Rs," were not reading, 'riting and 'rithmetic, but Rothschild, Rhodes and Rockefeller who conglomerated to exploit the riches. A secret society called the Broderbund of some 20,000 men swore to maintain power no matter what. This is what Mandela challenged!

Black History Everyday - Part One Photo. We Shall Not be Moved March.
Faces in the Crowd.

FREDERICK MONDERSON

Thus, "If there is a place for Reparations it is South Africa." "The Boers fostered unity among Europeans and divisions among Africans." They used the Zulu Mpande to kill his brother Shaka. The same way they "encouraged" Chief Buthelezi to ferment violence among Africans. This created a universal moral crisis. In their grab, that minority took 85 percent of the land. However, despite Mandela's victory, "We won the battle but they won the war" by remaining in control of the nation's economics.

Black History Everyday - Part One Photo. Faces and signs in the crowd for the 50th Anniversary March on Washington.

BLACK HISTORY EVERYDAY
PART ONE

Black History Everyday - Part One Photo. Walter Brown fixes his camera to get that important photo.

Black History Everyday - Part One Photo. Faces and signs in the crowd for the 50th Anniversary March on Washington.

FREDERICK MONDERSON

Dr. Jeffries shed light on Afrikaner examination of the role of the church in the struggle. They studied Archbishop Tutu's many speeches, dissecting the many times he mentioned the **ANC**. They realized they were fighting the church on the inside and the freedom fighters on the outside. Significantly, they entrapped and neutralized Rev. Boesak rendering him ineffective as a voice in liberation theology.

Dr. Jeffries explained further, "Politics is what you do to control your economics." His synthesis depicted a triangle compromising economics, politics and culture, the mind values, he called it. Importantly, he pointed out, the 1948 election victory of the Nationalist Party "set in motion the dehumanization process of Africans." This resulted in "The African people suffering from a shattered consciousness and a fractured identity." Again, emphasizing the need to organize economics, politics and culture, and the role of women - Winnie Mandela; children - Steve Biko; church - Archbishop Desmond Tutu and Rev Allan Boesak, Dr. Jeffries insisted, "To serve the people, the curriculum of inclusion is not sufficient, we need a curriculum of liberation."

BLACK HISTORY EVERYDAY
PART ONE

Black History Everyday - Part One
Photo. Atiim Ferguson in a somber mood at Sonny Carson's funeral.

Black History Everyday - Part One
Photo. Emma Monderson poses with Dr. Evelyn Castro at the **West-Indian-American Day Parade** on eastern Parkway on Labor Day.

"The absence of hope can rot a society from within."
Barack Obama, Noble Lecture.

FREDERICK MONDERSON

"Change will not come if we wait for some other person or if we wait for some other time. We are the ones we've been **waiting for; We are the change that we seek." Barack** Obama. *Speech on Super Tuesday, Chicago, Illinois* [February 5, 2008]

11. CALLING OUT OBAMA!
BY
DR. FRED MONDERSON

The "Britisher" who murdered the American hostage Tim Foley, in stating ISIL's message called out Mr. Obama, which in itself is an affront and challenge! It was terrible he committed an unspeakable horror but to specifically direct his invective towards "Obama" was a challenge that had to be met. However, we must first of all recognize the three-fold nature of this situation.

Black History Everyday - Part One Photo. We Shall Not be Moved March. Faces in the Crowd.

BLACK HISTORY EVERYDAY PART ONE

First, **ISIL**, in seeking attention to their much-lamented military action many have characterized as barbaric, needed to respond to American Iraqi bombing pushback enabling humanitarian assistance to Yazidis cornered on that Iraqi mountaintop. As bombings signaled America's repeated resolve in standing good and against tyranny and terrorism, Edmond Burke's universal admonition became more manifest. "The only thing necessary for evil to triumph is for good men to say or do nothing!" Thus, America's response to the siege was to bomb ISIL's targets in the vicinity.

Second, say what you will, but America is synonymous with championing the underdog and oppressed. This has become much more realistic when it comes to guarding and responding to the safety of its citizens facing harm abroad. Jim Foley, an American journalist, was captured by rebels some have labeled terrorists in Syria, more than two years ago. It is understandable, the dangers of being in harm's way in the middle of such a conflict. However, there is international law stating "Prisoners of Wars" should be treated humanely and this was expected regarding Mr. Foley. Well, the ISIL rebel did the unthinkable in beheading Mr. Foley. This unspeakable act sent shudders across the globe that, in this day and age; persons, in this case, terrorists, could act so inhumanly, especially boastful in public.

Ok. So, the ISIL terrorists have been rampaging across Iraq and Syria, pillaging, killing in murderous

FREDERICK MONDERSON

swaths and seizing territory. Then they beheaded Mr. Foley. In this final assault and insult, they called Mr. Obama's name as representative of the American people. They spoke directly to him in a threatening tone. Reasonable people will acknowledge, Mr. Obama must respond having being called out.

Equally, Lieutenant Colonel Robert Magennis wrote an **Editorial** critical of the President. A CNN program anchor asked Mr. Magennis to explain his statement that "Mr. Obama lacked the testicular fortitude to attack ISIL at their bases in Syria!"

Here again, the wherewithal Mr. Obama brings to the table as President, viz., a wonderfully active intellectual capacity grounded in an effective work ethic associates and assistants have characterized as frighteningly well-prepared on all issues of concern. All this is enhanced by an exceptional team of advisers, military and civilian, who contribute various expert viewpoints on issues that enlighten and encourage Mr. Obama to arrive at the most optimum decision regarding any issue under study.

BLACK HISTORY EVERYDAY
PART ONE

Black History Everyday - Part One Photo. Faces and signs in the crowd for the 50th Anniversary March on Washington.

Mr. Obama has always demonstrated his thinking style is not one to rush to judgment but to deliberate all the pros and cons before arriving at a consensus and then final decision. However, in case of ISIL, as the United States of America's **Declaration of Independence** insists, "After a long train of abuses," and if you add the personal touch the executioner added, the consequences should be expected. Add to this Mr. Magennis' dare, tons of "bricks" will descend on ISIL!

So, the President ordered surveillance over Syria to gather real-time information about ISIL's status. In some of former **NATO's** Supreme Commander

FREDERICK MONDERSON

General Clarke's comments, though critical at times, he stated: "The President ordered air reconnaissance to add to existing knowledge about ISIL." Here again is reinforced an aspect of Mr. Obama's thinking strategy. Make sure every step is on a firm foundation by studying all aspects of its ramifications. However, past experiences have taught Mr. Obama a great deal. President George Bush took a "go it alone attitude" against Saddam Hussein in Iraq in 2003 when the world admonished against such recklessness. This damaged the world's perception about America which Mr. Obama had to repair and reverse at the same time enabling him to learn many things.

Mr. Obama is not simply a passive thinker, for while he contemplates the "Syria scenario," he continues to pound ISIL movements in Iraq. All the while he strategizes to organize a coalition that will represent a broad consensus designed to eviscerate the "cancer" he spoke of. As caution rules his thinking, when pressed on Syria in a News Conference on Thursday August 28, 2914, Mr. Obama insisted he "did not have a strategy, yet!" He insisted this is because many, especially the press, had jumped ahead of him and were practically printing dynamics of his bombing strikes in Syria.

BLACK HISTORY EVERYDAY
PART ONE

Black History Everyday - Part One Photo. We Shall Not be Moved March. Faces in the Crowd.

Many quickly sought to characterize Mr. Obama as either weak or ineffective because he did not have a "Syrian strategy," but in clarification it became clear what he actually meant. As explained, his ISIL strategy was based on creation of a unified Iraqi government that was inclusive of significant elements of ethnic Iraqis. Once this is achieved, there would be support for Iraqi forces in armaments and training. He sought to engage regional governments to become involved because ISIL poses an even greater threat to them in the long run. He was working to engage global allies to support action against ISIL and then once these "ducks were lined up," he would consult Congress to authorize the use of more effective military force against ISIL in Iraq and then possibly in their home base in Syria.

Men of vision reason, the President "does not want to tip his hand," for as many would tend to believe, ISIL's supporters are also watching his press conference. However, what the President is showing by his actions are as follows.

1. The humility of the really powerful.

2. The integrity of a human being who respects the sanctity of human life which his critics do not have.

3. In his respect for human life, Mr. Obama is reluctant to risk the life of others without all legitimate consideration.

4. He recognizes Iraq is a sovereign nation and under international Law recognizes America does not preclude the sovereignty of every other nation.

5. When it became clear Osama bin Laden had taken up residence in a sovereign nation, he had the "Testicular Fortitude" to order military action that ended the life of the murderous mastermind, a feat which had eluded several presidents before him.

6. The leader of Al Qaeda in Somalia, Al-Shabab,

BLACK HISTORY EVERYDAY
PART ONE

Mr. Ahmed Godane, long on Mr. Obama's radar and his resulting demise says much for planning and strategy, equally Obama's "stick-to-it-ive-ness" which trumps the "Light" Colonel's contention. Making Somali Pirates unemployed is another example of President Obama's thinking and strategic effectiveness.

Perhaps when this is over, "Light" Lt. Colonel Magennis will have the "testicular fortitude" to eat "curry or stew" crow and admit sending Seal Team Six to pursue Osama bin Laden was indeed a courageous act as also did the Somali surgical strike.

Thus, Mr. Obama actions will not only address the Colonel's challenge but will answer the executioner's dare and punish him for his cruelty and upstart arrogance!

Black History Everyday - Part One Photo. Faces and signs in the crowd for the 50th Anniversary March on Washington.

FREDERICK MONDERSON

Black History Everyday - Part One Photo. Let's have **JUSTICE FOR ERIC GARNER!**

"It is commonly said in some quarters that 'Africa has awakened.' This cannot be accepted by conscious Africans, for to have 'awakened,' one must have been asleep. Africa was not asleep. Africa was wide awake, but her land, as well as her sons and daughters. Were subjected to the most barbarous treatment man has ever imposed on man." Yosef ben-Jochannan. *The Rape of Africa and the Crisis in Angola* [1958]

BLACK HISTORY EVERYDAY
PART ONE
12. CELEBRATING "DR. BEN" – PART I
BY
DR. FRED MONDERSON

When African people begin to count the stars in their heroic pantheon constellation, the large and small illumination emanating there from, Dr. Yosef Alfredo Antonio ben-Jochannan looms among the largest and most significant of these luminaries. While many of these "stars" manifest in politics, war, nationalism, religion, agriculture, education and civil rights activism, etc., Dr. Ben, as he is affectionately called, excelled in intellectualism, praise of African womanhood, cultural conscious raising, the challenging of western pillars of cultural genocide depicted in the form of historical distortion, omission of meaningful historical contributions of Africans, blacks, and the psychological damages to their heritage and futures. He pioneered in recognition of the significance of indigenous naming of themselves, their cultural attainment and the geographical locations in which their genius originated all the fundamentals of civilization, such as religion, architecture, writing, art, medicine, agriculture, science, river travel and transportation of large stone and economics, among other forms of intellectual creations. He challenged, at great peril, financial and stigmatic, the onslaught of so-called "EGYPTOLOGISTS, AUTHORITIES ON

FREDERICK MONDERSON

AFRICA, SEMITICISTS, HAMITICISTS, WHITE LIBERAL HISTORIANS, AFRICANISTS," and the like of them. Yet, "NUBIANS" were, supposedly, the only indigenous Ethiopians (Blacks) the "NEGROPHOBES" conceded were "N-E-G-R-O-E-S" whatever this disgusting and nauseating term meant to the 16th or 17th century Portuguese RACISTS who invented it; a term which some of the world's greatest "SEMITICISTS" and "CAUCASIANISTS" even breakdown to make the NUBIANS appear as "HAMITIC-TYPE CAUCASIANS, DARK-SKINNED CAUCASOIDS" and "NILOTIC HAMITES."

Black History Everyday - Part One Photo. We Shall Not be Moved March.
Faces in the Crowd.

He frowned on the "SEMITIC NORTH AFRICA MYTH" and the equally ridiculous "CAUCASIAN

BLACK HISTORY EVERYDAY
PART ONE

NORTH AFRICA" which was "NEGRO-LESS." He severely criticized 'EDUCATORS," "SCHOLARS," "AUTHORITIES ON AFRICA," characterizing them all as very sick minds! He was particularly incensed over "DARK SKINNED HAMITIC EUROPEANS" and Seligman's Races of Africa's religious bigotry and Semitic racism as perpetuated by "AUTHORITIES," "LIBERAL HISTORIANS," "BLACK STUDIES PROFESSORS" who parrot racist and outmoded ideas of Africans, Africa and Egypt in the Nile Valley. Dr. Ben chose to "ignore the RACISTS actions and RELIGIOUS BIGOTRY" of White and Black Jews, White and Black Christians, White or Black Muslims, in their bastardization and plagiarization of the history and heritage of my "MOTHER-CONTINENT" - Alkebulan. He spilled much ink on the Jewish myth of Noah's curse of Black people!

In *The Black Man's North and East Africa* (1971) by Yosef A.A. ben-Jochannan and George Simmonds, originally published by Alkebu-lan and now reprinted by Black Classics Press, the authors contend that there is much falsity and distortion in the manner in which the history of these regions is presented in the guise of "academic scholarship" by academicians, authorities and scholars, even men of the cloth as "Rabbi, Reverend, Minister, Priest, Iman." What is interesting about this groundbreaking critique of the presentation of African history beginning in the 1940s but published in the 1970s, the authors pull no punches but outline a

FREDERICK MONDERSON

scathing critique of academic falsity whose foundation is a complete distortion of the historical record whether preached particularly from the perspective of lay or religious history.

In this, *The Black Man's North and East Africa* is a wonderful tour de force challenge to western and American historical distortion and what the authors call religious bigotry and racial prejudice. They take to task, the manner in which Egypt and Nile Valley culture in general is presented to represent the indigenous creators of that magnificent civilization in Ancient Africa. They present a very cogent argument to show ancient writers, and they show a whole slew of them, viz., Herodotus, Aeschylus, Strabo, Eratosthenes, Homer in the *Iliad* and Odyssey, Philostratus, Statius, Philo, Eusebius, Manetho, Josephus, Diodorus, Lucretius, Poenuhis, Agatharclude, and even the Church Fathers of Christianity, such as Tertullian, St. Cyprian, St. Augustine, among others, who never used the term Negro, Semite nor Hamite to describe the people of ancient Egypt, Nubia, Kush, the Nile Valley. Equally, the name the people themselves and the ancients called the land, Africa, is a late Roman nomenclature rather than the names of Olympia, Hesperia, Oceania, Corpyle, Ortygia. The Greeks and Romans called it Africa and Libya and the Ethiopia called Africa Alkebu-lan.

BLACK HISTORY EVERYDAY
PART ONE

Black History Everyday - Part One Photo. Emma Monderson poses with Detective Pierre Louis and other officers of the 77th Precinct.

In textual analysis, he states "Xenophanes was the first to use physical characteristics as a point of racial identification of the Ethiopians rather than color of skin. Of this point, I cannot subscribe; for, what was it but "PHYSICAL CHARACTERISTICS" when Herodotus wrote "… the Colchians, Ethiopians and Egyptians have the most wooly-hair of all mankind." He continued that, "Herodotus wrote of the "BLACK FLATTEN-NOSED ETHIOPIANS I MET…" etc. Even Strabo 17.1.2 and 17. 1.5 cites Eratosthenes' works with regard to the Egyptians who fought against Cambyses and his Persian invaders of Merowe being BLACK (Ethiopian); this he wrote about c. 525 B.C.E. Further verification came from other Greeks who fought with the Ethiopians at the battle of Xerxes."

FREDERICK MONDERSON

Black History Everyday - Part One Photo. We Shall Not be Moved March. Faces in the Crowd.

Dr. Ben argued further: "It is written that 'Aeschylus was the first of the Greeks to place the Ethiopian" Kushites at a specific Geo-political "boundary in Africa." This may have been very much true; but Ionian merchants and mercenaries who served in the army of Psammetichus I (otherwise known as "Psamtik" **Biblically**), somewhere between the years 663-609 B.C.E., also described the Ethiopians they met in Africa, Egypt in particular, with respect to their "geo-political setting." He is concerned, contemporary with the Egyptians, these writers never used such terms as "Negro, Hamitic, Semitic," etc., to describe these ancient Africans and the authors show these are, and they criticize these, modern interpolations. In fact, the tone of the ancient commentators who used nothing but "Ethiopians" to

BLACK HISTORY EVERYDAY
PART ONE

describe the Africans, black people, contrasts remarkably well with the disparaging epithets moderns, fueled by racial hatred, distorted the evidence, omitted the facts and projected a description not found in the Egyptian, Greek or Roman lexicon. The racists invented disgusting terms as "Negro" not simply to disparage Africans and exclude them from Egypt, while misrepresenting even the religion the black man invented, claiming Judeo-Christian-Islamic origination and underscoring white, Caucasian, blond hair, blue eyed, superiority in all forms of human creation, whether religious, scientific or social. For the most part, modern teaching cast ancient Egypt in a Graeco-Roman mold, using Roman terms describing even Pre-Roman developments in the Nile Valley.

Black History Everyday - Part One Photo. Eric Garner's mother, Rev. Sharpton and a Nurse among many seeking Justice for Eric Garner!

FREDERICK MONDERSON

This little book is a powerful resource for its identification of classical writers who commented on Egypt, Ethiopia and Ethiopians as well as the modern writers whose listed books are key to creating the foundation of falsity permeating current academic teaching, historical writing, newspaper reporting and museum representation of a "Negro-less" or "white only Egypt" that is far from the truth. In this, Dr. Ben takes to task a whole army of wrong doing "authorities on Africa" such as M.D.W. Jeffries; Elsy Leuzinger - *The Art of Africa*; Basil Davidson - *Africa in History*; Donald Weidner; Hayes of the Met; James H. Breasted; Alan Gardiner; Bovril - *The Golden Trade of the Moors*; C.P. Groves - *The Planting of Christianity in Africa*; even Frank Snowden's *Blacks in Antiquity*, mentioning Waddell's Manetho, the traveler and commentator Leo Africanus, G.M. James's *Stolen Legacy*; James Frazier's *Golden Bough*; J.H. Lewis - *The Biology of the Negro* (Chicago, 1941); Posener's *Dictionary of Egyptian Civilization*, Count Volney's *Ruins of Empire* and Baron Vivan Denon commentary and painting a graphic image of the Sphinx before its facial disfigurement.

Whether the proponents of a "white Egypt" are ignorant of the facts of history or knowingly misrepresent the record to proclaim white supremacy in religion and culture while waging psychological and spiritual warfare against the black race, fearful that if the truth be told, the white race would be

BLACK HISTORY EVERYDAY
PART ONE

viewed as covetous, harmful and perpetrators of a gigantic fraud is the line of argument he pursues.

Among the things Dr. Ben states, "Herodotus divided the Ethiopians" into "MACROBIANS, ASMACHIANS" and "CAVE DWELLERS." As far as he was concerned, obviously, all the Ethiopians (Egyptians, Nubians, Carthaginians, Garamantes, Ghanaians, Kushites, etc.), at least those he was aware of, were basically the same in physical characteristics (thick lips, broad noses, wooly hair) and color (black or "burnt skin"). At no instance in his writings did he relate to any of them being SEMETIC or HAMITIC, nor even CAUCASIAN. He was equally certain that many of the Ethiopians could be found in goodly numbers in parts all over the Eastern countries (Arabia Felix - the Arabian Peninsula, Persia, India, etc.)."

The author writes, "Herodotus' anthropological descriptions of the Ethiopians (so-called "NEGROES") were not only verified by Aeschylus, who also delineated Ethiopia's geo-political boundaries; he also wrote about the Ethiopians of Kush beliefs and mythology."

The ancient writers, Dr. Ben holds, "made many references to the Africans' pigmentation, and of course made distinction in their remarks to the degree of BLACKNESS or variance of DARKNESS between different national groupings of Ethiopians ("Negroes" or "BLACKS") on the continent of

FREDERICK MONDERSON

Africa (Alkebu-lan). This factor was best observed by Philostratus in his description of "MEMNON" not being as "... BLACK AS OTHER ETHIOPIANS;" indicating that the Greeks were quite observant of the variance in degree of BLACKNESS among the Ethiopians."

Black History Everyday - Part One Photo. We Shall Not be Moved March. Faces in the Crowd.

As such, in Dr. Fred Monderson's **4th Annual Memorial Day Tribute to Dr. Ben**, June 3 and June 10, 2012, at True South Bookstore 492 Nostrand Ave, between Halsey and Hancock Streets 3:00 - 6:00 PM, the venerable and well-liked educator, Egyptologist, historian, Anthropologist, nationalist, etc., was praised for his **Avant Garde** championing of "Black is Beautiful," pioneering the wearing the Dashiki when in the 1970s Blacks faced

BLACK HISTORY EVERYDAY
PART ONE

a cultural crisis and his audacious effort to "take Egypt" to educate and enlighten African people of their heritage and the forces arrayed against them. He very early made it known how significant travel to Egypt really was and must continue in order to view the monuments where he often told such visitors, "Now that you have come to Egypt, seen what you have seen, what are you going to do with the knowledge!" Thanks to his efforts, conscious raising groups as the **Association for the Study of Classical African Civilization (ASCAC)** was born and today continue his identification. Let us not forget, Dr. Ben placed the Black woman on a high pedestal in praise and appreciation for her tremendous contribution as mother, spouse, nurturer and educator.

Black History Everyday - Part One Photo. Ladies on the Dancefloor at **CEMOTAP's** 31st Celebration.

FREDERICK MONDERSON

Black History Everyday - Part One

Photo. Faces and signs in the crowd for the 50th Anniversary March on Washington.

Black History Everyday - Part One

Photo. Amazing, and Kudos to the brains behind the idea of such a monumental and worthwhile project full of history chronicling Lynching of more than 4040 African-Americans, others still unknown and no one brought to justice for the heinous crimes!

BLACK HISTORY EVERYDAY
PART ONE

Black History Everyday - Part One Photo. We Shall Not be Moved March.
Faces in the Crowd.

Black History Everyday - Part One Photo. We Shall Not be Moved March.
Faces in the Crowd.

FREDERICK MONDERSON

Black History Everyday - Part One Photo. Brother Walter Brown and Brother Fred Monderson stand beside James Brown in his hometown, Augusta, Georgia.

Black History Everyday - Part One Photo. Brother Walter Brown of Atlanta, GA., in relaxing mood.

BLACK HISTORY EVERYDAY
PART ONE

Black History Everyday - Part One Photo. One of the many planks depicting the numbers of enslaved Africans lynched in the various counties of the South from 1870-1950.

FREDERICK MONDERSON
13. CELEBRATING DR BEN - PART II.

Dr. Yosef ben-Jochannan's life has been one extraordinary experience of intellectual trail-blazing, daring cultural nationalism on a global scale, heavy in praise of African womanhood and in dynamic process as author, lecturer, publisher, archaeologist, educator, historian and Egyptologist, among many others. Very few have done more extolling Africa in the forefront, lived as long and even many times challenged the angel of death, as the man lovingly called "Dr. Ben" by beloved fans and admirers worldwide. Ever wondered how Dr. Ben got his name? I made his acquaintance early in 1972 when a friend, Barney introduced me to this extraordinary individual through his classic *Africa: Mother of Western Civilization* at a time in the black consciousness movement when young people, even elders, were at a crossroad looking for leadership extolling nationalist sentiments, cultural patriotism, motifs, symbols, slogans and representing positive role models that the young could emulate. Since at first his name was puzzling to pronounce **Barney and I** began calling him "**Ben Jo**" in referring to his book *Mother*, and its message, imagery and bibliographic listing that exposed his readership to a new world of reference material. After I enrolled at New York City Technical (then Community) College and met **Curtis Dunmoodie**, Curtis said we needed to show more respect and so we young students began calling him "Dr. Ben." By the time I

BLACK HISTORY EVERYDAY
PART ONE

moved to Hunter College in 1974 the name had stuck. So much so, when he came to sit in for Dr. Clarke in the Black and Puerto Rican Studies Department the fellow students began calling him Dr. Ben, on a grander scale. It should be known Dr. Ben was not well liked at first, both by the general public and in academia particularly by black academics.

Black History Everyday - Part One Photo. Stairs to the panoramic view of the vast display recounting 4040 lynching murders chronicled by the Equal Justice Initiative Restoration Project in Montgomery, Alabama.

FREDERICK MONDERSON

Black History Everyday – Part One Photo. Faces and signs in the crowd for the 50th Anniversary March on Washington.

Having to defend his scholarship in challenge to Western and American distortion, omission, plagiarization and religious, cultural and historical racial bigotry in genocidal behavior towards Africa and Africans as well as the uncomfortable position he put black scholars in, many dismissed him, infinitesimally critiqued his work claiming "Dr. Ben has no PhD!" Well established publishers refused to consider his works. As such, he initiated Self-Publishing of his books, producing small amounts that young students and others bought as encouragement to enable him to continue the work. As a young student at NYCTC, an episode of "**Dr. Ben has no PhD**" made me cry. I ran to the A Train from school on Jay Street, rode to 125th Street and onto Lenox Ave where his office was located on

BLACK HISTORY EVERYDAY PART ONE

the second floor, opposite to Choc-Full-of-Nuts, and Professor Simmonds consoled me showing Dr. Ben's PhD in Anthropology on the wall!

Black History Everyday - Part One Photo. Ladies of substance and commitment to Black Upliftment being honored at **CEMOTAP'S** 31st Celebration.

As an avid supporter of Dr. Ben, I purchased every book he wrote in first edition, traveled first with him to Egypt in the 1980s where he held the first and only "Panel Discussion" under the theme "What has coming to Egypt meant to you!" Subsequently he asked me, "Monderson, now that you have come to Egypt, seen what you have seen, what are you going to do with the knowledge?" Enthused by the subject of Egypt, motivated by the gifted scholar and in

FREDERICK MONDERSON

seeking advice as to the direction of my studies as a young student, Dr. Ben told me, "Monderson, there are fifty nations in Africa, choose one and specialize in it. Be a specialist not a generalist on Africa."

Black History Everyday - Part One Photo. We Shall Not be Moved March. Faces in the Crowd.

Then he admonished, "In doing research on Egypt, get the oldest material you can find and work from there." In 1990, at a dinner in Dr. Ben's honor hosted by Dr. Lewis, the Ophthalmologist, at Mini-Sink in Harlem, and given the opportunity to speak before the Elders, I said: "Dr. Ben, as your vision becomes cloudy and you're looking for someone to pass the baton to, look for Monderson for I'll be there!" On two occasions Dr. Ben recognized my work in letter form!

BLACK HISTORY EVERYDAY PART ONE

Years later, aged and infirm Dr. Ben, sitting in a Harlem restaurant Dr. Ben asked me, "Monderson, can you take me back to Egypt one last time? I don't want to see the sights; I just want to sit in the hotel lobby and the people will come to see me!" This is because of the good work Dr. Ben has done for the Nubians and truly Egyptian Africans in that country. Everywhere he went he dropped envelopes. From baggage handlers, bus drivers, cooks in the hotels, cleaners, gardeners, you name it, everyone got something! He did so much for those people; Dr. Ben is well-liked in Egypt. Even today in Egypt, People still ask "Is Dr. Ben still alive?" "How is he doing?" Contacting his lawyer, he told me, "The Court will not permit me to allow Dr. Ben to travel." As such then, I began to promote the Annual Memorial Day Tribute to Dr. Ben and here we are at the fourth one, hopefully there will be many others. This year, 2019, we celebrated the 12th Memorial Day Tribute to Dr. Ben. In addition, I conducted three Annual Lectures in Dr. Ben's name at Karnak Temple, Luxor, Egypt in 2016, 2017, and 2018. With changes in the Administration of the temple, this was discontinued.

In the co-authored *The Black Man's North and East Africa*, Dr. Ben and Professor George Simmonds, there is a final chapter entitled "Things done by Africa before Europe," Dr. Ben lists accomplishments on which he elaborates.

FREDERICK MONDERSON

Before we begin today's Part two of this tribute, I wish to reflect on an aspect from the book, discussed in last week's discussion. It goes as follows: "In this article the author will very briefly show some of the many 'Things' the continent of Africa has given to the world before the coming of Europe into history. It is taken from the writer's much more extensive work **'AFRICANS INFLUENCE ON EUROPEAN FEAR AND HISTORY**,'" presently being edited for publication. The larger work shows the reasons why **TRUE HISTORY** has been suppressed and kept from the peoples of the world. Because of the old myths and teachings that **AFRICA** (Alkebu-lan) **HAS NO HISTORY**" this article is written from a point to that perspective. The reader in this context, can then see many reasons for the terrible fear of African History being taught truthfully in a white (European)-oriented society or setting."

"In order to control the numerous former chattel slaves, it was (from a white-European perspective) - **AFRICA**; and make him psychologically ashamed of himself and the color of his skin. Such controls make blacks think that they ought to be grateful and thankful to the whites for discovering" (a term Europeans love to use whenever they first find out that something, someone, or some places existed of which they knew nothing) them in "backward Africa" and taking them to "stolen lands" in what is commonly referred to in history and other disciplines

BLACK HISTORY EVERYDAY
PART ONE

as the "New World" (the Americas - both North and South, and the Caribbean Islands.)"

THE BIRTH OF MAN OR MAN-LIKE CREATURES - Man-like creatures, fossil man, pithecanthropus, erectus, sivanthropus, Zinjanthropus Boisie, are the oldest forms of the human species dating back millions of years old and found only in Africa.

THE STEP-PYRAMID - Created by Imhotep for Pharaoh Zoser of the Third Dynasty at Sakkara stands at the beginning of architectural history and attests to the ingenuity of ancient African science of building and organization, that early in time.

THE TRUE PYRAMIDS - The best examples are those at Ghizeh in terms of size, exquisite nature and preservation but they represent the highest form of organization of manpower, quarrying and transportation of stone, building to predetermined architectural planning, with accompanying logistics and ordinances for medical treatment of injured and sick workers, nearby housing for the workers, ordinances for their meals and the coordination of construction over great distances of a colossal nature.

THE PYRAMID TEXTS - Sayings and scriptures that are now ascribed to famous Hebrew prophets and other personages as Job, Jeremiah and

FREDERICK MONDERSON

King Solomon, had their origins in the Pyramid Texts.

Black History Everyday - Part One Photo. We Shall Not be Moved March. Faces in the Crowd.

THE COFFIN TEXTS - These grew out of the Old Kingdom Pyramid Texts in that now during the Middle Kingdom, the religious words of inspiration that accompanied the dead were placed on the inside and outside of coffins making such spiritual powers available to everyone who could afford it.

THE BOOK OF THE DEAD - Represents a New Kingdom compilation of the Pyramid Texts with additional spells and incantations accompanied by colorful illustrations of the journey in the Afterlife and the obstacles encountered there.

BLACK HISTORY EVERYDAY
PART ONE

THE WORLD'S EARLIEST NAVAL POWER - In a Riverain country, the first thing one had to do was conquer the Nile. Even in the mythology the gods traveled by boat and in the Pyramid Age boats were interred in the Pyramid Complex for the king to journey to meet the gods. Found in 1954 and reconstructed, one is now housed at Ghizeh in the Boat Museum.

PLANNED PARENTHOOD - The Kahun Papyrus discovered by Flinders Petrie and dated to the 18th Dynasty discusses birth-control methods. This important development, like so many new features of pharaonic cultural practice have been attributed to the time of Queen Hatshepsut.

KINGS AND QUEENS IN EGYPT - Kings ruled Egypt in an orderly manner for more than three thousand years and they were often shown in surviving examples with their queens in a state of equality. This is evident throughout the 3000-year period of dynastic rule. Queen Merneith of the Old Kingdom, Mentuhotep II's mother Queen Aam, Queen Tetisheri of the 17th Dynasty and her daughter Queen Ahmes-Nefertari, ancestress of the 18th Dynasty, Queen Hatshepsut and Queen Tiy, wife of Amenhotep III, and Queen Nefertari II wife of Rameses II were all beautiful and fabled ladies.

FREDERICK MONDERSON

BUILDING OF THE GREAT SPHINX OF GIZEH - Current evidence seems to indicate Khafre, builder of the Second Pyramid at Ghizeh did repairs to the Sphinx c. 2500 B.C. and that it is probably as old as 10,000 years based on water marks in the vicinity as planned by John Anthony West.

THE ONLY PERFECT GOVERNMENT RECORDED BY MAN - Rule by the gods who handed down their legacy to their son the Pharaoh but in time this dissipated.

THE ANKHS - Spiritual symbol of life often seen as an instrument of power in the hands of gods, when the gods imparted life to the pharaoh or when gods baptized the king before his entering the temple to conduct services.

Black History Everyday - Part One Photo. We Shall Not be Moved March. Faces in the Crowd.

BLACK HISTORY EVERYDAY PART ONE

SCOTTISH RITES - Secrets of the temple that migrated from Heliopolis and later the Grand Lodge at Luxor, built by Amenhotep III and expanded by Rameses II.

TRADES - **"SON LIKE FATHER"** - Crafts and knowledge were handed down as family secrets.

THE EGYPTIAN ALPHABET - This is truly indigenous to the Nile Valley, evidence demonstrated in Upper Egypt. While Winkler wants to attribute this writing to Mesopotamia, evidence of the flora, fauna, geographical features are native to Upper Egypt and even Diop affirms the Egyptian origin of their writing. So too does Budge.

THE EARLIEST KNOWN PAINTING - Not cave man scrawl but actual painting from the Old **Kingdom.**

COLLECTION OF TAXES - The first government to levy taxes on their citizens so that the work of government could progress as well as to replenish the royal treasury. Taxes were in the form of produced food, cattle, crafts, labor or precious instruments whether from citizens or as conquered booty and tribute.

FREDERICK MONDERSON

NAMING OF THE GODS - Ra, Osiris, Seth, Thoth, Amon-Ra, Montu, Khonsu, and many more who presided at the Judgment. There were national and local gods. At Abydos Temple of Seti I, in the corridor opposite the Abydos Tablet naming some 76 kings from Narmer to Seti I, on the opposite wall the names of some 300 divinities are listed. Elsewhere some 7000 gods are mentioned.

NAMING OF THE GODDESSES - Hathor, Isis, Mut, Maat, Selkis, Seshat, Neith, etc. These lady divinities, featured at different locations, were generally part of a triad of husband, wife and child, generally son.

MAKING OF THE OBELISKS - A single piece of stone quarried, transported and erected at a site hundreds of miles away from place of origin. It is decorated before erection. Many were dispatched to European and American cities. The Washington Monument is an obelisk but constructed of steel and cut-up stone. Generally, Obelisks had names.

BLACK HISTORY EVERYDAY
PART ONE

Black History Everyday - Part One Photo. Deep in the conundrum. How terrifying it feels to envision such a ghastly occurrence. Each plank contains a set of names of murdered victims and no accountability.

Black History Everyday - Part One Photo. Sister Betty Dopson, Co-Chair of **CEMOTAP** listens to praises being sung about her dynamic role in "Tag-Team" with Dr. James McIntosh.

FREDERICK MONDERSON

DEVELOPMENT OF THE SCRIBES - Scribes were intellectuals of their day and all forms of recordings were the domain of these men of letters, whether letter writing, instruction, accompanying military expedition to record ordinances and events, etc.

CENTERS OF LEARNING - Heliopolis, Luxor, Abydos, Asuit, Sakkara. Generally, any place where temples were located acted as some form of center of learning with some being more important and prominent than others.

DEVELOPMENT OF THE NEGATIVE CONFESSIONS - This moral and ethical imperative guided the society and its citizens' behaviors, so much so, upon death at the Judgment before the Assayors, the deceased confessed to the things he did not do while on earth. There were also positive confessions, listing good things the deceased confessed to doing.

CREATION OF MANY RELIGIONS - Religion grew out of the need to explain local phenomena within the context of original thinking about this world and the next.

DEVELOPMENT OF BULLFIGHTING IN EGYPT - Bulls played an important part in the social as well as religious life of ancient Egypt.

BLACK HISTORY EVERYDAY
PART ONE

INTRODUCTION OF THE WORLD'S EARLIEST KNOWN SOLAR CALENDAR - Depending on which scholar one reads the calendar was invented in 4241 B.C. as stated by Breasted, while Petrie gives 5701 B.C. and Maulana Karenga of Kwanzaa fame gives 6200 B.C.

> Visit the
> Augusta Museum of History
> and see
> The Godfather of Soul,
> Mr. James Brown,
> the only major exhibition
> about this
> international music icon
> in the country!

Black History Everyday - Part One Photo. The sign says it all.

FREDERICK MONDERSON

Black History Everyday - Part One Photo. Faces and signs in the crowd for the 50th Anniversary March on Washington.

In stating his philosophy of the "Quintessential Nile Valley African Man," Dr. Ben elucidates in The African Called Rameses (*"The Great"*) *II and the Africa Mother of "Western Civilization"* as a lecture he delivered on April 29, 1989 for **The Third Eye**, Inc., in conjunction with the Rameses (The Great) II Exhibition held in Dallas, Texas. This profusely illustrated 100 page book contains 97 illustrations and as part of a **Table of Contents** or Citations he lists as follows: Illustrations, Glossary, Foreword by Dr. John H. Clarke, a Retrospection, All in Statistics, Greetings, Opening, Origins, Questions, Background, Direction, Family, Manhood, Leader, Symbol, Tragedy, Architecture, Myth, Image, Syncretism, Education, Literature, The

BLACK HISTORY EVERYDAY
PART ONE

Craft, Belief, Guardian, Justice, Conclusion, End Notes, Bibliography and Index.

Black History Everyday - Part One Photo. **Public Advocate Jumaane Williams** at the **Podium** stating the case for the People at Sharpton's "Power and Policy Forum on Dr. King's Holiday.

Therefore, stating in a nutshell that he is "primarily a student and professor" of "Nile Valley and Great Lakes High-Culture of Africa with a major concentration on Ta-Meri," the Quintessential Nile Valley Black Man for Dr. Ben is embodied in Rameses II, "The Great," who is a pharaoh, King, courageous leader, father, husband, conqueror, militarist, Imperial colonizer, architect, engineer and builder, patron of the arts and learning, peace maker, devotee of the gods, whose history and heritage is greatly distorted as taught today in and outside of Egypt.

FREDERICK MONDERSON

Insisting that the continent of Alkebu-lan or Africa be "the first and most important land of call whenever we decide to travel" he admonished "Let's always be prepared to meet the foe in full knowledge of Ta-Meri's High Culture history before we visit, remembering always that among the Nubian population the truest seeds of the ancient Nile Valley African stock are to be found today in the 20th Century of the Common Era."

Black History Everyday - Part One Photo. This is where the civil rights struggle first began as these people chose to "Walk to protest segregation on Alabama's buses!"

On multiple occasions in 1955, black women were arrested for challenging Montgomery's law requiring racial segregation on buses. The arrest of Rosa Parks sparked a mass protest that launched the modern civil rights movement and brought to prominence a young pastor named Dr. Martin Luther King Jr. For nearly a year, black people in Montgomery boycotted the buses and challenged racial segregation in court, sustained by the courage of black women who collectively walked thousands of miles to end racial segregation in public transportation. You are standing in the neighborhood where modern civil rights activism in America was born.

Dana King (b. 1960)
Guided By Justice, 2018
Bronze

Black History Everyday - Part One Photo. The inscription tells the story!

BLACK HISTORY EVERYDAY
PART ONE

Black History Everyday - Part One Photo. The Capital Building with the emblem of Independence and Nkechie Taifa at Sharpton's Washington DC Conference on 9/6/2016.

"*On the Assassination of President John F. Kennedy*" - "It was, as I saw it, a case of 'the chickens coming home to roost.' I said that the hate in white men had not stopped with the killing of defenseless black people, but that hate, allowed to spread unchecked, had finally struck down this country's Chief Magistrate." Malcolm X. *The Autobiography of Malcolm X.*

FREDERICK MONDERSON

"You don't have to be a man to fight for freedom, all you have to do is to be an intelligent human being." Malcolm X. *Speech at the Audubon Ballroom.*

14. "CHICKENS COMING HOME" BY DR. FRED MONDERSON

The colonial climate that followed the **Berlin Conference** of 1884-85 **Partitioning Africa on Paper**, set the stage for an active **Partition of Africa on Land** campaign unleashing a thunderous military strategy to remove all forms of African resistance, contributed to the highest stage of imperialism resulting from Africa not simply being conquered and made Africa prostate. Ultimately, however, this imperial avariciousness led to World War I and the known "classic fascism" leading to Italian invasion of Ethiopia. In 1936, Haile Selassie, Emperor of Ethiopia, appeared before and appealed to the League of Nations denouncing Italian aggression and insisting the body must condemn such imperialist adventurism. In summing up his address, the Emperor prophetically reminded, "Today for me, tomorrow for You!" As such, in three years World War II broke out engulfing the world in the most cataclysmic devastation that threatened the very survival of nations and people. In present circumspect reflection, we must be careful not to

BLACK HISTORY EVERYDAY PART ONE

allow history to be repeated as elements of showmanship posture on the brink of such devastatingly threatening developments.

For nearly eight years Republicans from the highest leadership to rank and file have allowed, engaged in and meticulously and callously pilloried President Obama, staining the "Republican brand" and in the process the United States Presidency, the same position their compatriots hold in captivity today. From the 43 percent who voted against the "Black man," unending character assassination from "Nigger in the White House" to being unpatriotic, socialist, Muslim and "Palling around with terrorist," to lacking "testicular fortitude," "Poisoning the Well" and running a "Gangster Government" as well as the child-like charade of the "Birther Movement," such actions reveal an insidious and dangerously vindictive Republican underbelly. Even more, such unbridled "oral diarrhea" on part of Republicans Donald Trump, Michele Bachmann, Rick Santorum, "stupid" Senator Grassley, and "You Lie" Wilson in company of "Waterloo" DeMint and "Obamacare is worse than Slavery" Ben Carson, have now opened the gates for the "Chickens to come home." Only this time their bite is worse than those of Carson's "rabid dogs" and this casts a negative view on the nation as a whole. Today the world laments the tragic buffoonery of a once highly respected nation, seeming hopelessly and morally adrift in the cosmos as a Klingon ship after Captain Kirk a had dispatched it.

FREDERICK MONDERSON

First, the New York *Daily News* labeled Donald Trump a "clown" perhaps because of his "Birther charade;" one local paper recently labeled him "chump;" much of this due to his newly minted insulting callousness characterizing Mexicans as rapists, criminals and drug dealers; that he would "build a wall which Mexico would pay for;" mockingly attacked Carly Fiorina's face; blowing hard that "Iowans are stupid" for voting for Ben Carson; to his newest "Lulu" of "excluding Muslims" seems rescued fresh from the "dark strain of American conscience." Yet, many of the 30 percent see him as worth an applause, standing ovation, giving unquestioned support much of which Alan Dershowitz explained as being "inconsistent with the character of this country." Even more, and not surprising, as the verbal mayhem unfolded, the world watched and wondered, isn't the "ugly American" abroad or is he now at home?

Black History Everyday - Part One Photo. Faces and signs in the crowd for the 50th Anniversary March on Washington.

BLACK HISTORY EVERYDAY
PART ONE

Black History Everyday - Part One Photo. Faces and signs in the crowd for the 50th Anniversary March on Washington.

That designation and the active anti-Obama vituperative accusations with resultant threats to the President and his family, earned Republicans the designation "Party of No" particularly because they blocked every legislative initiative President Obama proposed; vociferously and vituperatively attacked his **Affordable Care Act** law; eviscerated his Jobs Bill; challenged the Asian Trade Deal he crafted; sought to block his immigration initiative; criticized his Cuban embargo breakout with establishment of mutual embassies all the while invoking a stale Republican pliant "Obama is Soft on Terror!" Equally they "try to make hay" that he is pursuing a failed policy on Iraq and Syria. In fact, as

FREDERICK MONDERSON

a thinker, President Obama has applied an analytically meticulous mindset in a new age of modern warfare in not falling for Isis and Al Qaeda "Hokey Dokey," while seeking to garner an active and effective Middle Eastern Coalition as he pounds their terrorist encampments proclaiming no significant "Boots on the Ground" is the way to go.

Black History Everyday - Part One Photo. Dr. Fred Monderson walks with the "Ladies" who started it all in the Civil Rights Movement as they unleashed the Montgomery Bus Boycott that crippled the city economically and led to reforms in segregation in that city.

BLACK HISTORY EVERYDAY
PART ONE

Black History Everyday - Part One Photo. Walter Brown mugs for the camera with the "Lynching Planks" of the Equal Justice Initiative Memorial at his rear.

Keen observers notice how statesmanlike President Obama appeared to be at the recent Global Climate Change conference. Espousing that presidential demeanor without question, observers believe none of the 16 2016 Republican contenders would probably have been perceived as resolute American ambassadors as President Obama appeared.

FREDERICK MONDERSON

Black History Everyday - Part One Photo. Luis and Carmen, mother and son, in a relaxing mood!

Nonetheless, recent developments point to, some believe, one frightening specter Donald Trump represents to the Republican Party and the facetious representative of the American brand particularly as a potential Commander-in-Chief. This is not only unsettling but can be more dangerous than America's most virulent enemies hope to be. Reason reveals, because over the last several years Americans did not turn off the Trump spigot, his bigotry is now full blown. Guess what? He needs to stop spewing such pathological and deep-seated polluted beliefs for such bigotry goes against and will pose a serious problem for the American brand going forward.

BLACK HISTORY EVERYDAY
PART ONE

Donald Trump's most vocal supporters need to take note, Fareed Zakaria spoke of the *Rise of the Rest* and President Obama recognized America's approach to the world and its challenges cannot be in the mold of Roosevelt's "big stick," but more of a "smart heart" being mindful of President Clinton's dictum, "America's greatness lies in its moral not military might." As such, current Republican "fools rush in where wise men fail to tread" strategy is more appropriate to the "horse and buggy" age rather than today's analectic post jet-age speed. Now, in view of such realities, while Republicans disagree with President Obama's incremental progression in economic and financial policy, the reality is job growth increased tremendously, housing starts have increased, the auto industry is now booming, research and development in education and science is very encouraging in fields of clean and renewable energy, even as unemployment figures declined towards the 5 percent historic lows; Wall Street DOW is beginning to bang the door at 18,000 up from 6500 when Obama began, and prevailing belief is many of Trump's supporters and associates are laughing all the way to the bank from this financial windfall; college enrollment is up and also Affordable Care Act registration has topped the 16 (now 20) million mark. In his studied and sure-footed approach, Mr. Obama has achieved a great deal despite Republican obstructionism and he has masterfully represented the nation in presenting a climate change proposal whose acceptance is practically a *fait accompli*; while real-politik dictates, the Iran Deal is in full-swing and the strange bedfellows of Mullahs, Assad, Obama and Putin must lay in bed with Hollande, Merkel and Cameron to effectively bring Middle Eastern states into coalition to defeat Isis. Taking the long view in a more sophisticated military strategy, in his policies Mr. Obama has remained actively and intelligently involved and must get credit for reducing American military casualties.

However, as the Trump "Pied Piper" keeps thundering towards the cliffs of oblivion carrying his loyal supporters into that chasm, we wonder where are the Republican men of substance demonstrating "testicular fortitude" to stand and condemn this new and dangerous foray.

Selassie's "Tomorrow for you" is now and as the old adage holds "when the enemy begins to self-destruct, stay quiet," so President Obama remains mum! Today some Republicans finally thinking about the predicament, including Dick Chaney, Paul Ryan, Jeb Bush, Nikki Haley, even Presidential historian Douglas Brinkley, have all come to realize, "We've let the dogs out, but they're biting left and right." But as old ideas die hard and thanks to Donald Trump's insensitivities many projected a possible Clinton occupancy of the White House again, but to no avail. More important, however, America's enemies have been handed tremendous propaganda ammunition and after he is "fired" Mr. Trump will have to explain his anti-Muslim statements to Middle Eastern Arabs and Muslim partners and business associates.

BLACK HISTORY EVERYDAY
PART ONE

It is interesting, a CNN anchor recently hosted a focus group and a two-term New Hampshire representative, a Trump supporter, went on *ad nausea* that President Obama is a "liar" and "when he spoke last Sunday he was lying to the nation." Turns out this woman was an active "Birther" advocate allied with Donald Trump's fool's errand. Today, t he said individual cannot up to the 12,209 lies Donald Trump has spewed so far. However, we're still counting.

Now, like a spoiled child, Donald Trump is threatening to run as an independent candidate and as his action will not only make the next president's job more difficult, Mr. Trump will go on to make more money in his business ventures. In this, he may forget the poor people who supported him and his notoriety in not only proposing impractical and hardly attainable but equally unconstitutional machinations and promises that "glitter but is not golden" which will continue to stain perceptions regarding this great nation.

And as such, thanks to Mr. Trump the voters may throw out the Republican bums at the next election. Unfortunately, this has not happened and we now have a President-Elect Donald Trump. Nevertheless, and say what anyone will, President Obama's legacy as per Paul Krugman's "Greatest President ever" assessment may ever further materialize because there is still much more to come and Obama

FREDERICK MONDERSON

continues to build up accomplishments, despite the actions and reactions of the "Party of No."

Black History Everyday - Part One Photo. **We Shall Not be Moved March**. Faces in the Crowd.

Black History Everyday - Part One Photo. Monument Park Admonition for racial terror lynching recognition.

BLACK HISTORY EVERYDAY
PART ONE

Black History Everyday - Part One Photo. Dr. McIntosh, Erik Monderson and Sister Betty Dopson at **CEMOTAP**.

"We are involved in a struggle for liberation: liberation from the exploitative and dehumanizing system of racism, from the manipulative control of a corporate society; liberation from the constructive norms of 'mainstream' culture, from the synthetic myths that control us as to fashion ourselves rashly without (reaction) rather than from within (creation)." [Milton Mirkin] Tone Dade Bambara. *The Black Woman [1970], preface.*

FREDERICK MONDERSON

"But they still took me from my home. They took me through the bush – raiding thieves. Fucking demons! 'She is for everyone, soup to be had before dinner,' that is what someone said. They tied me up to a tree by my foot, and the men came whenever they wanted soup. I make fires, I cook food, I listen to their stupid songs, I carry bullets, I clean wounds, I wash tier blood from their clothing, and, and ... I lay there as they tore me to pieces, until I was raw ... fighting for months. Five months. Chained like a goat. These men fighting ... fighting for my liberation. Still I close my eyes and I see such terrible things. Things I cannot stand to have in my head. How can men be this way?"

15. CULTURE FOR LIBERATION
BY
DR. FRED MONDERSON

Increasingly, and across the spectrum of African-American discussion, most commentators emphasize history and culture as a potent aspect of liberation. Today, when we contemplate Black Solidarity, and in keeping with this state of affairs, Egypt/ancient Kemet/Tawi looms even larger in the scheme of things because of its significant legacy in the evolution of ideas, methodology, achievements and influence. This notwithstanding, we ought to be mindful of the transposition of ideas and their potential damages particularly when their origination is based on a distorted perception.

BLACK HISTORY EVERYDAY
PART ONE

On October 16, 1995, while on the bus to the "Million Man March" we viewed a tape in which a young brother, articulate, sincere, revolutionary and committed, kept referring to the cliche' "Tell Pharaoh to let my people go." He was certainly not aware he parroted someone-else's history and that Pharaoh was one of "our people." For herein lies the need for solidarity in the methodology of liberation where we become more versed in our history and culture as this relates to the Nile Valley experience as fundamental to our spiritual, psychological, intellectual, cultural and physical freedom.

Black History Everyday - Part One Photo. Faces and signs in the crowd for the 50th Anniversary March on Washington.

FREDERICK MONDERSON

Black History Everyday - Part One

Photo. Faces and signs in the crowd for the 50th Anniversary March on Washington.

Therefore, and after an intellectually and spiritually uplifting pilgrimage to the ancient "Holy Land" of Kemet, now Egypt, it is only appropriate that this writer seeks "permission to speak" from the ancestors and elders on whose shoulders he stands. I can therefore praise their wonderfully creative spirit, that on the banks of the Nile, where that night, some of us stood, engineered the fundamentals of science, medicine, architecture, art-sculpture, painting, writing, astronomy, metallurgy, agriculture, philosophy, and mathematics. "Ma'atian principles" or equality, balance, order, propriety or goodness, undergirded these accomplishments that so influenced later civilizations. Today, our people simply need only let these shining examples of early African genesis of faith, and perseverance, help assist their path toward self-awareness, self-actualization, and intellectual and spiritual empowerment.

BLACK HISTORY EVERYDAY
PART ONE

Black History Everyday - Part One Photo. We Shall Not be Moved March. Faces in the Crowd.

Luxor Temple, the "Grand Lodge" of Masonic beliefs, was built by Amenhotep III of the Eighteenth Dynasty, and added to by Rameses II of the Nineteenth Dynasty. Today as one entrances the temple, from the north, pass the one standing obelisk and two seated and four standing statues of Rameses II, through the First Pylon, there is a small chapel in the northwest corner of the Great Court of Rameses II. This Kiosk was built and dedicated to the Theban Triad of Amon, Mut and Khonsu by Hatshepsut but later expropriated by Thutmose III and even much later by Rameses himself. On a wall in the southwestern corner of this court an interesting relief is depicted. Here Rameses II is seated in front of a

FREDERICK MONDERSON

procession of his sons going to the temple, along with cattle and priests in preparation for the offering.

No women are represented, that is to say there are none of his daughters were present. They are shown elsewhere since Rameses II like to depict his children as often as he could. In a way it could be argued this procession to greet the great king by his sons and priests' mirror in genesis the "Million Man March," where the brothers stood firm and the sisters understood and supported them. Thus, there is some precedence in African historiography for such a gathering of strong Black men, millennia later.

This notwithstanding, on any travel expedition designed to be educational, the crafters of the trip envision a general purpose as to what the trip hopes to accomplish. Thus, there are individual purposes for the many travelers. On my trip one summer, some fathers brought their sons and grandsons. Nuclear families, singles and families complete with grandfather and grandmother intact, were able to physically and collectively experience the monuments; and seek to learn some of the wisdom of their memories these monuments speak to.

My principal and personal reason for going on that trip, had been to take my sister Cherise, on that wonderful experience I have so often partook, along the banks of the Nile at Aswan, Luxor and in Cairo, Egypt, where the ancestral heritage reigns supreme. Dr. ben-Jochannan's book *From Abu Simbel to Ghizeh: A Guidebook and Manual* included Abydos,

BLACK HISTORY EVERYDAY
PART ONE

"where it all began." In that journey is encompassed the need for love of self, love of one's woman, and love for god. At the completion of the experience is reinforced love of self, love for thy neighbor, then we can appreciate love for god.

Except for Abydos, Luxor, the Ramesseum, Medinet Habu and Hatshepsut's temple at Deir el-Bahari; the others at Philae, Kalabsha, Kom Ombo, Edfu and Esna, were all constructed at the twilight in the history of the ancient land of Kemet, today's Egypt. More importantly, these temples were built on much older foundations, sites chosen for their ancient sacredness.

The greater vision would be to imagine a "High Holy Day" with temples lit at the cardinal centers of divinity worship, religious practice and theological learning, viz., Ptah at Memphis, Ra at Heliopolis, Osiris at Abydos and Amun-Ra at Karnak and Luxor. Then there's Abu Simbel. Such abounding religiosity! Imagine, the first great Egyptian African nation, at pray!

Now to picture Abydos with its splendid and beautiful depictions, wonderful collection of 3,000-year old paintings, that are housed in a magnificent architectural structure; where the power of Osiris manifested itself amidst the 7-deities to whom the temple was dedicated. These, in the Second, actually First Hypostyle Hall from right to left, consist of Horus, Isis, Osiris, Amon, Ra-Horakhti, Ptah and the builder and King, Seti I, deified. The first three comprise the Osirian Triad, the second three are the great gods of the Egyptian Empire, and third, the monarch who built the temple. What is also significant about the antiquity of the Abydos locale, in addition to the **Tomb of Osiris** or Osireion, it houses First and Second Dynasty Royal Tombs and remains of an old fortresses. In addition, Petrie identified the strata of 10 successive levels of temples at Abydos, dating back some 3200 years Before Christ. Therefore, evidence shows, in the architectural evolution of their religiosity and spirituality, the ancient African temple building practices evolved from use of simple materials as leaves, mud and daub, then to bricks, and finally stone. Those perishable materials cannot tell us how long our ancestors were "making joyful sounds unto the lord," "having sweet communion with deity," and "crafting moral and ethical standards for their children." As we were children, and our children will have children of their own, they too should know all this.

The ancestors carefully created conventions of wisdom, science and learning that benefited all. Today our children must enmesh themselves in the study of ancient African history with a methodological approach, through the development of its architecture, which tells of worship and ritualizing of the gods; festivals, frolics and flowers; the management of estates' wealth; imperial wars, conquest and endowments; advances in observational and instrumental astronomy; music and instruments;

BLACK HISTORY EVERYDAY
PART ONE

and the most fabulous raised, incised and painted reliefs of art together with other wonderful architectural accomplishments.

Black History Everyday - Part One Photo. Erik Monderson, a caring and concerned young man, all set for college.

This brings me to the statement: "The Fool says there is no God." In 1989, on one of his trips to Egypt, Dr. ben-Jochannan held a Panel Discussion, one of its kind; the members included a practicing minister, a former minister, a twelve-year-old lad, an assertive sister and a young couple. To begin the discussion, persons were asked to answer two simple questions. "What has coming to Egypt done for you?" and "Now that you have accumulated this much knowledge, 'What are you going to do with it?'"

FREDERICK MONDERSON

Black History Everyday - Part One Photo. We Shall Not be Moved March. Faces in the Crowd.

The assertive sister on the panel during the "Question and Answer" period said to the minister, "Rev. Dr. McNair," from Philadelphia, "How can you go back to your congregation and teach in like manner after what you have witnessed?" The astute Rev. McNair simply responded by saying: "I cannot teach my people there is no God. I can only teach them where God comes from." I thought that was the most revolutionary profound, yet sincere response, one could have expressed.

BLACK HISTORY EVERYDAY
PART ONE

Black History Everyday - Part One
Photo. Faces and signs in the crowd for the 50th Anniversary March on Washington.

Black History Everyday - Part One
Photo. Faces and signs in the crowd for the 50th Anniversary March on Washington.

To understand something about "African communion with Deity," one needs examine the temple. In this respect, the essential elements of ancient Kemetic temples, generally built along the river's banks, included a Quay where the royal boat would dock. Generally, but not always, a canal led from the Dock towards an Avenue of Sphinxes entrancing the Temple. Oftentimes, as at, say, Deir el Bahari, there is a Valley Temple at the Quay and from this building, instead of the Canal, an Avenue of Sphinxes leads directly to the entrance Pylon or Gate. As at Luxor, two Obelisks, two seated and four standing statues stood before the pylon. Generally, there is a court. The Hypostyle Hall has a varied arrangement of columns. There may be a second, though smaller Hypostyle and this leads to the Sanctuary that now stands atop a gradual incline upwards as one approached this sacred spot, the "Holy of Holies." This incline represents a sort of "hillock," a high ground, out of which legend has it, the God first emerged from the waters of chaos and sat upon his mound.

In front of the Sanctuary could be found sphinxes, kneeling and seated statues, obelisks, and inscriptional depictions somehow connected with the central worship. A place of spiritual transition from the profane to the sacred. The Hypostyle Hall, just before the Sanctuary, was generally depicted with images of the temple ritual arranged in succeeding panels. The columns were decorated with kingly and divine personal images. Some temples had an assortment of buildings nearby where a number of supportive functions were performed. There was generally a Sacred Lake fed through some underground spring. In the Graeco-Roman period, a "Mammisi" or "Birth House" of the god was added.

BLACK HISTORY EVERYDAY
PART ONE

As such, understanding these achievements in religious theory and practice, architectural and artistic constructions, and by extension of their influence and the fortitude and originality of their creators, allows both young and old to take pride in African genius. This awareness provides a significant beacon for knowledge of self and is a powerful source of inspiration and strength.

Black History Everyday - Part One Photo. Rev. Sharpton holds hands of Emma Merneith-Mitta Monderson on stage at **National Action Network's Fashion Show** and there she is again at the 25th-year celebration of **National Action Network's** activism.

"Any attempt by an African, or any person of African origin, to write Africa's history according to so-called 'ACADEMIC DISCIPLINE,' as established by European and European-American 'EDUCATORS' or 'AUTHORITIES ON AFRICA' (a la-western style), is tantamount to removing the African slaves as property of their European and/or European-American masters, without seriously damaging their economic interest. For at no time will the White slave masters, nor the children of the white slave masters, write of their Black slaves as their equal. This also holds true for the ex-slaves and the ex-slaves' children." Yosef A.A. ben-Jochannan. Yosef A.A. ben-Jochannan and George Simmonds. *The Black Man's North and East Africa.* [1971]

"In order to control the numerous former chattel slaves, it was (from a white-European perspective) necessary to keep the black man totally ignorant of his *'Motherland'* – AFRICA; and make him psychologically ashamed of himself and the color of his skin. Such controls make blacks think they ought to be *grateful* and *thankful* to the whites for 'discovering' (a term Europeans love to us whenever they first find out that something, someone, or someplace existed of which they knew nothing) them in 'backward Africa' and taking them to 'stolen lands' in what is commonly referred to in history and other disciplines as the *'New World'* (the Americas – both North and South, and the Caribbean Islands)."

BLACK HISTORY EVERYDAY PART ONE

16. Dr. YOSEF A. A. BEN-JOCHANNAN - A TRIBUTE BY DR. FRED MONDERSON

It is with great sorrow that I announce the death of my mentor, friend and world-renowned African historian, Egyptologist and humanitarian DR. YOSEF ANTONIO ALFREDO BEN-JOCHANNAN. At this time, AFRICAN PEOPLE HAVE LOST A CHAMPION OF GREAT MAGNITUDE, wisdom and intellectual fortitude. LET US WISH HIM A WONDERFUL RECEPTION INTO THE PANTHEON OF GREAT AFRICAN ANCESTORS who have never compromised in quest of the best for African people.

Among his many accomplishments, Dr. Ben placed the Black Woman on the HIGHEST PEDESTAL to be admired and respected in the hope she will continue to do what no Black man can ever do!

DR. BEN HAS BEEN A LIGHT and he has shown us the LIGHT!

FREDERICK MONDERSON

Black History Everyday - Part One Photo. We Shall Not be Moved March. Faces in the Crowd.

LET US ALSO HOPE PEOPLE, YOUNG AND OLD, WILL CONTINUE TO READ HIS BOOKS AND FOREVER DRINK FROM THE FOUNT OF HIS ENLIGHTENMENT EFFORTS as Tour Guide, archaeologist and national cultural spokesman whose 97 years on earth have been a tremendously wonderful and enlightening experience. He possessed a vision that looked far into the future. His efforts HAVE KNOWN NO LIMITS in quest for the very best for AFRICAN PEOPLE! Again, his books should be introduced into the schools to let young people understand the man and forces at work!

GOD BLESS DR. BEN-JOCHANNAN AND MAY HIS EFFORTS AND MEMORY CONTINUE TO BE AN INSPIRATION AND GUIDE TO US ALL!

BLACK HISTORY EVERYDAY PART ONE

Dr. Ben was an extraordinary man of many talents, but principally a man who held the African woman in the highest esteem. He taught us in the beginning was the African woman! Creation came out of the African woman! As the obelisk is a small pyramid on a tall base, this is the pedestal upon which Dr. ben-Jochannan placed the African woman. He honored the Black Woman who is the source of the Black Family! He taught us the Black Woman is a Goddess! He also led the light to the Nile Valley. He "took Egypt to challenge and destroy white supremacy!" It's like Marcus Garvey said, "the cubs are running free out there," and thanks to Dr. Ben, intellectual cubs are challenging the distortions, omissions and putting Africa in its proper place in world civilization history given its accomplishments in Nubia and Egypt, Nile Valley cultures, that gave so much to the world.

The Twentieth Century has been blessed with great African and African-American writers and historians. These include Dr. W.E.B. Du Bois, Dr. Carter G. Woodson, Dr. Kwame Nkrumah, Dr. Ivan Van Sertima, J.A. Rogers, Cheikh Anta Diop and Dr. Leonard James, Emeritus Professor of New York City Technical College of the City University of New York, among others. This enormous collection of brain-power equally extends into the Twenty-First Century. However, none of these giants singularly surpass the literary production, commitment, tirelessness, and sincere dedication of Dr. Yosef

FREDERICK MONDERSON

Alfredo Antonio ben-Jochannan. Outspoken visionary, iconic symbol and above and even ahead of his time; controversial and not afraid to take an iconoclastic and individual as necessary and a somewhat idiosyncratic point of view; Dr. Ben was always prepared to defend his positions, irrespective. His friends and students, affectionately call this father, teacher, historian, friend and Egyptologist, "Doc Ben." In fact, back there in the early 1970s when even "Black folks" did not readily accept "Dr. Ben," has anyone ever wonder how he got his name? It was a young man named "Barney" and myself, Fred Monderson, who first started calling him not "Dr. Ben" but "Ben Jo" and the name stuck and finally when a fellow student Curtis Dunmoodie picked it up and said we must be more respectful, we began calling him "Dr. Ben" in defiance of those "feather bedders" who said "Dr. Ben has no PhD!"

Ever cried for Dr. Ben? This odious statement once made me cry at New York City (Community) Technical College. I hurriedly took the A Train to 125th Street to their second-floor office on Lennox Avenue across from the Choc-Full-O-Nuts Coffee Shop in Harlem, before Prof. George Simmonds calmed me down, showing me Dr. Ben's Doctorate in Anthropology on the wall. That is what some of the "false prophets" still do today in academia to him and others! And so, you ask them to match their literary production with their in-clandestine vituperativeness and they cannot! Period!

BLACK HISTORY EVERYDAY
PART ONE

Here was a serious scholar, Dr. ben-Jochannan, who spent a lifetime researching, writing, and defending the integrity and intellectual capabilities of African people worldwide. Dr. Ben pioneered in indigenous ancient African terminology. Imagine a European-American scholar discovered the bones of a fossilized African woman in Ethiopia and named her "Lucy" after an Englishman's song "Lucy with Diamonds," then playing on the radio. Dr. Ben said "No! Her name is Denk Nesh, not Lucy!"

Black History Everyday - Part One Photo. Former Harlem Congressman Charles Rangel at the **Black Star News** Awards ceremony held in Harlem.

FREDERICK MONDERSON

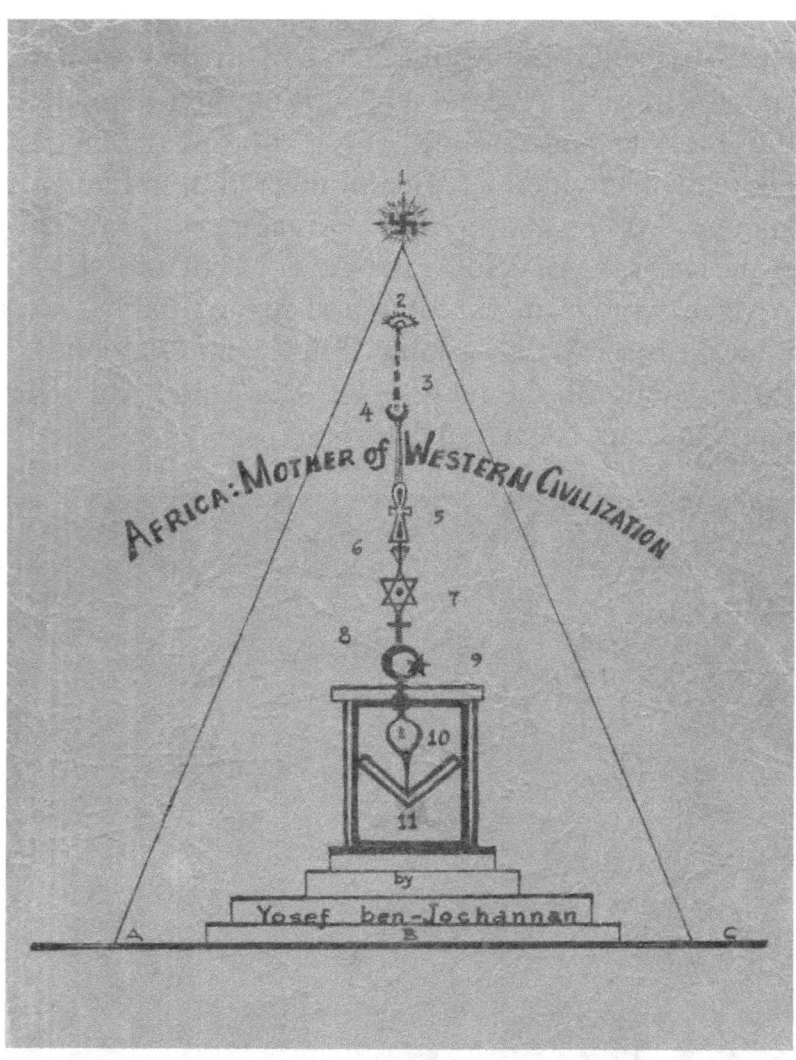

Black History Everyday - Part One

Photo. Dr. Ben's classic magnus opus, *Africa: Mother of "Western Civilization,"* as part of his "Trilogy."

BLACK HISTORY EVERYDAY
PART ONE

Black History Everyday - Part One
Photo. Faces and signs in the crowd for the 50th Anniversary March on Washington.

FREDERICK MONDERSON

Black History Everyday - Part One
Photo. Faces and signs in the crowd for the 50th Anniversary March on Washington.

In 1989, Doc Ben celebrated fifty years of visiting ancient Kemet, Ta-Merry (Egypt) and the Nile Valley cultures. This prolonged involvement has undergirded the basis of his researches, speeches, writings and educational tours. Equally, he began and for some time maintained archaeological digs on the Island of Elephantine and elsewhere. Alas, these have been discontinued.

This writer was happy to be a part of that epoch-making tour that marked Doc Ben's Fiftieth Anniversary visiting the ancient African "holy-land" and the next year for the First Nubian Festival. More importantly, I met "Doc Ben" in early 1972. This was right after the publication of his seminal

BLACK HISTORY EVERYDAY PART ONE

"Trilogy" works, *African Origins of the "Major Western" Religions* (1970), *Africa: Mother of Western Civilization* (1971), and *Black Man of the Nile* (1972), later Black Man of the Nile and his Family. The style of his writings, copious nature of referents employed to defend things African, and his Afrocentric pioneering approach made "Doc. Ben," a very well-respected elder, and in his later years a sought-after speaking attraction, a man who "tells it like it is!"

Black History Everyday - Part One Photo. Sister Betty Dopson, Dr. James McIntosh, Dr. Len Jeffries and Dr. Legrand Clegg III at **CEMOTAP**.

Dr. ben-Jochannan has compiled an impressive thirty odd publications that I am intimately familiar with. He helped set the stage for a whole new approach in

FREDERICK MONDERSON

interpreting Africa's contributions to civilization and its legacy. He lit the fire of intellectual and cultural consciousness in Africans worldwide. The Diasporan style of dress with an Afrocentric flavor is also credited to him. Establishing connections between Africans in America, the Caribbean, Africa, Asia and Europe are all attributed to Dr. ben-Jochannan, a man of vision, a seer, and intellectual giant. Many of his books challenged the distortions of Europeans in writing, publishing and disseminating knowledge about the arts, sciences, religion, etc., of the ancient people today called Egyptians and equally all along the Nile River. Dr. Ben has rightly included omissions and corrected distortions systematically implanted and perpetrated by racist Western, European and American historiography that has falsified the historical past with a prejudiced interpretation against African people. Dr. Ben dared to expose the hypocrisy of western scholarship. He attacked the foundational pillars upon which this false legacy rests. Naturally, he paid a price!

Very early he also expressed the view some scholars are confused because they were taught from a wrong premise. In his own right, and as a result of his teachings, he had no choice but to produce, publish and distribute his works without the aid of major publishing firms. He was thus a pioneer in self-publishing, launching Alkebu-Lan Publishing Company and appealing and winning the support of many upcoming nationalists as "they purchased his books in first edition form!"

BLACK HISTORY EVERYDAY
PART ONE

Black History Everyday - Part One Photo. Beyond a successful NYC City Council career, Mr. Jackson (center) is now a New York State Assemblyman.

Initiating a new approach to history, the end result was an exposition and critical analysis of dynamic forces of Europe and Africa in struggle to claim heritage of the ancient and modern historical record. Dr. Ben addressed professionals, laymen, clergy, students and educators. He stressed vitality, resilience and creative expressions that shaped the modern African personality and worldview. Such an approach found ready ears among a people yearning for enlightening factual information about their illustrious African past in effort to free their minds shackled by the European experience. These young and elder minds were enthused by the positive nature and potency of their cultural African heritage as "Ben" outlined it. He also took great pains to explain that there were lusterless pages in Africa's past but these must be remembered but discarded. Nevertheless, his concern fueled their emerging aspirations. This outlook brought Dr. Ben the adulation and respect of a grateful people, he for long deserved. They understood and welcomed his contributions among the litany of great African-American literary artists.

Black History Everyday - Part One
Photo. "Black Man of the Nile and His Family," the second part of Dr. Ben's "Trilogy" of books.

BLACK HISTORY EVERYDAY
PART ONE

Dr. Ben's writings, lectures and educational tours over the years have stressed two essential themes. The first is that the "emergence of civilization, viz., science, religion, government, architecture, agriculture, philosophy, and the arts, began in Africa." The mouth of these utterances became the conduit of today's Egypt and the Nile Valley. In his approach, Dr. Ben has shown how the structural foundations of western civilization developed from discoveries and scientific applications in this ancient African land. Lastly, he took great pains to show the writing and teaching of modern history has been distorted to elevate Europe and degrade Africa, which is clearly wrong and must be rectified. This fundamental view helped establish the need for African historical reconstruction and interpretation particularly as we navigate this new century and millennium.

The second of Dr. Ben's themes has been that "Africans worldwide should be proud of their ancestors' accomplishments. The arts and sciences that today govern the world are Africa's legacy. African-Americans should show great pride and dignity in their history and heritage." They must respect themselves and carry themselves with dignity and pride. Those who know can and should teach the young how to identify with Africa. In so doing, they must form study groups and visit Africa. Yet, they must also be aware of the machinations of cultural imperialism and cultural genocide constantly at work. Further the young must immerse themselves

FREDERICK MONDERSON

in an African-centric perspective and research, write and teach others in turn. They must study languages such as French, German, Swahili, Greek, Latin, Coptic, Arabic and *Medu Netcher* or Hieroglyphics. They must struggle to correct the recent distorted history of Africa's past. In this way, future leaders would help to better the lot of humanity and save the world from its impending moral, spiritual and scientific destruction. To accomplish these objectives the good doctor has supplied a reservoir of information and strategies from his life's researches in the arsenal of published works he has created. Of course, these works must be read, ingested and digested and returned to time and again. This is important for as Dr. John Henrik Clarke once said, "People buy but never read Dr. Ben's books." Herein then is the dilemma!

The author's major thesis of his *African Origins of the "Major" Western Religions* is that African religious practices were denigrated and called "fetishism" and "paganism." In fact, these early thought processes he showed are the fundamental bases of Judaism, Christianity and Islam. He argued that these ideas were first developed and nurtured in Central Africa among indigenous peoples and then migrated and extended throughout the Nile Valley. They found greatest fruition in Kemet (Egypt) and were preserved by its civilization advances and the nature of its geography. After thousands of years of mythological conception and oral practice, the early knowledge was first written down in such selections as the "Book of Gates," "Book of Knowing Ra,"

BLACK HISTORY EVERYDAY
PART ONE

"Book of Breathings," "Book of What is in the Underworld," etc. These were part of the earlier "Pyramid Texts" (Old Kingdom); then "Coffin Texts" (Middle Kingdom); and the later Book of the Dead or Book of Going Forth By Day (New Kingdom); and the "Mysteries of Sais" (Egypt). The fortunes of geography enabled Africa's second cultural daughter, Kemet, to rise to greater prominence than did the eldest, Ethiopia, Dr. Ben explained! He stressed and maintained to the day of his death, despite all the "new evidence," that civilization began to the south of Egypt! However, despite modern falsification of history and the insistent propagation of such falsity, his thesis is as credible as ever.

Black History Everyday - Part One Photo. Faces and signs in the crowd for the 50th Anniversary March on Washington.

FREDERICK MONDERSON

Black History Everyday - Part One

Photo. Faces and signs in the crowd for the 50th Anniversary March on Washington.

Another of Dr. Ben's seminal works is *Africa: Mother of Western Civilization*. Its major thesis holds that the "fundamental laws, principles, philosophies, ideas, arts and crafts that educated the west, are indigenous to Africa through the Nile Valley cultural experience." For critical teachers who face this dilemma he has some advice. As such, he wrote: "The only credentials necessary in the experience of African history, otherwise mis-nomered 'the Black Experience' and 'Black Studies' are the documented proofs and the sources from whence they are taken."

For this reason, *Africa: Mother of Western Civilization* is an enormous compendium of facts, sources, illustrations, and analyses that challenge scholars but can and does aid laymen. It suggests all educators and lay persons alike become involved in

BLACK HISTORY EVERYDAY
PART ONE

reclaiming the stolen heritage of Africa. This *magnum opus* opens new vistas for historical investigation and provides a wide array of references relating to the significance of Africa in world civilization.

Black Man of the Nile and his Family marks the third in the "trilogy of Dr. Ben's seminal works." This particular source represents the maturity of his thoughts and presentations for it focuses on the role Black men and women have played in bequeathing science, religion, arts, metaphysics, agricultural method, quarrying and stone transportation for erection at building site, boat building and Nile River navigation to the world through Africa's conduit in Nubia and Egypt. It also contains a number of objectives the author seeks to accomplish.

Black History Everyday - Part One Photo. We Shall Not be Moved March. Faces in the Crowd.

FREDERICK MONDERSON

The first of these objectives is, "an attempt to create in young African, African-American (Black person), and all other African people, a sense of belonging in the great African heritage." It is, writes Dr. Ben "specifically directed to those who have criminally demasculinized, denuded, and otherwise denigrated the Africans of their CULTURAL, ECONOMIC, POLITICAL, SCIENTIFIC, SPIRITUAL, and all other forms of their heritage and human decency." To this we should add the intellectual heritage as represented in Egypt and the Nile Valley; that is, through "acquisition methods," and teaching, writing and representation of the artifactual evidence in a distorted and misrepresented manner.

It also presents, "AFRICAN ORIGINS OF EUROPEAN CIVILIZATION" in a manner whereby, "scholars can find interesting use for it in their research; as much as the layman can for processing information."

Dr. Ben views his role as gadfly presenting, "pertinent information needed in the African peoples' RE-IDENTIFICATION with their great ancestral heritage." Lastly, he continued, the "major desired accomplishment this volume seeks to achieve, is to provide anthropological evidence in the ancient heritage of the Africans" and their contributions all over the world.

BLACK HISTORY EVERYDAY
PART ONE

Abu Simbel to Ghizeh: *A Guide Book and Manual* is in itself a useful piece of writing. But there are other books!

Black History Everyday - Part One Photo. *Abu Simbel to Ghizeh*: *A Guide Book and Manual* is another of Dr. Ben's important works.

FREDERICK MONDERSON

In the acquisition of knowledge, Sir Francis Bacon (1561-1626) reminded: "Some books are to be tasted, others to be swallowed, and some few to be chewed and digested." This much can be said of the trilogy of Dr. ben-Jochannan's works, *Black Man of the Nile and his Family*, *Africa: Mother of Western Civilization* and *The African Origins of the Major Western Religions*. The others are equally interesting! Everyone must buy and read these books and pass them on to others particularly their sons and daughters.

Finally, as a student of his, and based on observations and analytic critique, this writer would like to add a 15-point summation of how we can view Dr. Yosef Alfredo Antonio ben-Jochannan's contribution as an unselfish and fearless elucidation of the historical record systematically distorted to elevate Europe and denigrate Africa while wrecking psycho-social debasement on the African spirit and persona. Without question, whether through omission, distortion and even false presentation, the urban youth across America have most seriously been victimized in the systematic alienated educational process they have been subjected to. As such, the potent cultural lifeline Dr. Yosef Alfredo Antonio ben-Jochannan has provided is today critical in rescuing these young people adrift in the academic and intellectual cosmos of these modern times going forward. The critical prescription therefore is as follows:

BLACK HISTORY EVERYDAY
PART ONE

Black History Everyday - Part One Photo. Dr. James McIntosh at the Podium congratulates a youngster who completed one of the Computer Classes offered by **CEMOTAP**.

1. We must praise and show thankfulness for the man who, for more than half a century challenged the behemoth of western intellectual oppression of Africa and her offspring while enlightening many to the wonders of a creative African cultural heritage.

2. We must commend Dr. Ben-Jochannan for the humanitarian work he did among the Nubians in Egypt and Sudan, viz., Aswan, Daboud, Wadi Halfa, Dongola Province and Fashoda.

3. We must recognize his call to action to combat the cultural genocide in the African American studies

curriculum predating the Afrocentric insistence on multi-culturalism.

4.   We should continue to emulate his style of critical analysis of contemporary developments, whether it was historical omissions in Alex Haley's *Roots*; misrepresentation in King Tut's exhibition that has taken place several times in America; taking to task T. Eric Peet's "The Problem with Akhenaton;" Criticism of Father Temple's *Bantu Philosophy*; challenge to another writer's description that Rameses II had "badly abscessed teeth," and so forth.

5.   We can appreciate his identifying *"They all look Alike, All,"* thus linking African peoples across the globe who were victims of racial hatred and cultural aggression.

6.   His early clarification of the differences between the *Black Nationalist and the Black Marxist* was very timely and inspiring and still is.

7.   First to outline the *History of the Bible*, he challenged the *Black Clergy Without a Black Theology* and offered *A Black Bible for Black Spiritual and Religious Consciousness*.

BLACK HISTORY EVERYDAY
PART ONE

Black History Everyday - Part One

Photo. Faces and signs in the crowd for the 50th Anniversary March on Washington.

Black History Everyday - Part One

Photo Faces and signs in the crowd for the 50th Anniversary March on Washington.

FREDERICK MONDERSON

8. We must acknowledge as a human he may have made some mistakes; miniscule, as they probably were, outweighed the foundational reservoir of ethical, intellectual and cultural Ma'at or fairness he implanted in the consciousness of African people worldwide.

9. His insistence that all African Americans visit the Nile Valley to imbibe in the cultural heritage and grow from the intellectual exposure, but more particularly their dress code and mannerism among the people must not be construed as the "arrogance of Ugly Americans," was and is still timely and insightful.

10. His outspoken nature, love for *Marcus Garvey and his Philosophy and Opinions*, praise of Black women as Goddesses, critique of Academics who are "fifth columns," made him anathema to people with ill-intentions, black and white, in their views toward African people.

Black History Everyday - Part One Photo. We Shall Not be Moved March.
Faces in the Crowd.

BLACK HISTORY EVERYDAY
PART ONE

11. Dr. ben-Jochannan had little respect for people in high positions who never promoted the aspirations of their Black subordinates. He pointed to many in academic, business enterprise and even the military.

12. A staunch Pan-Africanist, he aspired to see accomplished sustained and measurable economic, political and educational empowerment for people of African heritage worldwide.

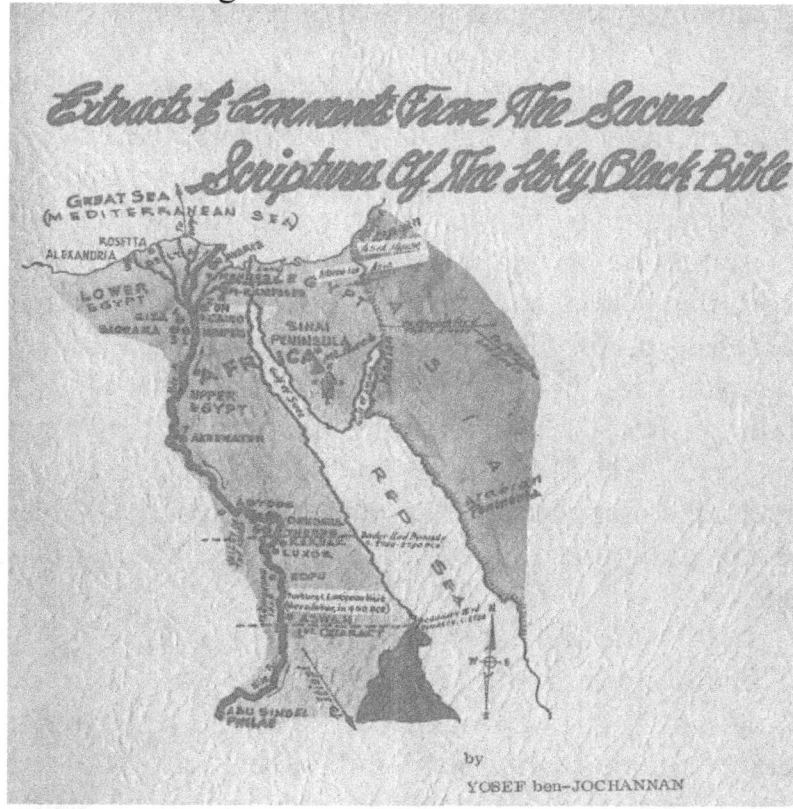

Black History Everyday - Part One Photo. *Extracts and Comments from the Sacred Scriptures of the Holy Black Bible.*

FREDERICK MONDERSON

13.   He said, "I took Egypt to show our people the proper way" and to challenge its misrepresentation, racism and projected religious bigotry.

14.   He insisted we not just read books and do research on Ancient Egypt in Africa, but also form study groups that debate and discuss these important issues raised by him as well as personally critique status quo's positions and most important, Academics who must "publish or perish."

15.   He asked us to standardize our learning and take responsibility for our own history. He stated: "Until African (Black) people are willing, and do write their own experience, past, and present, we will continue being slaves, mentally, physically, and spiritually to Caucasian and Semitic racism and religious bigotry." This latter we must never allow to happen, for as Dr. John Henrik Clarke has admonished, "African people must write their own history." That is because the "People who preached racism colonized history" and as a result, "When Europe colonized the world, it colonized the world's history."

Therefore, we must recognize that Dr. Yosef Alfredo Antonio ben-Jochannan has made a major contribution to African intellectual growth and consciousness. He created a cosmological vision over time that allowed us to see the light! His work has been seminal! In fact, he was our light! He taught us how to persevere to persevere! He asked that we

BLACK HISTORY EVERYDAY
PART ONE

establish and maintain a standard for our behavior, and don't fear, don't fear defeat, don't fear death!

"The Patrice Lumumba Coalition is a necessary and indispensable entity whose intent is the pursuit of liberation, human dignity and advancement of the interests of African people." Elombe Brathe.

"African people must forge ahead united under the Red, Black and Green symbolism of cultural syncretism, shared experiences and equal expectations of economic, political and economic advancement." Elombe Brathe.

17. ELOMBE BRATHE - ULTIMATE NATIONALIST SOLDIER BY DR. FRED MONDERSON

Accomplished Elombe; numbered among "one-name-revolutionary-giants" Che, Fidel, Malcolm, Sonny, Jitu, Stokeley; we mourn your passing at a time your keen consciousness is sorely needed to fend the ever-present oppressor's machinations, openly and inclandestine.

Immortal Black, proponent of a universal Pan-Africanist philosophic outlook manifested through the **PATRICE LUMUMBA COALITION**; your

FREDERICK MONDERSON

contributions inspired profound ideals in defense of Africa's sons and daughters' humanity and progress towards empowerment and freedom of mind, body and spirit.

"Little African man" wielding a powerful pen, big creative ideas, consciously and perennially nationalistic, when you spoke people listened, for the wisdom you enunciated earned you unmatched tribute from a grateful people who consistently recognized exemplary leadership in your efforts, decade after decade.

Indomitable Elombe, a name that will live in immortal glory, tasked to replenish the magnificent ancestor Brigade. How fortunate you were to be contemporary with Patrice Lumumba, Kwame Nkrumah, Sekou Toure, Nelson and Winnie Mandela, Carlos Russell, Oliver Thambo and the African National Congress as well as the "Freedom Fighter" Sam Njomo. We need not forget Martin L. King, Stokeley Carmichael, Malcolm X, Bob Marley, Paul Robeson, Sonny Carson, Jitu Weusi, Bill Lynch, Basil Patterson and Gil Noble; all exemplary nationalist beacons casting powerful rays illuminating the paths of African people's cultural consciousness and freedom quest!

BLACK HISTORY EVERYDAY
PART ONE

Black History Everyday - Part One Photo. We Shall Not be Moved March. Faces in the Crowd.

Resolute Harlemite in nicely fitted Dashiki Shirt-Jac, your memorial fits wonderfully well beside Harriet Tubman, whether statue or school, for your association has been nothing short of spectacular enlightenment, persistent champion of the Red, Black and Green!

Quintessential Son of Queen Mother Moore, Mother Jordan and associate of Betty Shabazz; departing for "ancestor glory," you charged Al Sharpton, Michael Hardy, Wyatt T. Walker, and Calvin Butts; as well as Gary Byrd, Herb Boyd, Bob Law, Len Jeffries, Leonard and Marilyn James, Job Mashiriki, Louis Farrakhan, Michael Hooper of **ROOTS REVISITED** and **CEMOTAP's** Betty Dobson and James McIntosh; to carry on your work of education and enlightenment to free the minds of African people worldwide as they rise to challenge oppression, in its sustained and manifold forms.

FREDERICK MONDERSON

Ingenious Elombe, your name should be enshrined "on street" in that glorious Harlem Community similarly as Dr. Yosef ben-Jochannan and Dr. John Clarke, W.E.B. DuBois, and A. Philip Randolph; Black nationalist and think tank, valiantly you kept the flame of African consciousness burning brightly while bearing the burdens of leadership Garvey spoke of.

Tireless man of vision, tenacity, courage, resilience and activist sustainability; Visionary who would not let Patrice Lumumba's memory fade as you challenged the oppressors of your people.

Resourceful leader whose visionary thought and deed propelled a movement seeking political, economic and educational empowerment consistent with the Civil Rights Movement's aspirations, you were a master tactician victorious on many fronts.

Black History Everyday – Part One Photo. Attorney Michael Hardy confers with Rev. Al Sharpton as members of the panel look interestingly at the Podium's speaker.

BLACK HISTORY EVERYDAY
PART ONE

Black History Everyday - Part One
Photo. Faces and signs in the crowd for the 50th Anniversary March on Washington.

Black History Everyday - Part One
Photo. Faces and signs in the crowd for the 50th Anniversary March on Washington.

FREDERICK MONDERSON

Mr. Brathe, you are the newest star in the Black Pantheon, where "Brother Gods" welcome your presence to further invigorate their efforts here and there, as we recognize the struggles must continue for our people's Civil Rights and human dignity worldwide.

Indefatigable Nationalist grandmaster, your flames powered Gil Noble's flood-lights awakening our people's intellectual, cultural and political consciousness through the powerful and educational **LIKE IT IS** TV program! Constructive statesman, theorist, master of strategic activism and blest with an enlightening penmanship, go assist Sonny and Jitu to organize heaven assuring our expected arrival in that blessed existence where ancestors earned their reverence and can still inspire our people as we meet challenges.

Incomparable Elombe Brathe, we who are yet to die recognize, praise and salute you for a fulfilling life of creative activism with measured attainments; a rich legacy, accomplished in advancing the cause of Africa and all humanity; recognizing we must stay the course you so eloquently and steadfastly charted in your constructive earthly existence. Good-bye and thank you, Beloved Brother Elombe!

BLACK HISTORY EVERYDAY
PART ONE

Black History Everyday - Part One Photo. Dr. Adelaide Sanford makes a presentation at **CEMOTAP**.

"The Committee to Honor Black Heroes was designed to bring recognition to and meaning for the work of the Great Ones we hold in reverence." Sonny Carson.

"We encourage cultural creativity in the music experience; encourage young artists to produce creative lyrics; but they must 'tone it down' regarding references of Black women. The music industry encourages such artists to think themselves as 'Gangsters' and to produce 'Gangster Rap' which in itself is a path of self-degradation and cultural annihilation. Sonny Carson.

FREDERICK MONDERSON

18. GOD SEND - SONNY CARSON AT NY CITY COUNCIL BY DR. FRED MONDERSON

"The spirit of the Lord moves in mysterious ways" is a Biblical saying.

First Don Imus, now Christine Quinn have unintentionally done more for Black unity than purportedly most of the activism has done in the last 40 years. We know Imus made his controversial statement disparaging Black women. Well, we subsequently learned his contract paid him millions of dollars to make such outlandish remarks and so he took the money and run back under his rock and rolled.

Black History Everyday - Part One Photo. We Shall Not be Moved March.
Faces in the Crowd.

BLACK HISTORY EVERYDAY
PART ONE

Fortunately, however, his actions galvanized New York's activist leadership bringing together diverse elements of conscious Blacks who in this new era were determined to say loudly, "We're fed up and not taking it anymore." Then along came the Sonny Carson affair and Speaker Quinn put her silver foot in her mouth by presiding over and removing Sonny Carson's name from an Omnibus Bill with 52 names. Therein lay the instrument of divine intervention!

However, pardon my explanation of the dance of events surrounding this issue.

Apparently, some three years after his passing the **December 12th Movement** along with members of the Bed-Stuy, now called "Abubadikaville," community wanted to name a four-block area along Gates Avenue for Sonny "Abubadika" Carson. They approached Councilman Al Vann who represents the district with their plan. His rightful response was, "Wait a minute, you have to get community Board 3's permission to do so." This they did! The Community Board advised them you have to get the people who live and do business in that community to sign petitions and provide letters of recommendation and in support. This they did, collecting some 10,000 signatures. Upon returning to the Board, the Transportation Committee of Board 3 voted to approve the measure and forwarded it to the full board. The full board voted 39-1 in favor of naming 4 blocks from Classon

FREDERICK MONDERSON

Avenue eastward in honor of Sonny Carson. This was sent to Councilman Vann, the community's representative in the City Council. Al Vann then made the Proposition to the Council that became part of an Omnibus Bill of 52 names for street naming.

For whatever reason, the Chairwoman of the Parks Committee of the City Council, a Black, voted for the measure but three whites voted against it.

Since the Speaker, in this case, Christine Quinn, is the traffic cop who permits passage or flags issues, Sonny's name was pulled from the lot. After this, a barrage of negative publicity was unleashed to paint Sonny in an unfavorable light. They claimed he was charged with kidnapping but he won that case. Next, he was accused of being a ringleader in the Ocean-Hill-Brownsville school desegregation battle of the 1960s but the community saw his uncompromising stance was one for their empowerment and self-determination in decentralization of the school system. Again, they accused him of being anti-white but Sonny argued all the pictures of Back men lynched and hanging in his office were done by anti-Black elements.

Fast forward to Wednesday May 9, 2007, at 10: 45 AM untold numbers gathered on the steps of City Hall to call for justice, fairness, equality, and fair share in this issue. The belief is that if the actions of Community Board 3 are undermined then the autonomy and self-determination of every other Community Board who takes a position on issues not

BLACK HISTORY EVERYDAY
PART ONE

popular with City Hall or the Council is equally undermined.

In the call to respond, and this was the only good thing about the Speaker's actions, the Who's Who in Black New York activism came out. They came from every walk of life, viz., the press, law enforcement, legal eagles, clergy, businessmen and women, council members, students and ordinary strangers.

Black History Everyday - Part One Photo. Faces and signs in the crowd for the 50th Anniversary March on Washington.

FREDERICK MONDERSON

Black History Everyday - Part One
Photo. Two of James Brown's outfits on display in Augusta, Georgia.

Black History Everyday - Part One
Photo. Faces and signs in the crowd for the 50th Anniversary March on Washington.

BLACK HISTORY EVERYDAY
PART ONE

Councilmember Al Vann was particularly incensed about how this issue has played out because it distracted from his concern about other serious issues facing his constituency that are more pressing. He cited: "Unemployment in New York City for Black men is an abominable 39.7 %. The rate of poverty is 30.2% for Blacks in New York City as of 2004-2005. The high school dropout rate in New York City among Black students is close to 50%. The high school graduation rate among Black students in New York City Public Schools is 42%. No statistics have been made available for the alarming dropout rate of Black students in New York City middle schools. Due to the disparities in access to health care, Black men are 6 times more likely to die from AIDS than white men, and Black women are 9 times more likely to die from AIDS than white women. At this very moment, there are 31,920 Black people incarcerated in New York State. Affordable housing has become a premium that most Black people cannot afford."

As such then, the message was clear from the podium:

1. When we're one we've already won.

2. The speaker's removal of Sonny Carson's name from the 52 names has racial overtones.

3. The action on the part of the Speaker of the City Council undermines the integrity and self-

FREDERICK MONDERSON

determination of the community who approved the naming of Gates Avenue for Sonny Carson.

Black History Everyday - Part One Photo. We Shall Not be Moved March. Faces in the Crowd.

4. Seems the rules change when it comes to Blacks. From full naming to co-naming to naming a few blocks to no-naming.

5. Concern was expressed that Council people who supported naming Gates Avenue for Sonny Carson may see a reduction of funding for their district in the City's new $53Billion dollar budget. This is tantamount to victimizing "whistle blowers."

6. One speaker said, in this Christian nation when we are asked to forgive slave owners, slavery, all manner of behaviors and atrocities committed against Blacks, why can't we

BLACK HISTORY EVERYDAY
PART ONE

forgive Sonny's uncompromising manner. It was all in response to Black self-determination and empowerment amidst police brutality, racial profiling, and drugs in the community, high black unemployment, poor schooling, inadequate housing and the prison industrial complex decimation of Black manhood. Based on the statistics quoted by Councilman Al Vann, not much has changed from the 1960s, but perhaps more Blacks are in jail.

7. Another speaker suggested we rename all streets in our community that reminds us of slave owners, slavery and racism.

8. Still another speaker reminded, the community appreciated Sonny's good works and chose to honor him and we're vehemently opposed to any one determining who our heroes will be.

Here, therefore, lies the goodness of the Council Speaker's actions. To use a biblical cliché, "Out of evil cometh good" for her actions have forged a coalition among all manner of conscious Black concerned citizens. These include but is not limited to: Pastor Jesse Sumbry, Fannie Barnes, Delores Jamison, Susie M. Landrum, Albee Barnwell, Catherine Manguie, Edward Barnes, William Fuller, Sandra Fuller, Charles Baron, Inez Baron, Emlyn Paul, Rebecca B. Hall, Miriam Francis, Herbert Oliver, Brother Bless, Abdul Hack, Baba Hodari Hakeem, Santina and Ofori Payton, Ali Lamont, Rev.

FREDERICK MONDERSON

Robert Townsley of the NAACP, Richard James, Morris Brown "Legend," Charles Jones, William Booth, Rev. Norman, SR., Bill Wren, Rev. Haller, Vice President 73rd Precinct Council, Pastor Eggleston, Paul Washington of Medgar Evers College, Eddie Ellis, Larry White, Oronde Takuma, Charlene Philips, Rev. Cheryl Anthony Mobley who spoke for the clergy, Ruben Pratts, First Vice President Community Board 3, Tomma Faulkner, Chair Economic Committee Community Board 3, George Murden, Job Mashiriki, Dr. Dexter McKenzie from the Black Brooklyn Empowerment Coalition, Rev. Herbert Daughtry, Connie Lesold, Pastor Waterman Chairman Transportation Committee Community Board 3, Elombe Brathe, Akin Labi Mackall, Peter Anderson, Dr. John Flateau of Medgar Evers College's DuBois Center, Mary Jackson, Gloria Boyce, Jesse Scott, Anthony Jordan, Arthur Niles, Una Clarke, Erik Stevenson, Omowale Clay, Jitu Weusi, Atiim Ferguson, Erik Mohammed, Roger Wareham, Viola Plummer, Esmerelda Simmons, Lem Peterkin, Solomon Quick, Rasheed Allah, Octavius Bamberg, Milton Allimadi, Publisher and CEO of *Black Star News*, and Andre Smith. Still, there were many, many more whose names are not here. They all came out to show support for not simply Sonny Carson but Black unity and Black self-determination and also to say 'when the roll is called down here, we'll all be there!'

According to the grapevine, the word is that "the genie is out of the bottle" and he is Black. Pandora's

BLACK HISTORY EVERYDAY
PART ONE

Box has been opened! The cry of "When we're one we've already won" filled the air.

Word has it the Council should have voted today on this issue but it has been tabled until May 30, 2007 and all are invited back. Al Vann explained he will introduce an amendment that Sonny's name be put back into the Omnibus Bill of 52. That must be voted on before the full measure can get its hearing. This is Protocol!

The question that a separate bill be made for Sonny to allow all the other names to go forward was rejected. It's all or nothing at all!

The cry of **No Justice**, **No Peace**, **No Justice**, **No Peace**, could be heard before the press conference adjourned until May 30, 11:00 AM.

"Tell the MTA I'm not finished with the Franklin Shuttle. I am disappointed with how the shuttle is kept. This is not a 'Ghetto enterprise.'" Jitu Weusi on *Reconstruction of the Franklin Avenue Shuttle and its Upkeep*.

FREDERICK MONDERSON

Black History Everyday - Part One Photo. **Jitu Weusi**, uncompromising iconic nationalist, educator, community leader, theorist, family man and friend, will forever remain in our hearts.

"Fred, the Chancellor is under pressure from the Mayor; the Superintendent is under pressure from the Chancellor; the Principal is under pressure from the Chancellor; Assistant Principals, parents and students are also under pressure. The most you can do is your best!" Jitu Weusi on *Pressure in the Educational Experience*.

BLACK HISTORY EVERYDAY
PART ONE

Black History Everyday - Part One Photo. We Shall Not be Moved March. Faces in the Crowd.

19. JITU WEUSI "MOUNTAIN OF A MAN" BY DR. FRED MONDERSON

Jitu Weusi, "Mountain of a Man," born Les Campbell, we mourn your passing but we rejoice for your presence and lasting contributions and we honor you as we have honored Malcolm X, Martin Luther King, Jr., Marcus Garvey, Rosa Parks and Sonny Carson your revered Brother in Struggle! Quintessential leader who would not accept the "thirty pieces of silver," who could not be bribed, you stood tall and firm as a resolute fighter for justice and social upliftment of Black African people,

FREDERICK MONDERSON

irrespective! You made your presence felt in many an arena. Educational activist, social critic and strategist confronting life's many challenges, your contributions to your people's march of progress earned you the "living legend" award and because of your vision, our people will not perish!

Indomitable spirit, leader in education, man of unbounded integrity and insightful thinking, we honor you because you fought the good fight, you kept the faith, and in this you were a perpetual light of social conscience. Creative genius of "The East" who innovated the African Street Festival among many creations, your place among revered ancestors assured, the pantheon of black champions now has a new star!

Black History Everyday - Part One Photo. Faces and signs in the crowd for the 50th Anniversary March on Washington.

BLACK HISTORY EVERYDAY
PART ONE

Black History Everyday - Part One Photo. Faces and signs in the crowd for the 50th Anniversary March on Washington.

Brooklyn Icon, from "The **East**" to Attica and Ocean-Hill-Brownsville Decentralization to the Franklin Avenue Shuttle struggle, and from the public-school classroom to the college campus and back to the public school as administrator making a difference, your unmatched contributions for educational excellence and social justice are too numerous to mention. With the desire for quality education as watchword and hallmark of your work of upliftment, educator, activist, headmaster, advocate, administrator, your efforts established the highest standards for intellectual development of our youth.

FREDERICK MONDERSON

Guiding light, visionary with clear sightedness, the influence of your classroom educational activities matched the brilliance of the brightest day, inspiring many to develop skills to achieve success. Resolute nationalist, Pan-African stalwart, your aspirations for your people's progress were seldom surpassed; and your equally untiring efforts as member of the "**Bones Committee**" helped assure Samuel Carson, "**The Runaway**," successful passage for internment in Ghana, West Africa, opening the "**Door of Return**."

Master organizer, unquestionably in education and in Black Solidarity Day activism, politics and jazz organization, your name resounds as an effective and successful strategist of exceptional note. Son of Brooklyn, man of integrity, fortitude and resilience, allow us to clone your image, persona and strategic thinking abilities as an effective tool in our ongoing struggle for social, political and economic empowerment for advancement of our people.

Man of action and boundless vision, though sorrowful at your passing, we celebrate your creative spirit with sweet melodic sounds similarly played by the Brooklyn Jazz Consortium you orchestrated and forever memories of you will be remembered through the African Street Festival, a contribution of immense proportions.

Revered leader, man of many seasons, it is our especial hope, your memory, image and name will

BLACK HISTORY EVERYDAY PART ONE

forever be a part of the history of struggle to uplift all people, particularly Black people. We also hope the children will remember you because we honor you as father, husband, tactician and community leader for your unrelenting struggle to advance our cause and make Brooklyn a better place for them and all other residents.

Brother, we salute you, we praise you, we honor you, and we thank you for a lengthy, constructive and successful life of meaningful service to the Brooklyn Community and African people worldwide. We are grateful you inspired us to persevere in the manner of Jitu Weusi's Way of integrity, stability and constructive service. This is the name Claever Place, the place of your origins, should be named, for your life has been an effective beacon that reflected the highest illumination, standards and aspirations of the Borough of Brooklyn and the best example of black manhood.

Black history Everyday – Part One Photo. "The Prisoners" on display on Pratt Institute's grounds.

FREDERICK MONDERSON

Black History Everyday - Part One Photo. We Shall Not be Moved March. Faces in the Crowd.

Black History Everyday - Part One Photo. Within the forest of inscribed columns naming African-Americans lynched in the South between 1870-1950.

BLACK HISTORY EVERYDAY
PART ONE

Companion at the Million Women March in Philadelphia, we are saddened you never lived to see the 50th Anniversary of the "March on Washington" but you would have been proud and active in concern for the safety and security of "The People."

Black History Everyday - Part One
Photo An award to "The Emperor of Soul, James Brown."

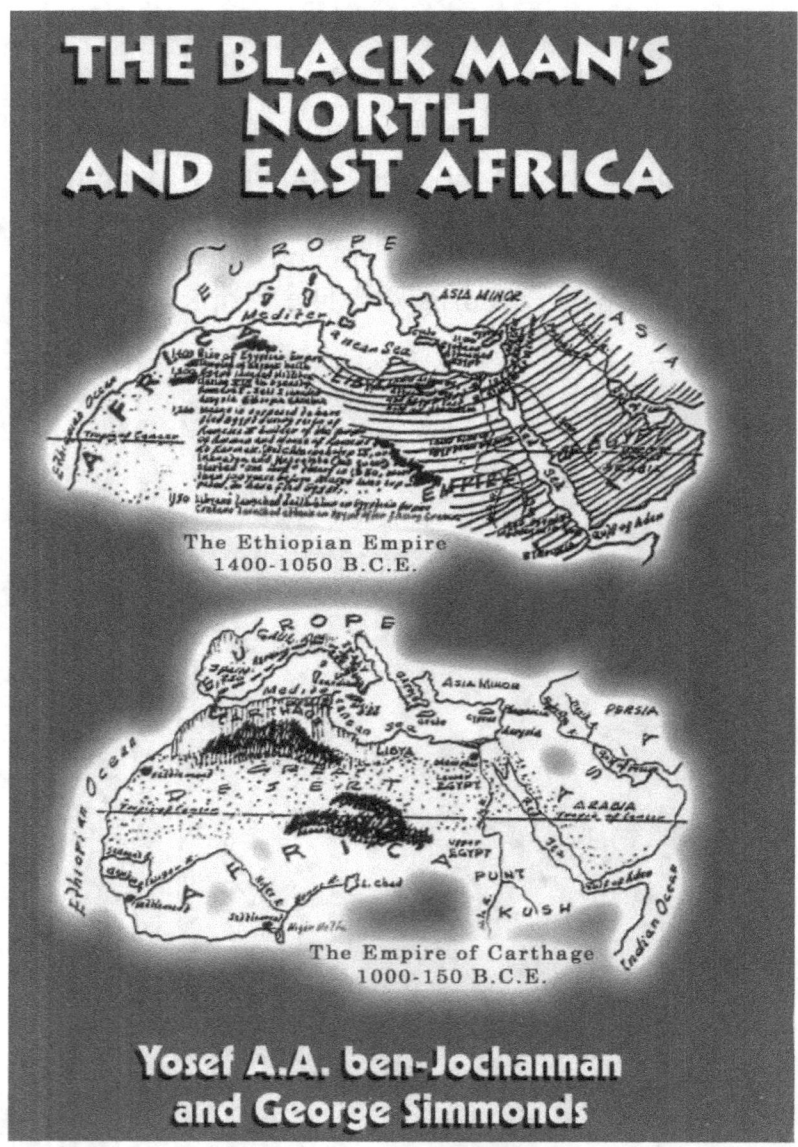

Black History Everyday - Part One
Photo. *The Black man's North and East Africa* by George Simmonds and Dr. ben-Jochannan.

BLACK HISTORY EVERYDAY
PART ONE

"It is a story that can never be told in all its gruesome details. Of the countless number of Africans ripped from the villages of Africa – from the Senegal River to Northern Angola – during the nearly four centuries of the slave trade, approximately one third of them died on the tortuous march to the ships and one third died in the holding stations on both sides of the Atlantic or on the ships. It is estimated that ten to twenty million arrived in the New World alive, to be then committed to bondage. If the Atlantic were to dry up, it would reveal a scattered pathway of human bones. African bones marking the various routes of the Middle Passage." John Henrik Clarke. From Tom Fellings, *The Middle Passage* p1995] introduction.

"Africa is a paradox which illustrates and highlights neo-colonialism. Her earth is rich, yet the products that come from above and below the soil continue to enrich, not Africans predominantly, but groups and individuals who operate to Africa's impoverishment." **Kwame Nkrumah**. *Neo-colonialism: The Last stage of Imperialism* [1965]

20. "LIKE IT IS" AND IMPERIALISM BY DR. FRED MONDERSON

A friend called Sunday March 19, 2006, just around Noon to say, watch **Like It Is**! This wonderfully

FREDERICK MONDERSON

educational, cultural, historical and intellectually stimulating program featured Adelaide Sandford, Vice-Chancellor, New York State Board of Regents.

Without really digressing, I certainly remember when Dick Clarke's New Year's Rocking Eve celebrated 30 years on air, and with great fanfare. Wow! Thirty years on air! Well, I also remember when Gil Noble's **Like It Is** celebrated 30 years and Elombe Brathe held an outstanding tribute to him in Harlem attended by Congressman Charles Rangel, Minister Benjamin Chavis Mohammed, Councilwoman Una Clarke, Rev. Calvin Butts, Dr. Lewis the Harlem ophthalmologist and Mrs. Lewis, Jitu Weusi, Publisher Tom Watkins, Dr. Ben-Jochannan, Dr. John H. Clarke and Mrs. Sybil Williams-Clarke, Sonny "Abubadika" Carson, Mrs. Mae Carson, Chief James "Barkim" Parker, Atiim Ferguson, Rasheed Allah, and Mr. and Mrs. Gil Noble and an auditorium filled with thankful and adulating friends of **LIKE IT IS**, all in praise of a show on air more than 30 years. The significance of **LIKE IT IS** rests in its tremendously powerful presentation of African developments relating to and covering the Black community in the most unimaginative manner. I also remember the struggles of activists including Dr. James McIntosh and Betty Dobson of **CEMOTAP** who fought to "**SAVE LIKE IT IS**." Why, then, adulation for one TV show, entertaining; and, efforts to eliminate the other with same longevity because of its inspiring, educational and ethnic features? Go figure!

BLACK HISTORY EVERYDAY
PART ONE

Black History Everyday - Part One
Photo. Faces and signs in the crowd for the 50th Anniversary March on Washington.

Black History Everyday - Part One
Photo. Faces and signs in the crowd for the 50th Anniversary March on Washington.

FREDERICK MONDERSON

Now to return! I turned the TV on just as the program was getting on the way and did not see the title. However, the guest Dr. Adelaide Sandford was responding to the situation.

Apparently, on a recent New York State Regents Examination, High School students were asked to answer two questions, "What were the benefits of Imperialism to Africa?" and on "Imperialism in India" but not mentioning "benefits" in the latter. Dr. Sanford, at her eloquent best, and this program should be re-run, mentioned the letters, phone calls and e-mails she received from parents, children and organizations complaining about the subjective and psychologically detrimental implications of the question and its impact on children, both white and black, many of whom refused to answer.

Black History Everyday - Part One Photo. We Shall Not be Moved March.
Faces in the Crowd.

BLACK HISTORY EVERYDAY
PART ONE

The Vice-Chancellor spoke on the loss of confidence in the educational system in New York State. She insisted that to ask students to justify benefits of imperialism in Africa was debilitating, with deleterious effects on both Black and White children. In fact, considering the seriousness of this matter, it was a failure of the people to stand up and demand accountability, she insisted. Dr. Sanford said many children wanted to critique the question but could not for they realized the liabilities of standing up. Insightfully, she indicated that education should provide the freedom and ability to think critically and analytically. The educator pointed out "no people of color who looked at the question" could answer without being upset. Since horrific imperialism and colonialism brutalized people in Africa, to ask the students to "eat from this foul cup," this "gall," may have long lasting psychological implications in damages to these young people.

The Host of **Like It Is**, Gil Noble next asked, "What can we do to ensure this type of question does not reappear?" She answered that the remedy will be worthwhile "only if there is sufficient recognition by the Board of Regents of the damage done to the children." Dr. Sanford next addressed the "rage directed toward young people." She insisted that "rage is development of a mode of behavior." "Our children turn rage internally." "We are not able to protect our children from physical, emotional, psychological damage because they have no maps, labs, books, as well as the posed social, human, economic and civil problems, etc., they faced. Still, we don't want to lower the standards for our children. However, we must retain standards and teach the adults who hold the budget strings, who write the exams and who teach our children."

Nonetheless, since the very nature of imperialism as a system involves victims and victimizer, conqueror and conquered, with attendant force, killing, intimidation, subjugation and exploitation, and there is a price exacted usually in the form of resources, to which can be added the psychological damages that can result. Kwame Nkrumah in *Towards Colonial Freedom* (1973: 13) quotes V.I. Lenin in his *Imperialism: The Highest Stage of Capitalism* who summarized the position thus: "Imperialism is capitalism in that stage of development in which the domination of monopolies and finance capital has taken shape; in which the export of capital has acquired pronounced importance; in which the division of the world by the international trusts had begun, and in which the partition of all the territory of the earth by the greatest capitalist countries has been completed." It also involved humiliation and loss of cultural esteem and destruction of social and other forms of institutions of indigenous people.

In evaluating the four evils or fundamental causes leading to World War I, nationalism, militarism, international anarchy and imperialism, the latter ranks pretty high among the four, perhaps the most

BLACK HISTORY EVERYDAY
PART ONE

significant driving force, because it was buttressed by colonialism and the implications of "holding territory," in the global scheme of empire in which white supremacy became the order of the day. Or, as the Englishman Oscar once remarked to this writer: "In any debate between a white and a black historian, all the Black has to do is to recount what white men have been doing all around the world and the white academic has to back up!"

Therefore, Nkrumah recognizing the role of economics at the root of imperialism discusses three fundamental doctrines. These are: (a) the doctrine of exploitation; (b) the doctrine of 'trusteeship' or 'partnership' (to use its contemporary counterpart); and, (c) the doctrine of 'assimilation'. The exponents of these doctrines believe implicitly and explicitly in the right of stronger peoples to exploit weaker ones to develop world resources, and 'civilize' backward peoples against their will." Thus, "imperialism is the policy which aims at creating, organizing and maintaining an empire." Unfortunately, these same "evils" became sledgehammers that ultimately cracked the edifice of white supremacy in its place of incubation and two decades later shattered the myth of invincibility of the white man in World War II and afterwards.

This essay therefore seeks to explore some aspects of the interaction between Europe and Africa with the resulting dynamics of imperialism in its "naked," "enlightened" and later "collective" guises with attendant implications for Africans and Africa. To this list we may also mention "Intellectual imperialism," for as Dr. John Henrik Clarke reminded, "The people who preached racism colonized history," to which we must add territory as well as, "When Europe colonized the world, it colonized the world's knowledge."

Europe's First Coming to Africa

Africa experienced two coming of Europe to her soils, both with detrimental results. The first occurred in the mid-Fifteenth Century and the second in the Nineteenth Century. In the Twentieth Century, "collective imperialism" emerged as an outgrowth of neo-colonialism in response to movements aimed at decolonization and independence. Nevertheless, the initial contact was a part of Europe's mercantile expansion to discover and colonize various parts of the world, to further its enrichment.

The major development relating to Africa in this first expansion was the Slave Trade. The Slave Trade began in 1441, when Africans were taken to Lisbon, Portugal, first as curiosities and later as captives. It did not end until the Portuguese in Brazil outlawed slavery in 1888, after the French in 1817, the British in 1838 and the Americans in 1865. Many nations were involved in the forced removal of African people to the "New World." The principal nations involved in the Slave Trade were Britain, France, Portugal, the Danes, Dutch, Brandenbergers

BLACK HISTORY EVERYDAY PART ONE

(Germans) and of course, Americans. Still, while the Spanish did not carry any Africans by virtue of Papal Proscription, they did, however, encourage their removal, through the infamous "Hacienda Treaty," to people their plantations in the Americas!

The mechanism of this removal of Africans was of a two-fold nature. The **Triangular Trade** represented the effective dynamics of the trade. The **Middle Passage** represented the affective nature of the experience. Equally too, discussions on the rape of Africa must also mention the work of the abolitionists whose efforts represented the best hope for the Africans and humanity, at the time.

The workings of the **Triangular Trade** were very simple. Outfit ships trading to African with what is tantamount to junk! This was exchanged on the West coast of Africa for Africans, in addition to those being kidnapped, who were then taken to the Americas. Here they would be sold as slaves to do manual labor on the plantations. In the "New World" the sale price was invested in tropical products of cotton, rice, indigo, sugar and molasses. These were taken to Europe. There, they fetched high prices and provided many jobs. In existence for several hundred years, this economic pattern created untold wealth for those nations involved. European nations created insurance institutions, and began metal industries, banking, cotton and textile manufacturing concerns

FREDERICK MONDERSON

and industries. They operated sugar refineries and rum distillation factories. Custom duties increased with expansion of boat building, shipping and enlarged ports serving the trade. Rifle and canons played an important part in the Slave Trade.

Black History Everyday - Part One Photo. LeGrand Clegg II, makes a Presentation at **CEMOTAP**.

To supply the demands of the trade it became necessary that ships sailing from Africa to America, on this second leg of the triangle, be loaded with Africans secured in whatever manner. "Get slaves honestly, if you can, if you cannot, get them anyway!" This was an old saying from Liverpool, one of the three principal trading ports in England. The other two were Bristol and London. Manchester and Glasgow were also involved in the trade but on a lesser level supplying merchandise for trade. These latter two cities were more interested in

BLACK HISTORY EVERYDAY
PART ONE

manufacturing commodities to exchange rather than actually carrying Africans in slaving ships.

The Middle Passage was a horrendous experience. The dynamics of the trade exposed the belligerent and exploitative nature of the European traders. The slaving industry wallowed in African defenselessness. Diseases, bad food, overcrowding, melancholy from fear of hopelessness and cruelty were part of the trans-Atlantic experience. Personal abuse of African women and a host of other sicknesses impacted negatively on the psyche of the African personality. The evolutionary process associated with man's development was reversed. The African suffered psychological damage almost beyond repair.

The abolitionists were vocal and keen observers of the Slave Trade. They finally stepped in and condemned the trade in fellowmen. In this undertaking, they researched the trade and put pressure on legislators, made individual efforts, and were active in courts and in church. Finally, the conscience of a Christian civilization was awakened. This was after Europe had reaped untold wealth from enslavement of humanity's African brothers. The Slave Trade was finally abolished among the British in 1807, though slavery was not abolished in the British Empire until 1834 with an apprentice period until 1838.

FREDERICK MONDERSON

Black History Everyday - Part One
Photo. Faces and signs in the crowd for the 50th Anniversary March on Washington.

Black History Everyday - Part One
Photo. Faces and signs in the crowd for the 50th Anniversary March on Washington.

The results of the initial contact between Europe and Africa were many. The first and most significant impact was the depopulation of Africa. Figures vary but Africa is thought to have lost more than one hundred million souls, according to the African-American scholar W.E.B. Du Bois. These include those killed in resisting the slave catchers, those killed in the march to the coast, those killed in the

BLACK HISTORY EVERYDAY
PART ONE

holding pens on the coast, those who died or mutinied and were tossed overboard and those who made it to the New World to be sold. In addition, there were those taken to Europe to be enslaved there. Significantly, the European nations benefited enormously from the trade. The trade helped to put Europe's economies on a more poised footing to launch the industrial revolution. This movement transformed Europe socially, economically, politically and scientifically. It extended into Europe's military institutions crafting its nature of warfare, that was then unleashed against the Africans and other non-white peoples.

The impact of the Slave Trade on African society is untold. In the depopulation, Africa's growth was eradicated. Her institutions cultural, social, political and religious, suffered tremendously. Unable to develop in a peaceful environment African society was encouraged to stagnate. Fortunately, there is a resilient dynamism in the African spirit and personality. In a way, clinging to the memory of Africa helped her sons and daughters to persevere in their travails abroad and at home. With some nurturing Africa began to grow again.

FREDERICK MONDERSON

Black History Everyday - Part One Photo. We Shall Not be Moved March. Faces in the Crowd.

Lastly, the African captives helped facilitate European retention and transformation of the New World colonies thanks to a profound ancestral heritage and an unconquerable spirit. This unconquerable psycho-spiritual resilience saved the Africans from extinction, for through *de Jure* and *de Facto* mechanisms the oppressor reversed the evolutionary process in crating chattel out of humanity. This is why young African people must know and still be proud of their cultural history. This knowledge will make them strong and resilient.

Despite the inhumanity of the experience, African efforts helped generate the impetus to develop and launch the Industrial Revolution in Europe and America particularly because they were not

BLACK HISTORY EVERYDAY PART ONE

compensated for their efforts. These then, were some of the elements of the "Naked Imperialism" that characterized Europe's first coming to Africa.

EARLY EXPLORATION OF AFRICA

The Rosetta stone was discovered in 1799 in Egypt and the Frenchman Jean Jacques Champollion deciphered Hieroglyphic writing in 1822. These two developments about the ancient Egyptians in Northeast Africa stimulated an interest in antiquarian studies. Then societies in Europe formed for exploration of Africa. In great fanfare, the explorers Burton and Speke sought to discover the source of the Nile River. This in turn generated further interest in Egyptian exploration and collection of antique artifacts. So, from its discovery the race to decipher hieroglyphics on the Rosetta stone, had begun and the science of Egyptology set in motion. This then opened the door for all forms of exploration of Africa.

This emerging science of Egyptology targeting Egypt in North-East Africa complimented various forms of exploration to discover the wealth, viz., geographical, mineralogical, agricultural, political, water resources, and cultural and religious practices. Even earlier, after 1600, there was much activity in East Africa. Traffic in the Indian Ocean, contacts with India and China, the role of the Portuguese and early trade made this area interesting for discovery and recording of this culture area. The Arab Slave Trade, for nearly a thousand years in progress, allowed such Africans as Tibbu Tib to make their name in the ghastly trade on the East side of the continent.

In South Africa, the British had secured their foothold at the Cape of Good Hope towards the end of the 18th Century. They began displacing the Boers who had settled here in 1652. The Boers in turn, had displaced the indigenous Africans they found there when they arrived. As far back as the end of the Fifteenth Century, the Portuguese Bartholomew Diaz and Vasco Da Gama had reported contacts with African "pilots" who assisted in their moorings and passage of the Cape.

In West African especially, the most concocted attempts were made at exploration. Success was dependent on curtailing the Salve Trade. The English Anti-slavery movement had pressured its government to use naval force, diplomatic persuasions, military pressures, legitimate commerce and missionary propaganda to end the Slave Trade in Africa. Many British missionaries and legitimate traders pushed inland to establish posts and cut the root off the trade. In this, they persuaded Africans to accept Christianity, legitimate commerce and to engage in practicing agriculture. The Africans were thus brought into the increasing demand for raw materials needed for the industrial revolution transforming Europe.

BLACK HISTORY EVERYDAY
PART ONE

To complement their expanding efforts, a number of early explorers converged on the continent. Mongo Park, Hugh Clapperton and Richard Lander came. Walter Oudney, Dixon Denham and Heinrich Barth were also among the early explorers who came to open Africa. Then there was also Henry Morton Stanley who came to find Dr. Livingston. The *New York Globe* newspaper sponsored his exploration. Private European organizations as well as governments, however, sent most explorers.

These forces converging on Africa in a many-pronged exploration strategy made many discoveries. They secured land concessions and did some scientific experiments. Others surveyed mineralogical possibilities. Still others did ethnological and tropical studies that made the new interest more enlightening. Many propaganda stories were told of exotic and primitive Africa. Newspapers published sensational articles in their "penny press" and the world simply loved Africa for its untapped wealth. As such, the Africans were caught up in a new reality where their culture was denigrated and their land and resources expropriated.

FREDERICK MONDERSON

Black History Everyday - Part One Photo. We Shall Not be Moved March. Faces in the Crowd.

EARLY COLONIAL SETTLEMENT

The anti-slavery movement gained momentum in the first decade of the Nineteenth Century. This effort resulted in the British Government outlawing the Slave Trade in 1807. The Americans had raised the question of the Slave Trade back in 1787. That year the constitution was drafted. However, a 20-year grace period was given for consideration of the issue. Popular belief held that the **Declaration of Independence** in 1776 and the revolution had not only freed the nation but also enlightened American thinkers. Some thought that slavery was dying out. Yet, Eli Whitney's **Cotton Gin** in 1793 changed this completely. The **Cotton Gin** revolutionized cotton processing and greater demands for cotton ensued. This innovation required

BLACK HISTORY EVERYDAY
PART ONE

more workers and increased the demand for enslaved Africans.

Following the British pattern, the American nation relented and outlawed the Slave Trade in 1808. It thus became illegal for Americans to carry Africans into the Americas. Importantly, the institution of slavery remained intact. An internal slave trade developed being fed from horrendous "slave farms" in the "deep south" where the African woman suffered the most horrendous form of humiliation and degradation in the master's demands that they produce more slave children to enrich his coffers. This was an especially terrible time for the African spirit. Consequently, many abolitionists felt Africans in America could not get equality in a nation that enslaved significant segments of its population. Many thought of overseas settlement for Africans. They examined the British model in Sierra Leone and approved it.

The Liberian experiment for colonization of American Blacks was considered as a feasible option. It would be located in West Africa, adjacent to Sierra Leone, the British nearby model. Efforts were made to relocate Africans and grant them the wherewithal to begin life anew. This experiment was begun between 1820 and 1822. In commentary on this fiasco, Dr. ben-Jochannan tells, many Black clergy voted one day against colonization; promised to be made Bishops in the church that night; they voted for colonization the next day! Thus, many American-

FREDERICK MONDERSON

Africans were resettled in Liberia, named Libertyville. Its capital Monrovia was named after the U.S. President, James Monroe. However, the native Africans were visibly upset by this colonization scheme. Several Chiefs sought to wipe out the settlement. It interfered with the slave dealing activities between some African Chiefs and European slavers. Interestingly, provisions were not made for the indigenous inhabitants who became victims of their American cousins.

Black History Everyday - Part One Photo. Faces and signs in the crowd for the 50th Anniversary March on Washington.

Black History Everyday - Part One Photo. Faces and signs in the crowd for the 50th Anniversary March on Washington.

BLACK HISTORY EVERYDAY
PART ONE

Black History Everyday - Part One Photo. Faces and signs in the crowd for the 50th Anniversary March on Washington.

More importantly, the settlers adopted an irritating and superior attitude towards the indigenous people. Many of the settlers refused to undertake agricultural enterprise. They preferred to trade which yielded quick profits. These profits were then spent on foreign goods that were bought in the United States.

Nevertheless, administration of the settlement became a crucial issue. Though Africans were in the majority, from 1822 to 1841 the colony's officials were white. In 1828, the elective process was introduced. In 1847 the colony got its independence with a Black government. Whites were, however, retained as advisors. This then, is how the process of practical colonization in Africa began. By the end of the century with the exception of these two territories and Ethiopia, all of Africa was colonized.

Black History Everyday - Part One Photo. We Shall Not be Moved March. Faces in the Crowd.

MINERAL RESOURCES OF AFRICA

The wide variety of mineral resources in Africa makes it the richest continent on earth. Unfortunately, Africans do not own the means of extraction and have very little influence on the world prices for their resources. Many African nations are today indebted to the extractive concerns dating back decades. However, it is safe to say, the Africans were very well aware of this factor. Also, they are concerned enough to use their leverage on extraction and sale of their minerals.

BLACK HISTORY EVERYDAY
PART ONE

Black History Everyday - Part One Photo. Resident artist at **CEMOTAP** makes a Presentation.

From the earliest days of the Nile Valley civilization, Africa's mineral resources have been worked. This allowed her craftsmen to develop and display their skill in the manufacture of jewelry and ornaments. Gold, copper, tin, brass, lead, silver, iron and many other semi-precious stones have been known and used by craftsmen from the time of antiquity.

Gold, iron and copper have featured prominently in the Trans-Saharan trade. According to known records, the Sub-Saharan nations exported 9 tons of gold annually in this trade. These minerals have helped to crown the "Golden Age of West Africa."

FREDERICK MONDERSON

From 1900 onwards, minerals transformed the South African economy into the continent's powerhouse. According to *Business Study: South Africa*, that nation produced and exported the following minerals. This also characterized various countries at different, perhaps smaller levels of production. South Africa has antimony, Asbestos, Chrome, Coal, Copper, Diamonds, Feldspar, Gold, Gypsum, Iron Ore and Iron Pyrite. There is Lead, Lime, Manganese, Nickel, Platinum, Salt and Silver. Further, Tin, Titanium, Uranium, Vanadium, Vermiculite, and Zinc are also produced. What a bonanza!

While concentrated in South Africa, these minerals are also scattered throughout Africa in the various states and in different amounts. Nevertheless, there are also other minerals not mentioned previously. These include Bauxite, Beryllium, Columbite, Graphite, Lithium, Natural Gas and Petroleum. There are additionally Phosphates, Tantalite, Thorium, and Tungsten. Additionally, there are other minerals that have not been discovered. Still, others, whose usefulness are not fully appreciated at this time.

Very few areas on the globe comparatively have a fraction of the mineral resources that Africa possesses. The enemies of Africa are afraid a strong continental government can harness the potential of this wealth of resources. They have the capacity to tap into the various sources of energy. In the *Black Africa: A Federated State*, Cheikh Anta Diop mentions forms of energy Africa has the potential to tap into include, "Hydraulic, Solar, Atomic,

BLACK HISTORY EVERYDAY
PART ONE

Thermonuclear, Wind, Thermal Energy of the Seas, Tidal Energy, Global Heat, Volcanic Thermal Energy, and Geothermal Energy." Such wonderfully diverse, bountiful and useful energy sources will make the position of Africa supreme on earth. That's why so much energy is expended to keep Africa and Africans from uniting.

PURPOSE OF FOUNDING COLONIES

The last quarter of the Nineteenth Century became the highest stage in European imperialism and beginning of formal colonization in Africa. This distinction was achieved during the period of "enlightened imperialism." "Enlightened imperialism" is the next stage after "naked imperialism." Ostensibly, the theory enunciates that Europeans help "less fortunate people" of the world. However, in receiving this "enlightenment" these colonial areas must pay for Europe's help by allowing Europeans to exploit the colonial areas' natural resources. In the climate of European geo-political and economic rivalry in the 19th Century, the Berlin Conference was organized and held 1884-85 to formally divide Africa among European "powers." This meeting helped effectuate the **Partition of Africa on Paper**.

Jules Ferrer was a distinguished Member of the French Chamber of Deputies, that nation's highest

FREDERICK MONDERSON

legislative body. He earned the nickname "master of imperialist logic." In 1885, in an address to the French Chamber of Deputies he outlined the rationale of the colonial policies of the French government. Hence, he laid down the operational dictum that European nations desired colonies for the following, principally, three reasons.

First, the policy was set in motion, in order that they may have access to the raw materials of the colonies. Europe was experiencing the industrial revolution and mass-produced goods chiefly for export. Europe needed raw materials to feed her industries. Therefore, she needed to effectively control the source of the raw materials. This required an active presence in the colonies.

Second, Europe needed to have markets for the sale of manufactured goods produced at home. These requirements created an insurance, shipping, shipbuilding and maintenance infrastructure to implement the operational policy. In this her missionaries, traders, merchants, marketing and shipping agents and their apparatus, as well as adventurers were considered the precursors to colonialism. In the colonies, these individuals, considered "imperialist activists" psychologically programmed Africans to "need and accept" products **MADE IN EUROPE**. The trade to Africa included clothing, furniture, clocks, radios, and other appliances that were novelties in a changing geo-cultural makeover. Naturally, Whites lorded it over the African Blacks!

BLACK HISTORY EVERYDAY
PART ONE

Black History Everyday - Part One Photo. We Shall Not be Moved March. Faces in the Crowd.

Imagine this scenario! The missionaries' homes were well-stocked with "modern" appliances. They would invite African wives to their "show-room" homes. The wives in turn would say to their husbands, "Honey we must have 'this' and 'that'" and so began the vicious cycle of appreciating European products over indigenous produce. The Africans needed to pay for these items in cash and levied taxes through the colonial administrations, in cash. Therefore, they were required to enter the money market and globally expanding cash-economy work-force. Here they earned cash, paid taxes, could purchase goods and continued to making the system work.

Unfortunately, however, industry was never encouraged in Africa. It was developed in Europe; raw materials shipped to Europe and finished products returned to Africa for sale.

Third, colonies were needed as a field for the investment of surplus capital. In a strategic move, Europeans invested their surplus capital in the colonies to construct railroads, roads, and ports and health facilities. The Africans had to underwrite these "development loans." The railroads and roads led to the ports built to accommodate ships bound for Europe loaded with colonial produce of raw materials. In time, port facilities expanded to handle more and expanded mercantile traffic. In many African countries, health facilities built were defensive in nature. They were designed to keep the African healthy and working to support the system. Some critical commentators have argued that hospitals were not truly built as a humanistic concern for the welfare and wellbeing of the Africans. These health facilities were part of the mechanism of enlightened colonial exploitation, the consequences of imperialism.

This was ingeniously thought out, so much so, when Europe was forced to relinquish its colonies, particularly after World War II, after all that transpired, the colonies were considered industrial backwaters. They lacked the technological, industrial and manufacturing infrastructure that would enable them to become viable independent nations.

BLACK HISTORY EVERYDAY
PART ONE

In addition, colonies served as outlet valves for surplus unemployed Europeans at home. Europeans could easily find some sort of employment in the colonies and "lord it over the natives!" In so doing, they transplanted the home culture abroad and thereby propagated and reinforced the "myth of white superiority." In order to accomplish this last, they built gulf courses, racetracks, encouraged the games of cricket and built European football or soccer fields and stadiums, tennis courts, etc. They were thus able to live in the tropics with the same amenities of home, even though many could not afford such lifestyles in their native countries.

Black History Everyday - Part One Photo. Faces and signs in the crowd for the 50th Anniversary March on Washington.

FREDERICK MONDERSON

Black History Everyday - Part One

Photo. Faces and signs in the crowd for the 50th Anniversary March on Washington.

Lastly, the colonies served as coaling stations to propel Europe's naval and military power abroad. These forces could help to safeguard Atlantic and Indian Ocean shipping sea-lanes. In times of war, navies engaged in hostilities abroad without returning to their homeports. A good example of the latter was Germany building an enormous transmitter at Yaoundé in the Cameroons. When World War I broke out, the German Navy operating in the Atlantic was able to communicate with Berlin using the transmitter as an intermediary. When Cameroons was invaded and conquered it was neutralized.

Therefore, imperialism and colonialism became the practices by which "mother countries" bind their colonies to support them. Through military maneuvers and political ties, they were able to assure a primary objective. This is considered the securing

BLACK HISTORY EVERYDAY
PART ONE

and promoting of their own economic advantages. As such, their economic policies and objectives for a "favorable balance of trade" held that national exports must exceed imports in value. In addition, that each colonial power must pursue a strict monopoly of colonial trade. Lastly, these efforts were pursued to build up the national power for the "mother country." Colonialism then was designed to help the richer countries get richer and pauperize those areas ensnarled in their colonial empires. These colonial holdings were not really poor because they contained natural resources needed in Europe. They did, however, lack the capital, technology and expertise to exploit their own wealth. This is what the Europeans took advantage of.

COLONIAL ECONOMICS

Any attempt to understand the nature of colonization must deal with the question of colonial economics. In order to comprehend further a sense of modern western economic history is appropriate. Equally too, the stages in the growth of the European economy is also important.

FREDERICK MONDERSON

Black History Everyday - Part One Photo. Dr. Leonard Jeffries makes a point in **Presentation** at **CEMOTAP**.

Mercantilism is an outgrowth of Feudalism, the medieval mode of economic production. Mercantilism developed in the commercial expansion of the seventeenth and eighteenth centuries. These were called the "centuries of trade" and the nineteenth century was called the "century of production." Throughout it all, nations were interested in "pursuing a favorable balance of trade." That is, maintaining the relationship of equilibrium between export and import trade. However, as stated, exports were required to exceed imports.

Now, in order to maintain a "favorable balance of trade," many times governments had to play a major role in their nation's economic system. Even though the West favored "free trade" and "capitalist

BLACK HISTORY EVERYDAY PART ONE

investment," the governments intervened through certain economic and political expedients. While encouraging a free enterprise system, government offered incentives as well as directly intervening in economic pursuits.

The first of the economic policies was to maintain high duties on imports. This discouraged other nations from selling goods in one's domestic market, including the colonies. Domestic production catered to domestic consumption. Equally too, there was a heavy reliance on the export of manufactured goods.

Black History Everyday - Part One Photo. We Shall Not be Moved March.
Faces in the Crowd.

FREDERICK MONDERSON

The nation interested in maintaining a favorable balance of trade received raw materials from other countries. She in turn exported finished products. Even more, the host nation placed severe restrictions on the export of precious metals. In so doing, she exalted foreign trade over domestic trade. Everything and everyone were concerned about manufacturing goods to sell abroad. This enterprise brought money and precious metals - specie - gold, silver, diamonds, etc., into the country. It also ensured full employment at home.

The social and economic infrastructure at home was greatly improved. Better roads were built. Bridges were constructed or improved on. The country's industries and factories expanded and became well organized at home. Schools in Europe trained administrators to govern colonies. On the other hand, schools in the colonial countries developed departments designed to foster better understanding and effective administration of the colonies they acquired. They studied the colonial culture, languages, soil, plant and animal life, rivers, geology and mineral resources. In addition, these mother countries stressed the importance of dense home populations. This provided an element of national strength to safeguard foreign trade and provide defense.

WHAT DID EUROPE DO FOR AFRICA?

Frequently the question is asked: "What did Europe do for Africa?" Admittedly, there is no one answer

BLACK HISTORY EVERYDAY
PART ONE

that could rightfully address such a profound inquiry. Rather, a number of plausible answers would create a better understanding of the unfolding circumstances in the colonial interaction dictated by imperialistic logic, tendencies and practices.

First, and unmistaken, Africa's mineral wealth was taken out by Europeans and used for Europe's own profit. Gold and diamonds in South Africa, gold and cocoa in Ghana and petroleum in Egypt, Gabon, Nigeria and Algeria, were used to supply European needs. Rubber, tin, diamonds and copper from the Congo, Zambian (Northern Rhodesia) copper and iron, phosphates, cobalt, platinum, etc., from other areas, were all part of the wealth extracted and shipped overseas. The mineral resources of Africa fed Europe's industry and military needs as well as provided personal adornment for the socially well-off.

In many places such as Southern Rhodesia (Zimbabwe), South Africa, Kenya and Uganda, large tracts of the most fertile lands were appropriated to white settlers. That is, control of colonial legislatures allowed European administrators to cede extensive tracts of land to their fellows. The only criteria for ownership were a white skin and the intent to settle and exploit the land. To encourage Africans to become part of the cash crop economy, tribes were separated and tribal customs and institutions were disparaged, disregarded or destroyed. Taxes were imposed on men, women, children, huts, animals, etc.

FREDERICK MONDERSON

Many Africans, with subtlety and through force by the Europeans, were made to relinquish their old customs. In the colonial system, they provided European farm labor.

Black History Everyday - Part One Photo. Faces and signs in the crowd for the 50th Anniversary March on Washington.

In many respects, the colonial countries introduced racial discrimination. The nature and type of this discrimination was totally unknown in "Africa before the white man."

As Europe developed the infrastructure of the industrial revolution extra-territorial holdings became a necessity. Africa, perhaps more than any other area, felt the full brunt of Europe's assault as mechanisms of the paradigms of imperialism. The

BLACK HISTORY EVERYDAY
PART ONE

emerging European nationalism clashed in efforts to secure colonies, and administer and exploit these lands. The prevailing colonial policy became one of "direct" or "indirect rule." Nations as France, Germany, Portugal and Belgium pursued "direct rule" requiring a greater colonial bureaucracy. This meant more Europeans were employed in the colonial administration. Britain followed an "indirect" policy. The "indirect" policy recognized indigenous or traditional authority as true leaders while the British tended to trade and external relations. If we add other Europeans who were merchants, planters, missionaries, tourists, adventurers, etc., this increased their numbers in Africa. All of these people impacted on the African continent in one way or another, whether in political, military, economic, religious, scientific, agriculture, health, tourism, journalistic or educational perspectives. From this and possibly other respects, the manner of Europe's impact on Africa can best be viewed.

Among the first things done with colonial possessions was to make geological, botanical, and mineralogical studies of the acquired territory. This done, millions of Africans were hired and trained to operate machines that dug their wealth out of the ground. New roads and railways were built. They led to the ports. Here the wealth was shipped overseas to be processed, pay bills or pay for the administration of the territory.

FREDERICK MONDERSON

Ostensibly, hospitals were built to safeguard the health of the nation. However, while they treated Europeans, it has been argued, they were built to keep Africans healthy to ensure work requirements were met on the plantations and government and private service. Schools were built to teach literacy because it facilitated communication between the European powers and residents in Africa and among African workers. Other types of buildings were also built, further employing more Africans. Questioned at school about events at home; inadvertently, African children by giving up information, unknowingly, were in fact spying on their parents. At first while the African people were working, paying taxes and buying goods made in Europe, the vicious cycle was not too obvious. Later during colonial agitation, World War I and II, and emergence of Pan-African activism as well as unionization that developed at home, new views began to educate the people to the perils of their condition created by European imperialism.

Missionaries did help to build schools in their Christianizing efforts. They also reduced African languages to writing and compiled dictionaries, which helped them, preserve these languages involved in reading the bible, etc. The missionaries also taught the European languages so Africans could communicate better with them. This helped well-to-do Africans to venture to study abroad. Thus, by learning to read and also write, and becoming familiar with basic knowledge of the world, African lives were transformed.

BLACK HISTORY EVERYDAY
PART ONE

Black History Everyday - Part One Photo. We Shall Not be Moved March. Faces in the Crowd.

The missionaries were helpful in many other ways. They improved methods of tropical agriculture. Better farming, irrigation and rotation practices increased the wealth, value and production of African soils that fed Europe's needs. The tribal warfare that grew out of the Salve Trade was ended by the work of the missionaries and colonial administrations because this was bad for the emerging business climate. Those Africans educated abroad returned home and helped in further moving their countries forward.

Overall, colonial rule did bring some material advantages of western civilization to Africa. There were however, many disadvantages. Firstly, the political structure of traditional Africa was transformed, being replaced by one imported from Europe. This also shifted power from rural to urban centers with attendant benefits and problems in the evolving scenario. Equally too, such things as poverty, illiteracy, and poor transportation infrastructure proved a problem. Many roads remained unpaved, dusty in summer and muddy in the rainy season. In Portuguese controlled areas such as Mozambique and Angola, there were no universities and, in some cases, only 1 or 2 indigenous doctors resided in the country in the whole country. When this Portuguese colonial power withdrew at independence there was either a lack of adequate service or all the Europeans removed everything, they could get their hands on, such as fridges, radios, pipes, toilets, you name it!

These were some of the factors associated with imperialism and the coming of Europe to Africa, colonial administration and the changing face of Africa. Therefore, when the question is asked, 'What did Europe do for Africa?' These, then are some of the facts! Let us not forget the many Africans lost in wars against European encroachment; the untold losses and suffering as Leopold's Belgians extracted rubber in the Congo; and, even more, the unending disrespect and psychological dislocation in one's home, land and country. Equally too, Africans were recruited to fight in wars among European nations. Fortunately, this involvement destroyed the mystique

BLACK HISTORY EVERYDAY
PART ONE

of the superiority of the white man when militarily trained Africans were now involved in acts of war.

Notwithstanding, we must never forget, for as Nkrumah (1973: V) puts it: "The aim of all colonial governments in Africa and elsewhere has been the struggle for raw materials; and not only this, but the colonies have become the dumping ground, and colonial peoples the false recipients, of manufactured goods of the industrialists and capitalists of Great Britain, France, Belgium and other colonial powers who turn to the dependent territories which feed their industrial plants. This is colonialism in a nutshell."

Finally, in *Neo-Colonialism: The Last Stage of Imperialism*, Kwame Nkrumah (1965, 1973: 43) associates the Rockefellers, Morgans, Rothschilds, etc., in the banking interests with oil concerns. In this he states: "Oil trust reserves run into the billions. Much has been used in investments abroad, America far and away exceeding all others. To financial reserves from oil must be added those amassed from metal and other raw materials' monopolies; from monopoly of food supplies and vast industrial and agricultural empires; from the monopoly network of distribution and distributive agencies; from military preparations and the several wars that have been fought with colonial peoples since the end of the second world war; from the development of nuclear instruments of destruction and the frenzied race for leadership in the realm of space research." Further Nkrumah added: "The European Community, of

FREDERICK MONDERSON

which the European Common Market is only one aspect, is by no means a new concept. It was foreshadowed by Hobson in his critique of imperialism as 'a European federation of great powers which, so far from forwarding the cause of world civilization, might introduce the gigantic peril of western parasites, a group of advanced industrial nations, whose upper classes drew vast tribute from Asia and Africa, with which they supported great masses of retainers, no longer engaged in the staple industries of agriculture and manufacture, but kept in industrial services under the control of a new financial aristocracy.' It is collective imperialism."

Black History Everyday - Part One
Photo. Faces and signs in the crowd for the 50th Anniversary March on Washington.

BLACK HISTORY EVERYDAY
PART ONE

Black History Everyday - Part One
Photo. Faces and signs in the crowd for the 50th Anniversary March on Washington.

"What political leader can stand up and say 'My party is a party of principles?' Where is our party? Where is the political party that will make it necessary to march on Washington? Where is the political party that will make it necessary to march in the streets of Birmingham? John Lewis. *Speech. March on Washington for Jobs and Freedom [August 28, 1963]*

"We are not against police. We are against police brutality." Rev. Al Sharpton. On *Going to Washington.*

"It is not a game of checkers. It is a game of chess." Benjamin Crump, accompanying Rev. Sharpton.

FREDERICK MONDERSON

21. SHARPTON AND CRUMP'S MARCH ON WASHINGTON BY DR. FRED MONDERSON

Saying "We're not anti-Police, we're anti-Police Brutality" Reverend Al Sharpton explained at the **National Action Network's** weekly rally in Harlem, on December 6, 2014, "Why we're going to March on Washington, December 13," "is to seek justice, to eliminate the smog of injustice in the air and force Congress to repair the broken Grand Jury system that miserably failed Black victims seeking justice. Many are disappointed in the Grand Jury System that seems manipulated in a conflict of interest scenario that exonerates police officers who should at least be indicted for the killing of Blacks!" Hopefully legislation will address this national problem.

Speaker after speaker spoke of the "sin and iniquity in the form of injustice being perpetrated against young Black men" and why "the campaign for justice must continue through marches." The speakers referenced the Civil Rights Movements' marches that brought about the **Civil Rights Acts of 1964**, the **Voting Rights Act of 1965**. To this they emphasized the significance and effectiveness of the **Montgomery Bus Boycott**. Quoting Dr. King

BLACK HISTORY EVERYDAY
PART ONE

that "the moral arm of the universe is long but it bends towards justice" the cry was "the issue is not simply civil but human rights." All insisted, "we must demonstrate dignity and perseverance in this movement until "righteousness rolls down like a mighty stream;" yet, "being mindful that change only takes place when you look in the face of injustice and force unbiased federal oversight."

Realizing, citizens from all over the country came together to address recent Grand Jury rulings, Congress must hold hearings and pass laws to protect citizens' rights. Thus, the legislative branch must step in. "The people must not be run like hamsters on single issues" they cried. Strategists and decision makers must connect all the cases as a sort of "class action," and they mentioned, among such cases those of Eric Garner, Michael Brown, Tamir Rice. "We must put the cases together to show police violence as we did in linking Rosa Parks with the Mississippi **Freedom Riders** and **CORE** and Dr. King cooperating for legislative relief."

FREDERICK MONDERSON

Black History Everyday - Part One
Photo. A lady of elegance at **CEMOTAP's** 31st Annual celebration.

The mother of Eric Garner thanked all, saying "You have stood with me from the beginning. I felt proud, to see people standing for my son. That makes my heart overflow with joy. Keep on doing what you're doing, but do it in peace." Esau Garner, his wife, was "overwhelmed" at the people's response. She spoke of the "gentle giant" and that this does not fully explain the wonderful man he was! She was elated people were saying, "Mrs. Garner we're marching for you!" Thus, she insisted, "Keep fighting this fight to get justice!" His daughter Emerald offered, "I must shout out the young people. Do it peacefully!"

BLACK HISTORY EVERYDAY
PART ONE

Black History Everyday - Part One Photo. We Shall Not be Moved March. Faces in the Crowd.

Equally, addressing the Press who have not been kind to him, Rev. Sharpton insisted he never got any "kick back" from any of the fights he has been in. All he wanted and wants is justice! He reminded "I have TV and Radio contracts and any kickbacks would jeopardize my livelihood!"

Joining the Reverend at the rally and in an Academy Award presentation, legal eagle Attorney Benjamin Crump eloquently made the case of "Why we are going to March on Washington!" Mr. Crump first of all thanked and congratulated Rev. Al Sharpton for "always answering the bell, whether the camera is there or not, he is there when it is not popular." Praising his fellow lawyers Jonathan Moore and Michael Hardy for their stalwart role in quest of justice, he praised "Young people who stood up!" and indicated the **National Bar Association**, the largest African American organization of lawyers, stands firmly behind Rev. Sharpton and this

FREDERICK MONDERSON

movement. Then he recognized "Eric Garner inspired and galvanized young people who crafted their own slogans," which the marchers chanted: "Hands Up, Don't Shoot" and "I Can't Breathe;" "Black Lives Matter;" "I am Michael Brown;" and "Justice for Michael Brown!"

Next Mr. Crump explained his "Theory of the case!" because "the system needs to be indicted!" He insisted, "The system is what breaks our hearts." He decried the "closeness in time" of the killings of Eric Garner, Michael Brown, Tamir Rice and pointed to the symbolism and seemingly inherent conflict of interest, "Even Stevie Wonder could see," when a local Prosecutor must investigate a local police officer. Calling Ferguson "a fraud" he advised, "We must be specific. It's about chess not checkers!"

He then proposed a precedence by which he questioned Ferguson! That is, for 30 years the Prosecutor has been presenting cases to the Grand Jury. All of a sudden, he changed his strategy!

Mr. Crump insisted the audience see what he termed "attempts to demonize young Black men" because as he pointed out, "Police officers are hired to protect and serve the community," but what you get is "Police protection for police and Police enforcement for Black victims." Searching for precedence he stated, "In 1982 the Supreme Court ruled, 'not to allow a suspect to testify!'" So, for 30 years the Ferguson District Attorney presented to the Grand Jury but did not allow any suspects to testify. "All of

BLACK HISTORY EVERYDAY
PART ONE

a sudden he wants to be fair," and in presenting to the Grand Jury, allows the suspect, Darren Wilson, to testify. He therefore asked, "Had he not been fair for 30 years?" His view of "police demonizing young Black men" is seen, first, where Officer Wilson compared his encounter with Michael Brown as "Hulk Hogan to a 5-year old." Then he pointed out how they use the terms "Supporters for Officer Wilson" but "Protesters for Michael Brown and Eric Garner!" Then again, three seconds after the police arrived, he shot Tamir Reid, yet he claims he told him to put down the gun three times. With Eric Garner they tried to play up he was arrested previously and that he was selling "loose cigarettes" which he was not doing at that time.

Vowing "Due Process" for Michael Brown, Eric Garner and Tamir Rice, Mr. Crump quoted former Supreme Court Justice Thurgood Marshall that "the Constitution guarantees the same equal rights to a Black, uneducated, poor, mother who gives birth in Mississippi to an affluent, educated, wealthy, white mother born anywhere in the United States. That is what being born in this country means."

Rev. Sharpton reminded all the National Action Network will provide free buses at different locations across the five boroughs but those interested must sign up for a seat. Go to **National Action Network.Net** or call and add your name. Buses will leave about 5:00 AM Saturday, December 13,

FREDERICK MONDERSON

2014, to rendezvous at Pennsylvania Avenue and 13th Street.

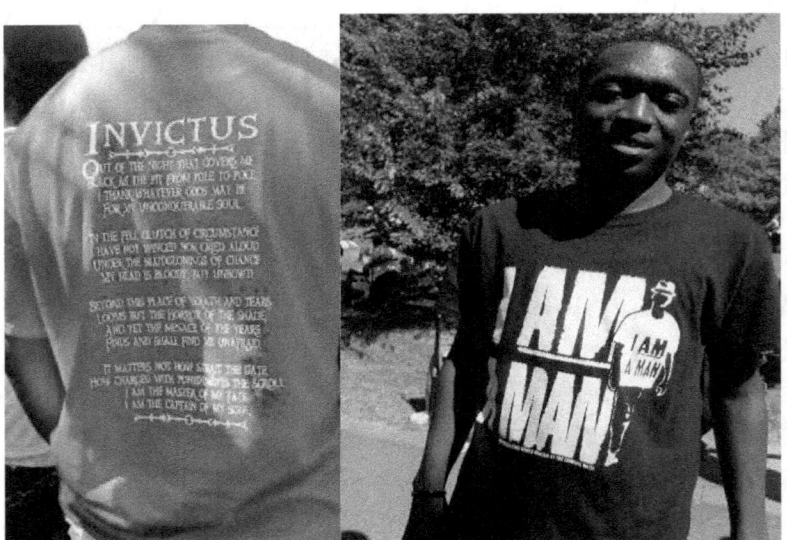

Black History Everyday - Part One Photo. Faces and signs in the crowd for the 50th Anniversary March on Washington.

Black History Everyday - Part One Photo. Faces and signs in the crowd for the 50th Anniversary March on Washington.

BLACK HISTORY EVERYDAY
PART ONE

"Heal the world, Make it a better place for you and for me, and the entire human race. There are people dying, If you care enough for the living, Make a better place for you and me." **Michael Jackson**. *Heal the World [1991]*

"Hold me Like a River Jordan, and I will then say to thee, You are my friend. Carry me, Like you are my brother, Love me like a mother, Will you be there?" **Michael Jackson**. *Will You Be There [1991]*

22. MICHAEL! "A SONG OF PRAISE" BY DR. FRED MONDERSON

"A wonderful song of praise to a gem of entertainment!"

Beautiful soul, man of love blest with the angelic voice, piece of divinity rests within you
For decades you created an inspiration with a delightful and elegant refinement of sweet musical poetry, seemingly guided by the highest spiritual authority, heart of a gentle lion
Ground breaking entertainer, the sweet melody of your wonderful craft was superhuman, spiritual, divine, and incandescent, master purveyor of a universal lyrical language

FREDERICK MONDERSON

Black History Everyday - Part One

Photo. Michael Jackson had a beautiful memorial send-off as this image shows.

Your inspired music reached across cultures and nations to harmoniously soothe souls of young and old, genius, your innocence is divinely beautiful with a soothing potency

Adorable and mystical spirit, Michael, archangel, child of exorbitant talent, maker of sweet music of happiness and healing, you are a master commander

BLACK HISTORY EVERYDAY
PART ONE

of musical arenas where your rhythm is classic and explosive, thunderous entertainer extraordinary

Man of boundless vision and magical creativity, how well you play those delectable keys of enchanting music, seeming whatever the poet writes is divinely inspired, professional

Cultural icon, though never echoing black is beautiful with your euphonic voice, existing above mundane issues of blackness

Your life and legacy are a manifestation of that forcefully creative shibboleth and the god of music, Thoth, is pleased with your iconic cultural contribution

An early view of the entranceway to the Harlem Shrine where well-wishing began to pay tribute to their idol that would later blossom.

Black History Everyday - Part One Photo. We Shall Not be Moved March. Faces in the Crowd.

FREDERICK MONDERSON

Purveyor of happiness through sweet music, imbued with spiritual creativity to create, virtuoso you are a giver of merriment to fans worldwide, your influence is unmatched

Possessing great spiritual grace, merry-maker, your vivid melody charms the soul, engulfs and makes the heart flutter, all wonderfully pleasing to the ear and bosom

Joy maker, your immortal lyrics awaken the dawn, salivates the sun, illuminates the heavens, and soothes evening bloom dressed in gleaming stars of your picturesque attires manifested in colorful garbs, zippers, glasses, white sox, gloves, glitter

Possessing great spiritual vitality, Moonwalker, the best of your superabundant musical charm is pleasing and joyful to the hearing with an original healing potency, unmatched, representing the joy of all humanity

Cultural celebrity phenomenon, your melodic dancing waves and musical expression is poetry in motion, exalting in its chants, everlasting in its blissful exuberance, classical

Great one blest with originality, your spirituality is incredible, your earned immortality is enshrined in photos, images, film, cards, race, music, entertainment, and much more since your talent was before and above your time

Very complicated, yet never racially or culturally controversial, you espoused godliness in your genius, gentle disposition and soft-spoken mannerism, yet

BLACK HISTORY EVERYDAY
PART ONE

endowed with powerful creative talents you are beyond legend, barrier breaker possessing a loving heart and wonderful disposition, philanthropist who cared for the poor across the globe
Forcefulness of you as symbol advanced the cause of blackness through culture, music and exquisite harmony that charmed the great mystical beauty and light of the universe
Not just a crossover artiste by any means, your intelligence, stature and persona, global in its consummate perfection, is a testimonial of impressive proportions, soul of genius, existing above our earthly concerns

Brilliant creator of exquisite sounds, you harmoniously impregnated cultural salt in the earth's consciousness, to rejoice and celebrate an enlightening symphony through an amazing body of music, the greatest testament to your extraordinary persona
Extolling love, brotherhood, and cultural syncretism, exalted in your delightful chants
You help others to see,
We are the world, where so many aspire to be

Cherubim transcending the realms of the most high, beautiful ornament, wonderful addition to the heavenly choir, your well-mannered, soft spoken nature is unique

FREDERICK MONDERSON

The euphoric melody of your elegant and graceful dancing footsteps partnering with the heavenly and dignified Alvin Ailey

Will forever virtuously echo, Michael, music maker, with the magnificent majesty of Marvin, Miriam, and Marley
As the sweet harmony of your lyrics resonate thunderously in the many mansions of the almighty's silvery universe, an audience of angels will welcome you into divine bosom

Black History Everyday - Part One
Photo. Nana Queen-Mother Camille Yarbrough in all her majestic splendor, "Doing her thing!

We mortals continue to sing you praises delightful one, you're more than a crossover star, you were beloved by all
So, we can never say goodbye, uniqueness

BLACK HISTORY EVERYDAY PART ONE

We will forever be grateful you provided intangible food for the human soul and spirit through your boundless and harmonious musical chords
Trumpeter of splendid chimes, the sweet resonance of your lyrics is like bells chiming musically in the heavenly Milky Way, all resonating into eternity without ending
Hounded in life because of envy, betrayed, yet not guilty, triumphant and martyred for pursuit of creative merriment that pleases the hearts of many cultures, your blessed talent is powerful and everlasting in the celestial firmaments you sang under unending

Today we mourn Knowing your sweet fire will forever burn in your comfortable global domain, soul man King of Pop, talented creator with exceptional artistic charisma, disciplined and a gentle person, man of love in search of love, the deathlessness of your silver sounds and golden harmony will live in musical remembrance for eons to come as the heavens proclaim the mystical and magical genius of your offers to aid humanity

Gifted beyond comparison, beyond legend, yours is music while music lasts, unrivaled, supreme because your mind is a musical instrument of great and melodious refinement, you're considered a universal pop culture icon, born to perform

FREDERICK MONDERSON

Thus, songbird, we give thanks you blest humanity's existence with creative expressions of joyousness, civility and soulful inspiration possessing a tremendously spectacular potency

Your musical and human contributions will echo for generations to come, because your chords reached deep into the universe helping create and echoing the food of divine love

Blessed as an angelic light your magic shined wonderfully bright as a young vigorous sun

Bells of heaven chimes as you are called home to embellish the heavenly orchestra

Sorrowfully, we know humanity is deprived when such a soft creative voice of love passes on!

Black History Everyday - Part One Photo. Faces and signs in the crowd for the 50th Anniversary March on Washington.

BLACK HISTORY EVERYDAY
PART ONE

Black History Everyday - Part One Photo. Faces and signs in the crowd for the 50th Anniversary March on Washington.

"We need to see One Million Black Men" in front of the Capital Building telling our story." Dr. Jack Felder on *The Million Man March*. [October 16, 1995].

"Many of you think I killed Malcolm. If I did, do you think I would still be here? Look who was giving him mouth to mouth respiration. It was an FBBI Agent. 'Justice or Else. The **'Or Else'** is up to You.'" Minister Louis Farrakhan on the 20th Anniversary of the **Million Man March**. October 16, 2015]

FREDERICK MONDERSON

23. MILLION MAN MARCH: "SUBSTANCE AND SIGNIFICANCE" BY DR. FRED MONDERSON

Riding in a DC cab the day after the March, the driver wanted to know the "Numbers! - A Million or so?" I responded, "Two million or more," based on my own unscientific observations looking out at the stretched-out masses of people within the barricades lining the Great Lawn, on adjacent streets, and the continuing streams entering from north and south conduits. Equally significant, even when leaving early, the late throngs of people pouring in and heading to the Mall certainly adds to an elevated assessment of how many people were there. I'm reminded 20 years ago of the controversy over the number of people who attended that first March. While Minister Farrakhan called for and acknowledged a million in attendance, the government downplayed this number offering no more than 400,000 to 500,000. On the other hand, others gave a figure of more than a million! However, while some folks may have arrived late, such as my daughter Keisha traveling with her family, who incidentally were in attendance at the **Million Family March** in 2000, the 2,000,000 number seems a real possibility.

Continuing the dialogue with the driver, he remarked, "I have been in this town 40 years. This town belonged to African-Americans but this has

BLACK HISTORY EVERYDAY
PART ONE

changed." I did observe a fair amount of destitute people on the streets and made contributions. On Sunday morning at McDonalds, to several of the persons nearby I asked, and answered the question, "Did you have your coffee this morning, brother?" To which several resounding "Thank yous" were heartfelt responses.

Notwithstanding, as the driver said, my mind reflected on a photograph at the Meridian Park, now renamed Malcolm X Park, showing a tremendous gathering of Marching African-Americans streaming out onto the street on **Black Solidarity Day** in 1972. Gathered in what appeared a military formation, an individual in "fatigues" led and directed persons in prominent Afro hairstyles and wearing dashiki shirts. This was a classic Black Nationalism moment! Perhaps this was the "golden age" the driver referred to.

Black History Everyday - Part One Photo. **We Shall Not be Moved March**. Faces in the Crowd.

FREDERICK MONDERSON

Nevertheless, though the "stomach may appear a bit soft," the stalwarts at the far reaches of the "Empire" are "no ways tired," because the substance and significance of the gathering inherent in the "ideology of the March" attracting the numbers in attendance as reflected in the many who announced their presence two decades ago, broadening of the multi-ethnic flavor of the gathering to include Whites, Native Americans, Asians, Latinos, LGBTs, in addition to those Black stalwarts who brought their sons and daughters, even wives; those who brought youngsters; and those returning to assert their manhood in support of the call; the need for, and the demands for **Justice or Else** going forward. Such is the essence of **Substance and Significance** of this most potent idea.

Thus, and without question, we must give praise and thanks to Minister Louis Farrakhan of the **Nation of Islam** for conceiving, executing and contributing to the "Million" idea. We know there are "forty something" million African-Americans in this country. They spend one million million (Trillion) dollars annually and there are perhaps a million Brothers and Sisters incarcerated, but Farrakhan's idea is different, tremendously revolutionary, and with continuous tweaking will remain a potent beacon of consciousness, soul searching and demands on government, all ripe for activism in nationalist assertion. Its crystal clear, in the most vital organ of the American system, Washington, DC, this genius planted a profound idea whose time has not

BLACK HISTORY EVERYDAY
PART ONE

only come but will endure for eons because of the power, substance and significance contained in the message.

The numbers, quality and receptivity of those who answered the call and as they return to their widespread areas of operation, the trees of this forest will in turn generate forests of their own who will creatively experiment with, carry forward, and sustain the message of **Justice or Else**, while making their own significant contributions not simply to advance the cause of Blackness but equally continue to make America a better place for all.

Living the legacy decades later, when One Million will become Twenty and Minister Farrakhan finally joins the revered ancestral pantheon; that is, among Jitu Weusi, Sonny Carson, Reverend Jones, Elombe Brathe, Dr. Ben-Jochannan, Professor George Simmonds, Dr. John Henrik Clarke, Bill Lynch, and the oldsters Malcolm X, Martin Luther King, Mary McLeod Bethune, Fannie Lou Hamer, Reverend Shuttlesworth, Dorothy Height, W.E.B. Dubois, Marcus Garvey, Elijah Mohammed, Kwame Ture, Herman Ferguson, Queen Mother Moore, Elijah Cummings, Nelson Mandela, Langston Hughes, Claude McKay, Forbes Burnham, Mitta Monderson, Ollie McClean, on the fiftieth anniversary and after, these will rejoice over the success of their efforts added to the **Million Man March** ideology and program's harvest of fruitful outcomes.

FREDERICK MONDERSON

Naturally much was said, but a most powerful theme Mr. Farrakhan evoked was the call for an economic boycott especially at holiday time. Investing in Black Enterprise is always an equally potent idea. However, for the longest our leaders have emphasized the importance of the economic boycott. They cite the successes of the Montgomery Bus Boycott and concurrent Boycott of Birmingham stores that brought that city's white supremacy to its knees! Equally, many features of early **Black Solidarity Day Boycott** were successful but for whatever reason that movement lost its way, as only a few groups across the country see the need for and continue the tradition.

When Sean Bell, on the eve of his wedding, was shot many times in Queens, New York, Reverend Al Sharpton called for an economic march along Fifth Ave on December 16th of that year, entering 50th Street in Manhattan and passing through the "Heart of Christmas," the intent was to "Shop for Justice." The theme was, "Hold your money, Don't Shop this holiday!" That is an equally significant theme Minister Farrakhan emphasized on this 20th Anniversary of the Million Man March under the shibboleth "Justice or Else!"

BLACK HISTORY EVERYDAY
PART ONE

Black History Everyday - Part One Photo. Faces and signs in the crowd for the 50th Anniversary March on Washington.

Black History Everyday - Part One Photo. Faces and signs in the crowd for the 50th Anniversary March on Washington.

FREDERICK MONDERSON

Again, Bob Law and Reverend Calvin Butts in New York have proposed and are currently pursuing a national economic boycott to redirect the more than **One Trillion Dollars African Americans spend annually**. Echoing Adam Clayton Powell's "Don't shop where you can't work" boycott dictum, down through the age's leaders have emphasized the same idea. Thus, Bob Law, also emphasizing the prevalence of "fast food" establishments in the Black community and the implications for long-term health concerns, has advised "redirect your burger and fries money," not necessarily your big spending habits. He emphasized, in these "fast food joints" that don't hire Blacks or support any nationalist initiatives that concern African-Americans, they should not shop there. However, when shopping they should ask proprietors of such establishments, "Where are the Black people who work here since we're shopping in your place of business?" Without question, "our dollars represent the margin of profit" for these businesses as Bob Law expressed, particularly so the big chains with their ubiquitous presence in or serving the Black Community. More specific, only about "8 percent of Blacks" need to withhold such spending to make a difference and these enterprises will recognize Black aspirations because **Black Lives Matter** in all of its manifestations! One sign at the march even advocated, "Make the Black Dollar circulate more in the Black Community!"

BLACK HISTORY EVERYDAY
PART ONE

Black History Everyday - Part One Photo. We Shall Not be Moved March. Faces in the Crowd.

A classic case was once observed in Maryland, famous for crabs. One Asian establishment selling crabs but not employing Blacks was servicing a line that stretched around the corner, "Because they make good crabs!" How foolish and counterproductive!

More importantly, however, in his two-hour presentation one pointedly important assertion Minister Farrakhan posed, "I know you all think I killed Malcolm! If I killed Malcolm, do you think I would be here? See who was giving him mouth to mouth resuscitation? It was an FBI agent!" The idea elicits a Hollywood analogy in the movie **Shooter** starring Mark Walberg and Danny Glover. When the

FREDERICK MONDERSON

hero and the FBI agent went seeking "Wisdom" from the old shooting expert, to the question, "Who killed Kennedy?" he responded, "Those boys on the grassy knoll were dead within hours." The FBI agent responded, "You know this for sure?" To which the expert responded, "I still have the shovels in the back!" This sort of lends credence to the Minister's denial. Notwithstanding, Sonny Carson and Herman Ferguson both thought he did it! However, he may not have been at the Audubon to pull the trigger but to feign ignorance of the "climate around Malcolm" and "the hit going down" is not a tenable position.

Nevertheless, the Minister pointed out the Honorable Gentleman had married the ladies and took care of his children, "not like some of you players out there." He equally criticized the many women who "let the players play" and "not hold them accountable" for their behaviors. He also made special note of black-on-black crime and killings as well police killing of Blacks. Others gave a litany of names of victims of such violence. Nonetheless, with these issues and the substance and significance of the March recognized in the numbers who came and the seeds they will plant to creatively organize and continue to demand **Justice or Else** then return at this idea of anniversary in five years to the **Million Family** in 2020; all the while the **Million Woman** in 2018 and **Million Youth** anniversaries remain on deck, certainly underscores the significance of the idea of the Black Community thinking in the millions as a tool of social and nationalist activism.

BLACK HISTORY EVERYDAY
PART ONE

Whatever, we must still acknowledge, praise and give thanks for Minister Farrakhan's vision in seeing the need, inspiring Millions to think in such mega proportions while participating in structured recurring like decimal anniversaries to encourage future youth to build on the multifaceted platforms of social activism he bequeathed them. Thus, the **Million Man March** idea, its history as ultimately will materialize in creative epic proportions is a self-help movement to uplift African people here and abroad; and, we have Minister Louis Farrakhan and his cadre to thank for the creatively brilliant concept.

Black History Everyday - Part One Photo. Brother Nova Felder and Brother Chris Noble at **CEMOTAP**.

FREDERICK MONDERSON

Black History Everyday - Part One
Photo. Faces and signs in the crowd for the 50th Anniversary March on Washington.

Black History Everyday - Part One
Photo. Faces and signs in the crowd for the 50th Anniversary March on Washington.

BLACK HISTORY EVERYDAY
PART ONE

Black History Everyday - Part One Photo. Faces and signs in the crowd for the 50th Anniversary March on Washington.

Black History Everyday - Part One Photo. We Shall Not be Moved March. Faces in the Crowd.

FREDERICK MONDERSON

Black History Everyday - Part One Photo. "**They All Look Alike! All?!**" Again, Dr. Yosef ben-Jochannan.

BLACK HISTORY EVERYDAY
PART ONE

Black History Everyday - Part One

Photo. Brother Walter Brown (top) and Brother Fred Monderson (bottom) meet in Augusta for a 50-year reunion.

FREDERICK MONDERSON

Black History Everyday - Part One Photo. Former Mayor of New York City, **David Dinkins** speaks from the Podium and then with two young gentlemen.

BLACK HISTORY EVERYDAY
PART ONE

"You are a patient people. You act as though you were made for the special use of these devils. You act as though your daughters were born to pamper the lust of your masters and overseers. And worse than all, you tamely submit while your lords tear your wives from your embraces, and defile them before your very eyes. In the name of God, we ask are you men? Where is the blood of your fathers? Has it all run out of your veins? Awake, awake, millions of voices are calling you! Your dead fathers speak to you from their graves. Heaven, as with a voice of thunder, calls you to arise from this dust." **Henry Highland Garnett**. *Address to the Slaves of the United States of America.*

Black History Everyday - Part One Photo. Party people getting down at **CEMOTAPs** 31st Celebration.

FREDERICK MONDERSON

Black History Everyday - Part One
Photo. Faces and signs in the crowd for the 50th Anniversary March on Washington.

BLACK HISTORY EVERYDAY
PART ONE

Black History Everyday - Part One Photo. Faces and signs in the crowd for the 50th Anniversary March on Washington.

FREDERICK MONDERSON

"We are standing on the blood of our ancestors. We are standing on the blood of those who died in the middle passage, who died in the fields and in the cells of their jailers, who died on the highways and who died in the fratricidal conflict that rages within our community. We are standing on the sacrifice of the lives of those heroes, our great men and women, that we today may accept accountability that life imposes upon each traveler who come this way." Minister Louis Farrakhan. *Speech to the Million Man March on Washington* [October 16, 1995]

24. MILLIONS MORE MOVEMENT: I WAS THERE! BY DR. FRED MONDERSON

The reason for my coming to Washington, DC to attend the **Millions More Movement March** was to celebrate the 10th Anniversary of the **Million Man March** of October 16, 1995. On that historic date I was on the bus with some friends, Dr. Jack Felder, Dr. James McIntosh, Dawad Philip and an arm amputee named Sid. When we arrived beside the Capital Building for a few minutes I left for the Library of Congress to deposit a book I had written. Sid said, "I want to make history twice this day" and so accompanied me to the Library of Congress, Madison Building.

BLACK HISTORY EVERYDAY
PART ONE

Black History Everyday - Part One Photo. We Shall Not be Moved March. Faces in the Crowd.

The book was entitled "**19 Letters to O.J. Simpson on Ancient African History**" that was deposited in 17 volumes and was designed to be an educational tool of enlightenment for black people and for all people seeking truth about ancient Africa, the Nile Valley Culture, ancient Egypt/Kemet. Ten years later like the **Million Man March**, the book has shown historical and creative direction in the intellectual and emotional growth of one individual. The book had nothing to do with Simpsons life or his case but simply a tool of enlightenment delivered during his incarceration. For the record, he never acknowledged my effort!

FREDERICK MONDERSON

Coming to the **Millions More Movement** March in 2005, I brought my daughter Keisha, son Erik and grandson, Bryce to be part of this historic gathering of their history and the individual and events that have given birth to his new movement of consciousness and direction for Blacks, Latinos, Native Americans and poor people here in America. In addition, the cultural and historical awareness fires lit in the minds of these and many more youngsters are designed to assist their rites of passage becoming conscious and strong black-men in America and to be able to live out their destinies. Hopefully, this waxing strength will make them better citizens to make America a better place because our destinies are tied to the destiny of this great nation.

While I do not agree with everything Minister Louis Farrakhan says, despite what is said about Minister Louis Farrakhan, it was tremendously visionary of Minister Louis Farrakhan to call for the *Million Man March* on October 16, 1995, for now people begin to think in terms of millions, viz., men, women, youth, moms, families, jobs, coalitions, anti-war advocacy, etc. When we consider the great parades, marches in America, viz., Columbus Day, Veterans Day, St. Patrick's Day, Firemen, Police and the many ethnic gatherings, someone started these parades/marches years ago and now these groups celebrate with great pride, pomp and gaiety. So, long before a century from now, as we gather on the **Great Lawn** in Washington, DC., the heritage and legacy of the

BLACK HISTORY EVERYDAY
PART ONE

Million Man March will have propelled Martin Luther Kings "Dream" that we shall overcome and America will become a true nation of equality for Native Americans, Black men and women, white men and women, Protestants, Catholics, Jews and Gentiles, Muslims and agnostics, atheists, handicaps, gays, straight, you name it. We will know this midcourse correction was designed to help America live out the true meaning of its creed, that all men (and women, people) are created equal. In the meantime, we must all work hard for harmony, equality, justice, peace, jobs, dignity, understanding, respect and an end to racism, discrimination and inequality and today's business as usual will be a thing of the past.

The almighty provided optimum weather, a dry, sunny atmosphere that was the first in a long train of success on this marvelous and memorable day. A number of speakers including **Dorothy Height** of the **National Council of Negro Women** and Kwesi Mfume, former chairman of the **National Association for the Advancement of Colored People** believed "racism, discrimination and anti-Semitism is wrong." Even further, he continued, "we understand that any bigotry is bad. We also understand that the time for action is now." Jesse Jackson, Benjamin Chavis, Russell Simmonds, Wycliff Jean, Viola Plummer of the **December-12 Movement**, Conrad Worrill, Erika Badu, Leonard Jeffries and his wife

FREDERICK MONDERSON

Roslyn, Ron Walters, the President of the Cuban Assembly, Jamaica's Prime Minister Patterson, congressional and religious representatives, women, Minister Louis Farrakhan's daughter, Amiri Baraka, and a whole lot of others too numerous to mention spoke at the podium. The Bush Administration was the chief villain for its policies based on arrogance, war mongering, insensitivity to Americas poor and minorities and in general poor leadership. Malik Zulu Shabazz of the **New Black Panther Party** charged Pres. Bush with several "Crimes" to which the crown responded "guilty as charged." Dr. Yosef Ben-Jochannan told the crowd, "look behind you" towards the **Washington Monument**. He said: "You built that," meaning your ancestors "built the obelisk" (a small pyramid on a high base), which the Washington Monuments represents.

Black History Everyday - Part One Photo. Ms. Hill. Secretary and Member of the Executive Committee of **CEMOTAP**.

BLACK HISTORY EVERYDAY
PART ONE

Rev. Al Sharpton, President of the **National Action Network** compared Dr. Kings 1963 march in which he made his "I have a dream" speech. Sharpton continued that: "What made the 1963 March is that we passed the 1964 Civil Rights Bill, and therefore, the success of this march will be that we take charge of our communities and make a difference in the next [2005, 2006] elections."

Dr. James McIntosh and Ms. Betty Dobson of **CEMOTAP**, Dr. Jack Felder and his son, Nova Felder, Dr. Blakely, Michael Hardy, Jitu Weusi and his wife Angela, Vincent Emanuel, Carlos Walton, and Kevin Mohammed were some of the people spotted at this event. Wycliff Jean had people singing on the lawn: "This is not a March; were building a movement. This is not a March; were building a movement."
[
Farrakhan was at his usual best, working the crowd, with a number of anecdotes, humorous, factual, on point. While the numbers probably did not equal the first Million Man March, they spoke for themselves. Nevertheless, with the same vibrancy, intensity, electricity in the air, seeking the same hope and promise, the unity and camaraderie, looking for leadership and guidance, the attendees this time were more diverse. Men, women, young people, children, whites, Asians, Native Americans, some say gays; all represented a beautiful mosaic of motivated individuals from all across America. They were just

FREDERICK MONDERSON

as peaceful, civil, cooperative, and respectful as ten years ago. Many people from different parts of the country vowed to return to their communities and to do good works. Many saw these marches as good outcomes for Blacks. Many who returned after the first march told of the changes they saw come about because of the intent, honesty and message of that historic time.

Black History Everyday – Part One Photo. "The Club of Mothers" whose sons were killed in senseless violence!

BLACK HISTORY EVERYDAY
PART ONE

Black History Everyday - Part One
Photo. Faces and signs in the crowd for the 50th Anniversary March on Washington.

FREDERICK MONDERSON

The closer to the Capital Building where the stage was located, security checkpoints greeted those who ventured this far. As this was a natural security precaution, most people remained on the lawn, sitting on folding chairs, on the grass, on cardboard boxes, milling around, taking pictures, buying buttons, T-shirts, CDs, and other souvenirs, making donations in containers passed around by FOI (Fruits of Islam) representatives, buying food, drink, water, ice-cream, etc. and viewing events and listening to the wide screens. There were lots of signs. One read: "Bush lied; people died."

A most beautiful and far reaching, yet fleeting moment was to see the Red, Black and Green, pasted against the Capital Building. Unthinkable, that the sons and daughters of former slave-forebears could gather in such numbers on the Capital grounds and to see the nationalist flag of Black America fly on the Capital Building shows how far we have arrived but only with the intent to challenge racism, discrimination, poverty, adversity, calamity, police brutality, joblessness, the behemoth of the Prison Industrial Complex and most important of all, the tremendous efforts of a well-organized and coordinated Movement whose success was very evident this day.

There was talk of forming a new political party, a coalition of Blacks, Latinos, and Native Americans to leverage power within both parties, to see which one will give more towards the cause of these constituencies. Fannie Lou Hamers name was

BLACK HISTORY EVERYDAY
PART ONE

invoked for her role in the Mississippi Democrats. In assisting, Farrakhan urged listeners to visit the **Millions More Movement** web site, register and make a $20.00 donation or how much you can give. In urging the participants to go home and do constructive things he said: "The measure of this day is not what we do today but the measure of this day will be determined by what we do tomorrow to create a movement, a real movement among our people."

Minister Louis Farrakhan spoke of a time during the Franklin D. Roosevelt Administration when Mrs. Roosevelt invited the great union organizer A. Philip Randolph to the White House. Mr. Randolph spoke at the dinner about discrimination, racism, black inequality in America, fear and intimidation, lack of jobs, education, health care, the whole litany of challenges facing African-Americans back then. The President listened intently then said: "I recognize what you say. I agree with what you say and the need for change." He sat quietly for a while, passed around cigars then said: "Now go and make me do it." Farrakhan then explained the body of government on whose steps he spoke was very lethargic about the general interests of minorities. They favored special interests and the rich and so have to be prodded through organized numbers empowering Black legislators who could build coalitions, block frivolous legislation from proceeding and move constructive legislation out of committee. That is why we must go home and organize our communities, register people to vote,

FREDERICK MONDERSON

fight drugs, illiteracy, ignorance, respect the elderly and even more, ourselves. We must recognize that "opposition is as necessary as the wind. Opposition tests our commitment and strength. We can prevail."

Saying that we cannot let another catastrophe as Katrina occur and not be prepared then what we say can only become flesh if we mobilize street, block, house and get lots of people on board. Saying that organizing is serious business, and that the rich hate anyone who can stimulate the poor, he gave another example of the rich and poor dichotomy. Quoting a biblical analogy using the body as an example he explained how the rich are few and the poor are many. With a head of gold, chest of silver, body of iron and feet of clay, the burden of support rests on the lower extremities while the substance of most value controls the vital regions. This explains how the rich exploits the poor and their antipathy towards anyone who points this out and mobilizes the poor.

Saying that there should be "regime change in Washington" he also indicated: "America is for sale; all she needs is to see more Benjamins" or $100 notes.

Speaking about Hurricane Katrina, the levees, reluctance to rebuild the 9th Ward (200 B for war in Iraq and not 14B for New Orleans) and further he spoke of a class action suit for those affected by Katrina. Today there are 75,000 foreign children as sex slaves in America and 2500 children missing in New Orleans. There is need for cooperation and

BLACK HISTORY EVERYDAY
PART ONE

coalition building with Native Americans, Black outreach to Africa and the Caribbean, need for a Caribbean Federation with Venezuela and Cuba, and to aid this he then proposed a 10-Point Plan saying the more organized we are the more demands we can make on this House. Organization begins at home! Here he spoke of POP. "Power of the People, Power of the Poor. We must demand and command what we want. We can demand that America do justice." By organizing, registering and voting this can be done.

Farrakhan then put the following questions to those in attendance, citing the need to create ministries that would cater to the needs of the people. He asked for:

1. A Ministry of Health and Human Services. Saying that leadership should build and not be master but servants. He wanted to be able to cater to the social and health needs of his constituency in America, that is Black, Brown, Native Americans and the poor. Here he mentioned Fidel Castro's offer of 700 doctors to assist Katrina health recovery and 500 scholarships to study medicine in Cuba that our government, proud, rejected.

2. A Ministry of Agriculture. Saying we must be able to grow what we need to eat and sell the surplus. He pointed out that pharmaceutical companies and other merchants of death who feed the American people, encourage genetic engineering of foods with chemicals and then turn around to develop medicines

FREDERICK MONDERSON

that would treat the diseases they engineered. The Native Americans who are considered a nation in this nation want to lease millions of acres for farming so we can control the foods we eat.

Black History Everyday - Part One Photo. Faces and signs in the crowd for the 50th Anniversary March on Washington.

BLACK HISTORY EVERYDAY
PART ONE

Black History Everyday - Part One Photo. Faces and signs in the crowd for the 50th Anniversary March on Washington.

FREDERICK MONDERSON

3. A Ministry of Education will unite to teach our children history, politics and philosophy so they would be better educated.

4. A Ministry of Defense. Our children are born soldiers but in the wrong war. They kill each other and should be taught to defend not destroy our community.

5. A Ministry of Art and Culture should have the responsibility of recording history and encouraging creativity.

6. The **Millions More Movement** should be involved in Africa and Caribbean trade. These countries will find it hard to exist into the future and hence the need to federate.

7. A Ministry of Justice is needed to solve our legal, social and police problems.

8. A Ministry of Information can create the proper trained reporters who will go and get the right news for us so we don't have to rely on United Press International, Reuters and the Associated Press.

9. There should be a Ministry of Science and Technology to keep abreast of fast changing developments in these fields.

BLACK HISTORY EVERYDAY
PART ONE

10. There should be a Ministry of Spiritual needs that combines Christianity, Islam and Judaism to cater to the religious needs of our people.

Black History Everyday - Part One Photo. We Shall Not be Moved March. Faces in the Crowd.

Finally, we must destroy the "Willie Lynch Syndrome" that has infected and destroyed as well as misdirected our people.

FREDERICK MONDERSON

Black History Everyday - Part One Photo. An important person, photographer, gets his groove on at **CEMOTAPs** 31st Celebration.

"The government which had made the Negro a citizen, found itself unable to protect him. It gave him the right to vote, but denied him the protection which should have maintained this right. Scourged from his home; hunted through the swamps; hung by midnight raiders, and openly murdered in the light of day, the Negro clung to his right of franchise with a heroism which would have wrung admiration from the hears of savages. He believed that in that small white ballot there was a subtle something which stood for manhood as well as citizenship, and thousands of brave black men went to their graves exemplifying the one by dying for the other." Ida B[ell] Wells-Barnett. *A Red Record.*

BLACK HISTORY EVERYDAY PART ONE

"Bullies are always cowards at heart and may be credited with a petty safe instinct in scenting their prey." Ana Julia Cooper. Voices from the South.

25. NO TO REPUBLICAN BULLYING
BY
DR. FRED MONDERSON

Everyone is familiar, from the inception of his Presidency, Republicans, not simply leaders but even obscure politicians and young upstarts have made a career, and however, short it has been, in defaming and bullying and disrespecting Mr. Obama. Some GOP lawmakers of whom you never heard because they have been irrelevant like Rep. King, not the New Yorker, who came out against President Obamas immigration stand and have and are now trying to impress the world with self-assumed political acumen, knowledge about current issues and electability. They wish to impress their fans how much they have "stood up" to President Obama. Perhaps it was Rick Santorum who in recent years, has coined the phrase, "Poison the well" and now Republicans are trying to pin this label on the President because he has issued an Executive Order on Immigration. Given "big money" problems, viz., health care insurance, immigration, bank collapse, auto industry woes, a lacerated economy bleeding untold jobs, Osama bin Laden running wild in addition to two concurrent wars, the nation's infrastructure in shambles and Republicans purposely incapacitated, then Barack Obama is forced to act decisively as he has done despite the "Party of No!" "Fighting him tooth and nail." Such behavior required bold action by the President on issues such as Immigration Reform as he has demonstrated through the issuance of Executive Action.

Some time ago, in frustrated exasperation from observing Republican treatment of the President, that famous New York Knickerbocker Spike Lee asked, "When will Mr. Obama take off the gloves?" In response to Republican behavior which tried to reduce Mr. Obama to as Denzel Washington said in the movie "Inside Man," where he was in an almost vulnerable position! The President consistently tried to work with Republicans whose mantra of "No" has earned them the deserved "Obstructionist" title.

Those two famed "One term" and "98 percent" lawmakers, Mr. McConnell and Boehner, were presumably numbered in that "Republican conspiratorial gathering" mentioned in *The New York Times* of October 6, 2013, and were also principals in the obstructionist movement which finally hoodwinked the American voting public such that the Republican right wing gained full control of Congress in the 2014 Mid-term Election. By completing the portrait caricature of Mr. Obama, as the earlier defamers Michele Bachmann, "Joe the Plumber, "You Lie Wilson," "Stupid Grassley, "Waterloo DeMint," and the many others intoxicated

BLACK HISTORY EVERYDAY
PART ONE

from drinking the toxic tea of racial fear and hatred including even "Palling around with terrorists," "Lipstick on a Pig" Sarah Palin, have tried unending to disparage President Obama. There is an old adage which holds that "Politicians are liars and cheats" who can be bought. They hypocritically "kiss babies then steal their lollipops." "Their goals in life are to get elected and then re-elected;" and they will say anything to further this aim. Let us not forget, it was Rick Santorum, a Republican, who said, "Anything gets said in a campaign." This Republicans do very well

Central to that hue and cry has been: Mr. Obama is an unpatriotic socialist, too Black, not a citizen, lying about his place of birth and to quote "Father Cruz," we should "send him back to Kenya!" As all of this unfolded, a "Light Colonel" in Republican leadership does not have the simple intelligence to realize and admit "Mr. Obama is a decent and knowledgeable, highly educated individual as well as the loving head of a family and full of empathy as a humanitarian," this is because they are too busy fighting him "tooth and nail." Using the threat of "being sued" and "impeached" they have played the stunt card. In fact, Mr. Obama is doing such an excellent job as Chief Executive, it is evident that he has rescued the nation from the economic quagmire ditch into which Republicans under George Bush, Dick Chaney, et al. drove the country. We must remain vigilant that history does not repeat itself in this behavior under this newest Republican Congressional leadership.

FREDERICK MONDERSON

Let's face it, it's stupid to assume that Mr. Obama, a highly intelligent Constitutional scholar, very well versed in the history of the office he now serves in and equally armed with a battalion of lawyers would propose illegal measures and or acts in an unlawful manner. He must certainly know how far his position allows him to act on behalf of the American people and those living within our nation's shores. If we care so much for one American being victimized abroad, can we care less for 50 million lacking health care protections and others who wallow in poverty? Are we so insensitive towards 5 million within our shores who generally do the low paying manual jobs which many Americans frown upon? Even much more important, functioning in an environment rife with racial prejudice and hatred, Mr. Obama certainly realizes as a Black man that he is and would be subjected to the most rigorous scrutiny and this would surely shape his behavior. As we await his biographical tell all book, one has to wonder how he will characterize the miscreant "B" and "C" political actors which he has encountered in recent years.

Most observers will admit, as Malcolm X reminded us: "History is a good teacher," and when later scholars scrutinize this "Obama Age" they will probably admit it was also an age of prejudiced and disrespectful "two-bit hustlers" and "chiselers," some not yet caught, but whose opportunistic intents didn't really consider the public good.

BLACK HISTORY EVERYDAY PART ONE

Black History Everyday - Part One Photo. We Shall Not be Moved March. Faces in the Crowd.

So, after "a long train of abuse" Mr. Obama "tightened his belt," donned his armament, expressed, "Damn the torpedoes, full speed ahead" and walked into the street on immigration reform. Calling out Republicans to "Pass a Bill!"

Black History Everyday - Part One Photo. Faces and signs in the crowd for the 50th Anniversary March on Washington.

FREDERICK MONDERSON

Black History Everyday - Part One
Photo. Faces and signs in the crowd for the 50th Anniversary March on Washington.

Perhaps some Baptist preacher can ask incoming Senate Majority Leader Mitch McConnell and Speaker John Boehner, "What is the value to a man if he gains the world but loses his soul?" Then again, there's only one truly "Soul" Brother in American leadership. This is Barack Hussein Obama, 44th President of the United States of America.

BLACK HISTORY EVERYDAY
PART ONE

"I am the son of a black man from Kenya and a white woman from Kansas. I was raised with the help of a white grandfather who survived a Depression to serve in Patton's Army during World War II and a white grandmother who worked on a bomber assembly line at Fort Leavenworth while he was overseas. Ive gone to some of the best schools in America and lived in one of the world's poorest nations. I am married to a black American who carries within her the blood of slaves and slave-owners – an inheritance we pass on to our two precious daughters. I have brothers, sisters, nieces, nephews, uncles and cousins, of every race and every hue, scattered across three continents, and for as long as I live, I will never forget that in no other country on Earth is my story even possible."

26. "OBAMA: A BAD YEAR NO!"
BY
DR. FRED MONDERSON

In *The Washington Post* of Sunday December 14, 2014, Chris Cillizza writer on "The Worse Week in Washington" wrote: "Congrats: President Obama, you had the worst year in Washington, again." Arguably this is another "hatchet job" on a good and decent leader swimming in a sea alongside gators, barracudas, and piranhas that see only his color, emphasize his failures not his brilliance and refuse to accentuate his accomplishments. Like so many others who see his glass half empty, in contradiction, many see his glass three quarters full, at least.

FREDERICK MONDERSON

In his beginning, this "hatcheteer" stated: "The year began with Obama issuing a set of reforms for the National Security Agency, a result of on-going National Security leaks and ended with mid-term elections that saw his party lose its majority because of the Presidents unpopularity. In between were continuing challenges to the **Affordable Care Act**, Americas re-entry into Iraq - a war the President had vowed to exit - and memoirs from former Cabinet officials questioning Obamas decision-making and judgment." This and much more was stated.

Who could forget the famous **Time Magazine** cover that "embellished O.J. Simpsons blackness?" In the same way, Mr. Bingo, the Illustrator for **The Washington Post** emphasized Mr. Obamas color" and traditionally this has been to cast such subjects in a bad light. Why did the artist waiting on No. 45 shout "Bingo" not color the "White guy" Dan Snyder - "Really Bad Year; the Secret Service men - "Bad Year;" and "Not so good year" Chris Christie! Governor Christie "lightened his load" by throwing his men under the bus, for after all, "The Buck Stops" with him who is responsible for the wrong-doing, notwithstanding!

Naturally, on the next page, both writer and illustrator cast Mitch McConnell as having the "best year." It is said, for McConnell, it was the realization of a life-long dream, a not-insignificant accomplishment for a

BLACK HISTORY EVERYDAY
PART ONE

man who has been around politics since the 1960s; that is half a century. "McConnell, like Harry Reid whom he will replace in the Senate's top job is not a flashy politician who surged through the ranks in record time. He is a plotter and strategist of the highest order, a man who always has a plan and executes is relentlessly."

The "founding fathers" were called "freedom fighters" but today such persons are called "terrorists." Sure Mr. McConnell is not flashy. He did, however, flask that "Thumbs Up" signal to cohorts watching his Code Expression: "I got that Nigger in the White House!" That he is a plotter is no doubt! Too bad *The Washington Post* people don't read *The New York Times*, in particular its article in October 6, 2013, depicting the treasonous or seditious plot by which high ranking Republican operatives and their backers tasked to derail Mr. Obamas Presidency. Nearly 20 NGOs were named as being funded, their operatives trained and deployed to "educate" the public about the evils of Obamacare! Former Attorney General Ed Meese under Ronald Reagan was named as a principal actor in the treasonous plot against the duly elected government of the United States of America under the leadership of President Barrack Hussein Obama, a Black man! As such, every Legislative or Executive initiative by Mr. Obama was scrutinized by Republicans to determine its legality. Edmund Burke admonished, "The only thing necessary for evil to triumph is for good to do or say nothing." Were there no good

FREDERICK MONDERSON

Republican men or women when all this transpired emboldened "B and C Actors" took it upon themselves to pile on the disrespect and generate racial hatred towards Mr. Obama.

An article on former Senator John Thompson was entitled as "When Politics Meets Art and Art Meets Politics." Consider this scenario! Given some ingredients, much remains "secret" or hidden, we must conjure the outcome.

Black History Everyday - Part One Photo. We Shall Not be Moved March. Faces in the Crowd.

Mitch McConnell "has been around politics since the 1960s." Who can count the deals he made, the toes he stepped on in his climb to accomplish his "lifelong dream of becoming Senate Majority Leader?" Did he ever entertain the thought of becoming President?

BLACK HISTORY EVERYDAY
PART ONE

Traveling on the same train he very well could have been a protégé of Ed Meese in his striking days. Now, along comes Barrack Obama, an upstart African-American who "Surged through the ranks in record time." This is troubling to Ed Meese and his knights at table charged with stopping Obama, resulting in undermining the Presidency, the well-being of the nation, and the welfare of the American people be damned! "Stop Obama by any means necessary!" Remember the sickening expression of the Naval Commander in that movie with Cuba Gooding and Robert De Nero, as he looked down on the Black naval recruit Bashir.

Possessing seniority in the Club, steeped in intimate knowledge of the workings of politics in Washington, Ed Meese recruited his combatants from the active field of powerful Republican operatives. From his office of high visibility as Senate Minority Leader, nearly 50-years in politics perhaps obligated to Ed Meese for chaperoning him along the way, Mitch McConnell was probably the first chosen for this first salvo of the character assassination of the President of the United States because of the color of his skin. Throw in "Waterloo" DeMint; "Stupid" Grassley; add "You lie" Wilson; poor Michael Steele; block Allen West from the inner portals; while were not sure about John McCain, let the uncontrolled, limelight seeking Sarah Palin earn her stripes, and don't trust "God told me to run" Michele Bachmann because "our actions may not set well with her, boss, the divine!"

FREDERICK MONDERSON

Given McConnell "failed in his famous goal to make Obama a one-term President" the operation evidently began after the 2008 election and by the January 2009 Inauguration though revealed in 2013 after the 2012 election. Equally, and given Mr. McConnell "is a plotter and strategist of the highest order, a man who always has a plan and executes it relentlessly," a failure in his primary goal does not preclude a secondary objective. Hence, Mr. McConnells "Party of No" well-choreographed track record of obstruction and blaming the other guy is finally rewarded by a hood-winked American public, aided by some failures on Mr. Obamas part, unrelenting "legislative Lilliputians trying to tie Gulliver" and the confessions of "insider foxes" who cry "sour grapes."

After Dr. Murray was released from prison, having served time as a responsible party in the death of Michael Jackson, he began making statements about his closeness with the singer even mentioning his "fixing Michaels Caterer." That astute comic and radio and TV host, Steve Harvey who conceptualizes so readily and well, responded, "Hell, he is shopping for a book deal!" Panetta and Gates certainly shopped for book deals. In all likelihood financial gain was their primary objective for they perhaps never donated the proceeds to favorite charities. But, more important, they were not courageous enough to "fall upon their swords."

One of Obamas problems was choosing "kiss and tell" guys like Panetta and Gates whose

BLACK HISTORY EVERYDAY
PART ONE

autobiographies were nothing more than insider gossip. So much so, "By the next morning, Republicans were using those lines in TV Ads bashing Democrats as Obama clones." So, what's new about Hillary? She started the route down the dusty trail and naturally could have refused the Secretary of State position that gave her the foreign policy credentials to be considered a credible 2016 candidate. Of the three "revealers," she is the only one as a potential candidate and for African-Americans who love this President, the jury is still out! Across the board, many should pay attention to a Biblical expression, "Where were you when they crucified my Lord?"

Black History Everyday - Part One Photo. Faces and signs in the crowd for the 50th Anniversary March on Washington.

FREDERICK MONDERSON

Black History Everyday - Part One

Photo. Faces and signs in the crowd for the 50th Anniversary March on Washington.

Notwithstanding, "Sizzling: Chris Cillizza," continued to bash Mr. Obama expressing, "The revelation that the IRS was targeting Tea Party groups for special scrutiny; the Edward Snowden leaks about NSA surveillance and the botched rollout of Healthcare.gov to name three that happened in 2013." Equally, "Obamas longtime pledge to reset relations with Russia was exposed as frighteningly naïve when President Vladimir Putin moved into Eastern Ukraine with impunity. Obamas response to Putin's aggression - Sanctions - was derided as using a spray bottle to put out a five-alarm fire."

Even further, the "Dumb War in Iraq," the Rise of ISIL, the two turncoats and finally Mr. Obamas confession: "I am not on the Ballot. These policies are on the Ballot. Every single one of them!" Finally, that famous Faulkner's line, "The past is never dead. It is not even past" the author uses to characterize Mr.

BLACK HISTORY EVERYDAY
PART ONE

Obamas political fortunes in 2014, the Past keeps Complicating his Present - and Clouding his Future."

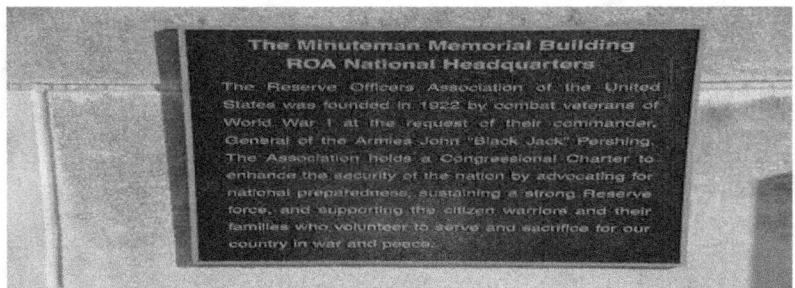

Black History Everyday - Part One Photo. We Shall Not be Moved March. Faces in the Crowd.

Separate rules are constructed for Mr. Obama! Mitch McConnells racist statements in the past has not complicated his present nor clouded his future. Kentuckians voted for the bacon Mr. McConnell could bring home as Senate Majority Leader as opposed to his fresh opponent.

Sure "Uneasy lies the head that wears the crown," but Obamas second, actually his first, jeopardy is his color. Sure, there is political opposition but political opposition worse than the Ferguson Police initial full-court press response to demonstrators is a low for this country that boasts of being at the apex of the political food chain. Something stinks below.

Perhaps if the articles author had not ended the year before December 15, he would have realized some of

FREDERICK MONDERSON

the myriad accomplishments of Mr. Obama merit a more positive critique. After all, he gave McConnell nearly 50 years to climb the hill that "Poor boy Obama" did in 4 and then again!

By the actual Calendar years end, the economy is better than good. Unemployment is down 26 percent with some 10,000,000 private sector jobs added even though Republicans refused to pass Mr. Obamas jobs bill. Somewhere in America gas prices may be lower than two dollars and Wall Street is booming with the DOW nearing 18,000, a height never before reached. That Putin fellow, well he is suffering from Obamas sanctions imposed after the invasion. Boastful as Iran's façade is, it too is hurting from sanctions. Obamas incrementalism has worked. The Presidential historian Doug Brinkley characterized President Obama as one who "doesn't over-react."

A consensus now is that Obamas new book on The White House Years, will perhaps be **Wisdom from My Father** warning to beware of snakes in the grass, or don't trust Washington shadows after noon, or is it 9:00 AM. Still, Mr. Obama is too decent a fellow to wallow in the mud. His opponents have already shown their shallowness.

History must judge Mr. Obama favorably for his climate agreement with China; his new Immigration initiative; and the vision to see and courage to chart a new course in Cuba. This particular act, futuristic in its intent like so many Obama initiatives will realign relations in the American and Western hemisphere. It

BLACK HISTORY EVERYDAY
PART ONE

has been described by the White House Correspondent Jim Acosta as "A major, major step forward." It's a pity the "Sizzle" missed the boat, I mean, did not get that e-mail.

Black History Everyday - Part One Photo. Queen-Mother Nana Camille Yarbrough and a stately gentleman at **CEMOTAP**.

FREDERICK MONDERSON

Black History Everyday - Part One Photo. Congresswoman Yvette Clarke (second from left) joins Yusuf Salaam, one of the "Central Park Five" now **Exonerated**, Gary Byrd and Milton Allimadi, Publisher of **Black Star News** with two other beautiful ladies.

"But the truth is, that isn't all that I know of the man. The man I met more than twenty years ago is a man who helped introduce me to my Christian faith, a man who spoke to me about our obligations to love one another; to care for the sick and lift up the poor. He is a man who served his country as a U.S. Marine; who has studied and lectured at some of the finest universities and seminaries in the country, and who for over thirty years led a church that serves the community by doing God's work here on Earth – by housing the homeless, ministering to the needy, providing day care services and scholarships and prison ministries, and reaching out to those suffering from HIV/AIDS."

BLACK HISTORY EVERYDAY
PART ONE
27. OBAMA AND EXECUTIVE ORDER
BY
DR. FRED MONDERSON

When President Obama issued his Executive Order regarding the immigration status of young immigrants brought to this country illegally by their parents, this act engendered great enmity by Republicans who never liked him to begin with and have vacillated on immigration reform though several influential Republican favor some form of comprehensive legislation. Mrs. Clinton once said, "If President Obama walked on water," former U.S. Ambassador to the U.N. under President Bush, "Bolton would say it's because he could not swim!" To examine this statement further reveals a lot about Mr. Obamas opponents. To "walk on water" is an extraordinary feat. Only one man in history has been able to execute this phenomenon, and he had divine connection. For Mr. Obama to accomplish the necessary far reaching legislation means he is exceptional versed on the issues, possibly possessing, at least, a tincture of divine essence. Given the above, his actions, activities, accomplishments must be of a higher standard; yet, in every iota it never matches up to Republican expectations. Whether this is purposeful or not, Republican behavior is a demonstrated fact! Even the killing of Osama bin Laden and dismantling of his terror network could

FREDERICK MONDERSON

not garner much praise from Republicans who only blinked momentarily then closed their eyes. The "blink" was necessary otherwise people would really see Republicans for the real hypocrites they truly are.

Now, that there was precedence in the issuing of an Executive Order and that this was Mr. Obamas first did not matter! Recently, some "What's his face" lawmaker said Mr. Obama was "stupid!" Imagine! A Doctor of Law, Constitutional scholar, graduate from two of the nation's finest Ivy League Universities, Columbia and Harvard, President of the Harvard Law Review and an individual possessing all the temerity and wherewithal to campaign successfully to become President of the United States, twice accomplish legislative and policy gains as he has, is "stupid." Equally, that he is a "tyrant" for leading not following seems more reflective of the person making the statement, for only a stupid individual could see such as he gazes in the mirror.

Black History Everyday - Part One Photo. We Shall Not be Moved March.
Faces in the Crowd.

BLACK HISTORY EVERYDAY
PART ONE

Nevertheless, this ad hominem claim is in keeping with Republican pernicious "bloopers." Remember "You lie" Wilson; "Waterloo" and "faulty numbers" DeMint; "the President should be ashamed of himself" Congressman; and the McConnell Mantra, "I intend to make Barack Obama a one-term President!" What Republicans need to do is borrow the Hubble Telescope to see they are dealing with a very intelligent, astute, strategically savvy-minded individual not only at the pinnacle of power but at the top of his game!

Much has been said about President Lincoln and the issue of slavery and Secession but at a time when the nations fabric was torn asunder, Mr. Lincoln issued the Emancipation Proclamation which was itself an Executive Order. His Order insisting Confederates should be tried in federal courts that was eventually overturned, constitute actions of a leader not afraid to take action in face of legislative sloth and inaction. Nevertheless, this latter act was overturned by the Courts. Faced with the calamity of the Great Depression and stymied by the "9 old men," President Franklin D. Roosevelt issued Executive Orders to inaugurate many programs to get the nation moving forward. In modern times, Presidents Nixon, Reagan, Clinton and George W. Bush issued Executive Orders. Some issued multiple such orders, especially Ronald Reagan, Republican darling and King of Executive Orders. Nevertheless, that this was

FREDERICK MONDERSON

Mr. Obamas first and few other Executive Orders and in keeping with the "Party of No" objection to the Presidents every action, Republican opposition to the order granting reprieve to immigrants who fit the discussed category, is not surprising. However, an explanation of what constitutes an Executive Order is in order.

Black History Everyday - Part One Photo. Faces and signs in the crowd for the 50th Anniversary March on Washington.

Black History Everyday – Part One Photo. The Audience at **CEMOTAP** on "King and Malcolm" influence forum.

BLACK HISTORY EVERYDAY
PART ONE

Black History Everyday - Part One Photo. Faces and signs in the crowd for the 50th Anniversary March on Washington.

In *The American Political Dictionary* Jack Plano and Milton Greenberg (8th Edition, 1989: 169) define an Executive Order as, "A rule or regulation, issued by the President, a governor, or some administrative authority, that has the effect of law. Executive orders are used to implement and give administrative effect to provisions of the Constitution, to treaties, and to statutes. They may be used to create or modify the organization or procedures of administrative agencies or may have general applicability as law. Under the National Administrative Procedure Act of 1946, all executive orders must be published in the Federal Register." They further state its significance (1989: 169) as, "The use of executive orders has greatly increased in recent years as a result of the growing tendency of legislative bodies to leave many legislative details to be filled in by the executive branch. The Presidents power to issue executive orders stems from precedents, custom, and constitutional interpretation, as well from discretionary powers given to the President by Congress when enacting legislation. This trend will likely continue as government involves itself further with higher complex and technical matters."

On Jack Caffery's CNN program, in answer to a question some two years ago, someone noted, "The 2012 election began on November 4th, 2008." Thus, given the methodology of Republican strategy towards Mr. Obamas administration, the "McConnell Mandate" and "lone wolf" legislators attacks on the very being of the president and Presidency; these people cannot yet comprehend the superior nature of the mind they are in contention with which stays ahead and continues to befuddle their pack. For example, for some three and a half years Mr. Obama has tried to govern effectively in the interest of the American people, reached out to create bipartisanship legislation but to no avail because of a predetermined treasonous plot to sabotage his administrative agenda. Yet, he was still able to accomplish significant legislative successes in the interest of the American people. Many of his followers wondered, after the manner Republicans treated Mr. Obama, in Spike Lee's words, "When is he going to take off the gloves?" Now, as Republicans boasted of the one billion dollars, they will raise to defeat Mr. Obama, the President finally

BLACK HISTORY EVERYDAY PART ONE

began to deploy his strategy, emphasize the power of incumbency and building coalitions among significant voting blocks, viz., women, gays, immigrants, Hispanics, labor, etc. In response to such actions, Republicans have accused him of playing "dirty pool!" Well, a close look under Republican fingernails will reveal the pool chalk accumulated over their years of "dirty pool!"

Black History Everyday - Part One Photo. We Shall Not be Moved March. Faces in the Crowd.

To recall, after the "Debt Ceiling" debacle, Senator Mitch McConnell was shown smiling giving his now famous "I got that Nigger" thumbs up; Speaker John Boehner refused to return Mr. Obamas phone calls but met with the Press and later, smoking, boasted "We got 98 percent of what we wanted." Nonetheless, people wondered, why is the President allowing "minions to think they're whales!" Then a *New York Post* political cartoon featured President

FREDERICK MONDERSON

Obama looking through the White House window as the New York Yankees relief pitcher Rivera approached asking himself, "I wonder why he sent for me!" Thereafter, "Gentleman Jim" Obama invited "Smoking Boehner" to a game of golf. As these gentlemen teed off in their golfing shorts, the President looked at the Speaker and thought, "Don't worry, Ive got something for you, Mr. Speaker!"

After the Osama bin Laden compound raid by Seal Team Six, *The Post* again featured a political cartoon showing Mr. Obama instructing the team, "The next compound you raid will be Trump Towers!" After the "Gang" of Karl Rove, the Koch Brothers, the TD bank official and other Super PACs boasted, "We will raise one billion dollars to defeat Obama" the President said, "Oh yes, well employers must pay for Women's Contraceptives." From the "Bully Pulpit" he preached, "Gays should be allowed to marry to protect the rights of such people in long term relationships," that the **NAACP** termed "a Civil Rights Issue." As Chief Executive, he challenged the Supreme Justices to rule on his challenge to the many features of Arizona's immigration law and his own Health Care Reform measure. To protect his Attorney General Eric Holder from a Republican "witch hunt" over "Fast and Furious" the President exerted "Executive Privilege" that Plano and Greenberg (1989: 169) defined as, "The right of executive officials to refuse to appear before or to withhold information from a legislative community or a court. Executive Privilege is enjoyed by the President and those executive officials accorded the right by the

BLACK HISTORY EVERYDAY
PART ONE

President. No legal means by which executive privilege could be denied to executive officials existed for many years, but in 1974 the Supreme Court established a landmark precedent (*United States v. Nixon*, 418) U.S. 683 [1974] by unanimously ordering President Richard M. Nixon to release recorded tape with allegedly criminal information on them that eventually led to his resignation." The significance of this action is explained further by Plano and Greenberg (1989: 169), where "Executive privilege in the American system is claimed as an inherent executive power under the constitutional separation of powers and on time-honored tradition. Although the right of the President to refuse to appear before congressional committees is generally unchallenged, the issue remains as to whether his major advisers should enjoy the same privilege. The right of Congress to obtain information for the lawmaking process and to investigate for possible impeachment actions, and the right of the courts to hear and decide cases involving executive officials, clash with the Presidents right to function as the head of a coordinate branch of the national government. Critics charge that executive privilege is often invoked to deny the American people information critical of executive policies."

Ronald Reagan had said of Walter Mondale, "I will not, for political purposes, exploit my opponents youthful age and inexperience." Now, in the 2012 political climate, as the Junior Senator from Florida, Marco Rubio, became intoxicated with hearing his

FREDERICK MONDERSON

name mentioned as a possible Romney Vice-President nominee, he started "pussyfooting" over an immigration bill Romney had decried in his "immigrants should self-deport," insult during the Primaries. The President, as Commander-In-Chief, soared like the American Eagle, legal and otherwise; fired on the "Rebels Camp" by issuing his new Immigration Executive Order, forcing Senator Rubio to abandon his idea. Mr. Romney argued Congress should offer a permanent solution but given his past stance and the House objection to Mr. Obama this was not to happen. Thus, Mr. Obamas discretion in issuing an Executive Order ahead of Republican stall, at least this decision temporarily eased the agony of the young immigrants.

Black History Everyday - Part One Photo. Dr. Molefi Asante waiting on deck to make his enlightening presentation entitled, "Embracing and Celebrating Who We Are" at **CEMOTAPS** 31ST Anniversary celebration."

BLACK HISTORY EVERYDAY
PART ONE

Instantly in their confused state of shock, Republicans cried "foul," the President is "playing dirty pool!" Imagine, after their nearly four years of unrelenting assaults on every legislative initiative, attacks on his integrity, leadership and judgment, these people forget they're dealing with the most powerful man in the world, the President of the United States and leader of the Western Alliance. Somehow Mr. Obama seemed to remind his opponents, "The circus may be in town, but I'm actually the ringmaster of Washington, DC."

Black History Everyday - Part One Photo. Faces and signs in the crowd for the 50th Anniversary March on Washington.

FREDERICK MONDERSON

**Black History Everyday - Part One
Photo**. Faces and signs in the crowd for the 50th Anniversary March on Washington.

All this notwithstanding, Ralph C. Chandler and Jack C. Plano in **The Public Administration Dictionary** (1982: 249-50) provide insights into the history of the Executive Order and its historic use that states: "The earliest executive orders were neither numbered nor issued in any standard format, and there was no requirement for official notices or publication. As the mechanism became more formalized, however, a chronological numbering system came into use in 1907, and all earlier orders were assigned numbers. The Federal Register Act of 1935 required all executive orders of general interest to be published in the Federal Register, with a later act requiring publication of all executive orders. Executive Order Number 1 was issued by President Abraham Lincoln in 1862. It concerned the establishment of military courts in Louisiana. Since that time, executive orders have been used in a wide range of policy areas, depending on the president's personal values and his perception of his constitutional responsibilities."

BLACK HISTORY EVERYDAY
PART ONE

Even further, the authors explained, "Beginning in the 1960s, executive orders were used more and more in controversial social and political policy areas. They were frequently issued as a result of recommendations made by task forces and special committees, which were first introduced by the Kennedy administration as new policy-making groups. Once a president has decided to make an authoritative policy statement, there are a number of factors involved in the decision to use an executive order, as opposed to some other means of proclamation. First, there must be a strong public demand for solution to a given problem. For example, **Executive Order** Number 11491 was issued in 1969 by President Richard M. Nixon in response to growing federal employee discontent over the limited provisions for public sector labor relations contained in **Executive Order** Number 10988, which had been issued in 1962. Second, the president must consider whether there will be funding for, and enforcement of, the directive. Both factors are crucial to the success of an executive order. Third, the president must consider whether Congress or the courts will effectively address the policy needs he has in mind. If they will act, perhaps he does not need to act. Neither Congress nor the courts seemed inclined to deal with discrimination in public housing in the early 1960s. **Executive Order** Number 11063 was therefore issued by President John F. Kennedy in 1962, setting the official national policy of nondiscrimination in federally assisted housing.

FREDERICK MONDERSON

Executive orders are subordinate to statuary law, to decisional law by the Supreme Court, and even to the legislative intent of Congress. An executive order can be declared invalid by the courts if it conflicts with any of these laws of higher authority."

To this the authors add (1982: 250-510) the significance of the measure, "The executive order is an important policy-making tool which is more flexible and adaptive than statuary law. It allows an opportunity to experiment with programs at the federal level without full-scale congressional involvement. The availability of the executive order serves a safety-valve function as part of the overall system of checks and balances. If a critical issue gets bogged down in Congress, the executive order is a mechanism available to fill a policy void until a statuary decision can be made. Some critics object to a President's use of the executive order, considering it a usurpation of legislative power."

Now, after Mr. Romney told the President to "start packing" and the Republican camp began writing his **Obituary**, in response Mr. Obama began flexing his muscle of incumbency, and like John Paul Jones reminded everyone, "Surrender, I have not yet begun to fight for the interest of all the American people. In my considered vision for this great nation and that of my children and grand-children will have a better and brighter future resulting from the environmental, educational, immigration, clean-energy and humanitarian policies he enacted. "I have to, I will bring Congress along, reluctantly or otherwise, into a

BLACK HISTORY EVERYDAY
PART ONE

clearer understanding of our combined responsibilities to all the American people because our system is of the people, by the people and for the people that is the one hundred percent not just the one percent."

After 6 years of Republican obduracy, two years of "Tea Party" influence in the House, untold challenges to Mr. Obamas legislative agenda, he has nevertheless moved the nation forward.

As things stand today, and in as much as congress has failed to provide Health Care coverage to some 50 million Americans; Congress has stalled on filling administrative leadership positions; sheriffs and other state leaders have targeted immigrants; there are un-ending challenges to the sanctity of the vote, etc., Mr. Obama as Chief Executive and leader of the American people, will go ahead and issue Executive Orders to serve the best interest of the nation. This he has promised; the opposition be damned!

Black History Everyday - Part One Photo. We Shall Not be Moved March. Faces in the Crowd.

FREDERICK MONDERSON

"Understanding this reality requires a reminder of how we arrived at this point. As William Faulkner once wrote, "The past isn't dead and buried. In fact, it isn't even past." We do not need to recite here the history of racial injustice in this country. But we do need to remind ourselves that so many of the disparities that exist in the African-American community today can be directly traced to inequalities passed on from an earlier generation that suffered under the brutal legacy of slavery and Jim Crow." Barack Obama. *Speech on Race.*

"People began to shout, to rise from their seats and clap and cry out, a forceful wind carrying the reverends voice up into the rafters…. And in that single note – hope! – I heard something else; at the foot of that cross, inside the thousands of churches across the city, I imagined the stories of ordinary black people merging with the stories of David and Goliath, Moses and Pharaoh, the Christians in the lion's den, Ezekiel's field of dry bones. Those stories – of survival, and freedom, and hope – became our story, my story; the blood that had spilled was our blood, the tears our tears; until this black church, on this bright day, seemed once more a vessel carrying the story of a people into future generations and into a larger world. Our trials and triumphs became at once unique and universal, black and more than black; in chronicling our journey, the stories and songs gave us a means to reclaim memories that we didn't need to feel shame about … memories that all people might study and cherish – and with which we

BLACK HISTORY EVERYDAY
PART ONE

could start to rebuild." Barack Obama. *Speech on Race*."

Black History Everyday - Part One Photo. Faces and signs in the crowd for the 50th Anniversary March on Washington.

Black History Everyday - Part One Photo. Faces and signs in the crowd for the 50th Anniversary March on Washington.

28. OBAMA AND LEADERSHIP
BY
DR. FRED MONDERSON

Of all-American presidents demonstrating outstanding leadership during challenging times, perhaps none has faced more difficulties than Barack Obama. Granted each President faced, for example, George Washington and foundation of the nation; Thomas Jefferson and the **Louisiana Purchase** and Barbary Pirates; James Monroe and his **Doctrine**; Abraham Lincoln and **Secession** and Civil War; Franklin D. Roosevelt and the **New Deal** leading up to World War II; Dwight Eisenhower and the **Korean War**; Ronald Reagan and the **Cold War**; and George W. Bush stung by September 11, 2001; but none, in time perspective, has faced the challenges meted out to President Obama. Thus, contrary to misguided belief fed by insidious propaganda, Mr. Obama had demonstrated exemplary leadership. Nevertheless, perhaps the doubting Thomases or Republicans need a Hubble Telescopic vision to see, understand and appreciate his accomplishments and this is what makes his tenure as the 44th President so exceptional.

George Washington and the founding fathers, in establishing the new nation and institutions, the parameters of its survival and sustainability viz., the constitution endowing institutions and a variety of

BLACK HISTORY EVERYDAY
PART ONE

powers to make the system work was indeed a formidable challenge. Yet, with the exception of a few Tory loyalists, everyone was rooting for the success of the President and his men to make the new nation a success. Upon realization that Jeffersons Louisiana Purchase not simply tremendously expanded the physical borders of the nation with the promise of the potential for great economic prosperity in both free and slave sections of the economy, many of the vast majority of movers and shakers lauded and aspiring property owners, hailed Mr. Jefferson for the nations extraordinary good fortune now that the **Haitian Revolution** under Toussaint L'Ouverture had forced Napoleon to bequeath that great largess to America for some $15 million, less than the price of some New York City apartments these days. Thus, Jeffersons work in writing the **Declaration of Independence** and launching the new nation, together with the **Louisiana Purchase** endeared the nation to support his presidency especially in his challenge to the Barbary Pirates.

FREDERICK MONDERSON

Black History Everyday - Part One Photo. The ever-vigilant, ever-creative, Dr. James McIntosh, Co-Chair of **CEMOTAP**.

Following cessation of hostilities in Europe ending the aftermath of the **French Revolution** and **Napoleonic Wars**; and in America, the War of 1812, the **Second War for Independence** against Britain that ended in 181; James Monroe faced the horde of European imperialists seeking to regain their New World recolonization. Again, this bold move that created a lucrative economic market for the US in Latin America was hailed as a great leadership strategy especially since it was backed by the power of the British naval might.

With a nation divided culturally, economically and politically, beating the potential drums of war, secession and actual war, the loyalists supported Mr. Lincoln and hailed his leadership at a time of great

BLACK HISTORY EVERYDAY
PART ONE

distress for the nation. Winning the day, or war, outlining a plan to bind the wounds of war and heal the nation then deploy a plan towards a path of economic development through **Reconstruction**, Mr. Lincoln was seen as a genius. Losing his life as he did, his greatness was amplified.

Black History Everyday - Part One Photo. We Shall Not be Moved March. Faces in the Crowd.

Franklin D. Roosevelt was elected in 1932 on a "New Deal" promise as the nation swelted under the trials and tribulations of the **Great Depression**. In a "damn the torpedoes, full speed ahead" attitude, Mr. Roosevelt challenged the nation from "Captain to Cook," to rescue his beloved land initiating untold numbers of programs, in a "If one does not a work,

FREDERICK MONDERSON

try another" mindset as frame of reference. Ahead of his time in recognizing the aspirations of all Americans, viz., labor, immigrants, power companies, blacks, women, FDR pressed ahead with his alphabet programs until finally challenged by the "9 old men" of the Supreme Court. Men of vision and tenacity are seldom stopped in their tracks but they either walk around or through obstacles. In time, even the Supreme Court came around and with lots of help from being drawn into World War II, Mr. Roosevelts p9olicies pulled the nation out of the Depression placing it on a path of economic prosperity with untold economic and other safeguards in place.

The size of the Roosevelt Memorial in Washington, DC is indicative of the expansiveness of the man's thinking and actions wherein all people lent their shoulders to his wheel as he rescued his nation from the clutches of its most catastrophic challenge initiated in the Great Depression. His vision and leadership set the stage for unparalleled transformation of the nation. It is no wonder Presidents Lincoln and Roosevelt proved to be Mr. Obamas greatest role models.

Dwight Eisenhower, a general in World War II became President from 1952-1960 and had to contend with the Korean War and also the communist threat leading to the Cold War. He was well liked and Americans rallied to his efforts to readjust in wake of the realistic dynamics of the post-World War II and Korean conflicts.

BLACK HISTORY EVERYDAY
PART ONE

Black History Everyday - Part One

Photo. Faces and signs in the crowd for the 50th Anniversary March on Washington.

Black History Everyday - Part One

Photo. Faces and signs in the crowd for the 50th Anniversary March on Washington.

FREDERICK MONDERSON

President John Kennedy came and left early but he transformed the Office of the Presidency and the nation and its image on the world stage. In meeting Khrushchev's challenge in the **Cuban Missile Crisis**, not only did President Kennedy diffuse the potential consequences of a nuclear conflict but he exemplified American resolve when all the marbles were at stake. This martyr's death emboldened his successor Lyndon Johnson to masterfully bring into legal fruition Mr. Kennedys "**Great Society's**" vision. This work in progress, prodded by challenges of the Civil Rights Movement and the emergence of African nations as players on the world stage at the United Nations, resulted in the 1964 Civil Rights Act and the 1965 **Voting Rights Act** that changed the nation in the most unimaginable manner.

Though he denied being "a crook," Richard Nixon created foreign policy masterpieces in establishing détente with China and Russia that were significant first steps in Ronald Reagans path to glory in confronting the Berlin Walls divide. Nevertheless, Ronald Reagan the actor and governor of California certainly endeared himself in the minds and hearts of the American people though a career that spanned several decades. As President, this "public capital" proved favorable in acceptance of his social and economic policies and his military build-up that resulted in collapse of the Soviet Union as they tried to match his level of military preparedness. So much so, no modern President received as enormous

BLACK HISTORY EVERYDAY
PART ONE

posthumous recognition as Ronald Reagan in his extensive funeral and in numerous naming of airports and public buildings in his honor. His 11th Commandment, "Thou shall not criticize a fellow Republican," became enshrined in American and Republican political lore and his aura continues to radiate from the shrine of his memory as Republican "wanna-bes" seek to exploit mileage of his blessings through association with Mrs. Nancy Reagan, identification with the Reagan Library or curry-favoring to Reagans lieutenants and even exploiting the notion through "I was in the room with Ronald Reagan" saying.

Black History Everyday - Part One Photo. We Shall Not be Moved March.
Faces in the Crowd.

FREDERICK MONDERSON

Pulling all the strings that got him into the White House, George Washington Bush lulled the nation into a false sense of security that Al Qaeda exploited in effectuating their 9/11 plan of an unprecedented attack on the homeland that killed thousands. It was foolish that conspiracy theorists blamed Mr. Bush for concocting the attack. Notwithstanding, he cherished his respect for history given his being named after the first George Washington and his oath to uphold the office. Sure, he made some faulty decisions and as a human being this is understandable, owing to poor advice and faulty intelligence. Some have argued Sadam Hussein's attempt on the life of the Senior Bush prompted George to invade Iraq after the Afghanistan "Shock and Awe" blitz. Nevertheless, the reality of two wars, especially the "go it alone Iraq escapade" the Bush Tax Cuts for his "base," a Prescription Drug Plan that was unpaid for as well as skull-duggery speculation in banking, runaway Wall Street downward spiral speculation and the unchecked housing market as a result of lax regulation brought America to the brink of economic disaster and failed-state status. Thereafter, and having laid low at the end of his tenure, Mr. Bush is being rehabilitated through exploitation of his good side. Nonetheless, the goodwill endeared to these great presidents, elected twice, did not include endowing such benefits upon Barack Obama.

With Mr. Obama, we have "a horse of a different color!" He broke the mold of 43 white-only presidents. None of the former presidents had risen from the humble beginnings of Barack Obama,

BLACK HISTORY EVERYDAY
PART ONE

struggled to acquire that "Million Dollar White man education" from Columbia and Harvard, "done business white but married black" and possessed the tenacity and wherewithal to challenge for, campaign and win the Presidency of the United States. As such, a credible argument can be made; losers wanted to shift the responsibility for the nations calamity and so acquiesced in Mr. Obamas victory in hopes to benefit from his cleaning out the "messy stables." However, it is still not inconceivable, in a nation of contingency planning from day one, if not before, elements probably hatched the plan to create his demise as he first tackled the problems, created constructive solutions and moved the nation from the brink of economic collapse and mounting disrespect on the world stage. Then, Mitch McConnell and his "Mandate" happened.

Despite his years in Congress, and though "a plotter," Mitch McConnell does not seem capable of single-mindedly originating his "I intend to make Barack Obama a one-term President" mantra. He must have had input, followed orders to hatch such a seemingly brilliant yet flawed, outwardly racist statement and assignment! "Original as it may seem, one has to wonder if he is capable of writing his own material even though he seems to have tried to do and did a good job executing such!" Unfortunately, god was on Obamas side.

It has to have been, for from that day-one seedling planted in the nucleus of the anti-Obamaites temple, a forest of ill-will germinated as countless off-shoots vied with each other to disrespect, threaten and block Mr. Obamas every legislative initiative designed to aid the broad masses of the American people. Republicans removed their focus from doing the people's business to ensuring Mr. Obamas tenure as President is a failure. Connecting the dots, it is evident racial animus has been a catalyst for all such behaviors. The interesting thing about Barack Obama is his demonstrating exemplary leadership as he chooses to see the "boys will be boys" nuisance as just that as he earnestly sought to execute the requirements of his oath of office. Nevertheless, he did remain relentless in keeping the wolves at bay, yet struggling to rescue the American economy despite purportedly started "front and back fires" scorching his path. After all, this unending sabotage was not by "angels with dirty faces" but "devils with clean faces!"

Nonetheless, according to a major front-page write-up in *The New York Times*, certainly after the 2012 election but more probably about the 2008, then the 2012 victory, an influential group of Republicans met and planned to treasonably sabotage Mr. Obamas term in office. However, his extraordinary leadership style enabled Mr. Obama to successfully navigate the Republican legislative and non-governmental organizations minefields, leaving them all in the dust. To this he could reasonably say, the and even now, "I know what you did last summer!"

BLACK HISTORY EVERYDAY
PART ONE

Mr. Obamas deliberative style, his tremendous self-preparation to be familiar with all the issues, unrelenting search and dispatch of Osama bin Laden; that Wall Street has tripled its worth under his watch; passage of Lilly Ledbetter; and Obamacare with untold millions registered for its privileges, some 9 to 10 million private sector jobs have been added during his presidency, two wars were essentially curtailed, and significantly, the Somali Pirates became unemployed. So much more attests to Mr. Obamas leadership skills and style. Unlike many who shoot first then sort later, Mr. Obama first deliberates in his leadership style. When Senator John McCain thought of military action in Eastern Europe, Senator Obama responded, "I have spoken with my advisors and we need to study the situation some more." This deliberation prevented American military involvement attesting to leadership skills. In Libya, Mr. Obama was accused of "leading from behind" but no American lives were lost. Since, many foreign policy issues continued to unfold testing Mr. Obamas leadership.

In the new episode of the downed Malaysian Airliner over the Ukraine Airspace, many persons want to instantly blame Russia under Mr. Putin's leadership. Rather than outright accuse Mr. Putin, President Obama has had a number of subordinates hint at Russia's complicity as Mr. Obama sorted out the intelligence. Rather than come right out, Mr. Obamas deliberative strategy connects the dots before outright laying the blame for the tragedy at Mr. Putin's

FREDERICK MONDERSON

doorstep. In this and so many ways, Mr. Obama exemplified extraordinary leadership.

Black History Everyday - Part One Photo. Cherise Maloney of Brooklyn and Dr. Leonard Jeffreys at **CEMOTAPS** 31st Anniversary Celebration.

Black History Everyday - Part One Photo. Faces and signs in the crowd for the 50th Anniversary March on Washington.

BLACK HISTORY EVERYDAY
PART ONE

Black History Everyday - Part One Photo. Faces and signs in the crowd for the 50th Anniversary March on Washington.

"To me black power must mean hard work, trained minds, and perfected skills to perform in a competitive society." Benjamin Elijah Mays. *Born to Rebel*.

"It must be born in mind that the tragedy of life doesn't lie in not reaching your goal. The tragedy lies in having no goal to reach. It isn't a calamity to die with dreams unfilled, but it is a calamity not to dream. It is not a disaster to be unable to capture your ideal, but it is a disaster to have no ideal to capture. It is not a disgrace not to reach the s tars, but it is a disgrace to have no stars to reach for. Not failure, but low ai is sin." Benjamin Elijah Mays. *Disturbed about Man* [1969]

29. PIPELINE WISE, INFRASTRUCTURE FOOLISH
BY
DR. FRED MONDERSON

Driving along the highway where Brooklyn-Queens Expressway (NY) intersects with the Belt Parkway going east, it's obvious the work being done to repair the deplorable roadway also known as I-287. Added to this a bridge collapsed in New Jersey and the ordering of hurried inspections to the several thousand such structures across that state, is symptomatic of the problem across the 50-states of this nation. In his recently delivered State of the Union Address, President Barack Obama drew attention to this problem as part of general infrastructure deterioration. Here he emphasized Republican incessant emphasis on the Keystone Pipeline, ignoring the significance of infrastructure repair of the nation's roadway, rails, ports, bridges, tunnels and the many jobs they provide to strengthen the economy as opposed to the measly, some say, 35 jobs the pipeline will provide.

BLACK HISTORY EVERYDAY
PART ONE

Black History Everyday - Part One Photo. We Shall Not be Moved March. Faces in the Crowd.

For six years a popular refrain has been, "If Obama favors it, then Republicans oppose it." That is, the foolish policy is, prevent "an Obama win" at all costs! As such, every initiative President Obama proposed to Congress, Republicans, especially in-control of the House of Representatives, in "group think" mode and like lemmings, they have all lined up to say "No to Obama!" Imagine, whatever proposal the Chief Executive initiates, by saying No, Republicans affirm it is not good for the country! An interesting and "hot out of the oven" issue surfaced when President Obama requested congressional authorization to declare war against ISIL (ISIS). When the question was put to Senator Lindsey

FREDERICK MONDERSON

Graham (R.N.C) he instantly declared, "I will vote for it!"

For six years the Senator could not see eye to eye and vote favorably to support any measure of the President but all of a sudden, he would support a War Resolution. Recognizing that war is costly, requiring great financial outlay in armaments, tanks, bullets, weapons, artillery, aircraft jets and helicopters, desert terrain vehicles, and most important American lives, Mr. Graham all of a sudden is in step with the President. No one can deny the danger posed by ISIS but this move is not about benevolence, humanitarianism; it is about financial outlay and profits of war! It will also be interesting to see how many of the Senators Republican colleagues, will see this as a "good Obama policy," that paradoxically "gives Obama a win!"

It is not unexpected Speaker John Boehner will support and expedite a vote on this resolution. Imagine, the Speaker of the House of Representatives representing the people of the United States not simply the Republican base. Again, at a historically important time as the State of the Union Address when the President of the United States addresses Congress and the American people with the world watching, rather than manifest a sedate, dignified, intelligent and attentive posture, the Speaker sits behind the President sniffling, sneezing, and rolling his eyes, hardly applauding most of what the Chief Executive proposed.

BLACK HISTORY EVERYDAY
PART ONE

Let us suppose, Mr. Boehner had the sniffles; which is a natural malady. For sure, it did not begin at 9:00 PM on January 20, when the Sergeant of Arm announced, "Mr. Speaker, the President of the United States!" So, earlier in the day, he calls up his doctor, "Let me have 2 Excedrin tablets" to stop this sniffling before I take the stage behind the President," rather than appear as a fidgeting Middle School student outclassed in his position. To his right, the counterweight, Vice President Joe Biden appeared so majestic, dignified, attentive with a pleasing smile. That is, Joe Biden as a "well-cooked steak" and John Boehner as a "chicken in the rough!"

Oh yes, so at the Roulette Table of this important issue, Republican put all their chips on Red unmindful of the actor Wesley Snipes admonition in the movie **Passenger 57**, "Always bet on black!" That is, they value the Keystone Pipeline much more than a Jobs Bill that will benefit the whole American landscape; will employ millions putting these people back onto the tax roll, benefitting families who shop at grocery and clothing stores, plan for their kids' education, pay doctor bills, buy new cars, gas at the pump, take a vacation after work gets into full swing and even put away a little for retirement.

Some have argued, the Keystone Pipeline only transits American terrain with the potential to unleash environmental harm and is really to bring Canadian oil to an Atlantic port for sale abroad, perhaps Asia, specifically China. This is more significant, for while this project may one day have long-time American significance, at a time when world oil is in a glut, prices are down, the global economy is in down-turn from declining oil prices, to place such great emphasis on the pipeline at the expense of a national Jobs Bill, seems not a wise decision but such actions are symptomatic of President Obamas towering brilliance over his Lilliputian rivals which forces the hands of Republican strategic thinking.

Much ink has been spilt on the pros and cons of the benefits of the Keystone Pipeline. Some myths explored in **Huffington Post** include, the "competitive advantage in processing compared to foreign refiners;" that "traditional sources of heavy crude are declining;" that "the US will need to import oil to meet its domestic demand for decades;" questions regarding "the number of jobs that will be created;" whether "declining gas prices will benefit American consumers;" whether "native Americans" are getting a fair share; and whether it is "cost effective for producers in light of falling oil prices."

All this notwithstanding, as the nation's Chief Executive and Chief Legislator, we must seek to understand the Presidents objection to the feasibility of the project. If the prevailing view from a Republican perspective is, "if Obama favors it, then its bad," then we must view the issue from a different perspective. So, if Republicans favor it especially so intensely, does the President have a better perspective in addition to the Power of the Veto!?

BLACK HISTORY EVERYDAY
PART ONE

Black History Everyday - Part One
Photo. Faces and signs in the crowd for the 50th Anniversary March on Washington.

Black History Everyday - Part One
Photo. Faces and signs in the crowd for the 50th Anniversary March on Washington.

FREDERICK MONDERSON

Black History Everyday – Part One Photo. Congressman Hakeem Jeffries (center) convers with Assemblyman Nick Perry (right) and another in rally for Justice for Eric Garner.

30. REFLECTIONS ON RACE IN AMERICA IN 2006 AND TODAY
BY
DR. FRED MONDERSON

At the conclusion of the National Elections and in view of the Republicans trouncing or thumpin and particularly regarding Blacks and Politics it is appropriate that some reflection be cast on the issue of Race in America with its ramifications on voting, leadership and office holding, responsibility and accountability as it contrasts with other voters,

BLACK HISTORY EVERYDAY
PART ONE

leaders and office-holders as we move along the arduous journey into the 21st Century. As such, a careful eye must be focused on the condition of Blacks and their allies, the poor, the challenged and the voiceless. Some have argued how in this "Age of Terrorism," the term "Terrorism" can equally be applied to "Nineteenth Century African American History." As such, the question that can be posed must be: "Is there evidence in the historical record of a biological determinant for race in America?" and "What have been the ramifications of this pattern of behavior?"

Black History Everyday - Part One Photo. We Shall Not be Moved March. Faces in the Crowd.

The **Voting Rights Act** is a corrective to Black disfranchisement in its many guises. The new mechanism of oppression is the use of prisons, that even though prisoners have paid their debt to society, they are denied the right to vote and Blacks in prisons are a substantial majority; thus, this is a potent weapon in the disfranchisement movement.

In answering, we can easily look to Gunnar Myrdal *An American Dilemma* (90) who mentions how President Thomas Jefferson, at the start of the 19th Century, enumerated the differences between Black and white in his time, a belief long and consistently held in this country since. He lists, "color, hair form, secretion, less physiological need of sleep but sleepiness in work, lack of reasoning power, lack of depth in emotion, poverty of imagination and so on. In all these respects he is inclined to believe that it is not their condition, then, but nature, which has produced the distinction." This view was further underscored by John Calhoun in his "Disquisition on Government" speech in the 1840s where he defended the institution of slavery as practiced in the south that essentially terrorized Blacks as if saying they were unfit for liberty. McKittrick's *Slavery Defended* (9-11) tells, according to Calhoun that liberty "is a reward to be earned, not a blessing to be gratuitously lavished on all alike; a reward reserved for the intelligent, the patriotic, the virtuous and deserving; not a boon to be bestowed on a people too ignorant, degraded and vicious, to be capable either of appreciating or of enjoying it." Even further: "Now, as individuals differ greatly from each other, in intelligence, sagacity, energy, perseverance, skill, habits of industry and economy, physical power, position and opportunity, - the necessary effect of

BLACK HISTORY EVERYDAY
PART ONE

leaving all free to exert themselves to better their condition, must be a corresponding inequality between those who may possess these qualities and advantages in a high degree, and those who are deficient in them." This was the racial mindset that permeated 19th Century America. And, according to the old adage, that "ideas die hard," such perniciousness is very much reflective of the behaviors of some purveyors of ill-will into this age.

Simply put, if there is no claimed biological determinant, then there would not have been a need for the 1964 **Civil Rights Act**! Decades after Jefferson and Calhoun, at the start of the 20th Century, W.E.B. Dubois stated pointedly, "The problem of the Twentieth Century is the problem of the color line (Race)." Importantly yet inappropriately however, many people view the issue of race and racial discrimination and its debilitating effects as one of prejudice but this is altogether wrong. Racial discrimination rightfully is determined by the allocation of rights, responsibilities, resources, privileges, immunities as well as reward and punishment. When these entitlements are not allocated and on the basis of equality, disrespect and inequity steps in and this become the basis for "second class citizenship" and the seed germ of racism, too often obfuscated in discrimination.

The concerned question is particularly cognizant since in his *2005 Inaugural Address*, the second President George Bush raised the issue by saying

FREDERICK MONDERSON

"We must work to end racism in America." More than a decade later, we could similarly argue, despite seeming Black gains, particularly in politics, not much has changed in race relations in America. Poverty, prison incarceration, joblessness, police brutality and killings, suspicion and prejudice are still factors of concern for Blacks in American life. Importantly, we cannot afford to forget Henry Kissinger had said "Let us put the Blacks on the back burner." However and significantly, we need remember in the 1950, 1960s and 1970s untold numbers of white scholars, viz., Kenneth M. Stampp, *The Peculiar Institution* especially Chapter 4, "To Make Them Stand in Fear" (1956), *The Era of Reconstruction* (1965); Erik L. McKitrick, *Slavery Defended: The Views of the Old South* (1963); John L. Thomas, *Slavery Attacked* (1965); David B. Davis *The Problem of Slavery in Western Culture* (1966); Eugene D. Genovese, *The Political Economy of Slavery: Studies in the Economy and Society of the South* (1965), *The World the Slaveholders Made* (1969); Alan Grimshaw (ed) *Racial Violence in the United States* (1969); C. Vann Woodward, *The Strange Career of Jim Crow* (1957); Albert P. Blaustein and Robert L. Zangrando (eds) *Civil Rights and the Black American* (1968); Gunnar Myrdal, *An American Dilemma: The Negro Problem and Modern Democracy* (1944, 1962); Thomas F. Gossett *Race: The History of an Idea* (1963); Robert William Fogel and Stanley L. Engerman *Time on the Cross* (1974); Richard C. Wade, *Slavery in the Cities, the South, 1820-1860* (1964); and Winthrop Jordan, Lothrop B. Stoddard, etc., were all awarded PhDs for

BLACK HISTORY EVERYDAY
PART ONE

researching, studying and writing about African and African-American history and the issue of race in America. Today this odious and pernicious practice is still a viable question of historical inquiry and should remain on the "front burner" because it bears upon relationships between Blacks and Whites in this country; yet, official and legislative discussion refuses to address the issue. However, because of the forcefulness of consistency concerns, some 2020 Democratic presidential candidates insist more attention must be paid the endemic social cancer. All should be reminded, the great American President Abraham Lincoln once said, "Silence in face of wrongdoing is to be culpable for that wrong."

All this is significant because the ancestors of Blacks in America have not only worked to build this great nation for free as kidnapped and enslaved Africans; who have fought in every American war from the *French and Indian Wars* in 1756-63; the *Revolutionary War* 1776-1783; the *War of 1812* from 1812-1815; the *Mexican War* 1845; the *Civil War* 1860-1865; the *Spanish-American War* 1898-1901; *World War I* 1917-1918 (1914-1918); *World War II* 1941-1945 (1939-1945); the *War against Communism* 1947-1996; the *Korean War* 1950-1952: *Vietnam War* 1964-1975; from *Grenada, Kosovo* and the *First and Second Gulf Wars*, to *Afghanistan, Iraq*. Reflecting on such effort, and despite the obstacles of gerrymandering, etc., when given the chance Blacks have voted to make democracy a living and practicable experience. Americas Black citizens have

FREDERICK MONDERSON

fought for an education to become better citizens who can contribute something worthwhile to society. Importantly, these patriotic citizens have become activists to help America live out the true meaning of its creed as Dr. Martin Luther King reminded: "We hold these truths to be self-evident that all men are created equal and are endowed by their creator with life, liberty and the pursuit of happiness."

Black History Everyday - Part One Photo. Two giants, Bernard White (left) and Dr. Len Jeffreys (right) at **CEMOTAPs** 31st Anniversary Celebration.

However, and regarding the recent elections, party house-cleaning is not altogether new, for this nation has a tradition of throwing the bums out every 8 to 12 years. If we look at a brief history of the pattern of party elections this is quite apparent.

BLACK HISTORY EVERYDAY
PART ONE

1860	Lincoln	(Rep)
1864	"	
1868	Grant	(Rep)
1872	"	
1876	Hayes	(Rep) disputed
1880	Garfield	(Rep) close
1884	Cleveland	(Dem)
1888	Harrison	(Rep) close and the Democrats could have won
1892	Cleveland	(Dem)

1896 to 1932 is considered the Age of Republican Supremacy.

In 1896 Grover Cleveland resigns. He refuses to support William Jennings Bryant.

1896	McKinley won (Rep)
1900	McKinley won. He was assassinated. Teddy Roosevelt succeeded to the Presidency.
1904	Roosevelt (Rep) elected
1908	Taft wins over McKinley (Rep)
1912	Teddy Roosevelt (Rep) wins to kick Taft out
1912	Wilson (Dem) wins because Republicans split between Roosevelt and Taft.
1916	Wilson re-elected owing to World War I.

FREDERICK MONDERSON

1920   Harding (Rep) won on restoring the country to normalcy after the war. He was succeeded by Coolidge.
1924   Coolidge (Rep)

1928 Hoover (Rep) defeats Al Smith.
1932 to 1968 is considered the Age of Democratic Supremacy and this is particularly aided by a wholesale change of party by Blacks who had started voting Democratic in defection from the "Party of Lincoln."

Black History Everyday - Part One Photo. We Shall Not be Moved March.
Faces in the Crowd.

1932   F.D. Roosevelt   (Dem)
1936   F.D. Roosevelt   (Dem)
1940   F.D. Roosevelt   (Dem)

BLACK HISTORY EVERYDAY
PART ONE

1944   F.D. Roosevelt (Dem). Roosevelt died in 1945 after being elected four times and was succeeded to the Presidency by Harry Truman.

1948   Truman (Dem) wins re-election

1952   Eisenhower (Rep) beats Adlai Stephenson.

1956   Eisenhower (Rep) re-elected

1960   John F, Kennedy (Dem) beats Richard Nixon. He was assassinated and succeeded by Lyndon Johnson.

1964.   Johnson (Dem) defeats Goldwater

1968   Nixon (Rep) defeats Hubert Humphrey. Wallace was a third party.

1972   Nixon(Rep) re-elected. He resigned owing to his involvement in the Watergate break in scandal, and was replaced by Gerald Ford.

There have been three significant moments of change in political parties in government. These occurred at approximately 36-year intervals.

1972   Nixon(Rep) defeats Humphrey
1972   Nixon (Rep) defeats McGovern
1976   Carter(Dem) defeats Gerald Ford
1980   Ronald Reagan (Rep) defeats Jimmy Carter
1984   Reagan re-elected (Rep)
1988   George Bush (Rep) elected against Michael Dukakis

FREDERICK MONDERSON

1992	Bill Clinton (Dem) defeats George Bush
1996	Clinton (Dem) re-elected
2000	George Bush (Rep) defeats Al Gore
2004	George Bush (Rep) re-elected by defeating John Kerry.
2008	Barack Hussein Obama (Dem) defeats John McCain (Rep) elected President (First Black President)
2012	Barack Obama (Dem) re-elected (Defeats Mitch Romney (Rep)
2016	Donald J. Trump (Rep) defeats Hillary Clinton (Dem)

Clearly, the nation does "clean house" every 8 to 12 years. Once in every 30 to 36 years there is a long-term division and shift in party alignment. Nevertheless, despite party change in Congress after the Mid-term national elections in 2010, 2014, 2018, all citizens must remain vigilant. Such a view is consistent with a recent issue of *Caribbean Life* newspaper, where the legendary civil rights activist and entertainer Harry Belafonte made a startling revelation that there are great similarities between politics, policies and practices of the Democrats and Republicans in terms of not helping the poor, those persons near and below the poverty line, within which a great many Black people fall. Usually, we must insist the democrats address certainly some of the pressing issues of these people.

BLACK HISTORY EVERYDAY
PART ONE

Black History Everyday - Part One
Photo. Faces and signs in the crowd for the 50th Anniversary March on Washington.

Black History Everyday - Part One
Photo. Faces and signs in the crowd for the 50th Anniversary March on Washington.

FREDERICK MONDERSON

The seriousness of the issue of second-class citizenship based on race in America is highlighted when, recently at the Martin Luther King Jr. Memorial Ground Breaking in Washington, D.C., as Andrew Young spoke, both he and Jessie Jackson broke into tears. They were not crying for Dr. King but for the condition of our people in America, many of whom were miles away from realizing "the Dream." While Dr. King had seen the "Promised Land," his dream was beginning to take on solid form with this Memorial but there were many obstacles to that reality. This is what drove these two great Black-Americans to tears at this momentous moment

I remember someone last year criticizing the commercializing of his birthday as stores hawked the "Martin Luther King Day Sale!" Dr. King was not about "Sales," he was about racial injustice, equality, segregation, jobs, housing, health care, and plight of the poor, dispossessed, and disfranchised, even about foreign policy in wake of his Vietnam concerns. Since his time the prison industrial complex has come to play a significant role in the life of Blacks. Jesse Jackson got a lot of mileage when he pointed out that the state of South Carolina had 35 state prisons and 1 state college! Naturally, the history of racial discrimination and psychological emasculation has spawned a form of racial hatred so much so that Black men are now killing Black men in unprecedented numbers. Perhaps Willie Lynch has won, somewhat!

BLACK HISTORY EVERYDAY PART ONE

Listening to "Barber Shop Talk" in the Deli back in 2006, one discussant said to the other, "Well, America is ready for a Black President, as Rev. Al Sharpton could have won in 2004 if he had more support." The other responded, "America is not ready for a Black President, man we cannot even get in the Fire Department, much more the White House. Yesterday, November 13, 2006, the (NY) *Daily News* showed the NY Fire Department is 91% white, with more than 200 firemen, only 12 are Black." Less than a decade ago, *Newsday* Newspaper ran a five-part series entitled "It's a White Man's World" and showed the untold numbers of businesses and institutions run by white men. In many respects, little has changed!

Black History Everyday - Part One Photo. We Shall Not be Moved March. Faces in the Crowd.

FREDERICK MONDERSON

Regarding Rev. Al Sharpton's run for the Presidency in 2004, he was a "winner" having completed the race, been a part of the debates, fund raised, enjoyed Secret Service protection, energized Blacks and raised their political consciousness, **established chapters of his organization National** Action Network nationwide, and encouraged Blacks to run for offices in their locality, all while understanding and being part of the American political and Presidential process. Despite the fact he was championing grassroots issues that affected broad masses of the population, he lost, perhaps, because of his color, and maybe his activism, since many other candidates ended up advocating his issues.

How many times have the movie "In the Heat of the Night" with Sidney Poitier and Rod Steiger been shown? Remember when the rich southerner Endicott slapped Virgil Tibbs in front of Chief Gillespie, and the Black Butler in Sparta, Mississippi. To recall, in an original showing, the Butler was shown telling other Blacks that Virgil slapped Mr. Endicott, but this was cut and not shown in recent showings. However, and particularly in the "2006 Era of Political Correctness," Gillespie was called "Nigger Lover" and told to "Get rid of the Nigger" and when Purdy brought his sister to the Chief to complain of her being pregnant by one of the Chiefs men, her brother Purdy would tell the Chief, "Not to Keep a Nigger in the Room." All this says, they would not show a

BLACK HISTORY EVERYDAY
PART ONE

Black man, no matter how respectable slapping a white man on TV, but they would show "White trash" calling a Black man "Nigger" no matter how respectable or professional he was. Consider that they would "Bleep" certain curse words on TV but would air the "N" word. A good example is the movie RFK where someone referred to a statement of Bobby Kennedy by responding "son of a B." While TV would bleep the "B Word," still it won't bleep the "N Word."

The early morning Steve Harvey radio show on Monday of Thanksgiving 2006, discussed the issue of a white comedian, Michael Richards, who played Kramer on TV, went on a racial diatribe at the Laugh Factory. His jokes were "flat" and were heckled by a Black member of the audience and he responded, "Nigger shut up!" "Nigger," "You're a Nigger" *ad nausea*. Perhaps if it was a white member of the audience he would simply have said, "Shut up." Being on stage in the public eye, entertainers should expect to be heckled if their material is "off base." What is troubling is the use of the "N" word in such a demeaning and psychologically emasculating manner, that is complimentary to denial of rights, responsibilities, privileges, immunities, rewards and punishments. A commentator said he was simply "caught." Well, what of the others who are not "caught!"

FREDERICK MONDERSON

Black History Everyday - Part One Photo. Cherise Maloney, Bernard White, a beautiful **CEMOTAP** member and Dr. Len Jefferies at **CEMOTAPs** 31st Gala.

Such behavior is commensurate with the mindset directed towards O. J. Simpson. As stupid as Simpson has been in airing his narcissistic and warped mentality as well as love for the limelight, the jury ruled that OJ was not guilty! Yet many people refuse to accept this. When the jury ruled in favor of others similarly charged, case in point, the Robert Blake "Beretta" character, everyone accepted the jury verdict, because they had ruled on the guilt or innocence of a white defendant. Yet they challenged the jury decision because it concerned a Black defendant. This in no way exculpates OJ Simpson for his disgusting mentality and behavior.

BLACK HISTORY EVERYDAY PART ONE

In a somewhat related story regarding race in America, *Caribbean Life* November 14, 2006, p. 3, entitled "Politics and Economics not favoring Blacks says Malveaux and McKinney" which holds, "Look at what is happening in the labor market right now" Malveaux said. "On the one hand you have a headline which says the unemployment rate (nationally) has dropped to 4.4 percent - for whites - but 8.6 percent for us (Blacks)." This is twice as much and in some urban areas the claimed percentage of unemployed for Black youth especially is between 40 and 50 percent.

Black History Everyday - Part One Photo. Faces and signs in the crowd for the 50th Anniversary March on Washington.

FREDERICK MONDERSON

Black History Everyday - Part One Photo. Faces and signs in the crowd for the 50th Anniversary March on Washington.

Now let's look at some recent developments of issues colored by race which begs the question of whether there is a double standard relating to black and white relations in this United States of America.

We remember Assemblymen Roger Green and Clarence Norman, because of their legislative prominence were persecuted, prosecuted and convicted for something like $5000.00 or less. When we contrast that with Comptroller Alan Hevesi, who according to his TV political campaign Ad said, "I am a good Comptroller who did a stupid thing" and clearly broke the law by using "a state-paid staffer who chauffeured his ailing wife for three years." He repaid New York State $172,688.00, and one has to wonder where are the Gung Ho prosecutors and when

BLACK HISTORY EVERYDAY
PART ONE

will Mr. Hevesi be tried? What will be his penalty? Will he go to jail? Perhaps there is a double standard based on race!

Harold Ford Jr., the Tennessee Congressman who ran for Senate in his home state, was by some accounts, a "Clean Negro." Remember this term J. Edgar Hoover used when he wanted to replace Dr. King as a reputable Black leader. Mr. Ford was well liked, he supported all the "Good" issues, viz., Gun Control, Anti-Abortion, he took a position on Stem Cell Research, etc. His campaign literature tells of his position on Reforming the Educational System; Affordable Health Care; Technological Innovation; Energy Self-sufficiency; Balancing the Budget; Making America Competitive Again; Protecting Workers Pensions; and Anti-Pork-Barrel Legislation, etc. Yet, when it came for the south to elect a Black Senator, the Republicans rolled out a "White Woman" from a Playboy Club who said, "Harold Call me!" This "strategy" is reminiscent of the "Willie Horton ambush" of the Democratic Presidential Candidate Dukakis when he was defeated by the Republicans and President George Bush, the elder in 1988 election. Willie Horton, a Black convict was either pardoned or released by Dukakis as Governor of Massachusetts. Subsequently, he committed a crime and the Republicans used this "Black syndrome" to defeat the Democrats. Let us not forget the Smith woman who drowned her two children and said, "A Black man did it!"

FREDERICK MONDERSON

Black History Everyday - Part One Photo. We Shall Not be Moved March. Faces in the Crowd.

The New York *Daily News* of Saturday November 4, 2006, p. 4 reported: "An Evangelist who advises President Bush and is an outspoken opponent of gay marriage dropped a bombshell yesterday when he admitted buying methamphetamines from a gay escort he was visiting, supposedly for a massage." He said: "I called him to buy some meth but I threw it away," "I was buying it for me, but I never used it. I was tempted. I bought it, but I never used it." No one would ever believe a Blackman if he said something like "I bought drugs and threw it away." More important, however, this moralist was probably delving in the "nut butter." Moreover, in his confession, he mentions his "dark side" and this is consistent with Webster's **Dictionary** that lists some 40 entries on Black and all are negative, except

BLACK HISTORY EVERYDAY
PART ONE

the one that describes being in business and making a profit which means being in the "Black." Equally too, *American Express* did have a Black gold credit card at $10,000.00 minimum. But these are only two examples of "Good Black!"

Several people echoed the view that it was "racism that robbed Attorney Alton Maddox of practicing law in New York State." More than twenty years later, he is still debarred.

The new "icon" "Flavor Flave" has been accused of debasing Black women on TV. Many have commented that this is a come down from his earlier revolutionary stance as a "Public Enemy." While his buffoonery is acceptable, intellectual and professional Blacks are not given their proper respect in terms of equal exposure treatment. Important, we must insist, this does not mean every white person practice racism, but many do! It's a sort of showcase of the "Super masculine menial" mentality.

"Mr. T," the "Super masculine menial" and buffoon has returned to the TV screen and despite the fact, "Lot wife turn a pillar of salt," Senator Trent Lott was being called the "Comeback Kid" in Washington D.C. as he tried to become a leader in the Senate again, despite his praise of Senator Strom Thurman, the Southern Segregationist who vilified Blacks while having and keeping a Black daughter under wraps. One thing is certain, neither Al Sharpton nor Jesse Jackson are considered "Good Negroes" and

FREDERICK MONDERSON

have taken their "hits" but like that famous "Bunny" they keep on "ticking" in civil and social rights activism. This is because they keep the interests of the people on the "front burner" and speak for those without a voice. One thing is certain, in this writer's mindset, there's nothing anyone can say to besmirch these "two great heroes."

As we move forward, think sympathize and suffer for the betterment of this great nation, we must work, pray, and advocate for the betterment of an America where "all children will be judged by the content of their character not the color of their skin." Until then, we must all fight in the schools, boardrooms, work places, hospitals, and legislative arenas, for until equality manifests and justice roll down like a mighty stream, the "Struggle Continues!"

Black History Everyday - Part One Photo. Dr. Wright surrounded by three very important Black men at **CEMOTAP**.

BLACK HISTORY EVERYDAY PART ONE

"Pan-Africanism looks above the narrow confines of class, race, tribe and religion. In other words, it wants equal opportunity for all. Talent to be rewarded on the basis of merit. Its vision stretches beyond the limited frontiers of the nation-state. Its perspective embraces the federation of regional self-governing countries and their ultimate amalgamation into a United States of Africa." George Padmore. *Pan-Africanism or Communism* [*1956*]

"From our knowledge of the history of man, from our knowledge of colonial liberation moments, Freedom or self-government has never been handed over to any colonial country on a silver platter." **Kwame Nkrumah**. *What I Mean by Positive Action* [*1949*]

31. SALVATION THROUGH PAN-AFRICANISM BY DR. FRED MONDERSON

Across the globe, the African World is in disarray! Forces in opposition are escalating sentiments of division to suppress and control the aspirations of African people whether in Guyana where racial division is a fact; across the African continent fanned tribalism creates suspicion and division; and in local

FREDERICK MONDERSON

communities here racists of all hues including militias, skinheads, even "Tea Party" types and associates racially stereotype as powerful an individual as President Obama. Let's not forget what's being propagated, Donald J. Trump is a principal miscreant in all this. Gentrification is not only displacing many long in residence of local areas but a pejorative mentality pervades the behavior of some new residents fed by divisive elements emanating from across the nation's highest offices. Significantly, as many recent "greats" in Black perennial struggle for salvation through economic, political and social empowerment join the pantheon of revered ancestors given "they came early," viz., Rev. Shuttlesworth, Sonny Carson, Jitu Weusi, Bill Lynch, Ossie Davis, Elombe Brathe, Maya Angelou, Ruby Dee, Et. Al., there is an ever-present need for a cadre of vibrant young leadership motivated by an active and effective philosophic orientation and modus operandi that will unite and advance the cause of African people's salvation. Pan-Africanism is such a philosophic ideology, its creators and proponents must be recognized. We cannot forget the work of Booker T. Washington, W.E.B. DuBois, Marcus Garvey, George Padmore, Sylvester Williams, Kwame Nkrumah, Sekou Toure, Mitta Monderson, for their efforts provided the foundation for the all-inclusive Pan-African philosophic brotherhood. Pan-Africanism was born and nurtured in the cauldron of African peoples struggles across chattel slavery, colonialism and imperialisms exploitation and racism. Such actions also gave birth to nationalist

BLACK HISTORY EVERYDAY
PART ONE

assertions in order to demand and secure equality and dignity for African people across the globe.

Viewing the 2014 Soccer World Championship in Brazil, its clearly evident, that once European elitist sport has "gone African," where such soccer powerhouses as England, France, Germany, Netherlands, and especially South American teams, are manned by players whose heritage is indigenous to the African continent. The unmistakable fact is: those teams striking thrusts and threats are significantly African in representation!

Nevertheless, oftentimes viewing contemporary developments we see a unique phenomenon represented in map displays highlighting significant occurrences. In football, the various stadiums across the host nation Brazil stand out on a representative sample.

Black History Everyday - Part One Photo. Faces and signs in the crowd for the 50th Anniversary March on Washington.

FREDERICK MONDERSON

Black History Everyday - Part One Photo. Faces and signs in the crowd for the 50th Anniversary March on Washington.

In that nation, there may possibly be 120 million people of African ancestry. This is the largest single number outside of the African continent. As such, it would be an important first-step if many Brazilians root for African teams taking the field to qualify as top contenders. Of course, we do not mean when their nation is playing, for then we saw the stands full of symbolic yellow and green Brazilian colors. After all, and notwithstanding, enlightened Brazilian intellectuals have insisted that their people learn more about and appreciate their African heritage.

BLACK HISTORY EVERYDAY PART ONE

Black History Everyday - Part One Photo. Cherie Maloney (right) and Mrs. Branch, whose husband John founded **The National Black Theater**, at **CEMOTAPs** 31st Gala.

The notion of Pan-African consciousness was first articulated and championed by W.E.B. DuBois and Sylvester Williams in 1900 although it dates back to the efforts of Paul Cuffe, Martin Delaney, Henry Highland Garnett, Frederick Douglass, Sojourner Truth and Harriet Tubman, Booker T. Washington, among many others. In the early decades of the 20th Century, Marcus Garvey was an ardent advocate for the unity of African people, at home and abroad, and thus founded the **Universal Negro Improvement Association (UNIA)** to advocate such a goal.

FREDERICK MONDERSON

Garvey came to America to meet Booker T. Washington, a staunch Pan-Africanist, who died just before his arrival in 1916, yet he continued the task of mobilizing and unifying African people under the banner of "**One People, One God, One Nation, and One Destiny**!" However, he was not alone in that era for Washingtons **Tuskegee Institute** that instituted the **Tuskegee Plan**, and the birth of the **National Association for advancement of Colored People** as well as the **National Urban League** as change agents have proved enduring institutions and testaments of constructive African unity, activism for uplift. Then in 1919, DuBois convened the **First Pan-African Conference** or Congress in Paris contemporary with the Versailles Peace Conference concluding World War One peace treaty. To contest the negative reaction to the conference from America and Great Britain especially, the latter quintessential imperialist and colonialist nation; DuBois appealed to Blaise Diagne, a Senegalese Delegate to the French Assembly during the tenure of Prime Minister Georges Clemenceau's government.

As evidence has indicated, during the war, as the German military hammer pounded France, Clemenceau dispatched Diagne to West Africa to recruit Africans to fight their German enemy. He successfully recruited some 120,000 Africans who

BLACK HISTORY EVERYDAY
PART ONE

helped stem the German onslaught thereby rescuing France. In payback, Clemenceau simply said, "Go ahead, have the Conference, but keep it low key!" So, once the go-ahead was given and venue secured, DuBois invited delegates from Europe, Africa, America North and South America and the Caribbean. There the flames of a unifying global African consciousness had been lit! During the inter-war years (1919-1939) three such conferences were held as DuBois, aided by George Padmore and others remained active in the struggle. Their efforts espoused the intent of Pan-African consciousness to combat the many years of systematic assaults upon the humanity and integrity of the African persona, long oppressed, at home and abroad.

Africans from all over, particularly the colonial possessions on the continent and in the New World, fought to check German World War Two rampage in Europe, North Africa and the Atlantic Ocean states. At wars end in 1945, then an elder and somewhat tired DuBois turned over leadership of the Pan-African movement to a younger and more vigorous Kwame Nkrumah of Ghana who chaired the **Fifth Pan-African Conference at Manchester**. In that city, Fredrick Engels championed the Labor Movement, and so reception to the conference was favored there. This time, the Pan-African movement had come of age. The ideological orientation and thrust was passed to the next generation of leadership who were empowered

FREDERICK MONDERSON

with a new ideological orientation to chart the movements course with a mandate to decolonize Africa and the other colonial areas in the Caribbean. In America, desegregation of the Armed Forces following World War II coupled with the on-going activism of such persons as A. Philip Randolph, Rev. Shuttlesworth and legal eagles such as Thurgood Marshall, kept the flame burning in the desire to seriously be free and equal!

As these delegates returned to their respective countries and began organizing their people to become more knowledgeable about colonial administration and politics, the one unifying idea was that of Pan-Africanism. The philosophy of Pan-Africanism essentially expressed; African people globally have been the victims of European and American aggression, political expansion, exploitation, racism and solely for the furtherance of these nations interests and privileges. In this climate, as people's consciousness evolved further animated by activism and unionization agitation, the colonial powers began incarcerating leaders of the new movement seeking to free their land. Nevertheless, within a decade of the **5th Pan-African Congress** of 1945, Kwame Nkrumah led Ghana to independence on March 6, 1957. With the colonial powers weakened by the war and the people united under a vibrant group of leaders, viz., Sekou Toure of Guinea; Namdi Azikwe of Nigeria; Jomo Kenyatta of Kenya; Gamal Abdel Nasser of Egypt; Tafawa Balewa of Nigeria; Et. Al. all espousing an equally vibrant strategy, dominoes began to fall and African

BLACK HISTORY EVERYDAY
PART ONE

nations became independent enmasse; thereby becoming members of the United Nations simultaneously and now empowered to play politics on the global stage. In America, reaction against Blacks in general, nationalists, the **Black Panthers**, the **Student Non-violent Coordinating Committee**, the **Republic of New Africa** and the **Southern Christian Leadership Council** under Rev. Joseph Lowery who pressed their case, protested, marched, sit-ins, and encouraged economic boycotts while seeking political rights and educational and social advancement drew condemnation on the world stage. All this occurred against a heightened and vehement backlash from persons seeking to "hold back the dawn" of civil rights. This group was represented especially by Southern racists and ante-bellum legislators, foremost among whom was the segregationist George Wallace of Alabama and other nefarious allies in the North.

Representative James Clyburn (D. SC), pointed out, the Confederate Flag so associated with Dylan Roof killing and the backlash in South Carolinas Mother Emanuel Church was a new motif in the backlash to the Civil Rights Movement.

FREDERICK MONDERSON

Black History Everyday - Part One
Photo. Faces and signs in the crowd for the 50th Anniversary March on Washington.

Black History Everyday - Part One
Photo. Faces and signs in the crowd for the 50th Anniversary March on Washington.

BLACK HISTORY EVERYDAY
PART ONE

The success of African and Latin American nations in winning their independence and being seated at the United Nations in the 1950s and 1960s, emboldened the Civil Rights Movement in this country. So much so, the reactionaries of "Bull Connors," the "White Citizens Council" and "Ku Klux Klan" demonstrated their inhumanity and unabashed racism against protesting African American men, women and children. This nation continued to be embarrassed on the world stage. There was also a "push and pull," challenge in emergence of young and persistent leadership in Jesse Jackson, John Lewis, Stokeley Carmichael (Kwame Ture), Rev. Abernathy who were bent on bringing social change. As a result, there was the assassination of key figures in the struggle such as Dr. Martin Luther King, Malcolm X and Medgar Evers. Clearly there seemed to be government complicity in unscrupulous behaviors against its citizens; nevertheless, hard won gains were accomplished. Just as the 1960s was the decade of African independence, concerted African-American effort in coalition with progressives and sympathetic activists, in and out of government, especially the Kennedy brothers, brought about important gains in voting, housing, education and solidarity with Africa.

FREDERICK MONDERSON

Black History Everyday - Part One Photo. We Shall Not be Moved March.
Faces in the Crowd.

The historic 1954 *Brown v. Board of Education of Topeka, Kansas* laid the foundation to desegregate the nations school system, and the election of John Kennedy in 1960 started America down a "no-turn back" road seeking equality for all Americans. The new philosophy Mr. Kennedy brought to the office was designed to transform the nation while looking to encourage its people to outdistance others in science and the various areas that measure global leadership. The president was naturally impressed with Dr. Martin Luther King's poor peoples "March on Washington" in August 1963 that was actually the brainchild of A. Philip Randolph, longtime worker in the vineyards of social activism. He, Dr. King delivered his famous "I Have A Dream" speech which was really about jobs! However, within months President Kennedy was assassinated and his successor, Lyndon B. Johnson, in the interest of

BLACK HISTORY EVERYDAY
PART ONE

"continuity," launched his "Great Society Program" which was actually Kennedys brainchild

Surprisingly, this master politician, Lyndon Johnson, a Southerner from Texas, was able to cajole, "push and pull," "give and take" compromise and emerged successful in passage of the 1964 **Civil Rights Bill**. The next year, the **Voting Rights Act** was passed and then Malcolm X was assassinated. This was a major blow to Black American nationalism. The Vietnam War was also a factor, though it produced a great many military trained Blacks who were and still are a counterweight in potential race riots or potential armed struggle in America. Nevertheless, the struggle continued and by the end of the decade, Medgar Evers and Martin Luther King were also assassinated. Throughout, several acts of brutality were committed against the African-American community including more than 100 unsolved civil rights murders for which no one was brought to justice! Then there was the Birmingham church bombing that took the lives of "4 young Black girls." Of course, in the southern "lynching states," for nearly a century after passage of the 13th Amendment outlawing slavery, these, by todays definitions, terrorists, lynched, killed, tarred and feathered, terrorized and intimidated African people and deprived them of society's protections and equal, human and civil rights in this nation. Meanwhile, the Africans continued to express concern at the United Nations regarding the condition of their brothers and sisters in America. We need not forget the nearly 4000 lynchings in the South from approximately 1870 to 1950 as *The New York Times* reported in 2017.

It is believed, that such behaviors continue today, often in clandestine actions and coded statements. Nevertheless, a wise theorist once said, "There are no permanent enemies, only permanent interests." Malcolm X, on the other hand, declared "History is a great teacher" and that we must learn about how other people addressed and solved their problems. As for example, without question, America was at war with Britain, France, and especially Germany in World Wars One and Two. In these conflicts, untold numbers of American citizens were killed. Yet, as of today, June 22, 2014, on Fareed Zakaria's Sunday Program on CNN, in an interview with the German Minister of Defense, and in response to a question, she is quoted as saying, "We share the same values as America." Therefore, that being so, and despite the war dead, the unmistakable fact is, if the above is true, then Africans worldwide, at home and abroad, should unite under the ideological philosophy of Pan-Africanism for this is a potent formula to strengthen African resolve and the only way the world will respect each and every one of Africa's sons and daughters!

BLACK HISTORY EVERYDAY PART ONE

Black History Everyday - Part One Photo. Cherise Maloney beside the Poet Mr. Mitchell at **CEMOTAPS** 31st Anniversary Celebration.

Black History Everyday - Part One Photo. Gary Byrd and Milton Allimadi at the **Black Star News** Awards.

FREDERICK MONDERSON

Black History Everyday - Part One
Photo. Faces and signs in the crowd for the 50th Anniversary March on Washington.

Black History Everyday – Part One
Photo. Congressman Hakeem Jeffries joins others on state seeking Justice for Eric Garner.

BLACK HISTORY EVERYDAY
PART ONE

Black History Everyday - Part One Photo. The message is clear: **Black Lives Matter**!

FREDERICK MONDERSON

Black History Everyday - Part One
Photo. Faces and signs in the crowd for the 50th Anniversary March on Washington.

"I am tired, vexed, by seeing images of Black men hanging from trees, lynched. That is why I keep such images front and center in my office to be reminded how far we still have to go, and how much more has to be done. This is why we must vote now! Sonny "Abubadika" Carson. *Call for a* **Million Vote Campaign** *particularly to oust Rudy Giuliani as Mayor of New York City.*

Black History Everyday – Part One
Photo. Hakeem Jeffries - Justice for Eric Garner.

BLACK HISTORY EVERYDAY PART ONE

"We will join hands with you as women of this country.... We will kneel-in, we will sit-in until we can eat at any counter in the United States. We will walk until we are free, until we can walk to any school and take our children to any school in the United states. And we will si-in, and we will kneel-in, and we will lie-in if necessary, until every Negro in American can vote." **Daisy Bates**. *Speech at the March on Washington for Jobs and Freedom [August* 28, 1963]

32. SONNY CARSON: AT THE GATES BY DR. FRED MONDERSON

Reflecting, one could well imagine Robert Sonny "Abubadika" "AB" Carson's arrival at the "Pearly Gates" of heaven and Saint Peter beginning to question him as to his credentials for admittance into the joys of this wonderful existence. Before answering, the observant Carson looked past the gate to a gathering of anxiously awaiting friendly faces who, informed he was on his way and in protest mood, kept shouting "Welcome, Brother Carson, Welcome," "Let him in! Let him in!" In this crowd, he could make out his ancestor the "Runaway Slave" Samuel Carson, Harriet Tubman, Nat Turner, Martin Luther King, Junior and Senior, Thurgood Marshall, Alex Haley, Adam Clayton Powell III, Langston

FREDERICK MONDERSON

Hughes, Rosa Parks, Charles Richard Drew, Rev. Shuttlesworth, George Washington Carver, "Allah You Akbar" Bramwell, Benjamin Banneker, Marcus Garvey, Percy Julian, Paul Robeson and Mary McLeod Bethune. Across from these he saw ancestors who had survived the Slave Trade and some ex-slaves still in rags but with their chains tossed to the side. Behind these all, he heard the most melodious singing coming from an orchestra composed of singers Michael Jackson, Teddy Pendergrass, Luther Vandross, Mahalia Jackson, Marvin Gaye and Bob Marley, while Miles Davis, Dizzy Gillespie, Charlie Parker, "Satchmo" Louis Armstrong and Count Basie, Thelonious Monk, Hassan Roland Kirk, who all played unbelievable and melodious sounds on their instruments.

Embolden by such familiarity Sonny Carson moved toward the questioning table at the gate to begin the process. He stated, he came from a poor South Carolina family who moved to Brooklyn in a significant population migration in the World War II era. Coming of age in Post-World War II America, Sonny, like so many urban black youths were "troublesome," indulged in drugs and all forms of illegal behavior including gang membership that landed him in prison and was forced to enroll to fight in the Korean War of the 1950s. After one stint in prison, perhaps becoming socially transformed by his experiences, Sonny Carson became a social activist.

The **Fulton Street Corridor** in the Bedford-Stuyvesant section, for the longest, had been the

BLACK HISTORY EVERYDAY
PART ONE

economic mainstream of that community. In that era of the Civil Rights Movement, all such businesses and their employees were White in a Black community. Sonny began advocating if Blacks shop and spend their money in these stores, then they should be able to work there. Here began his notion of the economic boycott that had gained so much for organized Black movements. As this idea caught on, in an era when "Black is Beautiful" was a meaningful mantra, Sonny began the long and arduous voyage of social transformation of himself and his community. As the good of this new idea caught on, Sonny began calling for "Black ownership."

Black History Everyday - Part One Photo. We Shall Not be Moved March. Faces in the Crowd.

This novel idea also led to opening of "Mom and Pop Stores" that sprang up in many places in the Black community, across the country. Thus, Sonny Carson had arrived as a civil rights/social/education activist, and soon he evolved into a nationalist activist who teamed up with the Republic of New Africa

FREDERICK MONDERSON

demanding nation status for Blacks. Such respectful advocacy did not preclude him being implicated and charged with kidnapping and labeled a rabble rouser as well as garnering the enmity of many.

From this time on Sonny Carson emerged as a leader who challenged the establishment because he was not satisfied with the condition of Blacks in this country and reactions to Black protest to address civil and human rights issues, all being fueled by the significance of the African decolonization movement sweeping that continent in the 1960s. As America blazed with the new activism, Sonny became an admirer of Malcolm X, the fiery Black Muslim Minister who wanted radical change for blacks in America and he was particularly moved by his assassination, never accepting nor forgiving those who committed the despicable act. With a number of others, he held high Betty Shabazz because she had to raise those children, but most important she was considered the queen of a fallen battlefield general. Nevertheless, at first, Carson was lukewarm towards Martin Luther King, Jr., who believed in non-violent social protest. Thus, with the assassination of first Malcolm X and then Dr. Martin Luther King, Sonny intensified his efforts for social change, extended his interest beyond America and raised his profile as a black-nationalist leader with international standing.

In broadening his interests, Sonny became an education activist and equally involved in institution building, advocating for the dispossessed, speaking up for many falsely accused and brutalized by law

BLACK HISTORY EVERYDAY PART ONE

enforcement as well as becoming a voice for many languishing and being psychologically emasculated daily in the prison industrial complex system. With such a resume of involvement; a visiting king of Ghana, West Africa, touring Brooklyn, New York, anointed Sonny Carson "Abubadika," which means "he who leads his people." For those who found the name difficult to pronounce, Sonny simply became "AB." From here on, Mr. Carson began "earning his stripes."

Carson appeared in court to show support for those "falsely accused" of a crime by police. He also appeared in court to support tenants victimized by unscrupulous landlords. He attended funerals and showed dislike for "Black on Black Crime." Like all good generals, Sonny passed on and had a parade from the Brooklyn Bridge and up Fulton Street and a wonderful "home going."

Black History Everyday – Part One Photo. Part of the audience for "King and Malcom at **CEMOTAP**.

FREDERICK MONDERSON

Black History Everyday - Part One
Photo. Faces and signs in the crowd for the 50th Anniversary March on Washington.

Black History Everyday - Part One
Photo. Faces and signs in the crowd for the 50th Anniversary March on Washington.

BLACK HISTORY EVERYDAY
PART ONE

As Sonny recounted such involvements, Saint Peter checked his books and replied: "These things I'm familiar with but what else have you done?" Thereafter, in that usually assertive manner Sonny Carson reminded the Saint he was a founding member of **Restoration Corporation** on Fulton Street in Brooklyn, designed to economically revitalize the Bed-Stuy community. He was a principal advocate for four-year status for Medgar Evers College of the City University of New York and was highly critical of its administration when he attended graduation ceremonies, finding no drums or other such African cultural motifs, and thought he was in Greece rather than in Africa. Sonny founded **Black Men Against Crack** to fight the scourge that was plaguing the Black Community and took to the streets to actively protest against the drug. When merchants acted improperly in the black community, "AB" led boycotts on Fulton Street and Church Avenue. Through all these developments, Mr. Carson testified and spoke out at Congressional Hearings and other such forums as at Medgar Evers College and other venues.

Still not satisfied and appearing somewhat sarcastic, St. Peter challenged Sonny Carson. Meanwhile his cheering section among the Black Pantheon within the "Gates of Glory" became more active as their champion was being put through the questioning rigors. Just then Sam Cook backed by Baby Huey broke into song: "A change is going to come" and this

FREDERICK MONDERSON

was followed by Brooke Benton who blurted out, "I who have nothing, I who have no one, adore you and want you so." As Hasan Roland Kirk, Charlie Parker, Gillespie and Miles blew their horns, the whole company burst into chorus emboldening Sonny, much to Saint Peters surprise. The Saint felt those people were interfering with the interrogation and selection process and should stay out of it.

Black History Everyday - Part One Photo. We Shall Not be Moved March. Faces in the Crowd.

The singing and instrumental music seemed to revitalize Sonny even further as he started St. Peter down "a dusty road." He blurted out, "I led the Ocean-Hill-Brownsville educational challenge to the New York City Board of Education that resulted in community control and a disproportionate number of Black and Puerto Rican teachers and administrators

BLACK HISTORY EVERYDAY PART ONE

being hired in a school system disproportionately minority. For this action they branded me an extreme radical and a racist. But all I did was to enhance the condition of my people, as Malcolm X would say, By Any means Necessary."

Saint Peter asked: "Does this mean you had no respect for law and order?"

"Quite the contrary" Sonny responded. "I respected law and order but disdained racists and all forms of exploitation and discrimination and disrespect for the community the police were sworn to serve."

"Never mind, just go on" Saint Peter, baiting Sonny asked, "What more can you add about hour miserable life?"

"Thinking, "What's with this M …?" Sonny held his tongue, but continued. He exclaimed, "Dr. Newman described a path similar to mine: After the fever of life; after weariness, sicknesses, fighting and despondings, languor and fretfulness, struggling and failing, struggling and succeeding; after all the changes and chances of this troubled and unhealthy state, at length comes death, - at length the white throne of God, - at length the beatific vision." Even more he added, "I attended funerals, stood up to uppity politicians, challenged Sony over Gangsta Rap, and founded **The Committee to Honor Black Heroes**. This enabled me to change streets

FREDERICK MONDERSON

as Malcolm X and Marcus Garvey Boulevards and lay the foundation for Harriet Ross Tubman Avenue, all in Brooklyn; I also changed the names of schools to honor Malcolm X as Malcolm X School and Toussaint L'Ouverture School."

Black History Everyday - Part One
Photo. Faces and signs in the crowd for the 50th Anniversary March on Washington.

"Sounds impressive to me" chimed Saint Peter.

Still Sonny continued, "But that's not all I did. I retrieved the Bones of my ancestor Samuel Carson, that fellow over there behind the "Gates of Heavenly Bliss," from his U.S. Navy segregated burial site in Brooklyn and transported it back to Ghana, West

BLACK HISTORY EVERYDAY
PART ONE

Africa, to inaugurate the **First Emancipation Day Ceremony** on August 1, 1998 and create a site of pilgrimage for African-Americans seeking roots in Africa. In this I was able to create the "Door of Return" opposing the "Door of No Return." As he continued to pour out his heart, Sonny Carson could hear the orchestra break out in chant, "We Shall Overcome; We shall Overcome" and even more, "Were gonna study this war some more, were gonna study this war some more."

"Even in my passing on transition to these Pearly Gates the Community I fought for so hard for so long, chose to honor my name in a section of Gates Avenue in Brooklyn as Sonny Carson Avenue. Yet, despite wide and demonstrated community support on the day of the vote, the reactionaries in the New York City Council voted to deny such. In response, the Community named **Linden Park (Sonny Carson Park**) on Linden Boulevard in my honor and even put up their own sign which the Parks Department removed. Similarly, on Gates Avenue they put up their own sign at Nostrand Avenue which was also taken down by officialdom. Finally, the good people of Bedford-Stuyvesant, Bed-Stuy, renamed that section of Brooklyn, "**Abubadikaville**!" The rest you know.

With that Saint Peter responded, "Mr. Carson, you have done well but you must understand my position,

FREDERICK MONDERSON

to fully examine every entrant. You deserve to enter this Company of Blessed Souls. God be with you!"

The Orchestra, patiently awaiting the results of the inquisition, broke out in thunderous applause and began singing, "Were gonna walk these streets of gold" before beginning to welcome and brief Sonny on extant conditions in heaven and on earth. Thereupon Sonny insisted, "Bring me up to speed on what's going on in Heaven." In response he heard, "Here are the issues and here's what need to be done!"

Black History Everyday - Part One Photo. Former Congressman Charlie Ranges and Dr. Rudy Crew, President of Medgar Evers College and former Chancellor of New York City Board of Education.

BLACK HISTORY EVERYDAY
PART ONE

Black History Everyday - Part One Photo. Sonny "Abubadika" Carson, "Bringing it."

Black History Everyday - Part One Photo. Faces and signs in the crowd for the 50th Anniversary March on Washington.

FREDERICK MONDERSON

"The world today needs a spiritual regeneration. If this can come from biology as biology it has a power in this age of science over those who see science as the end-all of life, and gives strength to others who know by faith alone. But spiritually poverty-stricken as the world is today, how few realize this plight! Where is there given adequate emphasis on things of the spirit? And yet, what is man and all his science but the reflected light of this inner flame." Ernest Everett Just. *Letter to John D. Rockefeller*, Jr.

"The Sociologist, The Philanthropist, the Race-leader are not unaware of the New Negro, but they are at a loss to account for him. He simply cannot be swathed in their formulae. For the younger generation is vibrant with a new psychology; the new spirit is awake in the masses, and under the very eyes of the professional observers is transforming what has been a perennial problem into the **progressive** phases of contemporary Negro life." Alaine Locke. *The New Negro* [1925]

BLACK HISTORY EVERYDAY PART ONE

Black History Everyday – Part One Photo. Sister Frederika Bey at the Podium while Dr. MacIntosh, Dr. Len Jeffries, Siter Rosalind Jeffries, Minister Hafeez Mohammed and professor Blake look on.

33. SPIRITUAL VALUES VERSUS SECULAR MATERIALISM BY DR. FRED MONDERSON

The Media has flashed information of various Anti-Obama groups such as Carl Roves Super-Pac that has spent some $10m in Advertisement against the President with another $15m more waiting to be spent and Rickets of TD Bank fame donating another $10m in essentially the same cause. There is too much effort and rapidity to defeat President Obama and in this, money becomes a primary God! After all,

FREDERICK MONDERSON

the motto of this nation is "One Nation under God, with liberty and justice for all." When oligarchic whites invest to gain profit from their investment, under the Judea-Christian religious and philosophic principle, the answer is privilege, profit and power. Since secular materialism buys the God, buys the government, the question becomes "Is it one nation under god or under material mammoth?" Equally, one has to ask, "What is the return and who gets it for such lucrative investments?"

Nevertheless, in the movie "Rocky" when confronted by the challenger who said, "I'm going to bust you up," Rocky simply responded, "Go for it!" These large sums spent to negatively paint Barack Obama will prove futile even though the forces arrayed against President Obama are wealthy, powerful, unrelenting and formidable representation of materialism. Thus, despite his position, in those respects, President Obama becomes an underdog and America loves the underdog. It's been said one man can become a majority if he believes in himself and his truths are immutable. Thus, as this situation reflects his state of preparedness, honest integrity and bold vision, Mr. Obama will win the election going away! This is equally a view expressed by Bill Clinton on CNNs Piers Morgan on Thursday, May 31, 2012.

We believe the win is predictable because President Obama is collecting vast but small sums of American money to wage his campaign and this is being undergirded by his trump suit of "Spiritual Currency"

BLACK HISTORY EVERYDAY PART ONE

generated through efforts of "Black Saints" with its dynamic potential miraculous effect. This secret weapon, enshrined and encapsulated in the Sunday morning prayers generated by the grandmothers, grandfathers, uncles, aunts, brothers and sisters and cousins across this land, invigorated by the good works of the ancestors who have seen and weighed in the balance the heart of the man of whom they have seen the illuminating beacon of his vision of the future. This is the idea and advantage Obama has had over his adversaries and competitors, and more especially Donald Trump. As such, if we follow some of the old aphorisms were told, "Money is the root of all evil;" though Rev. Ike often proclaimed "The lack of money is the root of all evil!" Yet, in the movie **Green Berets** starring John Wayne and Raymond St. Jacques, when the soldiers tried to solicit assistance and offer protection to a nearby village of Mountainards, they promised "Well give you money." The Chief asked "What is money?" Even these days, amidst much glaring Media fanfare, Mr. Zuckerberg launched his **Face Book** IPO with shares set relatively high. Word has it, so many billion dollars were made and days after he was being raked over a bed of flaming coals for some form of stock impropriety. Thus, money is not always everything. For one thing, money can't buy health and it cannot thwart the will of the people determined and united in a cause they deem correct and inclusive. Tell that to Donald John Trump.

FREDERICK MONDERSON

Obama supporters should take heart, there is a "spiritual force" at work in Mr. Obamas campaign, an unseen power; the obstinate and arrogant cannot comprehend its prevalence, for it undergirds the divine mission of Mr. Obama. Interesting, he does not flaunt his spiritual values; he lets it permeate his being in doing god's work. He upholds the nations and universal Christian philosophic admonitions to "love god, love yourself and love your neighbor." After all, the souls of the righteous are immortal and divine! Thus, in his humanity and social policy, Mr. Obama manifests the beatitudes Jesus admonished. These, according to Matthew 5: 3-10 are:

Blessed are the poor in spirit, for theirs is the kingdom of heaven

Blessed are the meek for they will inherit the earth.

Blessed are those who hunger and thirst for righteousness, for they will be filled

Blessed are the merciful, for they will be shown mercy

Blessed are the pure in heart for they will see God

Blessed are those who are persecuted because of righteousness, for theirs is the kingdom of heaven.

I could add, "Blessed are those who have no health insurance for they will have it under Health Care Reform" in the Affordable Care Act (ACA). Thus,

BLACK HISTORY EVERYDAY PART ONE

Mr. Obama adheres to the basic philosophic and moral tenets of this Christian nation. This the giddy multitude of anti-Obamaites could never envision nor comprehend!

However, while I cannot equate Mr. Obama with Jesus, his philosophy of leveling the playing field, giving everyone a fair shot, insistence that everyone pay their fair share, even his concern for the millions with no health insurance is consistent with the aspirations inveighed in Matthew 5, which is also, the Meek shall inherit the earth ....

As he gives hope to the masses, the spirit of god is upon Barack Obama! He becomes the salt of the American earth! This light of the world is a beacon, a light of that shines from the City on a Hill making manifest the American mission as the last hope for humanity. Compare the Presidents compassionate concern with the secular materialisms privilege, profit and power; we notice the nation has moved off its moral foundation; its moral compass, as Dr. Martin Luther King would say! This contradicts every spiritual value of one nation under god. His concern for the millions without health care, believing everybody is entitled to medical care forces us to ask, "Which stance or campaign worships secular materialism, which supports spiritual values?"

FREDERICK MONDERSON

Black History Everyday - Part One Photo. Faces and signs in the crowd for the 50th Anniversary March on Washington.

Black History Everyday - Part One Photo. Faces and signs in the crowd for the 50th Anniversary March on Washington.

Therefore, as the forces of history teaches us, Christian belief holds Jesus and the Saints have amassed an enormous amount of good will through

BLACK HISTORY EVERYDAY
PART ONE

their good works, that is stored in a container in the Vatican which the Pope can draw upon to carry through his mission of mercy and salvation in the world. Equally, the African-American ancestors who have toiled unpaid in the fields of the institution of slavery, suffered the indignity of that emasculating experience, been victims of racial discrimination and terror; yet, created and experienced the joys of Negro Spirituals to ease their suffering while caring for the young, old and infirm, all the while still looking toward emancipation and salvation. These are the people who, with faith in the future, could only bank "spiritual capital," "spiritual currency." Believe it or not, their good works keeps America buoyed and "still standing!" Their prayers, dreams, aspirations and expectations of these martyred visionaries, for all we know, foresaw the rise and elevation of Barack Obama. This long vision has also recognized the challenges to Mr. Obama as he seeks to complete his mission and contribute to the elevation of their progeny through educational advancement, economic empowerment and political practicalities. That is why the ancestors bequeathed the potency of a "spiritual currency bank" for Mr. Obama to draw on to contend and conquer the forces of materialism and evil committed to derail his divine mission. Thus, the peoples champion will prevail because through god "Spiritual capital" will win out against the financial prodigiousness of mammoth designed to thwart the will of destiny and the divine, while continuing to expand their wealth and riches at the people's expense!

FREDERICK MONDERSON

Black History Everyday - Part One
Photo. Within the "forest of planks!"

Black History Everyday - Part One
Photo. We Shall Not be Moved March. Faces in the Crowd.

BLACK HISTORY EVERYDAY
PART ONE

Black History Everyday - Part One Photo. Faces and signs in the crowd for the 50th Anniversary March on Washington.

"Who will revere the Black woman? Who will keep our neighborhoods safe for Black innocent womanhood? Black womanhood is outraged and

FREDERICK MONDERSON

humiliated. Black womanhood cries for dignity and restitution and salvation. Black womanhood wants and needs protection, and keeping, and holding. Who will assuage her indignation? Who will keep her precious and pure? Who will glorify and proclaim her beautiful image? To whom will she cry rape? Abby Lincoln [Anna Marie Wooldridge] *Who Will Revere the Black Woman? Negro Digest [September 1966]*

Black History Everyday – Part One Photo. Congressman Hakeem Jeffries, Rev. Al Sharpton and four mothers whose sons were murdered in senseless violence, seeks Justice For Eric Garner.

BLACK HISTORY EVERYDAY
PART ONE

"Unity does not require that we be identical to each other. Black women are not one great vat of homogenized chocolate milk." Audrey Lorde. *I Am Your Sister* [1985]

34. THE BLACK WOMAN BY DR. FRED MONDERSON

The Black Woman is a unique specimen in all facets of the human experience. While admired for her intellect, charm, beauty and supportive motherly sensitivities, she has yet been the most maligned and abused of all persons down through history. Tremendously sexually attractive, she has been admired for these gifts by the male species across all races for all time and equally despised concomitantly by the opposite sex of the same sets. As such, that paradoxical situation visited upon the Black Woman has manifested in thought and action in both ancient and modern times and the scars, visible and invisible, bear testimony to this assertion.

The first Black Woman we know of was a young female discovered in the Hadar Region of Ethiopia and dated at some 5 million years old. The contradiction in this wonderful find by the anthropologist Johanson was calling the beauty out of her name! Listening to a song playing on the radio by the British rock group "The Beatles" entitled "Lucy

FREDERICK MONDERSON

in the Sky with Diamonds," Mr. Johansson named the Black Beauty "Lucy." The venerable and well-respected anthropologist and African historian Dr. Yosef A.A. ben-Jochannan said no! Call her by her African name, **Denk Nesh**!

In Ancient Egypt in North-east Africa, as the legend goes, the wife of an Old Kingdom priest was visited by the Sun God and promised progeny who would become kings in that ancient land. The fourth Dynasty kings Khufu, Khafra and Menkaura whom the Greeks renamed Chufu, Cheops, and Mycerinus are thought to have issued forth from her loins. The Great Pyramid builder Khufu buried his mother Hetepheres with great pomp and splendor. Her tomb was discovered early in the twentieth century by George Reisner on an expedition for the Boston Museum of Fine Arts which exhibited some of the wonderful funerary furniture buried with the beautiful lady. Unfortunately, grave robbers had disturbed the Queens resting place, perhaps defiled the body which was never found and they robbed the tomb. However, four wonderful alabaster Canopic jars were found indicating the missing deceased was mummified at that early date. Fearful that Khufu would have a fit to know his mother's tomb was desecrated, the priests simply reburied the remains without telling him.

Neithhotep was the last pharaoh of the Old Kingdom but scholars dismiss her reign, whether short or otherwise, perhaps it was because she was a woman who dared to rule this early in time. In modern times,

BLACK HISTORY EVERYDAY
PART ONE

perhaps in calypsonian tribute, Black Stalin sang, "The more Africans they gun down, the more Africans keep coming!"

After the Old Kingdom, Egypt entered a state of serious instability through the Seventh to the Tenth Dynasty and it was not until the Eleventh Dynasty that order and stability was restored by Theban dynasts. Behind these kings were strong Black women, the mothers of Intef and Mentuhotep, for example, whose rationality and influence enabled these kings to unite rather than fight. Consolidating their power, they won back the country, and found the Eleventh Dynasty ushering in the Middle Kingdom.

Mentuhotep II built an enormous and attractive temple at Deir el Bahari, the oldest surviving Middle Kingdom temple at Thebes and the best-preserved structure of that age. It proved to be a transitional architectural form linking the Old and New Kingdoms in Egyptian building practice. This temple also proved to be a tomb for female members of the Kings household. However, one lady Kemsit, because she was painted black as opposed to several servants painted red, scholars argued she was Negro, Negroid, etc. Nevertheless, while the king's statue was painted black and dressed in Heb Sed attire wearing the Red Crown of Lower Egypt as discovered nearby, a line of argument developed stating he was "so painted for the funeral ceremony." Seriously, she painted Black as a Negro but he painted Black for the funeral ceremony! What a ridiculous proposition in itself. What a contradiction! This false line of reasoning was also applied to the two statues later discovered guarding Tutankhamon's burial chamber. Nonetheless, the two kings' Mentuhotep and Tutankhamon are classic examples of falsity clothed in obfuscation for distortion. Two kings painted Black yet rationalized as so for the funerary ceremony; yet, o Caucasians are shown, certainly as kings, but we must conjure them for "some unknown reason" as possessing a "superior intellect." That is to say, we must discount the Black evidence, but accept the white evidence that does not exist! Sop much for our reasoning!

Nevertheless, as the Middle Kingdom waned, unable to field strong leadership, the nation disintegrated and foreign invaders; Hyksos, seized the land and founded the fifteenth and sixteenth dynasties. After a century or more of brutal and over-lordship rule, their insolence motivated Theban princes of the Seventeenth Dynasty to challenge these occupiers and so waged a protracted 50-year struggle to oust them. While these early African nationalists were up north waging the battle, a Theban opportunist named "Tety the Handsome" sought to seize the throne in a palace coup and so fermented a rebellion. However, they underestimated the resolve of the Dynasty's matriarch Tetisheri and her daughter Aahotep who rallied the faithful at Thebes then put-down the revolt. Her son, Aahmes later immortalized his mother Aahotep with a stele in Karnak temple, praising her tenacity and revolutionary fervor. He

BLACK HISTORY EVERYDAY
PART ONE

also donated lucrative utensils and jewelry to the temple in her name establishing a hereditary title and endowment for the family.

Black History Everyday - Part One Photo. Faces and signs in the crowd for the 50th Anniversary March on Washington.

Black History Everyday - Part One Photo. Faces and signs in the crowd for the 50th Anniversary March on Washington.

FREDERICK MONDERSON

His wife and sister Aahmes-Nefertari, not simply beautiful but also astute as Queen-mother was later deified along with her son Amenhotep I in the Theban necropolis and a temple was erected there in their honor. One modern commentator argued she was only painted Black by workers in Ptolemaic times but not really so in her time! Of course, Heinrich Brugsch-Bey in *History of Egypt Under the Pharaohs* described her as Ethiopian! Her painted image is in the British Museum with another in the Berlin Museum.!

No woman was more villainized in the ancient world than Hatshepsut because she dared to seize the throne of power and rule a nation state at the apogee of its power. An assertive woman whom destiny placed among Thutmose I, II, and III, Hatshepsut proved tremendously astute and resourceful in the "art of the possible" contending against stiff opposition. "Alliances with strong men in the kingdom," not only empowered her politically but also enabled her artistic and creative abilities to impact heavily on Egyptian society and history. She was thus able to initiate many cultural innovations that became standard pharaonic practices down through dynastic times particularly giving new impetus to the ancient Heb Sed festival. The anger and hatred of her successors is evident in her treatment once removed from the helm of the state.

BLACK HISTORY EVERYDAY
PART ONE

Black History Everyday - Part One Photo. We Shall Not be Moved March. Faces in the Crowd.

Her successor, Thutmose IIIs adherents attacked her mortuary temple at Deir el Bahari, smashing her statues; he enclosed her Karnak obelisks in a manner hiding it from general view; her tomb in the Valley of the Kings was firebombed; the "Red Chapel" Bark Sanctuary in Karnak she built was smashed and buried. Wherever these fanatics found the Queens name they were expunged to erase her memory from history. In apartments adjacent to the replaced sanctuary at Karnak her image in association with Amon/Min and being baptized by Thoth and Horus, was chiseled out neatly. Her mummy was displaced and remained unknown until recently positively identified through scientific and dental sleuthing and now we know her true identity and possess her mortal remains! Fortunately, some of her cartouches escaped the destroyer's eyes and hands.

The dastard deeds notwithstanding, same as that Angelic phenomenal woman Maya Angelo penned, "Still I Rise," the Queens name, instead of being forgotten by history, resounds well with modern art and architecture lovers, in "after years" as she declared.

Rameses II in the next dynasty, the nineteenth, was credited with completing his father Seti Is temple at Abydos; perhaps it was Seti himself who created the **Abydos Tablet** depicting 76 kings in cartouche from Menes to that deified monarch, was unkind to the queen. Five of the cartouche names were left blank. Four of these names, Amenhotep IV or Ikhnaton, Akhenaton, and Smenkare, Tutankhamon and Aye, associated with the "Amarna Revolution" at the end of the eighteenth dynasty, were never inscribed in the sacred oval.

Hatshepsut, whose reign was much earlier was proscribed because as a woman she sat on the throne of Egypt claiming to be "Son of the Sun God." That she wore male attire; a false beard and constructed a temple at Deir el Bahari greater than that of her ancestor Mentuhotep II nearby; generated much enmity. Though she had a tomb built in the Valley of the Queens while a young princess, she had another hewn in the Valley of the Kings which Seti probably thought was heresy. Even more revolutionary, while New Kingdom monarchs had their mortuary temples

BLACK HISTORY EVERYDAY
PART ONE

distant from their tombs, Hatshepsut planned and began constructing a tunnel linking her Deir el Bahari temple and tomb in the Valley. She intended to be taken directly from the temple's funeral ceremony to the tombs eternal resting place. Unfortunately, the ground halfway through the mountain was unstable and not able to support the enterprise, thus it was abandoned.

Notwithstanding and despite all the adversity, the Queens name lives today through her temple, a gem of architectural construction. Her obelisks at Karnak of which one still stands while another lie broken near the Sacred Lake were significant logistical and artistic accomplishments. We know from Deir el Bahari she erected four obelisks altogether but the whereabouts and location of the other two are unknown, though thought to be east of Thutmose III's Festival Temple the Akh Menu. In addition, she did repair work on temples and other structures throughout the country following Hyksos occupation and destruction. Much more significant, however, the depicted images in her temple of transporting two obelisks on the Nile; the expedition to the "Land of Punt" on the Somali Coast in East Africa; and the revolutionary conception of her divine birth underscores her household name today encouraging many young women wanting to be like the "first queen."

Need it be said, Hatshepsut took great pride in being a Black Woman! When challenged she underscored

FREDERICK MONDERSON

her relationship and descent from her father Thutmose I's relationship with his grandmother Aahmes-Nefertari, the Black-skinned Queen and divinity. This Ethiopian beauty's image wearing white, red and blue is featured in the British Museum.

Runoko Rashidi in *Uncovering the African Past: The Ivan Sertima Papers* (2015: 96) depicts another image of the queen in the Berlin Museum showcasing her black features.

Black History Everyday - Part One Photo. We Shall Not be Moved March. Faces in the Crowd.

The next great Black Woman of history was Queen-Tiy, wife of Amenhotep III and mother of Amenhotep IV. She was well-liked by the king, wielded a great deal of influence in, besides, around and from behind, the throne. Many scholars credit her with initiating the concept of Aten worship. Dr. John

BLACK HISTORY EVERYDAY
PART ONE

Henrik Clarke spoke glowingly about this Black Beauty but more poignantly about her response to those critical about her sons Aten revolutionary movement.

She is stated, according to Dr. John Clarke, to inform all such, "You may criticize my sons beliefs and actions as much as you want, but if you harm one hair on his head, I will send you to the infernal regions;" or words to that effect. Naturally and not surprising, modern critics of Egypt and Black influence therein sought to link her to Syria; this "So Nubian" queen! Her tomb was discovered in the Valley of the Kings in 1905 and revealed resplendent artifacts and jewelry attesting to her status at burial. The Syrian connection has been over used, particularly by such scholars as A.E.P.B. Weigall, who, in fact, held the blacks in contempt.

Black History Everyday - Part One
Photo. Sister Nickey and the Poet Brother Lading

FREDERICK MONDERSON

Kalibah at **CEMOTAPs** 31st Anniversary celebration.

Though Queen Tiy was the principal wife of Amenhotep III; Nefertiti, a Syrian princess came to Egypt to marry the old king in a political marriage, but ended up marrying his son Amenhotep IV, Akhnaton, Akhenaten. Certainly, with Queen-Tiy as a mother-in-law, Nefertiti needed big shoes to fulfill her mission. This she accomplished admirably-well, being seen participating in Aten worship festivities, being in her husband's company on festival and formal occasions and bearing him five daughters. All this contrary to modern critics questioning her husband's manliness and virility that essentially impugned her integrity and character as a dutiful, faithful and loving wife.

Black History Everyday - Part One Photo. Faces and signs in the crowd for the 50th Anniversary March on Washington.

BLACK HISTORY EVERYDAY
PART ONE

Black History Everyday - Part One Photo. Faces and signs in the crowd for the 50th Anniversary March on Washington.

In the 19th and 20th Century German assault on Egypt, thousands upon thousands of artifacts were unethically removed from the antique land. In one swipe Lepsius shipped 15,000 pieces of artifacts to Berlin. Add to this the great numbers that understandably belonged to Brugsch, Brugsch-Bey, Erman, Mariette, etc., and multiply this by the thousands of adventurers, explorers, consuls, archaeologists and antiquity lovers who collected untold artifacts in their work and sojourn. To this we may add collections in Germany, England, Italy, France, Turkey, and the United States, among others. Collectively, this is simply a part of what Brian Fagan called the "Rape of the Nile." One significant piece in Berlin, the Nefertiti head, is important for a number of reasons. It is a prized piece coming from an artist's workshop from the time of an important era in the history of Egypt and also since she was the wife of the great reformer. It was removed from Egypt at a time when there were no restrictions against such an important piece being taken out of Egypt. The queen looks "so Caucasian," some pointed out but this is simply because she was Syrian, Even more important she fits the false-razzle-dazzle notion that the "Egyptians were Caucasian."

A modern Egyptian official familiar with the contemporary negotiations on behalf of the Egyptian government seeking return of this valued piece, among others, informed of the complex and frustrating experience in the process, still to no avail. A similar situation occurred in getting the Sphinx's beard back from the British Museum. Consider that Mariette sent 15,000 pieces to Berlin and that Theodore Davis sent some 400 boxes to the University of California, then multiply such by the thousands who excavated and collected, the adventurers who worked for private collections in addition to themselves, museums, governments etc. To return any such piece as the Nefertiti bust would open the flood gates demanding that all such artifacts be returned. So, the British returned the Sphinx beard on a "permanent loan" basis. So much for diplomacy and linguistics in negotiations.

We know Rameses IIs most favorite wife Nefertari was Nubian. They always choose the beautiful, best and brightest! But he himself was a serial womanizer.

BLACK HISTORY EVERYDAY
PART ONE

Cleopatra, the seventh queen so named, is another African woman confronted with changing realities, at the end of the Ptolemaic dynasty. She was the only one in her line who understood hieroglyphics and spoke the native language. Confronted with the geo-political and military dynamics of a changing era and in the Harriet Tubman tradition, chose to "Live Free or Die!" So, she killed herself rather than become the love toy of Octavian, the future Roman Emperor Augustus! Two respected African scholars, Dr. Yosef ben-Jochannan and Dr. John Henrik Clarke offered different perspectives on the Queen. Dr. Ben argued she was the last of a line of hated Ptolemaic dynasts. While Dr. Clarke explained, she was an astute African Queen faced with the realities of her time and acted in the best interest of the African state with dignity and uncompromising determination. Critics also contest her image at the rear of Hathors Temple at Dendera while others contend the artists of her time certainly knew more about the Queen than speculative theorists two millennia removed.

FREDERICK MONDERSON

Black History Everyday - Part One Photo. On the Knoll a view of the tremendously creative nature of the layout.

Black History Everyday - Part One Photo. We Shall Not be Moved March. Faces in the Crowd.

BLACK HISTORY EVERYDAY PART ONE

The many acrimonious assaults visited upon the Egyptian, African, queen chronicled above in no way compares to the extant defacement and destruction evident on the walls of temples in Egypt. Art lovers around the world will attest Egyptian art is probably the greatest in its genre for its originality, longevity and abundance. Many may speculate divine inspiration and guidance was foundation in creating such masterpieces that continues to excite and amaze, whether the expert or novice who travel from far and wide to appreciate and wonder about their majestic and timeless creative beauty.

A valid question, therefore, is "Why would anyone want to deface and destroy such splendid works of art?" "Would an art lover stoop so low?"

Visit any Egyptian temple or tomb that can be reached today and behold practically every image of the beautiful Black Woman has been defaced or destroyed. Again, why would anyone want to disfigure the face of a beautiful woman represented in art? In India rejected suitors throw acid in a woman's face disfiguring natures art. Many consider such actions sinful, full of hatred, spiteful and certainly illegal. In Egypt, however, hateful, spiteful designation, most certainly illegal may also apply. But there may be an even more sinister motive behind such actions. In fact, it may very well be part of the "Conspiracy Against ancient Egypt!" Let us admit, there are experts and there are experts and even when that first expert points to his discovered observation, we ask, why should the other experts continue to deny that immutable truth. Thus, this action in itself raises more far reaching questions particularly about the ethnicity of the ancient Egyptians and what was the principal role of Africans in the Nile Valley?

For example, several commentators had observed and commented, all Egyptian art, certainly its human figures are created in an African mold! Yet, many continue to deny this observed fact. Perhaps it is because the images of females on the walls of Egyptian temples and tombs, be they wives, mothers, sisters, daughters, are all created in the African mold projecting African features and therefore challenges and defeats the false notion of a Caucasian dynastic Egyptian. They were certainly created in the most meaningful periods of Egyptian history when Egypt excelled in art, architecture, science, medicine, government, militarism and religion. The important question, however, is 'How could some observers notice this African mold concept in art, and others not or deny such?

Perhaps then, this outlook is generated out of envy and in hatred to hold fast the waning and false belief and view of white supremacy that is continuously being challenged into extinct. The sad part of all this is, practically every statue or wall image has had its nose or mouth attacked and disfigured. To wit, another one of these lame excuses reads as such: "Well, the brains of the mummy was extracted through the nostrils!" How pathetic! Presently two mummies repose in glass cases in the Luxor Museum

BLACK HISTORY EVERYDAY
PART ONE

where one is thought to be Rameses I. The face is not broken! The nose is still intact. There are many beautiful statues in the same Luxor Museum under tight security, and their noses are not disfigured. However, in foreign museums, in Britain, Brooklyn, the Met, statues "after being dressed" have their noses broken. The question is why?

Black History Everyday - Part One Photo. Faces and signs in the crowd for the 50th Anniversary March on Washington.

FREDERICK MONDERSON

Black History Everyday - Part One Photo. We Shall Not be Moved March. Faces in the Crowd.

Still, this assault on the Black Woman is not germane to Egypt. The Ethiopian Queen of Sheba has also been a victim of equally nefarious assaults.

One of the supposed great love stories of all time is that of Solomon and Sheba, though the king had some 600 women in his harem! Of course, "he scored," but he never married the Queen to make an honest woman out of this Black Beauty. Some have argued, her kingdom was ten times the size of his and his "love play" was really an opportunistic gambit for political opportunistic consolidation.

BLACK HISTORY EVERYDAY
PART ONE

Black History Everyday - Part One Photo. We Shall Not be Moved March. Faces in the Crowd.

Though often shown in contemporary times as a White Woman, we know the Queen of Sheba boasted "I'm Black and Comely!" More importantly, however, perhaps it was one of the six hundred disaffected women who began saying the Queen of Sheba said instead, "I am Black but Comely!" Then a further disaffected descendant picked up the falsity and continued into contemporary times, in itself a contradiction considering extant images. Thus, this negativity in perception of the Black Woman, buttressed by the daily observed defacement and destruction of the facial images evident in the Egyptian temples and elsewhere, causes thinking persons to wonder why injure such beautiful masterpieces of art created by nature and also man-made. The sad thing about this, it has been done; yet it remains constant reminders of inhumanity and envy of man to man and totally un-divorced from the role of the Black African, man, woman and child in the formation, creation and perpetuation of the permanence of the Nile Valley Civilization and human achievement in general.

In the Medieval period, Islamic scholars arriving in West Africa commented positively on the friendliness, beauty and good nature of African Women who greeted travelers crossing the desert. The hospitality they extended was superb, but within a few centuries the same women were dragged off to the New World in a horrendous system called Slave Trade. The horrors of that Middle Passage psychologically scarred the Black Woman in unimaginable ways through the trauma of personal abuse; inhuman conditions of trans-shipment; and the unchecked behaviors of many sailors on board such vessels or slave ships often called sailing coffins.

Arriving in the New World, in the Caribbean and North, South and Central America, for centuries the Black Woman was mercilessly treated less than human. **Roots**, **Twelve Years a Slave**, **Django Unchained** and Ruby Dees narration of **The Fight Against Slavery** graphically depict the inhumanity meted out to the Black Woman. When in 1808 the American Congress outlawed the Slave Trade, the Black Woman was consigned to the

BLACK HISTORY EVERYDAY PART ONE

beastly behavior practiced on "Slave Farms" designed to produce off-springs to enrichen the slave holding value of owners. Clearly there was a difference in the stature and treatment between the Black Woman as house servant and the Black Woman as field hand. Still there was a difference between the Black as keep woman and the young woman as fair game to the owner and overseers' desires. Sure, Phyllis Wheatley may have had it a little better, able to write poetry; but Sally Hemmings was not freed by President Jefferson upon his death even though he fathered several of her children. The story is told of one Black Woman from "slave farm" days who was promised freedom if she made so many children; yet she died a slave having produced 36 children. Oh MY God!

Harriet Tubman would not have any of this and insisted "I must live free or die!" In the 19th Century days of southern white terrorism the Black Woman suffered tremendously as young and beautiful but also as wife and mother of lynched and terrorized husband and son. In the 20th Century, a young man was lynched and his mother protested. That day the racist mob lynched both mother and son. And so, it was and worse!

During the Civil Rights Struggle **4 little Black girls** were killed in bombing of a Birmingham church. Significantly, however, Malcolm X railed against the police officers "sicking dogs" on men,

FREDERICK MONDERSON

women and children protesting for human and civil rights. Malcolm X, "Our Shining Black Prince," also singled out the police officer who planted his knees in the chest of a Black Woman lying prostrate on the ground as he assaulted her and the FBI stood nearby taking notes!

We can therefore argue, the Black Woman down through history has remained a unique and original specimen of Gods creation! Importantly, she has been blest with beauty and attractiveness; ingeniously demonstrated intellect and knowledged assertiveness; exhibited love, compassion and sensitivity; and been courageous, supportive and faithfully loving while simultaneously rising above the challenges of greed, malice and envy. Still more significantly, as mother, wife, sister, aunt and friend, the world must be thankful and is a better place because of the forgiving nature, wisdom and tenderly and loving companionship of that wonderfully created, divine spirit, the Black Woman!

BLACK HISTORY EVERYDAY PART ONE

Black History Everyday - Part One Photo. Dr. Molefi Asante and **CEMOTAPs** resident Poet Laurate Lading Kalibah.

Black History Everyday - Part One Photo. Faces and signs in the crowd for the 50th Anniversary March on Washington.

FREDERICK MONDERSON

Black History Everyday - Part One
Photo. Faces and signs in the crowd for the 50th Anniversary March on Washington.

Black History Everyday - Part One
Photo. Faces and signs in the crowd for the 50th Anniversary March on Washington.

BLACK HISTORY EVERYDAY
PART ONE

Black History Everyday - Part One Photo. **We Shall Not be Moved March**. Faces in the Crowd.

Black History Everyday - Part One Photo. The message is clear: **Black Lives Matter**!

FREDERICK MONDERSON

"I'm not the average girl from your video, and I ain't built like a supermodel, But I learned to love myself unconditionally, Because I am a queen." India. Arie [India Aire Simpson, 1975]

"Any woman who counts on her face is a fool." Zadie Smith. *On Beauty* [Kiki]

35. THE ILLUSTRIOUS QUEEN MOTHER
By
Dr. FRED MONDERSON

With the passing of Queen Mother Moore, African nationalism suffered a serious setback. This matriarch of African liberation left indelible impressions on the consciousness of those struggling against imperialism, colonialism, de-colonization and racism. Whether through Garveyism, Nkrumahism or Afrocentricity as well as what is the future direction of Pan-African identification, strategy and struggle, Queen Mother Moore provided a significant role, influenced many and stood as a flaming star. In reflecting on a life of commitment to African liberation, the climax of her experiences is somewhat reminiscence of Marcus Garvey's classic statement: "You have caged the tiger, but the cubs are running loose out there." For certain, Queen Mother Moore has been a cub and she has raised and encouraged cubs! For sure, she has encouraged, supported, trained, and left cubs and young and old

BLACK HISTORY EVERYDAY
PART ONE

lions and lionesses, who are today committed to ideals, aspirations, and philosophic outlooks that motivate and fuel the efforts and desires of African people worldwide. As a result, she has earned her revered place in ancestral heritage and will be welcomed in the heavenly abode of the pantheon of African heroes and heroines. This state of affairs now forces us to consider the successor to Queen Mother Moore's august and respected place of leadership.

As an early follower of **Marcus Moziah Garvey**, **Queen Mother Moore** was influential in founding, sustaining and leading organizations such as the **Universal Association of Ethiopian Women**, Inc. She was the Founder of **Addis Ababa, Inc.**; Founding Matriarch of the **Ethiopian Orthodox Coptic Church**; Founder and President of the **African-American Cultural Foundation**, Inc.; and Founder and President of the **Harriet Tubman Association**. She was a Life Member of **Negro Women**; Member of the Founding **Committee 1970 Conference**: **Congress of African People** and she was also the first woman to formally address the **Organization of African Unity (OAU)** in Addis Ababa, Ethiopia. Several organizations were also formed to aid her or

FREDERICK MONDERSON

as a result of her influence on others. She is now indeed a Great Ancestor!

Though Winnie Mandela had been crowned **Queen of the Black World**, candidates for the title of Queen Mother needed to be identified, considered, chosen, and installed to provide leadership of causes affecting African people worldwide in memory of Queen Mother Moore and to keep her spirit alive and working. Dr. Delores Blakely is recognized as "Queen Mother of the Middle Passage."

To fully understand the position and significance of the title "Queen Mother," a historical reflection needs to be made of individuals who have filled this post, particularly in Nile Valley and later African culture. As such, one of the most celebrated of the "Queen Mothers" is the ancestress of the Eighteenth Dynasty, Aahmes-Nefertari, whose portrait is in the British Museum. This stately beauty is shown wearing a long flowing gown of white, red and blue, 1500 years Before Christ. In addition, she is depicted bejeweled and wearing the Vulture Headdress or the "Queen Mother Crown." This is a golden headdress, with uraeus, sun disk, and plumed feathers that sit atop a mortar. Another colorful portrait of a queen with the Queen Mother Crown is that of Rameses II's Nefertari of the Nineteenth Dynasty. This queen is shown in her tomb in the Valley of the Queens, where she offers two vessels in praise of the Hathor deity. However, while pictorial examples of the Queen Mother Crown may be lacking, the spirit and personality has survived in the lives of queens who

BLACK HISTORY EVERYDAY
PART ONE

influenced their husbands, sons, grandsons, families, communities, and been forces of inspiration who in turn were praised and revered.

Black History Everyday - Part One Photo. Faces and signs in the crowd for the 50th Anniversary March on Washington.

In the "Myth of Isis and Osiris," out of jealousy the king was killed by his brother Seth. The faithful wife Isis, together with her sister Nephthys, set out to recover the body. Once found and retrieved from a tree trunk in the Lebanon, Isis, with the aid of Nephthys, Anubis and Thoth, through magic, was able to impregnate the goddess to bear a son whom they named Horus. Right after, Set again found the body and dismembered it into several pieces, some say 13 or 14, and scattered it throughout. Then again, the goddess searched the land, finding a piece of the body in a particular location, she buried it there. This accounts for different regions where claims were made as being in possession of the body, or in actuality, a piece of the body buried in their location. The head, however, was buried at Abydos and the heart was buried at Philae, temple of the goddess.

Black History Everyday - Part One Photo. We Shall Not be Moved March. Faces in the Crowd.

Grown to manhood, Horus was able to avenge his father by capturing the despicable uncle after a protracted struggle and then slay him at the spot where the Temple of Edfu was built to mark the victory. Some versions of the story report Horus made a claim to the gods in their great Hall of Judgment where he was defended by Thoth, the "legal eagle" and god of writing and wisdom. This intervention resulted in the great judge's ruling that

BLACK HISTORY EVERYDAY
PART ONE

Osiris was wrongfully executed and that Horus should be installed in his father's stead as king of Upper and Lower Egypt/Kemet. Through it all, Isis, grand-daughter of Nut, stood by her son as she had done with her husband. Her influence, therefore, is traceable as a "Queen Mother" who gained great fame for her compassion, commitment, sincerity and faithfulness. From this mythological experience we can start with the individuals who constitute the human side of the dynastic experience.

If we begin with Narmer at the founding of the first dynasty, we first encounter his African queen in a majestic position of respect, certainly if not equality, within the domain of the husband and son. Narmer's wife was Queen Neithhotep, whom we encounter on the Narmer Macehead, a ceremonial weapon that has provided an enormous amount of factual information enabling scholars to arrive at some firm conclusions about this early period. Narmer and Neithhotep's son was Hor-Aha, who followed his father as king. He built an enormous tomb for his mother, several times that of his father. We are led to believe that the influence of the Queen Mother may have begun to be exercised from this early time. In addition, because of the special role of the Queen in transmitting divine genes, she came to hold a special place in the society, as power behind the throne and when that august position was threatened, she exerted her influence to diminish whatever threats there may have been.

FREDERICK MONDERSON

Snefru was probably the last king of the Third Dynasty and his wife was Hetep-Pheres who gave birth to a magnificent dynasty, the 4th with its illustrious kings, Khufu, Khafre, and Menkaure. These three pharaohs of the 4th Dynasty built the great pyramids on the Giza plateau.

When an expedition from the Boston Museum of Fine Arts discovered her tomb in the 1920s, they were soundly impressed with the burial remains of Queen Hetep-Pheres, mother of Khufu. Clearly the influence she enjoyed as "Queen Mother" can be deduced from her remains, including efforts at preservation of her body. This incidentally was one of the earliest examples of the process of mummification being employed.

Black History Everyday - Part One
Photo.   Dr. Molefi Asante, Cherise Maloney and Lading Kalibah, **CEMOTAP's** resident poet.

BLACK HISTORY EVERYDAY
PART ONE

The First Intermediate Period followed the collapse of the Old Kingdom and power was exercised between Memphis in the North and Assiut in Middle Egypt. This period of internal disunity was comprised of the VIIth-Xth Dynasties. Theban princes who united the South, before attempts were made to march northward to unify the country, began the formative era of the Middle Kingdom with consolidation of power. The German Archaeologist von Bissing tells in the *American Journal of Archaeology* of a conflict between two of these Theban princes, Intef and Mentuhotep. Apparently, Intef had planned an attack on Mentuhotep's force and as he came out of the pass onto the Plains of Thebes, he encountered Mentuhotep with a superior force deployed and awaiting him on the field of battle. Intef had his mother Queen Achtothes intercede with Mentuhotep's mother Queen Aam, to bring about a cessation of hostilities to "save the day." Clearly, these "Queen Mothers" were significant political and moral influences on their respective families, for, as we, as a united force, know Mentuhotep was particularly successful in his efforts to unite the land. He founded the Eleventh Dynasty, defeated the northern monarchs and their allies, the Princes of Assiut, and again united the land. He consolidated his power, reorganized the domain and expanded the cultural, economic and artistic institutions of the society and founded the Middle Kingdom. Though not much is subsequently

FREDERICK MONDERSON

known about his mother after this, we could well imagine the level of influence she exercised.

Black History Everyday - Part One Photo. We Shall Not be Moved March. Faces in the Crowd.

The next significant "Queen Mothers" were considered to be Queen Tetisheri and her daughter Aahotep. At the collapse of the Middle Kingdom, the Hyksos, an Asiatic people, invaded Kemet and ruled the land for a century from their stronghold in the Delta. The Princes of Thebes and the Upper Kingdom recognized these conquerors as their overlords and paid tribute to them. As with all such invaders, they were haughty and ruthless. After ruling as the Fifteenth and Sixteenth Dynasties, a Hyksos king sent a rather arrogant message to the Theban princes. He claimed the "hippos" grazing in the Nile at Thebes were making so much noise that

BLACK HISTORY EVERYDAY
PART ONE

the Hyksos rulers in the Delta, nearly 500 miles away, could not sleep at night. Therefore, "Shut up your hippopotamuses!" Such arrogance generated an intense response from the Thebans, of the "fighting province." They mobilized their forces and began a protracted war of liberation that lasted for some 50 years and ended with the expulsion of the Hyksos.

Queen Tetisheri's husband was Sekenenra-Tao who began the war of liberation. His son, Sekenenra-Tao was felled by a battle axe blow to the head and his mummy is now in the Cairo Museum. While the husbands were away fighting in the war of liberation, a palace coup broke out led by "Tety the Handsome." The gallant queen, perhaps with the aid of her mother Tetisheri rallied the faithful and put down the rebellion, saving the throne for her progeny. In that ongoing war of liberation, Kamose her husband, expelled the Hyksos and his son Ahmose completed the job of expulsion. This latter founded the XVIIIth Dynasty and New Kingdom. Ahmose or Aahmes married his sister, Aahmes-Nefertari who became ancestress of the Eighteenth Dynasty. Clearly, for her gallantry Aahotep was rewarded handsomely with a hereditary title and came to exercise the requisite influence as "Queen Mother." Significant gold and silver utensils were donated to the temple of Karnak, including a stela in her name by Aahmes.

FREDERICK MONDERSON

Black History Everyday - Part One Photo. Faces and signs in the crowd for the 50th Anniversary March on Washington.

We get an early glimpse of the Queen Mother or Vulture Crown being worn by her daughter Aahmes-Nefertari; whose influence was in itself far reaching. She was a black skinned beauty who gained legendary status. Both herself and son Amenhotep were deified as deities of the Theban necropolis, even having a temple in both their names. Years later, when Hatshepsut was on the throne of Kemet, and faced with questions regarding her legitimacy to rule, she boasted of her heritage that was tied to this queen.

Hatshepsut herself was Queen or should I say "King" of Egypt/Kemet. She had a daughter named Nefru-re; whose tutor was Senmut her architect. She had another daughter named Hatshepsut and this daughter

BLACK HISTORY EVERYDAY
PART ONE

married Tuthmose III. As such, Hatshepsut could be considered both Queen and Queen Mother, though her influence as the latter was much curtailed.

The next significant "Queen Mother" was Queen Tiy, wife of Amenhotep III and mother of Amenhotep IV, Ikhnaton, the revolutionary. This Queen, who looked "so Nubian," was thought to be everything but African and yet credited with having too much power and influence. She held a position of reverence and equality with her husband Amenhotep III, the "Magnificent," who built Luxor Temple, the "Grand Lodge." She sat on the throne beside him in equality. He also built a palace called Malcata, the "place of rejoicing" for this "Queen Mother." What a praise for this African Queen. Her influence on her son Amenhotep IV, Ikhnaton, and his religious revolution was significant, though Hayes believed reactions to the Amarna Revolution absolved her of any involvement.

On a scarab she is shown wearing the vulture headdress or "Queen Mother Crown." The queen of Tutankhamon, the next king in this dynasty, is shown wearing this crown with a menat and sistrum in a small shrine of her husband.

During the Nineteenth Dynasty, the great pharaoh, military strategist, father, husband, builder, high priest, etc., Rameses II, built the Abu Simbel temple in Nubia. Adjacent, he built another temple for his beloved Nefertari, the Nubian. Some thought he built

FREDERICK MONDERSON

his and her temples to solidify his relations with the people of Nubia after marrying one of their princesses.

Nevertheless, despite having several wives and untold numbers of sons, one could well imagine his favorite Nefertari as playing the role of Queen Mother with its attendant responsibilities and influences as their nation dominated the ancient world. Rameses II left ample evidence of their relationship. More than two thousand years later, in the time of the empires of the Western Sudanic empires of Ghana, Mali, and Songhay, Ibn Battuta wrote of the equality, freedom and independence of the women of these societies.

Black History Everyday - Part One Photo. We Shall Not be Moved March.
Faces in the Crowd.

BLACK HISTORY EVERYDAY
PART ONE

Yaa Asantewaa was a respected and significant heroine in Ghanaian and West African history. In the heyday of British imperialism in Africa, she was appalled at the performance of her nation's troops against a British army who had sought to desecrate the "Golden Stool," symbol and soul of the Ghanaian people. Following their defeat in one of a series of wars, she motivated and galvanized the warriors who were ultimately victorious against the British. Here is another unique example of black troops defeating a disciplined and more heavily armed European army. In this case, however, it was commanded by a Queen as in the case of Candace of old Ethiopia and Queen Nzinga against the Portuguese during the days of slave trade and ultimately slavery.

"Given the increasing diversity of America's population, the dangers of sectarianism have never been greater. Whatever we once were, we are no longer just a Christian nation; we are also a Jewish nation, a Muslim nation, a Buddhist nation, a Hindu nation, and a nation of nonbelievers. And even if we did have only Christians in our midst, if we expelled every non-Christian from the United States of America, whose Christianity would we teach in the schools? Would we go with James Dobson's, or Al Sharpton's? Which passages of Scripture should guide our public policy? Should we go with Leviticus, which suggests slavery is ok and that eating shellfish is abomination? How about

FREDERICK MONDERSON

Deuteronomy, which suggests stoning your child if he strays from the faith? Or should we just stick to the Sermon on the Mount – a passage that is so radical that it's doubtful that our own Defense Department would survive its application? So, before we get carried away, let's read our bibles. Folks haven't been reading their bibles." **Barack Obama**, Speech, November 2008

"A good compromise, a good piece of legislation, is like a good sentence; or a good piece of music. Everybody can recognize it. They say, 'Huh. It works. It makes sense.'" Barack Obama

36. THE OBAMA LEGACY II BY DR. FRED MONDERSON

Just before the 2014 mid-term election season began, a high-ranking Democratic senator was asked to define the Obama Legacy in which she responded, "It has not yet been written." What she actually meant, "Mr. Obama was making his list, checking it twice, crossing his eyes and dotting his tees, while being mindful of those who have been especially naughty." Then came the 'shellacking' of 2014 and 'talking heads,' 'pseudo-pundits' and certainly Republicans particularly "Tea Partyers" began singing Mr. Obama's "swan song," even christening him "Lame Duck!" Mr. Romney advised, "Mr. Obama should start packing!" To their great surprise, whether while from pontificating about Mr. Obama's leadership

BLACK HISTORY EVERYDAY
PART ONE

demise or distracted in a drunken euphoric party of his political legacy. They were certainly surprised by his re-election. So much so, though Republicans entered the 114th Congress in control of both Houses of Congress, they were left holding the bag as Mr. Obama triumphantly rode into the realm of history as one of the greatest presidents this nation has ever had. Notwithstanding, the ungrateful and fickle-mindedness of some of the American people, no matter how you wash their dirty linen, every 8-12 years they clean house and change party leadership. This is an unintended consequence of a viable system. Nevertheless, because of the forgiving nature of its people America eventually rehabilitates those initially proscribed. Much more important, young as he is, with his compounded wisdom and having proved a master of navigating Republican minefields, not only was Mr. Obama immune to their "dirty pool" but his cue stick, full of "English," proved to be very interestingly enlightening and will be for decades to come. Given that one man can become a majority and given the sum total of his assets, Mr. Obama, now out of office can exert moral leadership as an elder statesman of integrity and experience.

FREDERICK MONDERSON

Black History Everyday - Part One
Photo. Faces and signs in the crowd for the 50th Anniversary March on Washington.

Astute commentators and persons of vision certainly acknowledge Mr. Obama's legacy has been long in the making. Today, in the pugilistic business, most fights are 10 or 12 rounds, but in the classic contest, "Frazier-Ali" 15 rounds were the norm. In that long contest Mr. Obama was "still standing" at the final bell, showing he had taken hits and returned more with even greater ferocity. As such, though his opponents chose to celebrate their pyrrhic victory, even they will come to acknowledge Obama was a formidable opponent.

A cursory look at Mr. Obama's legacy will reveal, given circumstances as they unfolded, a photograph or two should suffice but not the chapter and verses more rightly volumes that recount the many episodes in a distinguished career. First and most significant, Mr. Obama did not commit ethically or

BLACK HISTORY EVERYDAY
PART ONE

morally reprehensible acts and as such this category is out. Using a baseball analogy, we are reminded statistically, if a batter hits the ball three times out of ten times at bat, he is considered a 300-hitter and headed to the Hall of Fame.

Black History Everyday - Part One Photo. We Shall Not be Moved March. Faces in the Crowd.

In viewing Mr. Obama's legacy, a number of factors can be considered, viz., What he did positively; What he did negatively; What was done to him; How he handled negativity directed towards him; What he brought in terms of decision-making strategies; and, how Americans benefitted from his leadership; and finally how the nation's enemies, domestic and foreign, feared in the Age of Obama. In sum, the record has shown, Mr. Obama stamped his imprint not only on America but significantly on the world stage. Despite the partisan naysayers and their

FREDERICK MONDERSON

directed negativity, at home, even abroad, considering where the nation was upon his arrival, all that has transpired where he left it upon his tenure's end, there is no question his legacy is strong, firm and indelible. That erstwhile adviser to Presidents, David Gergen in commentary when discussing Mr. Obama's accomplishments in the economy especially on how Wall Street is doing responded, "Yes, but a lot of people are still doing terribly."

Black History Everyday - Part One Photo. Dr. Asante in company of beautiful Black women at **CEMOTAP's** 31st Anniversary Celebration.

In response, here's a scenario. A graffiti artist inundates a wall with his colorful handiwork and a clean-up crew is assigned to erase all evidence of the saturation. This is not an easy task. Now, see this in human-societal interaction. Given the state of the nation when Mr. Obama won the Presidency. The economy was in shambles loosing 500,000 to

BLACK HISTORY EVERYDAY
PART ONE

800,000 jobs per month for the longest. Banks were in disarray. Wall Street had plummeted to 6500, the Auto Industry had lost its market share, "first responders" jobs were on the chopping block, the nation's infrastructure was in shambles and then only people making money were the gun merchants supplying the war effort in Iraq and Afghanistan. At a past Al Smith Dinner, former President George W. Bush described these and similar entities, "They call you the wealthy, I call you my base." Nothing has changed!

In addition, the price of imported gas was more than four dollars per gallon. Today that is halved. Not much has changed even though the car remained in the ditch; George Bush's base became the Republican base.

Mr. Obama set about strategizing on how to deal effectively with the wars in Iraq and Afghanistan, reform the nation's economic and financial system, securing "first responders" jobs, bailing out the auto industry despite stiff opposition, rescuing banks and Wall Street, offering incentives for clean energy initiatives, revamping education standards and providing security for teachers' jobs while emphasizing the important role of Community Colleges and encouraging parents to return to school. Laws were made to ensure equality of women in the work place and the long-delayed discrimination against Black Farmers was settled, though it took some time for them to be compensated. Interesting,

FREDERICK MONDERSON

Mr. Obama did not single out Black Americans for special favors lest it be said he was a "Black" rather than American President. While campaign rhetoric haggled with white unemployment rates at 8-10 percent, Black rates were double. Black youth unemployment rates were staggering high at 40-50 percent. These people were certainly not premier in Mr. Gergen's account!

The hunt for Osama bin-Laden, Somali Pirates, the shenanigans of Iran and North Korea and the heavy burden of the Presidency Mr. Obama bore like Atlas holding up the globe. As a racist seed germ mistakenly then dubbed "Tea Party" ramped their questionable behavior, equally racist militias were armed to teeth were preparing for their manufactured "race war." Much of this was generated as race fodder. In all of this, racist propaganda, a climate of disrespect and threats to the President's safety mounted. The false patriots exposed their jagged under-belly for the world to see. Now that a white man "threatens the nation's institutions and way of life, they are silent. The Secret Service realized they could not lose President Obama. Pleasing their handlers, Mitch McConnell and John Boehner exposed their dirty drawers and the world stood in awed astonishment over American sanctimoniousness.

BLACK HISTORY EVERYDAY
PART ONE

Black History Everyday - Part One Photo. We Shall Not be Moved March. Faces in the Crowd.

"How come you ain't got no brothers up on the wall." [Sheldon] Spike Lee. *Do the Right Thing* [*Movie*]

"We are determined that the great government that gave us liberty and rendered its gifts valuable by giving us the ballot shall not find us wanting in a sufficient response to any demand that humanity or patriotism may make upon us; and we ask such action as will not only protect us in the enjoyment of our constitutional rights, but will preserve the integrity of our republican institutions." Blanche Kelso Bruce. *Speech to United States Senate.*

FREDERICK MONDERSON

37. THE "SOUTHERN FIREWALL" BY DR. FRED MONDERSON

A new classification, not a new concept or reality, has emerged in the current political debate, namely the "African-American firewall," and it has never been truer. The iconic Malcolm X, waxing philosophically and realistically, pointed out the national electorate is so evenly divided, the African-American vote makes the difference and determines "who goes to the White House and who go to the Dog House." In the current scenario, as the Democratic contenders Bernie Sanders and Hillary Clinton vie, with Mr. Sanders projected a potential winner in both Iowa and New Hampshire, pundits have begun pointing to Hillary's "African-American Southern Firewall" in South Carolina, Georgia and Mississippi especially. This is certainly interesting that the Clinton camp recognizes the importance of the African-American vote and is, first of all, weighing heavily on South Carolina's "Firewall" where the African-American constituency does not have the same appreciation for Bernie Sanders. It is also strange that an African-American, Ben Carson, is also on the 2016 Presidential landscape but ironically cannot "drink from this important political fountain." So, what then is the Quid Pro Quo? Is there a Quid Pro Quo? How do African-Americans benefit from this scenario?

However, we must first distinguish between Henry Kissinger and Richard Nixon's "Southern Strategy"

BLACK HISTORY EVERYDAY PART ONE

and the current "Southern Firewall." The former was a master stroke to undergird a ticket and secure votes in the southern states, while the latter is a defensive mechanism to block a surging candidate, bolstering another and placing much faith in the African-American constituency's Democratic Party loyalty to reinforce former Secretary of State Hillary Clinton's "Grassroots" inclusion program. South Carolina is thus early and pivotal in this unfolding political drama and it should be noticed the Clinton camp seems all "wrapped up in the Obama colors" because the President is a "favorite son," not simply here but throughout the South to which the Democratic primary now focuses. However, this demonstrated loyalty is never handsomely repaid and any concessions and privileges are only relinquished under duress and hard-won circumstances.

Nevertheless, we need carefully examine the American political landscape to understand how the African-American constituency has risen from "King's footstool to King maker." As such, it has been a slug-fest, fighting for every inch of territory from the time the United States Political establishment recognized the enslaved African as $3/5^{th}$ of a man to the Constitution's **1965 Voting Rights Act** and the subsequent coming of age of the Black vote in persons such as Representative Charles Rangel and the gentleman Rep. Conyers from Michigan. Thus, a quick perusal of the American political landscape demonstrates:

FREDERICK MONDERSON

1. The **1787 Compromise** or the **3/5th Compromise Clause** - recognized and counted 5 Africans for 3 whites for political representation purposes and to secure southern support to ratify the Constitution.

2. The **1793 Cotton Gin of Eli Whitney** - made stripping the cotton seed much easier thereby increasing produce and facilitating a greater demand for Africans to plant and pick cotton.

3. The **Fugitive Slave Acts** empowered Slave Catchers to return runaways in which free Blacks were often entrapped and re-enslaved.

Black History Everyday - Part One Photo. Faces and signs in the crowd for the 50th Anniversary March on Washington.

BLACK HISTORY EVERYDAY
PART ONE

4. The **1808 Outlawing of the Slave Trade** - after a 20-year wait from 1787-1807, the British first outlawed the Slave Trade in 1807 and the Americans followed the next year in 1808. However, this prohibition led to an "**Internal Slave Trade**" practiced in the "deep south" in which "slave farms grew humans" and sent "coffles" of hapless Africans being taken to market to be sold.

5. General Andrew Jackson's 1819 foray into Florida to **punish Native American Seminoles** for aiding and giving sanctuary to enslaved Africans who ran away from slavery and made it to their territory, was an act of genuine brutality.

6. The **Missouri Compromise of 1820** banned slavery in that part of the Louisiana Purchase.

7. **David Walker's 1826 "Appeal"** to enslaved-Africans exhorted, "Throw off your chains, resist your enslavement and help overthrow the evil institution of chattel slavery."

8. The **1832 Nullification Act of South Carolina** and attempts to secede from the Union were severely rejected by President Andrew Jackson

FREDERICK MONDERSON

who mobilized federal forces to place the state under martial law.

9. The **Compromise of 1850** encouraged the later Lincoln/Douglas Debates of 1858 at the time the nation stood as "a house divided." The new law specifically enabled California to enter the union as a free state, strengthened the Fugitive Slave Acts and by popular sovereignty allowed people to determine if the **Mexican Cession** territory was to be free or slave.

Black History Everyday - Part One Photo. We Shall Not be Moved March. Faces in the Crowd.

10. The **1857 Dred Scott Decision**, in denying the humanity and political status of the African person on the eve of the Civil War, helped underscore the brilliance of President Abraham Lincoln's "House Divided" speech. In the Supreme

BLACK HISTORY EVERYDAY
PART ONE

Court's decision, Chief Justice Roger Taney essentially ruled "a master did not lose his right to property regardless" and that "Blacks were not citizens and could not bring suit in US Court" and even more, Blacks "had no rights a white man was bound to respect."

11. At Civil War's end, the "Party of Lincoln," the **Radical Republicans**, won unanimous support of the Freedman through their championing the 13th Amendment that freed the slaves; 14th Amendment which gave citizenship to persons born in the United States of America; and the 15th Amendment gave the right to vote to all such Americans. That is, males only, Black and White. The Freedman's Bureau doled out support in food, clothing, fuel and health services to the destitute regardless of race. Land was given to create some of the famous **Black Colleges and Universities** such as **Fisk University** (the Black Harvard), **Howard University**, **Atlanta University** and **Hampton Institute** were all beneficiaries of land grants.

12. While Reconstruction sought to "level the playing field," the 1877 "Betrayal" that brought the Southerner Rutherford B. Hayes to the Presidency, unintentionally, perhaps intentionally, gave "official" support to terror groups as the Knights of the Ku Klux Klan, Knights of the White Camelia, White

FREDERICK MONDERSON

Brotherhood, The Jayhawkers, Black Horse Cavalry, etc., who terrorized the Freedman with beatings, tarring and feathering, mutilations, threats, lynchings, and more while the White Citizens' Councils conducted and regulated "White Primaries," etc., undergirded by Jim Crow's *de jure* and *de facto* legislation and practice. When, during slavery, Blacks were economic property they were protected by the master; freed and lacking such protections, they were terrorized, lynched, held in economic peonage and other forms of servitude and in a vigorously orchestrated campaign kept from the polls. In this era, the racist South Carolina Senator Bill Tillman said in Congress, "We have done our level best. We have scratched our heads to find out how we could eliminate the last one of them (the Black voters). We stuffed ballot boxes. We shot them. We are not ashamed of it."

13. The **1896 Plessy v. Ferguson** decision of the Supreme Court gave legal sanction to "Jim Crow" segregation and racial discrimination under cover of "Separate but Equal" which was in fact, "Separate and Unequal," in both social and economic standing, and especially in education.

14. Overturning the "**Grandfather Clause**" in 1915, the Supreme Court slowly began to chip away at the mountain of oppression built up especially in the half-century from 1865 to 1915, which was a continuation of centuries of ghastly Slave Trade and Slavery wherein masters created a racial hierarchy among "House Slaves" and "Free

BLACK HISTORY EVERYDAY
PART ONE

Slaves." In that relationship, the House Slaves served the master in the capacity of maids, cooks, butlers, footmen, coachmen, grooms, valets, nurses and launderers. Equally, a skilled group of Blacks functioned as gardeners, brick-makers, weavers, carpenters, shoemakers, blacksmiths, and masons. Some slaves had mastered their skills and their master got the praise and money they earned and doled out pittance to the workers. Yet, out of this, thrifty African saved and purchased their freedom, even that of family members. Even more important, from the demonstrated skills, many US government patents were made by Blacks, registered by owners and these cheated the creators out of the benefits.

The Field Slaves did the work of staple crop production. They worked from dusk to dawn; both men and women working the same hours. There's evidence of personal abuse of the African woman by masters, their sons, overseers and even fellow slaves happened often.

After winning the vote from 1868 to 1928, Blacks voted, those who could, for a single party, the Republicans, Lincoln's Party. Though promises made were never kept, lynchings escalated resulting in forced waves of migration northward seeking to escape the climax of 19th and 20th Century American terrorism attest to conditions for flight. However, while Teddy Roosevelt only promised a "**Fair Deal**" and Woodrow Wilson betrayed his promises,

FREDERICK MONDERSON

Franklin D. Roosevelt generated a "**New Deal**" which encouraged Blacks to flock to the Democratic ticket, helping to ensure the Depression victory of 1932. However, it was FDR's wife Eleanor who helped bring about relief by listening/addressing Black concerns of inequality.

15.   Whatever may be said of A. Philip Randolph, as a quintessential activist and resolute civil rights leader of his age, he proposed the 1941 "**March on Washington**," because, 9 years after the Black vote solidified FDR's 1932 win and again in 1936 and 1940, Blacks fared dismally in securing jobs especially in the expanding war industry. Only fear of such an untimely show of coordinated Black force and its political impact, did President Roosevelt address this issue, with an Executive Action banning discrimination in the war industry job recruitment program. Seventy-five years later Black leaders can learn from this master stroke as a political demand especially as the "Southern Firewall" had begun to manifest.

BLACK HISTORY EVERYDAY PART ONE

Black History Everyday - Part One Photo. Another beautiful lady along with Dr. Len Jeffreys joins Dr. Asante and the Beautiful Ladies at **CEMOTAP's** 31st Anniversary Celebration.

16.   While Harry Truman desegregated the military at the end World War II, it took another decade of legal and civil rights agitation before passage of the 1954 landmark *Brown v. Board of Education of Topeka, Kansas* case championed by the later Supreme Court Justice Thurgood Marshall. Yet, Blacks still had to wait another decade for the 1964 **Civil Rights Act** and the 1965 **Voting Rights Act** with their promised universal application. However, while these laws were enacted, enforcement became another matter and every election since shenanigans characterized Republican attempts to eviscerate the Black vote. This was particularly so as late as the 2008 effort to derail

FREDERICK MONDERSON

Senator Obama's successful run for the presidency. In subsequent Republican controlled statehouses actions across the nation, efforts were made to erect roadblocks through Gerrymandering and other measures to nullify the Black vote. Between 2008 and 2016, the Justice Department under Eric Holder was continuously employed in litigating Republican controlled statehouses seeking to curtail the Black vote.

Black History Everyday - Part One Photo. We Shall Not be Moved March. Faces in the Crowd.

In conjunction, the Republican playbook was repeated in the 2012 "Stop Obama" effort and conspiracy that revealed both Republicans and Democrats tied President Obama's hands especially when Republicans swept to legislative control in the 2010 and again 2014 mid-term elections. Then, in control of Congressional funds, they not only continued to block the President's every initiative, it

BLACK HISTORY EVERYDAY
PART ONE

turned out the tremendous effort against President Obama was fueled by a treasonous gathering of high-level Republicans going back to January, 2009 if not sooner. These plotted to block the legally constituted government from functioning under President Obama's leadership. While only 20 Republican funded Non-Governmental Organizations were named in the conspiracy along with former Attorney General Ed Meese in *The New York Times* October 6, 2013 "big write up" article, it stands to reason anyone in the Republican high-echelon "Who's Who," especially those publically vocal against President Obama were involved in the treasonous conspiracy. We can't exclude Donald Trump, "the Birther King," whom some have described as fascist (like Hitler and Goebbels), recognizing the White establishment is letting him get away; for as Lincoln reminded, "To be silent in face of wrongdoing is to be culpable of such evil." Even more, Edmund Burke had echoed the same, "The only thing necessary for evil to triumph is for good men to say or do nothing." So, Ben Carson, as well as Herman Cain, J.C. Watts, Allen West, etc., should realize, swimming in dangerous waters can be costly, but equally, Black-Americans will always remember their actions. It's as Rev. Al Sharpton recently said to Kanye West, "Donald Trump will be out of office one day, but we will remember these developments for a long time."

FREDERICK MONDERSON

Black History Everyday - Part One Photo. Faces and signs in the crowd for the 50th Anniversary March on Washington.

Black History Everyday - Part One Photo. Young men attending the 20th Anniversary of the **Million Man March** in 2015.

"Probably he [the white historian] thinks it has something to do with economics, or with greed, or with lust; most likely he thinks the effects of the Trade can be seen in the shift of the worldwide balance of power.... To an extent, he will be correct.

BLACK HISTORY EVERYDAY
PART ONE

But he will also believe that the African Slave Trade [Atlantic Slave Trade, European Slave Trade] is over, that whatever its effects were, they are existing now in and of themselves, waves spreading across a pond, the stone that ca used them long ago come to rest. He will think this because to understand otherwise involves dealing with something so basic, so elemental, so fundamental that it can be faced only if one is forced to face it: death. For that is what the Slave Trade was all about. Not death from poxes and musketry and whippings and malnutrition and melancholy and suicide; death itself." David Bradley, Jr. *The Chaneyville Incident* [1981]

38. THE TRIANGULAR TRADE
BY
DR. FRED MONDERSON

The "Triangular Trade" is considered the effective or economic component of the Atlantic or European Slave Trade from Africa to America. Together with the "Middle Passage" and the "Institution of Slavery," history records four centuries of European and American inhumanity towards Africans, man, woman, child. The degradation of this experience has been called a "crime against the human spirit." In fact, it was a crime against Africa, African people and against humanity in general. So, we need to understand how logistics of the trade operated in a triangle that began in Europe, involved Africa, and the Americas and returned to Europe. Picton's view (1873: 222) is an apt description for he has written: "The ships sailed from Liverpool to the West Coast of Africa, where they shipped the slaves from depots where their living freight had been collected; thence to the West Indian islands where the slaves were sold, and the proceeds brought home in proceeds of sugar and rum."

Davidson (1966: 204-205) helps in understanding this even more when he wrote: "There developed what was to become known as the triangular trade, a commercial system which greatly helped to build the continued industrial and technical progress of western Europe in the eighteenth and nineteenth centuries." Equally, DuBois (1971: 227-228) added his take of this phenomenon, particularly in the British areas of the Caribbean, when he wrote: "If we confine ourselves to America, we cannot forget that this nation was built on African backs. From being a mere stopping place between Europe and Asia or a chance treasure house of gold, America became through African labor the center of the sugar empire and the cotton kingdom and an integral part of that world industry and trade which caused the Industrial Revolution and the reign of capitalism."

This operation started with the opening up of America and continued well into the Nineteenth Century. Portugal and Brazil were the last colonialist nations to outlaw the institution of slavery in 1888, and by some were among the cruelest.

BLACK HISTORY EVERYDAY PART ONE

The "Triangular Trade" got its greatest boost in the commercial expansion of the eighteenth and first decades of the nineteenth centuries. This is very well documented. Admittedly, historical evidence consists of primary and secondary sources. While a number of primary sources are consulted in this piece, a small but powerful book entitled *Capitalism and Slavery*, by the late Dr. Eric Williams, is a good secondary source. This prolific and very analytic writer on African experiences in the New World, was former Prime Minister of Trinidad and Tobago. Published in 1944, his work stirred the imagination of the academic and lay worlds. Erudite scholarship, profuse documentation, and a blockbuster thesis focused on the British involvement in an important aspect of world commerce in the centuries following America's discovery. The major thesis of his book is very interesting. The position argues essentially, the "abolition of the slave trade and ultimately slavery was an economic necessity rather than a humanitarian venture." This is to say, as the world changed particularly from the time of the Industrial Revolution, slavery became too expensive to maintain and not as efficient. This view, during and after World War II, provoked many an anti-thesis. Especially, before and still after the publication of *Capitalism and Slavery*, some scholars have tried to over emphasize the role of the abolitionists in outlawing the slave trade, and ultimately slavery. Williams' thesis notwithstanding, the work of abolitionists must be given serious consideration for without their unrelenting efforts the demise of the

FREDERICK MONDERSON

horrific institution would have been prolonged. In defense of his thesis, Eric Williams provided documented proof that socio-economic transformations, in Europe and America, intertwined with the enterprise of slavery and slave trade probably required labor supply devices that were tremendously profitable, particularly since labor costs were basically minimal. Nevertheless, the struggle against slavery, then and today, whether physical, emotional or psychological, had to be and needs be waged in Africa, Europe and America. For that matter, worldwide racism, discrimination and prejudice must get similar treatment.

Black History Everyday - Part One Photo. We Shall Not be Moved March. Faces in the Crowd.

His argument that the slave trade provided one of the main streams of labor, which in turn generated the capital to launch the industrial revolution in Europe, is a credible one. It eventually followed, changes

BLACK HISTORY EVERYDAY
PART ONE

brought about by an emerging industrial economy in Europe and later America, made the trade in forced slave labor inefficient. More precisely, the industrial revolution resulted in transformation of the economic, social, political and military systems of the west. This change also escalated the basis, structure, process and methodology of research and the scientific nature of the western world. As such, in a credible and defensible argument he has shown, the slave trade helped to finance social, scientific and industrial change in Europe and America. This institution itself became obsolete; that is, the slave involvement in the growing cash-economy of the west.

A good example of how the "Triangular Trade" operated is explained in this way. Imagine an English trader operating out of one of the main British slaving ports of London, Bristol or Liverpool. This merchant would outfit a ship's voyage, with what by today's standards, can be considered junk, yet precious in the economies to which it was destined. Wells (1902: 95) described the "manifest of a Bristol ship named **Dispatch**, which left the port on a slaving voyage in 1725. The cargo included 1,330 [British] pounds worth of copper rods, cotton goods, a cask of cowries, 2000 rangoes, 206 cwt. of iron bars, 10 barrels of gunpowder, 12 cwt. of glass beads, 207 gallons of brandy, 37 gallons of cordial gin, 18 hats edged with gold and silver. The return was 240 choice slaves, between 10 25.... A cargo of slaves might be worth 6,000 pounds."

FREDERICK MONDERSON

Gomer Williams (1897: 680) supplied another view of this trade when commenting on the price paid for a Negro man at Bonny, Nigeria, in 1801. The sale amounted to "one piece of chintz, eighteen yards long. One piece of baft, eighteen yards long. One piece of chelloe, eighteen yards long. One piece of Bandanoe, seven handkerchiefs. One piece of nicannee, fourteen yards long. One piece of Photae, fourteen yards long. Three pieces of Romalls, forty-five handkerchiefs. One large Brass pan, two muskets. Two bags of shots, twenty knives. Four iron pots, four hats, four caps. Four cutlasses, six bunches of beads, fourteen gallons Brandy. These articles cost about 25 British pounds."

Eric Williams helps further in his example by listing exports to Africa for the year 1787, as part of the goods in the "Triangular Trade." These were "cotton and linen goods, silk handkerchiefs, coarse blue and red woolen cloths." The British also sold "scarlet cloth in grain, coarse and fine hats, worsted caps, guns, powder, shot and sabers." Even further, they shipped "lead bars, iron bars, pewter basins, copper kettles and pans." Other items included, "iron pots, hardware of various kinds, earthen and glass ware, hair and gilt leather trunks." English merchants and traders sold the Africans "beads of various kinds, silver and gold rings and ornaments." Finally, the trade included, "paper, coarse and fine checks, linen ruffled shirts and caps, British and foreign spirits and tobacco." Such workings contributed to full

BLACK HISTORY EVERYDAY
PART ONE

employment in a society fueled by the dynamism of emerging industrial and economic institutions.

The commodities were put on board ships bound for Africa, and exchanged for Africans who were then shipped to the Americas. Here they were sold or exchanged with further investment being made in tropical products that were taken back to England. A handsome profit was realized all round. Again, a ship sailed outfitted for Africa with, for example, 500 British pounds of good was able to exchange this for something like three times its worth, say 1,500 British pounds of commodities in Africa, mostly humans.

Black History Everyday - Part One Photo. Faces and signs in the crowd for the 50th Anniversary March on Washington.

In an analogous argument, according to Williams' 1944 work, *Capitalism and Slavery*, in the New World, 1,500 British pounds of African goods fetched about 4,500 British pounds when sold. This

FREDERICK MONDERSON

sum was reinvested in tropical commodities. The Caribbean islands produced sugar, rice, indigo and rum to be shipped to England. At home the returning entrepreneurs sold their tropical products for about 7,500 British pounds. Therefore, according to some sources, as much as 6,000 to 7,000 British pounds could be made on one such venture. Imagine several hundred ships from several ports, of one nation, operating for one, two, three, four hundred years. Multiply this by the various ports of other nations involved in the trade, with their various ports. The profits and accumulated capital were enormous and guaranteed, from enslaving persons of Africa. This then is what is meant in the argument, particularly made as **Introduction** to the *TV Documentary*, **The Fight against Slavery**, narrated by Ruby Dee, when she said "The Slave Trade provided one of the main streams of capital that launched the Industrial Revolution.

Black History Everyday - Part One Photo. Rev. Al Sharpton leaves a gathering of "Keepers of the Dream" honoring Dr. M.L. King.

BLACK HISTORY EVERYDAY
PART ONE

Black History Everyday - Part One Photo. We Shall Not be Moved March. Faces in the Crowd.

The role of the British in the Slave Trade resulted in tremendous financial gain to tat nation. This is also a view clearly enunciated by Dr. Eric Williams' *Capitalism and Slavery*. This classic text showed how the "Triangular Trade" was fueled because "England, France and Colonial America supplied the exports and the ships; Africa the human merchandise; the plantations the colonial raw materials" worked by the human capital.

Williams further explained how the Triangular Trade gave a triple stimulus to British industry.

FREDERICK MONDERSON

Black History Everyday - Part One Photo. Everyone minding their own business at **CEMOTAP'S** 31st Anniversary Celebration.

"The Negroes were purchased with British manufactures; transported to the plantations, they produced sugar, cotton, indigo, molasses and other tropical products, the processing of which created new industries in England; while the maintenance of the Negroes and their owners on the plantations provided another market for British industry."

Clearly, such impact of the Triangular Trade on British industry was experienced in many areas. The first important gain occurred in shipping and shipbuilding. British shipping industry benefited tremendously by building bigger and faster ships to carry more Africans. Seaport towns expanded as ports developed to handle the prodigious increase in

BLACK HISTORY EVERYDAY
PART ONE

British shipping. Also, participation in the slave trade had become a "nursery" for British seamen and Britain's merchant marine. During times of war, these seamen aided the British Navy. Equally important, building crafts, techniques, and skills got a tremendous shot in the arm from their involvement in the trade, that was described not as actual trade but murder and robbery. Still, it meant, individuals were employed, wrote Williams, "in ancillary trades as carpenters, painters, boat builders, tradesmen and artisans connected with repairs, equipment and loading of slaving ships, both in Europe and America." These industries benefited.

Commissions, dock duties, and insurance increased from the trade in Africans, to fund other enterprises. Many British seaport towns expanded from the slave trade. Bristol, London, Liverpool, and Glasgow benefited enormously from their involvement. Port facilities expanded to accommodate the increase in shipping. This is noted above. Such expansion was experienced, more-so, in the latter decades of the eighteenth and early decades of the nineteenth century as the engines of industry progressed.

In *The City of Bristol*, Wells (1902: 95) noted, "the trade of the port was so great in 1725 that two new quays were built one at St. Augustine's back and one near King Street. In 1736 Corporation dues ... at 40 shillings on each 60-ton ship; ... dues ... worth 1000 pounds a year in those times."

FREDERICK MONDERSON

Customs payment of Liverpool and Bristol for the years 1753 1757 were:

Year	Bristol	Liverpool
	[In British Pounds]	
1753	170,361. 13s. 1 1/4d.	45,479 1s. 1 1/2d.
1754	156,717. 9s. 1 3/4d.	59,766 6s. 0 3/4d.
1755	177,894. 15s. 4 1/2d.	49,661 0s. 8 1/2d.
1756	155,951. 5s. 5 d.	49,976 11s. 1 1/2d.
1757	151,516. 1s. 1 1/4d.	60,263 15s. 10 1/2d.

In 1764 Bristol's contribution as a revenue producing port was, 195,000 [British] pounds and Liverpool 70,000 [British] pounds. The dues paid to the Society of Merchants by vessels of 60 tons and upwards increased from 918 British pounds in 1745 to 2000 in 1775."

More particularly, *The City of Bristol* boasted rather questionable beginnings for, according to Wells (1909: 381) its "first overseas trade was in white slaves, and the early prosperity of the trade was due to that nefarious traffic." In fact, Wells (1909: 382) again pointed out: "Bristol men kidnapped or bought the best of the youth of both sexes whenever they could. In the Bristol market strings of young men and maidens stood tied together waiting to be bought." If this is how "merchants" treated their own people, imagine how they treated Africans who were "different."

BLACK HISTORY EVERYDAY
PART ONE

Black History Everyday - Part One
Photo. Faces and signs in the crowd for the 50th Anniversary March on Washington.

Following John Hawkins' exploits two centuries earlier, Wells (1909: 383 84) informs: "In 1764 Charles II gave a body of London Merchants a monopoly to trade with Africa .... A flagrant injustice to the Bristol Merchant Venturers who had chartered rights in the trade.... Bill of Rights (1689) ... put an end to that monopoly ... gave great impetus to Bristol African Commerce. In 1696 London Merchants formed the Royal African Company tried to get the monopoly back .... The Royal African Company could not ship more than 3000 slaves per annum."

"Parliament passed an Act in 1698 virtually establishing free trade in slaves .... an Act of Parliament in 1759 threw the trade open to anybody

FREDERICK MONDERSON

willing to pay a registration fee of 2 [British] pounds, and thenceforth Liverpool became an important slave trading port .... By 1752 Bristol was the leading port in the trade. London came second and Liverpool third."

Black History Everyday - Part One Photo. We Shall Not be Moved March. Faces in the Crowd.

"300,000 [British] pounds per annum from slaves, 74,000 shipped a year from Africa. The price of slaves in Jamaica were about 5 [British] pounds for boys and girls. On the West Coast of Africa, they could be bought for 20 shillings each." Twenty shillings equaled one British pound.

In 1753 there were at least 20 sugar refineries in Bristol. John Latimer's *The History of the Society of Merchant Venturers of the City of Bristol*, (1903:178

BLACK HISTORY EVERYDAY
PART ONE

86) recounts: "Traffic in slaves ... trade to be of the most advantage to this kingdom of any we drive, and as it were all profit; the first cost being little more than small matters of our own manufactures, for which we have in return gold, [elephant's] teeth, wax and Negroes, the last whereof is much better than the first, being indeed the best traffic the kingdom hath." That is, Negroes were worth more than gold.

"Royal African Company, monopoly of trade with Africa granted them by Charles the Second in 1764."

"Merchant Venturers of Bristol .... Surreptitious traffic between the West Coast of Africa and the English plantations in America. That the prosperity of the West India planters depended upon a plentiful supply of Negroes ...."

"An act was passed in 1698, leaving the trade entirely open, the first nine years of open trade the Merchants of Bristol and Liverpool dispatched no less than 160,950 Negroes to the British Plantations."

"Petition to the House of Commons in 1713, ... that the subsistence of Bristolians chiefly depended on this trade, which gave employment to great numbers of seamen, shipwrights, weavers, metal workers, and other artisans, a large part of whose manufactures were exchanged for Negroes."

"A similar Petition from the Society affirmed that many of their ships were suitable only for the African

FREDERICK MONDERSON

trade and they would be ruined by exclusion from it .... In 1725 the African company, offering the Government a loan of one-million-pound sterling if their monopoly was restored ... rejected ... the trade was solely in the hands of individual merchants or firms. A bundle of loose papers throwing a strange light on the proceedings of some captains in the Royal Navy commanding ships of war stationed on the African coast was found. It appears from these documents, which are affidavits of the masters and sailors of Bristol slave ships, that in the year 1737, whilst the deponents were trying to procure cargoes on the coast, officers and crews of three royal vessels, the Diamond, Greenwich and Spence, lying there ostensibly for the protection of the trade, were actively engaged in the purchase of Negroes, gold dust and elephant's teeth, each of the ships being provided for trafficking with large stores of cotton goods, spirituous liquors, gunpowder and other merchandise, ... while 32 pound per head was given for slaves or 4 pounds above the ordinary rate."

One affidavit state that the Greenwich sailed for Barbados with 200 Negroes and another that the Spence, a small war sloop, carried off fifty or sixty more ... the Society cooperated with the Friends at Liverpool in forwarding a strong remonstrance to the admiralty which apparently succeeded in its object."

"The African Company ... (sponsored a) determined effort in Parliament to secure the trade exclusively for themselves .... that traffic on the Slave Coast could not be protected against foreigners unless a large

BLACK HISTORY EVERYDAY
PART ONE

number of additional forts were built and garrisoned; that the government grant for that purpose (10,000 British pounds a year) was wholly inadequate; and that the charge could only be sustained by a company enjoying exclusive privileges."

"The Common Council in a Petition to the House of Commons, alleged that the trade from this port to the West Indies and America by way of Africa was the Principal and most considerable branch belonging to the City, and that since such trade has been free and open it has greatly increased, much better supplied with Negroes and large quantities of the manufactures of this kingdom exported."

"The average number of human beings yearly being torn from their homes had then reached the appalling total of 74,000; ... Liverpool ... that town alone was making 3000 [British] pounds per annum by the traffic." The value of the British pound in that day was enormous.

"April 13, 1789, at a crowded meeting in the Hall, Mr. William Miles Presiding, an influential Committee was appointed to defend the traffic, "On which the welfare of the West India Islands and the commerce and revenue of the Kingdom so essentially depend."

So, tariff and revenue from the trade also multiplied. For example, Williams indicates: "British customs duties rose from 10,000 [British] pounds in 1634 to

FREDERICK MONDERSON

334,000 pounds in 1785. Wharfage dues payable on every vessel above sixty tons, increased between 1745 and 1755."

Black History Everyday - Part One Photo. We Shall Not be Moved March. Faces in the Crowd.

John Latimer (1893: 270 72) mentioned how the African Company was practically insolvent and unable to raise capital without legislative help.

"(1753) in Liverpool 101, in London 135 and in Bristol 157 merchants who were members of the African Company .... Bristol list dated June 23, 1755 ... 237 members resided in Bristol, 147 in London and 89 in Liverpool .... In 1750 the price demanded of native dealers was from 28 to 32 [British] pounds a head .... that the Bristol and Liverpool shippers could

BLACK HISTORY EVERYDAY
PART ONE

carry the trade 10 or 15 percent cheaper that London."

Black History Everyday - Part One Photo. Faces and signs in the crowd for the 50th Anniversary March on Washington.

This African Company exerted significant influence in the halls of parliament when efforts were made to regulate the trade in Africans. According to Latimer (1893: 476) the "measure was vehemently opposed by the African Merchants in London, Bristol and Liverpool."

Latimer tells (1893: 478) further, "the Bells of the Bristol churches rang merry peals on the news being received of the rejection of one of Wilberforce's motions .... [a Jesuit priest] Reverend Raymond Harris of Liverpool produced 'Scriptural researches on the licitness of the slave trade, showing its conformity with the sacred writings of the word of God' and of course the work was liberally patronized.... The trade was inconsistent with reason, religion and humanity."

Davidson (1971: 19-20) makes a comparison with the then capitalist schemes of things and another pariah state in the modern world where "attitudes allowed no respect either for the victims or for the peoples from whom they came." To those who condemned the trade, British governments of the day replied that it was far too profitable to be stopped. "We cannot," said Lord Dartmouth, Secretary of State for the Colonies in 1775, "allow the colonies to check or to discourage in any degree a traffic so beneficial to the nation." The argument was persuasive, "just how much so we ourselves are well placed to understand today. Nearly two centuries after Lord Dartmouth had enunciated his views on the indispensable benefits of the slave trade, another Conservative British government returned almost exactly the same reply to critics who condemned the sale of arms to the Republic of South Africa. The sale might have its unfortunate side; it was far too profitable to be stopped."

Aggregate import of slaves to Jamaica from 1700 to 1750 numbered 408,101 of whom 108,000 were transferred to other islands, leaving 300,000 settled laborers. Even more significant, growth was experienced in the textile industry. Wool became an enormously profitable business. Perpetuanas, Arrangoes, Bays, Bridgewaters, and Welsh Plaines

BLACK HISTORY EVERYDAY
PART ONE

were all manufactured for sale in the Africa trade. Petitions were received by the government regarding, "Suffolk, Essex, Woolen Traders of London, Woolen Merchants of Plymouth, Woolen Dealers of Totnes and Ashburton, Woolen Manufacturers of Kidderminister, Merchant Adventurers of Minehead" who were all involved. Eric Williams further added, "Wakefield, Halifax, Burnley, Colne, Kendal, were interested in the manufacture of woolen goods for Africa and the West Indies." Can you imagine, the brothers and sisters of Africa wearing "British wool" in the hot tropical sun? This raises the question of psychological programming to desire "foreign goods." Cotton manufacture too was big business. Liverpool, Cottonopolis, Lancashire, and Manchester were heavily involved. The tremendous dependence on the Triangular Trade "made Manchester." So much so, cities not directly involved in outfitting ships for the trade were tied to and benefited from feeder industries.

According to a study by the British Privy Council in 1788, wrote Eric Williams, it was estimated: "Manchester exported annually to Africa, goods worth 200,000 pounds, 180,000 pounds of this for Negroes only; the manufacture of these goods represented an investment of 300,000 pounds and gave employment to 180,000 men, women and children." Even the kids got in on the act!

FREDERICK MONDERSON

The British banking industry was another significant beneficiary from the slave trade. Banks were involved full scale by accepting deposits and helping underwrite much economic development at the time. Particularly, in the Eighteenth Century, a number of banking institutions were begun as a result of the slave trade. Coupled with insurance such "infant industries" found fertile opportunities for growth, development and expansion. The names of banks in the trade included Heywood Bank, Bank of Liverpool, Banking Firm of William Gregson, and Sons, Parke and Moorland and the Manchester Bank. Then there was the Thomas Leyland Bank, the Banking Firm of Charles and Roscoe, and the North and South Wales Bank, Ltd., Hanly's Bank, the Banking Firm of Charles Caldwell, Co., and the New Bank were all involved. Lastly, named were Miles Bank and Barclay's Bank. Yes!

Black History Everyday - Part One Photo. While Rev. Al Sharpton addresses the Rally from the podium, Rev. Herbert Daughtry sits among other dignitaries including Rev. Norris at his rear.

BLACK HISTORY EVERYDAY
PART ONE

Ships' Bank, Arms Bank, Thistle Bank, and William Deacon's Bank, all began in and serviced the Triangular Trade. However, while many of them did not survive or moved on to other enterprises, some banks as Barclay stayed in the same business.

Insurance was needed to cover the cargo whether commodity or humanity. Lloyds of London and Liverpool Underwriters insured the trade. These insurance magnates also helped to finance heavy industry involved in making metal instruments such as canons, anchors and artillery. In addition, attendant metallurgical industries produced fetters, chains, padlocks, and branding irons used for psychological and other forms for behavior modification. These latter were red hot when applied to the skin of anyone. *An Historical Account of Liverpool* tells (1884: 24) of the African "Chief Accra" who "was one of the principal men catchers and slave dealers in Old Calabar," and most used some of these same instruments.

FREDERICK MONDERSON

Black History Everyday - Part One Photo. "Together We Have Power!" **Million Man March** 20th Anniversary.

Black History Everyday - Part One Photo. We Shall Not be Moved March. Faces in the Crowd.

BLACK HISTORY EVERYDAY
PART ONE

Further (1884: 27 28) we are informed: "In the year 1769, Capt. Paterson, of a Liverpool slaver, while lying off Bristol town, induced his men and natives to set fire to two villages and during the conflagration the poor blacks, crying out for help, P's men seized the Negroes, branded them and made them slaves. Another method of obtaining slaves was by inviting traders to come on board ship to dine with the captain, ... supplied with drink, the ship be got under way, ... traders on awakening ... stripped, branded and put down the hole to share the fate of other slaves."

The slave was made to kneel down, the branding iron was red hot, then it was stamped on the poor Negro's forehead, breast, buttock or back, according to the fancy of the brander.

We are told again in the same (1884: 31 32) source, "as many as 800 have been stowed in the holds of these infernal ships ... remaining in for a four month's voyage to the W.I. The white man arrogating to himself the supreme privilege of being lord and master of the blacks; to buy, to sell, to torture and kill as he pleases .... Baron Montesquieu affirmed "It is impossible to allow that the Negroes are men; because, if we allow them to be men, it will begin to be believed that we ourselves are not Christians."

FREDERICK MONDERSON

Black History Everyday - Part One

Photo. Faces and signs in the crowd for the 50th Anniversary March on Washington.

"It's been funny to watch some of these politicians completely rewrite history now that you're back on your feet. These are the folks who said if we went forward with our plan to rescue Detroit, "You can kiss the American automotive industry goodbye." Now they're saying they were right all along. Or worse, they're saying that the problem is that you, the workers, made out like bandits in all of this; that saving the American auto industry was just about paying back unions. Really? Even by the standards of this town, that's a load of you-know-what. About 700,000 retirees saw a reduction in the health care benefits they had earned. Many of you saw hours reduced, or pay and wages scaled back. You gave up some of your rights as workers. Promises were made to you over the years that you gave up for the sake and survival of this industry, its workers, and their families. You want to talk about values? Hard work — that's a value. Looking out for one another —

BLACK HISTORY EVERYDAY
PART ONE

that's a value. The idea that we're all in it together — that I am my brother's keeper; I am my sister's keeper — that is a value. But they're still talking about you as if you're some greedy special interest that needs to be beaten. Since when are hardworking men and women special interests? Since when is the idea that we look out for each other a bad thing? To borrow a line from our old friend Ted Kennedy: What is it about working men and women they find so offensive?" *Barack Obama, Addressing United Auto Workers* in Washington DC, February 2012

"I reject the idea that asking a hedge fund manager to pay the same tax rate as a teacher or a plumber is class warfare. I think it's just the right thing to do. Both parties agree that we need to reduce the deficit by the same amount, by $4 trillion. So what choices are we going to make to reach that goal? Either we ask the wealthiest Americans to pay their fair share in taxes or we ask seniors to pay more for Medicare. We can't afford to do both. Either we gut education and medical research or we've got to reform the tax code so that most profitable corporations have to give up tax loopholes that other companies don't get. We can't afford to do both. This is not class warfare, its math." **Barack Obama**, during a speech, September 19, 2011

FREDERICK MONDERSON
39. TRUMP AND OBAMA I
BY
DR. FRED MONDERSON

Donald Trump and President Obama see the world differently because of their responsibilities and interests. Mr. Obama sees the world from his position as President but more particularly as Commander-In-Chief, Chief Diplomat, Chief Legislator and leader of his political party and more important as an African-American leading this great nation. The huge responsibilities that come with the many "Hats" the President wears are crafted by the notion of what Republican Condoleezza Rice, former Chief of Staff and Secretary of State exclaimed, "The world looks different in the view from behind the Oval Office desk." There is so much the President has to balance in executing his oath of office and equally maintaining diplomatic relations with most of the world's more than 190 nations. In these nations' representative visits to the White House to discuss relations, the contents are for the most part announced or an "Open Book."

Mr. Trump on the other hand sees the world from behind the desk of Trump Tower No. 1 and No 2, and so on as a businessman. While Mr. Obama has to answer to the American people who elected him and the press who follow him, his every word is watched and carefully scrutinized and at a cost he is held answerable to a multitude of constituencies and therefore must be wise in every respect; Mr. Trump

BLACK HISTORY EVERYDAY
PART ONE

answers to no one except his bank account manager, perhaps not even him or her. While Mr. Obama's every action is subject to legislative and judicial scrutiny, not least his constituency, the American people; as an insurgent Mr. Trump is not so constrained and remains unrestrained in his speeches and behaviors as he continues to trumpet, "Make America Great Again."

If we begin by analyzing the two men's response to the recent developments both at home and abroad, in Europe, especially, the night and day differences between the two outlooks becomes clearly evident. Of course, in this instance, these developments do not seek to underscore, and an example of one man seeking the other's job.

First, if we begin with the recent Brexit development, the DOW Jones Average "fell" nearly 600 points. Mr. Trump and similarly displeased pundits emphasized this significant one day loss on the stock market in the plunge from nearly18,000. Strange, but the 600 was quickly regained and the **DOW** is again above 18,000. No one said much about the precipitous rise of the "market" from 6500 in 2008 just before Mr. Obama took over, to the historic high then hovering at 18,000. Thus, this stark contrast and the evident reality must remain clear in every arena the two men are compared in. However, let readers not forget, the role of personality in the two views; for, while Mr. Obama is open and looking positively outward, Mr. Trump is closed and seeming pessimistic in his rants

FREDERICK MONDERSON

against Muslims, women, Mexicans, Mr. McCain, Mr. Khan, the disabled, a federal judge and let's not forget his disparaging and demolishing Republican presidential contenders and not to forget Mr. Obama himself. Calling Hillary Clinton, the devil, even railing against the Republican establishment and many of its top echelon members who publicly disfavor the man. Even more, to show empathy for the grief felt by families who have lost loved ones in the ongoing tragedy, we must focus on the man given his fool's errand "birther" escapade that may be dormant but not defunct.

Black History Everyday - Part One Photo. We Shall Not be Moved March. Faces in the Crowd.

Second, as head of the nation, in aftermath of every shooting that kills Americans on its soil, the President

BLACK HISTORY EVERYDAY
PART ONE

feels the pain and must commiserate with grieving families who clamor for gun ownership, or purchaser, controls, but more particularly responsible ownership and use of firearms. Mr. Trump and his Republican counterparts single-mindedly focus on the National Rifle Association's unequivocal insistence on the Second Amendment's right to bear arms guarantee regardless of any reckless behavior that results therefrom. Of significant note, however, the application of this pristine right is different from the Constitution's original enactment and the proliferation of weaponry given today's many dynamics. However, in their control of the House of Representatives, the most Republicans do is "offer a moment of silence," following tragedy after tragedy, after tragedy and the fundamentals of gun violence remain a deadly reminder, we must seek a responsible solution to gun violence and senseless firearms killing. This is especially so when people under scrutiny and on a "No Fly List" can still find shelter under the Second Amendment.

FREDERICK MONDERSON

Black History Everyday - Part One
Photo. Faces and signs in the crowd for the 50th Anniversary March on Washington.

Another remarkable issue of note is, classic gun owners possess arms from the time of the "Old West" and this is unmistaken. However, and as an example, in January 2009, when President Obama assumed his office, insidious propaganda held, "Obama wants to change the Constitution;" "Obama wants to take your guns;" "a race war is coming;" so, militias and the gun owners began or should I say, continued stockpiling arms and ammunition year after year. Since, given guns never go out of style, "How many weapons can one person shoot at one time?" Or is it simply the sale of guns to benefit the economic bottom line. Thus, President Obama has to respond after each shooting but Trump and Republicans, avid supporters of the National Rifle Association and gun owners' rights, never do. Still, another case in point with much relevance, after the Orlando nightclub shooting, Mr. Trump insisted "If gun owners were 'carrying' in the club they would have been able to

BLACK HISTORY EVERYDAY PART ONE

stop the madman who executed so many." Well, a Black man with a carry permit was recently shot in his car reaching for his identification in front of his wife with a child in the back seat.

Third, in seeking to execute and in response to the war on terrorism, Mr. Trump wants to impose a "complete and total ban on all Muslims entering the country." With some "pushback" this has been modified to "only Muslims coming from countries with known terrorists" actively engaged in such activities. Even more, he would reintroduce Waterboarding, go after terrorist families, even carpet bomb them. These potential policies have forced many high ranking and retired military personnel to question whether, the US military would obey such illegal practices. The modified Terrorist "pushback" would now apply to "any country compromised by terrorism" which includes France and Germany, American allies. Heaven forbids a terror incident occurs in Britain, America's staunchest ally, then the proscription would apply there also. Logically then, the position seems ridiculous and not thoroughly thought out even though Mr. Trump's base supports it steadfastly. Another example in which this megalomaniac loyalty tarnishes the American Brand, Mr. Trump once said, "If I stand on Fifth Avenue and shoot someone, I would not lose any votes." If so and such an action presents no consequences, but puts Mr. Trump above the law for firing a weapon within city limits and the consequences of actually shooting someone,

FREDERICK MONDERSON

especially if unarmed, then America is already in the pits!

Black History Everyday - Part One Photo. Erik Monderson and Gary Byrd, New York Radio Personality.

Black History Everyday - Part One Photo. Rev. Al Sharpton and the young members who are the future at **NAN's** Saturday Rally.

BLACK HISTORY EVERYDAY
PART ONE

President Obama, who really understands the "big picture" acquired through eight years of high-level security briefings as the head of state recognizes such positions have "pushback" of global proportions. That is, what may sound palatable to a few may have negative consequences for the many in response to any arrogant behavior. We must never forget how a "go it alone" mode of conduct sullied the American image in the world community when George Bush (43) led the nation into Iraq.

Fourth, conventions are a time when political parties invite their members to come together, present and debate platform issues then crown their party's standard bearer to contest the Presidential Election sometimes 3-4 months later in November. This 2016 Presidential Election has been described as like no other. The Democratic and Republican campaigns to succeed Barack Obama as President have been exercises in stark contrast. It's interesting, both Donald Trump and Barack Obama ran against Hillary Clinton. However, while Barack Obama ran a resolutely civil campaign it was purely based on brains, while Donald Trump waged his on brawn. While Obama's was civil, speaking on the issues of loss of jobs, deplorable condition of the housing industry, America's loss of face on the world stage, etc., Trump's was uncivil, spewing hatred, animus, bigotry, racism, even ignorance and lacking policies and programs of substance. As an African-American

FREDERICK MONDERSON

seeking the office of the president, Barack Obama had to offer sound policies, economic, social, educational and energy-wise which he delivered upon. All Mr. Trump wanted to do was "jail Hillary" and call her bad names, nothing but negativity that have won him disfavor with Republicans of Note. Still, Mr. Obama wonders why Republicans as John McCain, Paul Ryan, Mitch McConnell, while rejecting many of Mr. Trump's stated views, yet still endorse and support him. Their position seems, "No matter what, he's still our boy!" That is, Trump is white as opposed to Obama who is Black and whom "we objected to vehemently!" The sad commentary is, some have expressed concern, given Mr. Trump's outlandish, bigoted, some say racist statements and his solid support among his base, there is an alarming realization of how many Americans share his questionable and odious behavior and views. After all, in the outlandish statements he uttered, Donald Trump was compared to many ultra-right wing, even Neo-Nazi groups in Europe particularly those objecting to immigrants changing the face of their nation but also the potential for terrorist action. We can't lose sight of the fact many nationals of these nations fought for Isis in Syria then returned home with a desire to further that cause of terror and mayhem. There is no question loose rhetoric and "gloom and doom" declarations of Donald Trump's stoke such cauldrons.

BLACK HISTORY EVERYDAY
PART ONE

Black History Everyday - Part One Photo. We Shall Not be Moved March. Faces in the Crowd.

Fifth, because Mr. Obama is a principled man, presided over a unified party in 2008 and again in 2012, he was able to operationalize an orderly and constructive convention and with a tremendous work ethic he waged a successful campaign to become president. Mr. Trump, on the other hand, rode a bulldozer roughshod against a field of 16 others amidst an unusually rancorous climate of hate, insult, disrespect and speaking out of turn. As the RNC wound down its 2016 Convention, New Jersey Federal Senator Corey Booker took to the airwaves to denounce the hate spewing out of the Republican Convention. Imagine Christian Conservatives behaving in a manner that savaged Hillary Clinton, perhaps forced the on-looking world to wonder if this behavior reflects the true nature of America, going to hell in a handbasket.

FREDERICK MONDERSON

Sixth, the two men's spouses came under scrutiny in the manner in which they shared the spotlight with their husbands. In the 2008 campaign Michelle Obama, a potential first-lady, proved a class act. So much so, "Mighty Michelle" became an effective fashionista ambassador and asset for Barack Obama and America on the world stage. Michelle is an attorney by trade who writes her own material while Ivanka has a hired speech writer. However, while Melania publicly claimed ownership for the speech, another fell on her sword in claiming she is the culprit. A good example of how the world pays attention to developments in America, Wednesday August 3, 2016, under the timeline, "Trump's Wife Melania's Photos Make A Splash," quoting Monday's *New York Post*, expose of "Potential first lady, Melania Trump's naked 'Ménage a Trump," which "The picture shows a nude Melania being hugged by another nude woman as she is in bed. Even further, "On Sunday *The Post* ran a front-page picture of a nude Melania with stones covering her breasts, under the title "The Ogle of Office, The Republican Presidential campaign appeared to shrug off the pictures. Trump's adviser told CNN Sunday that there was "Nothing to be embarrassed about with the pictures. She's a beautiful woman."

"The *New York Post* endorsed Trump for President in Mid-April, describing him at the time as 'a potential superstar of vast promise, but making rookie mistakes." "Some wondered how conservative Evangelical Christians would react, while others

BLACK HISTORY EVERYDAY
PART ONE

wondered if Murdock, who also holds conservative views, had turned against Trump."

Black History Everyday - Part One Photo. Faces and signs in the crowd for the 50th Anniversary March on Washington.

In an interesting comparison, back in the day when Vanessa Williams, a beautiful African-American woman won the Miss America pageant crown, when similar nude photos surfaced, she was stripped of her crown. Melania was sent to the White House. As a beauty queen, Miss America does not have the same influence as the first lady at home or even on the world stage as she accompanies her husband on those important global summits. Remembering the "Shoe thrown at George Bush," one cannot fail to wonder how Mr. Trump will react at one of these high-powered global gathering when persons disparagingly comment on America's naked first lady.

FREDERICK MONDERSON

Black History Everyday - Part One Photo. Brothers conversing at **CEMOTAP's** celebration.

"Contrary to the claims of some of my critics and some of the editorial pages, I am an ardent believer in the free market." Barack Obama, *Business Roundtable*, February 24, 2010

Black History Everyday – Part One Photo. Part of the crowd seeking Justice for Eric Garner.

BLACK HISTORY EVERYDAY PART ONE

"A good compromise, a good piece of legislation, is like a good sentence; or a good piece of music. Everybody can recognize it. They say, 'Huh. It works. It makes sense.'" Barack Obama, *The New Yorker*, May 31, 2004

40. WHEN MCCONNELL MEETS OBAMA!
BY
DR. FRED MONDERSON

It wasn't a beer summit! It wasn't to a fish-fry when President Obama invited Senator Mitch McConnell to the White House to discuss the nation's business. With a number of pressing issues facing the incoming 114th Congress of which Mr. McConnell will now replace Senator Harry Reid as Senate Majority Leader, the meeting promised to be intense, crucial and will mark a new chapter in White House/Congressional cooperation for negotiations of substantive issues. After all, a history of relationships between the two leaders has been marred by party rivalry and much more; but the Senator, while donning his poker face wants to appear defiantly business-like yet conciliatorily cordial, with the nation's future at stake. Thus, Mr. McConnell arrived at the White House door as a myriad of questions began cascading down that percolating waterfall mind of his; without question, he is experienced in the art of the possible! Yet, he remained mindful he

FREDERICK MONDERSON

is coming up against a big one! He is then ushered into the room where such important and pressing issues are discussed and hammered out. Once there, waiting for the President, however, rather than take a seat, the Senator paces the room, admiring the photographs of great men gracing the walls and for a moment wondered, then dismissed, "Nah!"

Black History Everyday - Part One Photo. **We Shall Not be Moved March**. Faces in the Crowd.

Before entering the room, President Obama, on his part, having anxiously worked on the invitation, nervously pondered the encounter. For a moment, he thought of donning his "imperial décor" and making "a grand emperor's" appearance. That is, crown, gown, scepter, jeweled arms, a dagger in his waist, just in case, and accompanied by his fan bearers and entourage! He, however, dismissed this form of

BLACK HISTORY EVERYDAY
PART ONE

appearance as too "over the top" and decided to appear just as businesslike as the Senator. Then he entered the room, greeted the Senator with a handshake and advised he take a seat. At table, the President offered, "Coffee or Tea" but thought "he must not getter the better of me!" The Senator accepted coffee and both men prepared their own from "fixings" previously placed.

There was a deafening silence in the room as each man sipped his java, as the two great minds raced breathtakingly over hill and dale to arrive at ice-breaking consensus getting to negotiations. The President again greeted, "Hello Senator, welcome!" Mr. McConnell replied, "Hello Mr. President, I hope Michelle and the girls are well! Give them my best!" A curt thank you and a smile by Mr. Obama seemed a tremendous ice-breaker. Both men then sat at the sparklingly polished conference table.

Mr. Obama, realizing Mr. McConnell is in a much more powerful position than previously, ponders how he will get him to come aboard and help pass some of his pressing legislation.

As Mr. McConnell sipped his coffee, black with two sugars, he peered over the cup's brim, thinking! "What an uncomfortable position I'm in! I laid my cards out early and he trumped me. Now he's here in his second term and though I'm incoming Majority Leader and must work with him in the people's interest, I'm not sure how he feels. I know he's a good

FREDERICK MONDERSON

guy but my people have not been kind to him. If only we could take back some of what was said! I know there is a lawsuit pending and there is talk of impeachment but I'm sure our people **don't** want to shut down the government, again." Mr. Obama, on the other hand, studying Mr. McConnell thought, "He's a smooth operator who has thrown everything at me including the kitchen sink. Still, I must avoid letting him have his way with me as he and the Speaker did in our previous encounters."

Mr. Obama then spoke. "Senator you know we must work together for the good of our country. People sent us to Washington to pass laws to benefit the nation."

"I agree, Mr. President!"

"Still," Obama added, "even as some 10.9 million private sector jobs have been added to the work force, your party members in the House have blocked my Jobs Bill. Persons such as Senator Cruz in your House have blocked my Executive and Judicial Nominations. Your party members also refuse to permanently extend tax credits for working families."

"Well Mr. President, it's not like you think" the Senator responded. "I know my fellow Republican Representative King from New York labeled Mr. Cruz a 'fraud' but we represent a wide spectrum of Republican thought and if you try hard enough, I will try to work with you."

BLACK HISTORY EVERYDAY
PART ONE

"Sure" Obama replied, but thought, "You pay more attention to the interest of the one percent."

"Like I said, my constituency is wide ranging."

"Let us talk about the vote to fund the government." He seemed to touch a sore spot.

Silently, the Senator again thought, "I know we lost favor with the American people when we shut down the government the last time. We cannot afford to act in a similar manner but Mr. President you must give us something." "Mr. President," he continued, "if you scratch my back, I'll scratch yours."

"Ok, Senator. What would be your primary request?"

Black History Everyday - Part One Photo. Faces and signs in the crowd for the 50th Anniversary March on Washington.

"How about scaling back Dodd-Frank financial regulations to give banks some relief. To which I

FREDERICK MONDERSON

would add, environmental regulations that reduce EPA funding and preventing the agency from regulating the lead content of ammunition or fishing tackle and exempting life-stock producers from greenhouse gas regulations?"

"That is a really tough request," the President replied. "How about moving forward on my Surgeon General and other nominations and no substantial challenges to my **Affordable Care Act**? As you know, practical governance in the history of our nation has been the willingness to compromise. I want funding for the Homeland Security Department, Medicare payments for doctors and a more vigorous Highway Transit Fund. "

"Mr. President I will have to do a lot of arm twisting but I will push to fund the government until next September, but you must strengthen the military and there should be no funding for the District of Columbia Marijuana legalization effort.

"But I must get funding to fight Ebola at home and abroad and to fight in Iraq, Afghanistan and against ISIL (ISIS) as well as to train Syrian rebels."

"Sir, let us get something done and then we can work on the others."

"Ok!"

BLACK HISTORY EVERYDAY
PART ONE

Black History Everyday - Part One Photo. Rev. Al Sharpton and the author, Dr. Fred Monderson, at **NAN's Saturday Rally at the House of Justice** on W145th Street in Harlem.

"It is clear that the Caucasian problem is painfully real and practically universal. Stated briefly, the problem confronting the colored people of the world is how-to live-in freedom, peace and security without being invaded, subjugated, expropriated, exploited, persecuted and humiliated by Caucasians justifying their actions by the myth of white racial superiority."
George Samuel Schuyler. *The Caucasian Problem*. From **Rayford W. Logan**, *What the Negro Wants* [1943]

FREDERICK MONDERSON

"We are involved in a struggle for liberation: liberation from the exploitative and dehumanizing system of racism, from the manipulative control of a corporate society; liberation from the constructive norms of "mainstream" culture, from the synthetic myths that encourage us to fashion ourselves rashly from without (reaction) rather than from within (creation). [Milton Mirkin] Toni Cade Bambara. *The Black Woman* [190], preface.

41.   DEFENDING A MYTH!
BY
DR. FRED MONDERSON

On Monday June 22, Congressman James Clyburn (D. SC), appearing on CNN's Wolf Blitzer's **Situation Room** was interviewed regarding Governor Nikki Haley bi-partisan support and statement regarding removal of the Confederate flag from the grounds of the South Carolina State Capitol in which he praised this "idea whose time has come!" It is interesting that just prior, Mr. Blitzer had interviewed a gentleman of the League of the South in which he went on and on about the virtuous defense of the flag because of the 100,000 South Carolinians who died fighting an invader under that flag. Mature, he still seemed nervous, "defending the seeming indefensible!"

BLACK HISTORY EVERYDAY
PART ONE

Black History Everyday - Part One Photo. We Shall Not be Moved March. Faces in the Crowd.

Nevertheless, in his response to "Blitz," Mr. Clyburn explained his researched understanding regarding the Confederate flag. First, he reminded this flag did not come from the battlefield at the end of Civil War hostilities. He did indicate the current Confederate Flag was hoisted in opposition and response to progress made during the Civil Rights movement of the 1960s. Even more significant, he correctly identified the Confederate Flag not as belonging to South Carolina but Tennessee as created by General Forest Beckford, founder of the Ku Klux Klan. The version flying in South Carolina was actually that of West Virginia. Thus, theirs is truly "Defense of a Myth!" He went on to explain the people defending the flag did not even know their own history! Fact is, "they did not know they did not know!"

Black History Everyday - Part One Photo. Faces and signs in the crowd for the 50th Anniversary March on Washington.

However, this idea of defense of a myth is not new. In fact, down through recorded history, people, not necessarily misguided, but they have, through circumstances and cultural custom, been inculcated in defense of a myth and such resulting way of life. And, as "practice makes perfect" and "repetition is the bane of learning," these individuals became psychologically ingrained in believing their myriad bits the whole of reality. As such, if we examine myths in historical perspective, we would realize Mr. Clyburn's subjects are subscribing to beliefs in which they stand as the majority of one, or, perhaps a small sum.

BLACK HISTORY EVERYDAY
PART ONE

First, even though there are problems of reality as portrayed in the movie **Ten Commandments** starring Charleston Heston and Yul Brynner, a scene in the movie depicts King Seti I of the 19th Egyptian Dynasty, when confronted with the prospects of a "Messiah" instructed his son, the next Rameses II, "If it is a myth bring it to me in a bottle. If it is a man, bring him in chains!" This admonition began events throughout history where myths have sustained people, led them falsely in beliefs and been stanchly defended. Sometimes it led the wrong way at the fork in the road!

The story of the **Donation of Constantine** is another of those fascinating but intriguing historical documents involved in an issue of great controversy. Purportedly put to analytic scrutiny because it's an extant document justifying certain types of actions, problems were observed in its wording. Accordingly, Roman Emperor Constantine was on the verge of a major battle and the night before he had a dream involving a bishop's miter and other religious symbolism. Successful in the next day's battle, he attributed his success to divine intervention and as a result ended persecution of Christians and accepted Christianity as an official religion within the Roman Empire. In good faith, he convened the Council of Nicaea in 325 A.D. when a great many bishops were summoned and prepared the way for the church going forward. As such, to create a unified front and solidify the magnanimous developments, the Emperor ceded great tracts of land to the church and produced a document, a Deed that became the **"Donation of Constantine."** Held in great reverence, some 800 years later, linguists and other scholars, examining this prized document were alarmed it was forged, a fake, possessing no legitimacy!

What these sleuths were able to ascertain, there were words and phrases in the document that were not "invented" at the time of its issuance. That is to say, linguistically speaking, new words and phrases are added to language every day and others, by virtue of not being used, are dropped. A good example explaining this phenomenon is best understood in the following analogy. Let us, for argument sake say, we have a document written in 1920 after the **Versailles Peace Conference** of 1919. Sometime in the 1970s a popular phrase "Where's the beef?" appears in a TV commercial. Given this is a later creation, to have it appear in an earlier document when it was "not yet coined" or in use tells scholars it's a later insertion and so, the authenticity of the document becomes questioned and it is deemed a forgery. This is what happened in the case of the **Donation of Constantine**.

In the emergence of that "superior, Western, European mental capacity," a great number of historical falsifications were perpetuated to the detriment of many people and cultures. Even more

BLACK HISTORY EVERYDAY
PART ONE

important, science especially was led in the wrong direction for the longest until meticulous scholarship, *al be it* too late to prove the forgery; and, sad to say, the people concerned or benefitted from the hoax remained vociferously committed to proclaiming and defending the stated situation. Hence, we could end up with Mr. Clyburn's "Defense of a Myth!"

Black History Everyday - Part One Photo. We Shall Not be Moved March. Faces in the Crowd.

In the great religious swindle denying African involvement and playing a significant role in the formative efforts to establish Christianity, untold energy was expended omitting the influence of Africans as church fathers even popes. We know in the classical world, "everything African was

African!" However, within the modern mind influenced by the falsity of white supremacy, even when the person, through historical evidence, was proven to be born in Africa, the spurious argument held, "Yes, he was born in Africa but of European parentage!" Undoubtedly, while this denial is more modern than ancient, it's been part of the overall methodology and strategy not only to contribute to the myth of white supremacy; that is, elevating white and denigrating black; but it has caused untold psychological damage on the one hand and fooled many people on the other. The issue with the fathers of the church, notwithstanding, the case of Priscian is another prime example. This North African born individual dominated all forms of western grammatical structure for more than 1200 years. Born in the 7th Century, he wrote and taught in Europe all aspects of grammar with only minor adjustments being made to his method at the end of the 18th Century. Still, little is known of the man as an African and the significance of his work and this is considered a major historical distortion, especially though omission of his ethnic heritage.

The "**Myth of Prester John**" is significant for the African and the resources of Africa. It is a well-known fact, just prior to Columbus' voyages of discovery to the New World, Portuguese explorers Bartholomew Dias and Vasco Da Gama began explorations southward along the West African coast. As prospects for riches, trade and otherwise intensified, the "Myth of Prester John" was created possessing "end of the rainbow" attractions of

BLACK HISTORY EVERYDAY
PART ONE

adventurous integrity and promises of wealth as rewards. The myth held, Prester John was considered a white, Christian king, ruling a kingdom peopled by Africans. And so, adventurers of every hue and cry set out to find this individual. Well, they came searching; missionaries wearing religious garb as the first wave of imperialist colonizers, then traders, consuls and soldiers. Before long, while still searching for the king, "spheres of economic influence" were created, trade encouraged, land concessions secured and consuls sent to protect the missionaries and traders. To aid these, soldiers were sent to protect the consuls and then they recruited locals to form "frontier forces" commanded by white officers whose role was now to establish law and order. Naturally, these locals became spies breaking down their own cultural norms and acted as interpreters and so dramatic changes began to take place.

In all of this, propaganda labeled Africans as "killing and eating the white man." As Prof. John Clarke correctly reminded, "We invited the white man to lunch and we became the meal." Others opined, "If we had eaten the white man, we would not have the problem today!" Or, even the insight offered by King Menelik II of Ethiopia who defeated the Italians at the Battle of Adowa in 1896. "I know the strategy of European governments," he explained as indicated in Robert July's *A History of the African People* (1975), "First they send missionaries, then consuls, then soldiers to protect them both." Still even more as

FREDERICK MONDERSON

Jomo Kenyatta wrote in his book *Facing Mount Kenya*, "When the missionaries came, they taught us to close our eyes and pray. When we opened our eyes, we were holding the Bible and they the land." In similar but more viciously blatant fashion, the **Bible Study Group** at "Mother Emanuel Church" invited young Dylann Roof into their religious circle and the killer committed the most unspeakable act. So, some have argued, in as much as Prester John was not found, there may very well be individuals still searching the bushes of Africa for him to this day in the 21st Century.

Black History Everyday - Part One Photo. Faces and signs in the crowd for the 50th Anniversary March on Washington.

The "**Myths of the Phantom and Tarzan**" got much traction from that astute English mind, Edgar Burroughs, etc., who fabricated superhuman white individuals overcoming and outwitting untold

BLACK HISTORY EVERYDAY
PART ONE

numbers of Africans and as Hollywood got into the act, we laughed heartily in movie theaters as Africans caricatured, reinforced the "Cigar Store African" image. Even Calypsonian Mighty Sparrow sang how British Education Minister Cutridge's educational curriculum was intended "to create comedians" in the Colonies.

That assiduous European mind, quick to explore and exploit every situation, offered all forms of rationalizations for the Slave Trade. Starting with African culture being different from that of Europe; Noah's curse condemns Africans to "obey your masters;" the Slave Trade was just that, instead and widely believed robbery, murder and mayhem. The rationale was Africans sold their brothers into slavery; trans-shipment was not that bad, they arrived refreshed and ready for New World sale; instead of the physical and psychological brutalities of the Middle Passage experience, they were plied with skin oils and fed a last hot meal before being let off ship; "tight packing" and "loose packing" demands of the Triangle Trade justified expected profit margin; the terror of separation and fears of an unknown future; refusal to acknowledge all such atrocities were in preparation "To Make Them Stand in Fear" of the white man! Yet, many believe the impact was not as psychologically damaging generally thought, though the ramifications are clearly evident to this day.

A similar not too different case headlined the *News of the World* newspaper some 35 years ago. A By-line read, "Scientists discover the Home of Queen of Sheba, in Nigeria." Lo and behold, the centerfold showed the image of a white woman, despite the fact the Queen's famous words were "I am Black and comely!" Ivan Van Sertima argued, the Queen's empire may have stretched across the belt of Central Africa, from east to west. This meant her empire was many times the size of Solomon's tiny country. Nevertheless, that an Editor could publish such a false photograph, in this day and age, is an equally significant hallmark of distortion to defend a myth. Let's not forget, Malcolm X reminded, "They know how to put it!"

Black History Everyday - Part One Photo. We Shall Not be Moved March.
Faces in the Crowd.

The "**Myth of a Caucasian Egypt**" is one of those contemporary issues strangling this aspect of

BLACK HISTORY EVERYDAY
PART ONE

African history because for most of the 19th and 20th Centuries, unchallenged interpretations of the evidence have created a false, ossified belief. Without question, fathers of the foundation of Egyptological archaeology, linguistics, and anthropology did exceptional analytic work in reclamation, analysis and identification and interpretation of the new data emerging from the bowels of the earth. However, since these were humans and there was no African scholar as erudite as Dr. Diop as critic, involved in analysis, mistakes were made in interpretation of the data. But ideas gone abroad are difficult to recall particularly since they were ingrained in an era of white supremacy chauvinism and imperialism's clamor. That is also why "Moderns" as Derry, Emery, Wortham could claim "The Egyptians are Caucasians." That is why, such scholars as Elliot Smith, even C.G. Seligman's *Races of Africa* (1930), could claim Caucasian penetration not simply in the Delta but as far as into Nubia, almost Central Africa. Conversely, however, while David O'Connor could pronounce, "The Egyptians were not white," William Arnett in *Evidence for the Development of Hieroglyphs in Southern Upper Egypt* (1982) asserted, "While Dr. Diop proved the Egyptians were not Caucasians, the bones could not prove they were Negroes." However, the mummies do as Dr. Diop's analyses of mummy skin's epidermis proves. Even more important, despite Arnett giving only half a loaf, Diop did provide tremendous evidence to prove "Africa in

FREDERICK MONDERSON

Egypt" and "Egypt in Africa." Nevertheless, the Myth lives as one of a Caucasian Egypt.

The **"Myth of African contributions to American culture"** not only flies in the face of reason but insidiously questions the role of the fundamental pillars of music, sports, science, invention, agriculture, religion, even entertainment. More particularly, the importance of religiosity, compassion, healing and the power of prayer on behalf of America and its leaders are without question among this nation's most valuable and cherished resources. Black scientists and inventors and their inventions, mathematicians, and much more are not only undercounted but were omitted for much of the 19th and 20th Centuries. Even more important, for the last 50 years, school science texts across the curriculum, have totally ignored the black scientist, thereby underscoring the myth and falsity in American education, veritable and orchestrated systematic exclusion, providing justification for a curriculum of inclusion.

BLACK HISTORY EVERYDAY
PART ONE

Black History Everyday - Part One Photo. We Shall Not be Moved March. Faces in the Crowd.

Today the "**Myth of the Confederate Flag**" seems to be dissipating as smoke in open air. Across the nation, not simply citizens but state houses with links to the flag are now experiencing a groundswell to distance themselves from the odious atmosphere now revealed in association with the flag. A glaring irony was pictured on Wednesday, June 24th, 2015, when the caisson carrying Reverend Clementa Pinckney to "Lay in State" at the State Capital building, after Dylan Roof's horrible act. The martyr passed the Confederate flag fluttering in the wind. Meanwhile, many gathered nearby chanting, "Take it Down!" However, and because of the legislative maneuvering involved, in a clever ruse, an important South Carolina legislator proposed, for the

FREDERICK MONDERSON

Reverend's funeral, "We could take the flag down to clean it!"

Black History Everyday - Part One Photo. Rev. Herbert Daughtry, the venerable and iconic warrior, of "They will have to carry me out, then I'll carry on my activism while waiting for you in heaven" fame, hugs a supporter at Rev. Sharpton's Saturday Rally!

It is a sad tragedy throughout the continued progress of America, lives were lost, suffering ensued, perpetrators of evil acts have, for the most part, gone unpunished and remain unrepentant having committed untold terrorist acts against Black-Americans. Nevertheless, whatever may be said by the nefarious, some have branded racist, bigoted, inconsiderate, evil, the magnanimous humanity of African Americans' un-measurable commitment to religious tenets of love, forgiveness and commiseration for fellow man are significant anchors proudly buoying the American ship of state boosting

BLACK HISTORY EVERYDAY
PART ONE

the nation's tricolor flag's image among the many nations comprising the human family.

Black History Everyday - Part One Photo. Faces and signs in the crowd for the 50th Anniversary March on Washington.

"Only free men can negotiate. Prisoners cannot enter into contracts." Nelson Mandela. *Statement from Prison* [February 10, 1985].

"There is a view that the past is forgotten. Some criticize us when we say that whilst we can forgive; we can never forget …. The choice of o ur nation is not whether the past should be revealed, but rather to ensure that it comes to be known in a way which promotes reconciliation and peace. *Address for the Truth and Reconciliation Commission* [February 13, 1996]

FREDERICK MONDERSON

42. MR. MANDELA'S LONG WALK BY DR. FRED MONDERSON

When Jesus hung on the cross it was reported, one of the Centurions uttered, "What manner of man is this?" When activist Sonny Carson died, this writer called a friend to inform him of such and he replied, "Sonny Carson dead, God help us!" When Nelson Mandela passed on to his historical and heavenly glory, the world felt its moral compass shift and the terrain below its feet shutter. Whether the parallels may be appropriate or not; the life, times and passing of "Maida" Nelson Mandela are like a dashing comet plunging into the deep abyss of the universe, never to be seen again in many lifetimes. But this personal experience is part of the reason the world mourns the loss of this man of courage, endurance, resilience who possessed unifying, ethical, moral and philosophic rectitude embodied in a bright mind, a gentle soul, as a universal champion of freedom, humility and equality. Even more astonishing, this preacher of reconciliation was blest with a funny side that in totality makes him tremendously human though many think him divine. Having ascended the world stage as a great ambassador of South Africa, his principal aspirations achieved, this towering figure of world history, like Cincinnatus, he stepped down from power after a single term as President.

BLACK HISTORY EVERYDAY
PART ONE

When the "Powers" of this world show their true selves in their magnanimous tributes to Mr. Mandela, this giant of history, it says much of the man, his tenacity, ability to stand as a pillar for his principles and the tremendous influence he has and will continue to exert on many over the past and decades to come. He is without question the embodiment of one man becoming a majority because he stood for and laid it all down for principles of his ideal, universal franchise of one man, one vote! Recognizing the "moral necessity of racial justice" in his beloved land, he sought and achieved the abolition of the vicious system of Apartheid. Now the world, even his enemies have come around to recognize he was right from inception and his lack of recrimination, reconciling black and white, inspired untold millions around the globe, and especially those at home.

While the word enemy is a harsh term, it also embodies the state of an unalterable opposition evolved from the arrogance of an imperial onslaught that manufactured the intractable and challenging reality of racism and discrimination molded in the false belief that some persons are of an inferior/superior nature because of the color of their skin. This falsity has failed to recognize that Osiris was Black! Jesus was Black! Isaiah and Jeremiah were Black and many other religious and spiritual minds and souls who enlightened humanity were also Black. J.A. Rogers' 2 volume *World's Great men of Color* (1947) and *Sex and Race,* 3 volumes, are

FREDERICK MONDERSON

fascinating points of departure in this topic. It's acknowledged, no one race is responsible for the total progress of this world, not forgetting science confirms the earliest humans were Africans. Somewhat strange but even the concrete sidewalk in an urban environment can give birth to and nurture a beautiful flower.

Black History Everyday - Part One Photo. We Shall Not be Moved March. Faces in the Crowd.

The legacy of imperialism and colonialism in Africa created the lasting conditions that gave birth to the needs of a person, revolutionary savior, a Mandela, to address and correct the situation, requiring both wisdom and humility.

It is also interesting, when persons, institutions, even heads of states are allowed to view the awesomeness

BLACK HISTORY EVERYDAY
PART ONE

of the shadows they cast, when they finally come around, sometimes they even question themselves: "How could we have gotten away with it?" But, unlike many such individuals, Mr. Mandela mastered the art of success and succeeded by studying not simply his history but that of his enemies so he could communicate and negotiate with them on a level they could understand. He was fluent in Afrikaans, the language of the oppressor.

For centuries, the rapaciousness of the European mindset unleashed in Africa laid the foundation for thievery, racialism and resource exploitation and brutality visited upon that continent and its people. The resultant and appalling "rape of Africa," exile of her sons and daughters beyond her shores, and theft of her real estate and wealth are phenomena as wide as a solar system, philosophically speaking, and as dangerous as the dynamics of a black hole! As an example, at the 1981 Oxford University International Summer School held at Exeter College, an English Tutor exclaimed, "If we only knew how wealthy Africa is back in 1900 there would have been no decolonization and independence after World War II."

It is, however, amazing that the year 1900 was the time of the Boer War between Britain and its South Africa Cape Colony peopled by British expatriates, Africans, "colored" and Dutch Boers. The land at the southern tip of Africa, that Bartholomew Diaz and Vasco Da Gama in 1498 praised its pilots for helping them navigate the Cape, would later attract the Boers in 1652. They settled there to escape the horrors of the religious reformation sweeping Europe and would in turn visit similar brutality on Africans. These religious zealots would later falsely claim upon their arrival the land was devoid of Africans, when in fact Blacks occupied that area for hundreds of thousands, if not millions, of years. We know, for sure, Africans were mining hematite, an iron ore, in South Africa as early as 41,000 years Before Christ. In 2011, *The New York Times* newspaper reported discovery of a paint pot still containing red paint with a mixing device inside probably used as a stirrer and paint brush. This was carbon-dated to 107,000 years. Such evidence settles the argument as to who came first!

After 1814, when the British annexed the Cape of Good Hope and forced the Boers inland to begin their "Great Trek," they encountered the Zulu Chieftain Shaka expanding his territory and organizing his nation. The Boers bribed and tricked his brother Mpande offering promises he would become chief.

BLACK HISTORY EVERYDAY
PART ONE

Black History Everyday - Part One Photo. Faces and signs in the crowd for the 50th Anniversary March on Washington.

He then stabbed Shaka in the back. With the great African general removed from the scene, this paved the way for the "Great Trek" to move further inland with little or no resistance. In no time these Dutch Boers had seized much of the land, beginning to consign the Africans to being landless menials in their place of birth and ancestral lands. Still, a number of Zulu leaders including Cetewayo began struggles against the whites whose firearms ensured victory against the poorly armed Africans. In aftermath of the many clashes, Moshesh, an astute African leader, gathered many strands of Africans fleeing both Zulu and Boer explosiveness and formed the Basuto nation on a high Veld in South Africa. As events unfolded,

FREDERICK MONDERSON

before he died, he entrusted his land to the British as a protectorate to be defended against the Boer encroachment and the small enclave became Swaziland in the South African balkanizing scheme of things.

By 1870 gold and diamonds were discovered in South Africa and after the enormous mayhem of competing European and American miners laying claims, the Africans were sidelined. Cecil Rhodes and big conglomerates prevailed in consolidating claims to the fields and so began the systematic exploitation of the nation's wealth. To this Dr. Leonard Jeffries decried, "The three R's were not 'reading, 'riting and 'rithmetic,' but Rhodes, Rothschild and Rockefeller." Elsewhere, this was also a time of developing "spheres of influence" as "precursors" to the **Partition of Africa** ultimately set the stage for colonial control. The wealth of South Africa encouraged expropriation, rape and pillage of the land and the evolution of a mindset that by the turn of the century had initiated the genesis of the evil system later called apartheid, becoming "legal" in 1948 under Paul Kruger, the "father of Apartheid." His disciples among the Afrikaner nationalists were Malan, Vorster and Botha, all succeeded by De Klerk, the last white ruler. However, from 1872 to the start of the Boer War in 1898, discovery of precious metals of unimaginable reservoirs tremendously increase world supplies. This "outpost of the British Empire" found itself fighting with the "Mother Country" for control of the wealth and this led to the Boer War (1899-1902).

BLACK HISTORY EVERYDAY
PART ONE

Soon after the two parties "kissed and made up," then agreed on a mechanism to extract the resources for export mainly to Britain, advantageously rewarding whites and disadvantageously exploiting Blacks. In 1910, with Jan Christian Smuts playing a significant role, Britain acceded to the creation of the Union of South Africa comprising Transvaal, Pretoria, the Orange Free State and Cape Coast Colony.

Moving quickly, from 1910 to 1931, a number of draconian laws were enacted to further restrict and control the movement of Africans and to consolidate white control of the nation as well as to exploit Black labor. All this Britain acceded to, because South Africa was part of the British Commonwealth and Britain wanted access to the South African mineral wealth.

Essentially, from 1910 to 1948, spanning World War I and World War II era, South Africa mercilessly exploited the resources of that part of the African continent with Britain benefitting enormously from handling the gold and diamonds and enjoying the enormous benefit of being principal and favored trading partner. They supplied the newly declared nation's major industrial equipment and other trading items. However, in response to Britain recognizing establishment of the Union of South Africa in 1910, the **African National Congress (ANC)** was also formed in 1910 to advance the status of Africans in the land of their birth. Eight years later, in 1918, Nelson Rolihlahla Mandela was born in Qunu in the

FREDERICK MONDERSON

Eastern Cape Province, where he spoke the Xhosa language.

At the conclusion of World War II, the **5th Pan African Congress** was held at Manchester, England. There, W.E.B. DuBois ceded leadership of the **Pan-African Movement** to the Chairman of the Conference, Kwame Nkrumah, who accepted a mandate to organize and decolonize Africa. Along with Namdi Azikwi of Nigeria; Julius Nyerere of Tanzania; Jomo Kenyatta of Kenya; and Sekou Toure of Guinea, these African leaders vowed to wrest control of Africa from white rule and they ultimately succeeded in freeing the continent.

Black History Everyday - Part One Photo. We Shall Not be Moved March.
Faces in the Crowd.

BLACK HISTORY EVERYDAY
PART ONE

On March 6, 1957 Ghana became the first African country to gain independence and a whole slew of others followed suit by the mid-1960s. However, white control in South Africa was more entrenched from being buttressed first by German then Anglo-South Africa control of Namibia; by the Portuguese in Angola and Mozambique; and the British in ill-gotten Rhodesia, essentially under rule by Ian Smith and his predecessors from whom Robert Mugabe ultimately wrestled power. The struggle for South Africa was thus much more difficult than what transpired across the other parts of the continent.

After Manchester, within three years in 1948, the system of Apartheid became a reality as a result of white control of the legislative process in South Africa. In a work entitled The *United States and Africa* by the American Assembly at Columbia University (1958L 149-150) the authors write regarding "The South African Racial System?"

"The system of race relations in the Union of South Africa is a product of history, not merely the creation of a Malan or Strijdom. It has developed over the past three hundred years." This behemoth, global pariah, then, is what Mr. Mandela sought to overthrow, and to do it he had to become a martyr and convert his enemies into friends. Sort of, "Kill them with kindness."

FREDERICK MONDERSON

Black History Everyday - Part One Photo. Faces and signs in the crowd for the 50th Anniversary March on Washington.

Accordingly, "The two crucial features of the system are separation and subordination. Separation (or apartheid) means keeping non-Europeans (particularly Africans) apart from Europeans in housing, education, religion, public amenities, conveyances, recreation, and social life. Subordination means the consistent placement of Africans (and other non-Europeans) in an inferior position in all their relationships with Europeans. The system is rationalized by a complex ideology, rooted in the conviction that the non-European is not only different but inferior. In addition to the sanctions of custom, the system is enforced by an elaborate body of statutory laws designed to exclude Africans and other non-Europeans from social and political life,

BLACK HISTORY EVERYDAY
PART ONE

control their movements (the pass laws), and regulate their activities (the **Riotous Assemblies Act** and the **Suppression of Communism Act**, for example). In practice the system does not work perfectly; apartheid is only partial, and subordination is not invariably prevalent. Non-Europeans do occasionally share aspects of European life and exercise (extremely limited) influence on government; and not all Europeans accept the prevailing theologies about Africans."

More significant, however, is the need to reinforce separateness and inferiority coupled with the need to earn cash to fend for one's families and still be in white areas where such could be earned. "Apartheid is the best-publicized feature of the system." It is an Afrikaans expression meaning "separation" or "separate development." It symbolized the ultimate objective of the Nationalists (who came into power in 1948) to separate the races in all spheres of life: residential, economic, sexual, social, educational, religious and political. Ideologically, the emphasis is on differentiation of the races, not assimilation or integration. This objective is expressed in a large body of laws passed since 1948 such as the **Group Areas Act** (1950) designed to enforce residential segregation in urban areas; the **Mixed Marriage Act** (1949) and the **Immorality Amendment Act** (1950) which makes intermarriage illegal and interracial sexual intimacies a crime; the

FREDERICK MONDERSON

Reservation of Separate Amenities Act (1953) reinforcing existing segregation patterns in transportation and public places; the **Bantu Education Act** (1953) which strengthens the traditional system of separate education and gives the central government greater control over African education; the **Separate University Education Bill** (proposed in 1957 but not yet law) designed to provide separate universities for the races and to debar non-Europeans from the two "open universities" which they may not attend; and other laws which aim to restrict or eliminate all contact between Africans and Europeans."

Black History Everyday - Part One Photo. Sonny Carson, Atiem Ferguson and James "Chief" Parker.

BLACK HISTORY EVERYDAY
PART ONE

Black History Everyday - Part One Photo. We Shall Not be Moved March. Faces in the Crowd.

Subordination is in some respects a more basic feature of race relations in South Africa that is separation. Subordination, not separation of the total apartheid variety, characterizes the economic relationships. In theory, and largely in practice, the African is consigned to lower-level jobs while positions requiring skills, management, and direction are assigned to Europeans. This policy has been operative in the great mining industry, is reflected in the White Civilized Labor Policy dating back to 1924, and is expressed in the determination of the present government to secure the skilled and more highly paid jobs for Europeans in the clothing and secondary industries where the color bar was less rigid in the past. Thus, despite protests from industry,

FREDERICK MONDERSON

the **Minister of Labor** (under the authority of the revised **Industrial Conciliation Act, 1957**) intends to proceed with his plan to reserve for Europeans certain occupations in the clothing industry. The Minister was apparently unmoved by the claim of leading industrialists that, if this policy was extended, thousands of non-Europeans would lose their jobs and the development of industry in South Africa would be greatly hampered.

Complete separation is not actually possible. It neither existed in the past nor exists now. Subordination of the non-European in all relationships is easier to enforce and at the same time serves the major objective of the Europeans: to maintain their prestige and supremacy."

This practice then instituted and enforced a system of **Pass Laws** that not simply separated the races, black and white, by creating white areas and consigning blacks to what became regulated black areas called "Bantustans." These were essentially economic backwaters with nothing, only providing enormous numbers of Africans who could be hired as laborers in white areas. To get from the "Bantustans" (Black towns) or "nations within a nation," Black Africans needed a **Pass Book** that essentially contained every bit of information about the holder. As the system became more and more enforced, Africans were reduced to contract laborers who had no rights and needed permission to be in white areas. They could be accosted by anyone, must produce

BLACK HISTORY EVERYDAY
PART ONE

their Passbook on demand, and if not correct in all aspects they could be arrested, fined or sent packing back to the "Bantustans."

Black History Everyday - Part One Photo. Faces and signs in the crowd for the 50th Anniversary March on Washington.

Under the pretext of a practicing democratic system upheld through laws, the white minority of South Africa viciously discriminated against and oppressed the Black majority through the Pass Law mechanism enforced under a brutally oppressive system of imprisonment, murder, banishment and fines. Persons were also banned. Both Mr. Mandela and his wife Winnie were separately banned.

First and foremost, the law required every Black person to have a **Pass Book**. This was not a requirement for whites! The **Pass Book** was more

FREDERICK MONDERSON

than a passport, it recounted one's entire life history, from birth to the time it was demanded by a white person or law enforcement agent. Even more important, the Blacks were oppressed through a system of taxation that required them to work. To work and earn cash to support their families and to pay taxes, they had to be in white areas. In white areas they needed to have a valid pass and authority to perform contract labor. At the expiration of the contract, the African had to vacate the white area or face arrest. Once arrested for "trespassing" in their country of birth, it was stamped into the passbook and visible to anyone who demanded to see it, which meant it was more difficult to secure employment the second time around.

Now, as the society expanded, the demands for labor increased and a system of "influx control" regulated the movement of Blacks. This impacted where they came from, whether from Bantustans, the impoverished and over-crowded areas to which Blacks were consigned and from which pools of labor were contracted; or from outside the country in neighboring lands. Whether to work in the mines, to work on farms and to perform all forms of menial labor within South Africa, Blacks were contracted on an annual basis and upon completion of the contract, they had three days, sometimes 24-hours to return to their place of origin. Because of the society's demands for laborers were more than the Bantustans could provide, neighboring states such as Rhodesia and Mozambique and as far as Malawi were contracted to supply workers whose wages were

BLACK HISTORY EVERYDAY
PART ONE

remitted directly to their home governments, themselves glad to earn the badly needed foreign exchange. In turn they paid the family of the worker in local currency.

This is the South Africa Nelson Mandela came of age in, became educated as a lawyer and activist having joined the **African National Congress** in 1946 as one of its political operatives. It was also the age of continental African agitation and organization of decolonization strategy. What British Prime Minister Harold McMillan called "the winds of change" sweeping the British Empire and the world at the start of the 1960s decade, forced the South African government under its system of apartheid, to become harsher in treatment of Blacks and enforcement of the draconian laws in hope to forestall majority rule in that wealthy country, of untold poor Blacks. Economically speaking whites would work and be entitled to insurance, health and dental care and otherwise, even receive unemployment benefits which were practically non-existent since whites enjoyed full-employment from completion of school to retirement upon which time they were entitled to a pension. All these amenities were denied the Blacks who left their families in the Bantustans to eke out a wage, were not entitled to anything when either unemployed or in old age, and therefore unable to provide the back-breaking labor. This inequity still endured because they had to provide for their families.

FREDERICK MONDERSON

Black History Everyday - Part One Photo. We Shall Not be Moved March. Faces in the Crowd.

Since only males could work in the mines and farms, they needed a labor force that was housed in oftentimes substandard dwellings whether in urban hostels or on farms. In hostels especially, the most unsanitary and unhealthy conditions predominated, encouraging homosexuality and sickness. Such conditions Blacks were consigned to had the most deleterious effect on their psyche and on families back home in the Bantustans where the government and private enterprise further cultivated fresh crops of strong young men to replace the worn-out ones "on point."

These conditions are what Nelson Mandela and the African National Congress actively sought to change. By the mid-1950s, Mr. Mandela was constantly

BLACK HISTORY EVERYDAY
PART ONE

monitored, finally arrested he was charged with treason, a trial that lasted for several years. For the duration he was "banned." This was a form of punishing prohibition in which a person was prevented from having contact with more than one person at a time and restricting their movement. Though Mandela and his colleagues were found not guilty at first, by 1960, they were forced to go underground and on the run.

Some two years later he was again arrested and charged with subversion, for publicly burning his **Pass Book** in defiance of the system and accused of trying to overthrow the South African government. Finally convicted, sentenced to life in prison, he was sent to Robben Island, one of the most draconian prisons in the country where he spent 18 years and another 9 in a variety of prisons.

While **Nelson Mandela** managed his prison sentence, his wife **Winnie Mandela** kept up the struggle through her own activism. She too became a "banned" person who could only be in touch with a few people at any one time. She was constantly harassed and her home monitored. Winnie, however, would not be silenced. She traveled abroad, coming to the United States but could not speak as condition for her visa. Nevertheless, many spoke for her as she stood firm as a symbol of opposition to apartheid and as a pillar of what African womanhood stood for. In America and elsewhere she was regarded as a Queen

FREDERICK MONDERSON

of the Black World. **Queen Mother Moore** took her under her wings and the world loved and adored this beautiful fighter for freedom and justice. One particular and later front page of the New York *Afro Times* featured a picture of Minister Louis Farrakhan beside a seated Winnie Mandela and below words on the beginning of a series on Thebes, the city of Ancient Egypt, begun by *Daily Challenge* and *Afro Times* columnist Fred Monderson.

All the while in prison Nelson Mandela's image continued to enlarge. He became the first and only global icon of the 20th Century. Michael Jackson was known for his music but people demonstrated, held sit-ins, wrote, acted and demanded an end to Apartheid and freedom for Nelson Mandela.

As more African states became independent, attention began to focus on the plight of South Africans. Before his imprisonment, Mandela, had launched the armed wing of the **ANC**, called the "Spear of the Nation" and empowered it to wage an armed struggle against the government. Secretly he left the country, perhaps for guerilla training. Surreptitiously African governments and others began to train and supply the **ANC** with arms and the wherewithal to continue to struggle to Free South Africa. Libya under Mohmar Khadafy provided training-grounds, arms and money; so too did Fidel Castro of Cuba; even Yasser Arafat of the **PLO** aided the African cause. A most significant development occurred in the 1970s. For more than a century

BLACK HISTORY EVERYDAY
PART ONE

Germans, French, Italians, Belgians and British had deployed soldiers to Africa. In 1974 when Fidel Castro deployed Cuban troops to aid Angola under threat from Jonas Savimbi acting in concert with the marauding South African Army threatening liberation movements in Mozambique, Rhodesia, Namibia and Angola, the pariah Apartheid state's "Achilles heel" became evident. This signaled the final push to rid the continent of the white settle minority regimes in Rhodesia (Zimbabwe), South-West Africa (Namibia) and South Africa (Azania).

Black History Everyday - Part One Photo. Faces and signs in the crowd for the 50th Anniversary March on Washington.

FREDERICK MONDERSON

Black History Everyday - Part One Photo. We Shall Not be Moved March. Faces in the Crowd.

Across the globe young people and elders, from college campuses to local governments, all began to demand divestment from investment in the apartheid state. Professors taught classes and demanded term papers on "Apartheid," "Nelson Mandela" and the "History of South Africa." Movements sprang up and began targeting any and all-American institutions that invested funds, whether for business, unions, pension funds, insurance companies and insisted that American technical know-how must be withdrawn. The Free South Africa Movement gained steam in Europe and everywhere. The "Fight Apartheid" and "Free Nelson Mandela" buttons appeared everywhere. The might of South Africa was

BLACK HISTORY EVERYDAY
PART ONE

threatened. Rev. Herbert Daughtry and his **House of the Lord Pentecostal Church** on Atlantic Avenue in Brooklyn became a bastion of anti-apartheid sentiment. The **SASAA** Movement (**Sisters Against South African Apartheid**) was born at the Church and held meetings there.

Western nations that depended on mineral resources which South Africa had in abundance were caught in a dilemma having to satisfy their citizens' insistence that ties to Apartheid be cut. The world was awaked to the evils of apartheid and Nelson Mandela became a symbol of the opposition to the racism and brutality practiced in that country. As this movement escalated, divestment, protest, calls to end ties, sports boycott, etc., world leaders of major nations such as Margaret Thatcher and Ronald Reagan were caught in a bind. Ronald Reagan, as President of the United States and his Secretary of State Chester Crocker of a nation whose citizens, in many respects, lead the fight, pursued a policy of "constructive engagement" with the pariah state. The "Iron Lady" stalled on sanctions but the Commonwealth of Nations forced her hand. Importantly, persons such as the American Rev. Leon Sullivan began to be more vocal in efforts to squeeze and bring down the government. The image of Nelson Mandela grew further. Hugh Masekela sang a song "Bring Mandela home to Soweto."

FREDERICK MONDERSON

Black History Everyday - Part One

Photo.   A seated and smiling Jitu Weusi is surrounded by an associate, State Assemblyman Al Vann and Councilwoman Una Clarke.

South Africans such as Walter Sisulu were active in the country. Young Steve Biko, an activist was arrested and killed mercilessly by South African Security Forces. Donald Woods, a white friend of Biko was hounded and had to leave the country. In America, such nationalists as Jitu Weusi, Conrad Worrill and Sonny Carson certainly were engaged in raising the conscience of their brothers and sisters. Harry Belafonte continued to organize on-going protests in front of the South African Embassy that resulted in Major Owens, Walter Fauntroy, Mrs. Effie Barry and Reverend Herbert Daughtry, pastor of the **House of the Lord Church** which

BLACK HISTORY EVERYDAY
PART ONE

became the epicenter of the Anti-apartheid Movement were arrested. An Anti-Apartheid organizer at Hunter College, Charles Barron was married to his wife Inez at Rev. Daughtry's Church. Here too was centered **Sisters Against South African Apartheid (SAASA)** of which Barbara Emanuel was a member who also coordinated this through the Maurice Gumbs political campaign for School Board 17 and later the 21st State Senate, with Cherise Maloney and Fern Greenberg as operatives. Conrad Worrill of Chicago was an ardent anti-Apartheid proponent. Rev. Jessie Jackson, Randall Robinson of Trans-Africa, Cleveland Robinson and Jim Bell, union leaders, galvanized unions across the nation and world to protest that workers of South Africa had no representation. In churches, on college campuses, especially in Brooklyn at Medgar Evers College, student Manuel noted, "Everybody was working!"

Black History Everyday - Part One Photo. We Shall Not be Moved March. Faces in the Crowd.

FREDERICK MONDERSON

As the pot boiled, the racist South African regime that slaughtered untold numbers at Sharpsville in 1962 did the same thing on June 16, 1976 in Soweto as the youth took to the street to protest the evil system. All this aroused the conscience of the world that apartheid must go. More and more Mandela's release from prison became a top priority as the sanctions against South Africa escalated; squeezing the nation; the system began to crack from the pressures without and within. In response, the government sought an escape from the vicious and debilitating web they had woven. Prime Minister Pieta Botha tried to bribe Mandela with early release from prison if he would renounce the armed struggle, he initiated under *Umkhonto we Sizwe* or "Spear of the Nation." This offer was rejected, according to Mandela because prisoners cannot negotiate.

The **Free Nelson Mandela Movement** saw the revered leader released in 1990, a day the world sang praises in triumph against the evils of apartheid. By that time, David Dinkins had been elected Mayor of New York City and along with other operatives as New York Secretary of State Basil Patterson, radio personality David Lampel and others, including Elombe Brathe and members of the American Committee on Africa all welcomed Mr. Mandela to this city and nation. Bill Lynch, a Deputy Mayor in the David Dinkins administration orchestrated a parade for Mr. Mandela within the "Canyon of Heroes" in down-town Manhattan. Betty Shabazz, wife of Malcolm X was given a rousing embrace by

BLACK HISTORY EVERYDAY
PART ONE

Winnie Mandela as they stood on the podium in Harlem. Mandela visited Boys and Girls High School in Bedford-Stuyvesant and he gave speeches. Appearing on Television, when asked by Ted Koppel of Nightline, 'Why did he associate with and invite to his Inauguration such persons as Khadafy, Castro, Arafat, Mugabe, Farrakhan,' he replied, "These people helped us when apartheid oppressed us" as the West only extracted and benefitted from the wealth. And so many felt proud of being part of something greater than themselves!

Black History Everyday - Part One Photo. Faces and signs in the crowd for the 50th Anniversary March on Washington.

While Jesse Jackson pointed out Mr. Mandela's vision and outlook was shaped by persecution, the world praised him for seeking reconciliation in the

FREDERICK MONDERSON

best interest of the nation. Along with F.W. De Klerk, the last white ruler of the apartheid state, Mr. Mandela was awarded the Noble Peace Prize in 1993. After serving as the nation's first Black President, he was succeeded by his Vice President Thabo Mbeki, followed by Jacob Zuma who announced Mr. Mandela's death at 8:15 PM, December 5, 2013.

Mr. Mandela's legacy, besides the dissolution of apartheid was relentless against AIDS, poverty and African educational upliftment. He was against the US invasion of Iraq. However, while many have praised his conciliatory gestures towards the perpetrators of the crimes of apartheid, others have pointed out, he may have been too conciliatory but he never forgot his experiences and the revelations of the Truth and Reconciliatory Committee that chronicled the brutality the South African government prosecuted against its citizens.

Black History Everyday - Part One Photo. We Shall Not be Moved March.
Faces in the Crowd.

BLACK HISTORY EVERYDAY
PART ONE

"Nelson Mandela, giant," **Editorial** New York *Daily News* Friday, December 6, 2013, p. 30.

"It is true, all true. Nelson Mandela led the fight against an evil, racist regime; went to jail for a quarter-century; emerged from that dark place a stronger, wiser man; and, with quiet strength, led his nation toward peace, democracy and prosperity. His story is a rousing personal journey that conveys the boundless potential in every life, no matter how battered. It affirms the moral power that a single extraordinary person can exert on history by being better than his oppressors, and by ultimately embracing reconciliation over revenge."

In 1964, on the eve of prison, he gave one of the century's greatest speeches, concluding: 'I have cherished the ideal of a democratic and free society in which all persons live in harmony and with equal opportunities. It is an ideal which I hope to live for and to achieve. But if needs be, it is an ideal for which I am prepared to die.'"

It is an ideal he embarked upon once becoming President of South Africa by expanding health care to children, radically improving education, protecting workers, lifting people out of desperate poverty and settling thousands of land claims. This hero of history had his flaws. All men, great and small, do. They are of no moment. Today, brought short by his death, we revere Mandela for saving a nation's soul and for galvanizing the global conscience as a beacon for the

FREDERICK MONDERSON

proposition that all people are created equal." "A true hero passes into history," New York *Daily News*, Voice of the People. Saturday, December 7, 2013, p. 21.

Brooklyn: We cherish the stars - actors, athletes, etc. - and mourn their death when we know nothing about them. Nelson Mandela was a man - yes, a real man - who never showed bitterness or hatred for the 27 years he spent in prison. He won the presidency of a country where there were no gray areas, only black and white. Yet he did everything to bring his nation together. He is a true inspiration. Mandela has my ultimate respect, and my sympathy goes out to his family and friends. A true hero has passed away. David J. Gushue.

Bronx: Nelson Mandela was a good and great man who became revered by freedom-loving people throughout the world. His refusal to be broken by the vile apartheid government of South Africa will serve as an inspiration for generations to come. What a great voice he was, as opposed to those hucksters and hustlers, Al Sharpton and Charles Barron. They could learn a lot from Mandela's example. Kim Theobald. Both men parted feeling they had accomplished something through talking and compromise.

DECLARATION OF THE RIGHTS OF THE NEGRO PEOPLES OF THE WORLD.

We complain:

BLACK HISTORY EVERYDAY
PART ONE

1. That nowhere in the world, with few exceptions, are black men accorded equal treatment with white men, although in the same situation and circumstances, but, on the contrary, are discriminated against and denied the common rights due to human beings for no other reason that their race and color.

2. "... Our children are forced to attend inferior separate schools for shorter terms than white children, and public-school funds are unequally divided between the white and colored schools.

Black History Everyday - Part One Photo. We Shall Not be Moved March. Faces in the Crowd.

3. We believe in the freedom of Africa for the Negro people of the world, and by the principle of Europe for the Europeans and Asia for the Asiatics; we also demand Africa for the Africans at home and abroad.

FREDERICK MONDERSON

4. We believe all men should live in peace one with the other, but when races and nations provoke the ire of other races and nations by attempting to infringe upon their rights, war becomes inevitable, and the attempt in any way to free one's self or protect one's rights or heritage become justifiable.

5. Whereas the lynching, by burning, hanging or any other means, of human beings is a barbarous practice, and a shame and disgrace to civilization, we therefore declare any country guilty of such atrocities outside the pale of civilization.

Black History Everyday - Part One Photo. Faces and signs in the crowd for the 50th Anniversary March on Washington.

6. [We demand] That the colors Red, Black and Green be the colors of the Negro Race. Marcus Garvey. *Philosophy and Opinions*. [1967] Edited by **Amy Jacques Garvey**.

BLACK HISTORY EVERYDAY
PART ONE

Black History Everyday - Part One Photo. The motto of the **Million Man March** 20th Anniversary was **JUSTICE OR ELSE**.

43. "LYNCHING AS RACIAL TERROR" BY DR. FRED MONDERSON

For decades scholars have taught and activists labeled 19th century Southern white behavior towards African-Americans as terrorism. Equally, in a serious

FREDERICK MONDERSON

but humorous manner a popular "T-Shirt" depicts images of Native-Americans as "Fighting Terrorism since 1492." However, as "radical Islam" began attacking American personnel and interests, the issue of terrorism, brought home this reality and it has now become a household word. More important, an article published in *The New York Times* and dated Tuesday, February 10, 2015, p. A-11 and written by Campbell Robertson entitled "History of Lynchings In the South Documents Nearly 4000 Death." Essentially the article focused upon the work of an organization entitled **Equal Justice Initiative** under the praise-worthy leadership of civil rights attorney Mr. Bryan Stevenson and his group who chronicled and identified some "3,959 victims of racial terror lynchings in 12 southern states from 1877 to 1950." Equally significant, the year 1877 is very important in American history for many characterize it as a "betrayal" in which Rutherford B. Hayes, a Southerner, was spuriously placed into the Presidency to succeed Ulysses S. Grant ending Reconstruction that followed end of the Civil War. This artificial installation of the new President removed the protections of federal troops from the South, ended Reconstruction and opened the doors of ascendency to white supremacy that began to unleash unspeakable horrors against the freed, African American, peoples.

BLACK HISTORY EVERYDAY
PART ONE

Black History Everyday - Part One Photo. "Young Charles Baron" (right) sits alongside Carlos Russel author of **Black Solidarity Day** and "Thinking it Through" with another gentleman and the *Daily Challenge* frontpage headlines read: "Sonny Carson Day."

Campbell Robertson's article notes that while the states of Texas through Louisiana, Mississippi, Alabama, Florida, Georgia, South Carolina, North Carolina, Tennessee, Arkansas, Kentucky, and Virginia were numbered, Arkansas, Louisiana and Mississippi, often called "The Deep South," had the most such killings. In Phillips County, Arkansas, for example, 237 people were lynched in 1919 during the Elaine race riot alone for a total of 243 listed death for that year. Next came Louisiana with Caddo Parish (54), Lafourche Parish (50), Tensas Parish (4) and Ouachita Parish (35). In "73 Years of Lynchings" the article continues, "The most recent data on lynching, compiled by the Equal Justice Initiative shows premeditated murders carried out by at least 3 people from 1870-1950. The killers claimed to be enforcing some form of social justice. The alleged offenses that prompted the lynchings included political activism and testifying in court." These are fundamental rights guaranteed by the Constitution and required for good citizenship; yet they were systematically and forcefully denied these citizens. However, what Mr. Stevenson intends to do in his project is to erect markers on every possible lynching site to identify the place where each gory crime was committed. Naturally, pulling back the covers of this vicious part of the nation's history and exposing the involvement of families, farms and personnel in these racial tragedies do not sit-well with current white supremacy property owners, politicians and ideologues for the implications they present.

A good example of this "denial" is reminiscent in the 2012 Republican campaign to deny Barack Obama a second term as President. It came out, Governor Rick Perry of Texas is the owner of a piece of land named "Nigger Head Mountain." He claimed some time previously his father had "painted over the sign" that was prominently displayed. Naturally, then, concerned citizens had wondered whether on that site, a famous memorial had been erected to an equally famous Black man who had benefitted that community or whether that was a killing site where many a "Nigger Heads" rolled! Now, persons can see

BLACK HISTORY EVERYDAY
PART ONE

the inherent implication of marking such sites for the embarrassment this silent yet deadly legacy presents.

The history books have taught American heritage is traceable mainly to British colonists who settled the land. In their brightest moments Presidents such as Ronald Reagan and Jimmy Carter traced their family heritage to illustrious individuals and proudly boasted of this connected badge of honor. One wonders how many will willingly allow such markers on their property and be publicly associated with those murderous packs Ms. Constance Baker-Motley and others experienced and wrote about from the time of the "1877 betrayal," when federal troops, removed from the South, enabled and resulted in formation of the Ku Klux Klan, White Citizens Council, Knights of the White Camelia, "Jim Crow" legislation and practices particularly aided by the **Dred Scott historic Supreme Court decision of 1857**, in which Chief Justice Roger Taney ruled, "A Black man has no rights a White man is bound to respect." During "Jim Crow" times, such practices weighed heavily to influence the 1896 *Plessey V. Ferguson* ruling that in fact formally established *de jure* and *de facto* segregation as "Separate but Equal" which was actually "Separate and Unequal." That ruling was finally struck down in *Brown v. Board of Education of Topeka, Kansas* in 1954.

FREDERICK MONDERSON

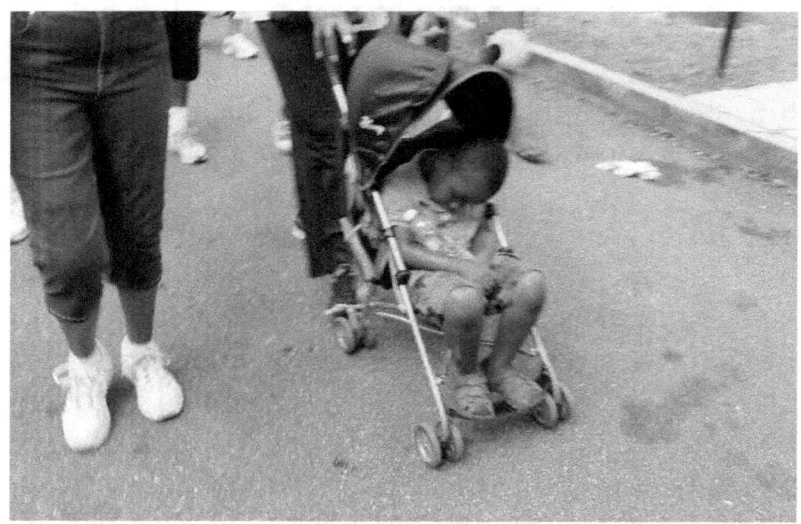

Black History Everyday - Part One
Photo. Faces and signs in the crowd for the 50th Anniversary March on Washington.

In this "hell on earth" experience, lynching was not the only tool in the repertoire of the racists who perpetrated these heinous crimes against African-American citizens finally granted America's momentous protections under the 13th, 14th, and 15th Amendments as enshrined in the United States Constitution. That is, after two centuries of horrendous chattel slavery, that fundamental and hard won right to vote was denied through orchestrated chicanery, intimidation, threats, tar and feathering, killings and economic peonage perpetuated through "share cropping" and crop lien, agricultural tyranny. But most brutal was lynching which became a spectator sport entertaining whole families such as the image depicted in the **Black**

BLACK HISTORY EVERYDAY
PART ONE

Book showing a Black man being roasted on a bed of coals. This was an extremely agonizing death much more different than the "Roasting" Whoopi Goldberg's boyfriend gave her on television. This was indeed a horrifying experience to see and smell a human being burnt to the delight of pictured White men, young children and old people, gleefully enjoying the ghastly spectacle. This is the history partially hidden that needs to be told!

Black History Everyday - Part One Photo. We Shall Not be Moved March. Faces in the Crowd.

Importantly, seldom is an article in *The New York Times*, "the paper of record," followed by a lead Editorial the next day, but this story was so compelling that it did under the title "Lynching as Racial Terrorism." For sure, many persons of all

FREDERICK MONDERSON

political and social persuasions across the country have criticized *The New York Times* for being a vehicle of liberal bias. However, even though persons have a problem with such quality reporting, *The Times* serves as an agent of the social conscience of this nation, raising significant and deep-rooted human concerns while the greater political leaders and ethical champions turn a blind eye and deaf ear to the plight of these and other victims of social, economic and even political injustice, despite victims constantly crying out for relief.

The lead paragraph of *The Times* **Editorial** states, "It is important to remember that the hangings, burnings and dismemberments of black American men, women and children that were relatively common in this country between the Civil War and World War II were often public events. They were sometimes advertised in newspapers and drew hundreds and even thousands of white spectators, including elected officials and leading citizens who were so swept up in the carnivals of death that they posed with their children for keepsake photographs within arm's length of mutilated black corpses." Even further, "These episodes of horrific, communitywide violence have been erased from civic memory in lynching-belt states like Louisiana, Georgia, Alabama, Florida and Mississippi. But that will change if Bryan Stevenson, a civil right attorney, succeeds in his mission to build markers and memorials at lynching sites throughout the country to confront an era of racial terror directly and recognize

BLACK HISTORY EVERYDAY
PART ONE

the role that it played in shaping the current racial landscape."

Seldom, if any whites at all were held accountable for such unspeakably horrific behaviors. President Nelson Mandela after 27 years of unjust incarceration empowered a "Truth and Reconciliation Committee" to record, chronicle and forgive the ghastly behaviors of some 85 years of Apartheid South Africa. Yet, it is unthinkable for such a panel to be assembled in this country in order to officially look into and record, then to seek the forgiveness of the victimized and their descendants. Perhaps it is because the victimizers past and present time memories are too horrendous to forget.

As Mr. Stevenson argued, "Lynching declined as a mechanism of social control as the southern states shifted to a capital punishment strategy, in which blacks began more frequently to be executed after expedited trials. The legacy of lynching was apparent in that public executions were still used to mollify mobs in the 1930s even after such executions were legally banned." Recognizing the powerful role lynching played in shaping Southern society, the report continued, "Most Southern terror lynching victims were killed on sites that remain unmarked and unrecognized." Nevertheless, in contradictory and wicked irony, the Southern landscape is cluttered with plaques, statues and monuments that record, celebrate and lionize generations of American defenders of white supremacy, including public

FREDERICK MONDERSON

officials and private citizens who perpetuated violent crimes against black citizens during the era of racial terror."

That is to say, the heroes of the "Rebel South" must be known and their memories perpetuated while the memories of associated terroristic horrors must not be. Or, put another way, we know of them in "Glory" but we should not know of them in "Savagery!"

Black History Everyday - Part One Photo. Councilwoman Una Clarke (left) with daughter Yvette later elected Congresswoman from Brooklyn, Elombe Brathe and others in a photo-op.

BLACK HISTORY EVERYDAY
PART ONE

Black History Everyday - Part One Photo.   Faces and signs in the crowd for the 50th Anniversary March on Washington.

Black History Everyday - Part One Photo.   **We Shall Not be Moved March**. Faces in the Crowd.

FREDERICK MONDERSON

Black History Everyday - Part One Photo. Walter Brown stands at the Front elevation of the Peace and Justice Memorial Center.

Black History Everyday – Part One Photo. BLACK LIVES MATTER!

www.ingramcontent.com/pod-product-compliance
Lightning Source LLC
Chambersburg PA
CBHW070156240426
43671CB00007B/468